# Communication
# in the Classroom:
# A Collection of G.I.F.T.S.

# Communication in the Classroom: A Collection of G.I.F.T.S.

**JOHN S. SEITER**
UTAH STATE UNIVERSITY

**JENNIFER PEEPLES**
UTAH STATE UNIVERSITY

**MATTHEW L. SANDERS**
UTAH STATE UNIVERSITY

bedford/st.martin's
Macmillan Learning
Boston | New York

**For Bedford/St. Martin's**

*Vice President, Editorial, Macmillan Learning Humanities:* Edwin Hill
*Program Director for Communication:* Erika Gutierrez
*Program Manager:* Allen Cooper
*Marketing Manager:* Amy Haines
*Director of Content Development:* Jane Knetzger
*Senior Development Manager:* Susan McLaughlin
*Developmental Editor:* Jesse Hassenger
*Content Project Manager:* Pamela Lawson
*Senior Workflow Project Supervisor:* Joe Ford
*Production Supervisor:* Robin Besofsky
*Media Project Manager:* Sarah O'Connor
*Manager of Publishing Services:* Andrea Cava
*Project Management:* Lumina Datamatics, Inc.
*Composition:* Lumina Datamatics, Inc.
*Permissions Manager:* Kalina Ingham
*Permissions Associate:* Claire Paschal
*Design Director, Content Management:* Diana Blume
*Text Design:* Books by Design, Inc./Lumina Datamatics, Inc.
*Cover Design:* John Callahan
*Printing and Binding:* LSC Communications

Manufactured in the United States of America.

2   1   0   9   8   7
f   e   d   c   b   a

*For information, write:* Bedford/St. Martin's, 75 Arlington Street, Boston, MA 02116

ISBN   978-1-319-10925-7

**Acknowledgments**
*Acknowledgments and copyrights appear on the same page as the text and art selections they cover; these acknowledgments and copyrights constitute an extension of the copyright page. All student activities appear courtesy of their authors.*

*At the time of publication all Internet URLs published in this text were found to accurately link to their intended website. If you do find a broken link, please forward the information to Jesse.Hassenger@ macmillan.com so that it can be corrected for the next printing.*

# Contents

To Robert H. Gass. Long before we were friends, you remarked on one of my exams, "With writing so illegible, you should consider a career in the medical profession." Indeed! But imagine all the fun we'd have missed! My chunk of this book is dedicated to you as coauthor, teacher, mentor, and friend. The point guard part of you doesn't deserve a dedication.

—*John Seiter*

To the teachers. I am fortunate to have learned from some truly incredible educators and thankful to have been introduced to so many more during the creation of this book.

—*Jennifer Peeples*

To Scott Hammond and Wayne Boss. Both of you kindly mentored me despite my inexperience, gave me opportunities to spread my wings in the classroom, and most importantly modeled for me what it means to be an influential teacher. Every success I've had as a teacher can be traced to what I learned from the two of you.

—*Matt Sanders*

# Introduction

## GREAT IDEAS FOR TEACHING STUDENTS: AN ORIENTATION

Quick, name one thing you can do to avoid getting trampled at a communication conference. If you said, "Steer clear of the hotel elevators, especially between sessions," give yourself a point. If you said, "Bypass Starbucks on the way to an early-morning session," chalk up another one. If you said, "Practice dodging and head-faking before attending a G.I.F.T.S. (Great Ideas For Teaching Students) session," you're not alone. Indeed, some time ago, one of the editors got bumped around a fair bit in one of these sessions, emerging from a crowd of rambunctious teachers with the idea for this book—a story we'll return to in a moment.

First, however, for those not familiar: G.I.F.T.S. sessions at conferences are presentations of a wide array of class-tested exercises, case studies, techniques, simulations, and other activities that teachers can use to facilitate or assess learning. These sessions, a staple of most communication conferences, use a variety of formats including panels and roundtable discussions. Our favorite format sets up a number of different stations, one for each teaching idea. Reminiscent of musical chairs, attendees visit these stations one at a time for ten minutes or so in small groups until prompted to move to the next station. This format provides opportunities for a lot of interaction, and as such we find them highly rewarding and productive.

In our experience, G.I.F.T.S. attendees are delightfully eager to gather as many ideas as they can. At one session, for example, one of the editors was asked to bring thirty copies of an activity to distribute to attendees, and brought extras just in case. After the session, presenters were asked to place extra handouts on tables in the back of the auditorium. That's when the crowd pressed in, sandwiching the editor and grabbing copies off the pile before they were set down. But who could blame them? With so many stations, it was impossible to attend them all. For someone who had previously presented papers to rooms with plenty of empty chairs, it was exciting. Over the years, we have watched with more careful attention the enthusiasm and eagerness of teachers as they gather new ideas from these sessions.

This avid response to the presentation of teaching ideas prompted the question: If G.I.F.T.S. activities were in such high demand, why not a book? Why not a collection of excellent G.I.F.T.S. that can be used as a resource for teachers dedicated to finding new ways to inspire their students? That was our motivation for working on this project—teachers' desire, enthusiasm, and need to both share and learn from each other. But before presenting the collection of teaching ideas, we offer a few words about active learning and the process behind this book.

## The Gift of Active Learning

Plenty of teachers prefer to rely primarily or exclusively on their own lectures in the classroom. But communication is a practical discipline (Craig, 1989). The information we teach deserves to be explored, discovered, experienced, practiced, and reflected upon. Its value does not lie in whether or not we simply know it; it is what we can do with the information to improve our relationships, organizations, communities, and societies that ultimately demonstrates why studying communication is worthwhile. Our goal as teachers is to help students think more deeply about the role of communication and engage with the world differently. Active learning requires that students comprehend through reading, discussion, and/or lecture and then *do* something with that knowledge to make it stick and demonstrate its utility (for further reading on active and/or experiential learning, see Kolb, 2015; Meyers & Jones, 1993; Wurdinger & Carlson, 2010).

We imagine that most teachers who read this book will not need to be persuaded that an active learning approach is valuable. We think that teachers looking for additional creative ways to enrich their classroom will be pleased with the G.I.F.T.S. in the pages that follow. Whether you're a new teacher or a veteran, we hope you and your students will enjoy these activities, share the excitement of their authors, and gain new knowledge about engaging students much as the editors have through the process of putting together this book.

## How to Approach These G.I.F.T.S.

Perhaps the greatest value in the G.I.F.T.S. in this book is that they keep us engaged in our classes. Let's face it: If we aren't engaged, our students aren't, either. When considering adopting specific activities, we recognize that it can feel uncomfortable. That's good! We often ask our students to be uncomfortable, stretch themselves, and experience new things; teachers need to be willing to do that, too. So we encourage you to experiment. Challenge yourself to grow as a teacher. However, that doesn't mean you should change everything at once. The Cornell University Center for Teaching Excellence advises instructors to start small. Implementing too many active learning techniques in one term, or worse, in one class period, may discourage the student engagement you seek. They recommend that you "focus on engaging *more* students in *more meaningful* ways" rather than simply making changes for the sake of change.

Another way to approach these G.I.F.T.S is to ask, "Who am I as a teacher?" Not all of the activities in this book will fit your style or tastes. Indeed, even we as editors didn't always agree about which activities work best in our own individual classrooms—nor should we. With over one hundred contributors, this collection represents a diverse range of courses and approaches. We consider this diversity one of the collection's great strengths, and some activities will fit your teaching style better than others. With that in mind, we encourage you again to stretch your boundaries

## About the G.I.F.T.S.

To be considered for inclusion in this volume, teaching activities needed to have been presented at a communication conference (NCA, ICA, WSCA, ESCA, CCSA, SSCA, etc.). After having cleared that initial disciplinary hurdle, the activities had to pass the rigorous reviews of the editors and our publishers. Many of the activities included won awards from the conferences where they were presented. Additional instructors reviewed many of the activities and topics discussed here, and we must thank them for their time and efforts:

Angela Blais, University of Minnesota-Duluth
Leslie A. Bates, Los Angeles Film School
Shannon Bates, Highline College
Amber Davies-Sloan, Yavapai College
Ashley Edwards, Northwest Arkansas Community College
Stacy Fitzpatrick, North Hennepin Community College
Jodi Gaete, Suffolk County Community College
Carla Gesell-Streeter, Cincinnati State Technical and Community College
Carla Harrell, Old Dominion University
Krista Hoffmann-Longtin, Indiana University–Purdue University Indianapolis
Christa Tess Kalk, Minneapolis Community & Technical College
Holly Manning, Laramie County Community College
Penny J. O'Connor, University of Northern Iowa
Danielle Parsons, University of Rhode Island
Andrea Pearman, Tidewater Community College
Narissra Punyanunt-Carter, Texas Tech University
Curt VanGeison, St. Charles Community College
Kristine S. Williams, Hocking College

These G.I.F.T.S. represent our discipline's vast array of styles and approaches, touching on theories, concepts, methods, and skills from courses that are part of most typical communication curricula. As a collection, the quality of these activities can be measured by the extent to which they provide more frequent and immediate feedback to students, address different student learning styles, create personal connections to the material, allow students to practice important skills, build self-esteem through conversations with other students, and create a sense of community in the classroom through increased student-student and instructor-student interaction. All of these qualities increase student engagement, motivation, and willingness to learn.

The activities in this book follow a similar format. Each begins with background information on the concepts it teaches, the courses it can be used in, and its history as an activity. Each entry then has a purpose, an explanation, and a debrief section followed by references and appendicies with copy-ready material for teachers to use. This similar formatting allows instructors to look through the book more easily to figure out if an activity works for a specific classroom. To aid in finding the appropriate activities, we have arranged the book by course (see the table of contents, p. v). As many concepts are taught in multiple classes and many activities can be used to teach a variety of subject matter, the index makes it easy to search for a G.I.F.T.S. by concept or course. In addition, the activity authors have provided contact information and are willing to receive emails with further questions.

In the current world of Google where obtaining facts is just a mouse click away, the evolution from a traditional "sage on the stage" classroom to a more active learning approach seems especially relevant. Effective teachers actively engage students in ways that help them think, analyze, interpret, and apply. For those looking to invigorate their teaching, we think that the activities in this book contribute greatly to that prospect—and we hope they enrich your teaching experiences. Enjoy!

## Acknowledgments

In addition to thanking the eager conference-goers who sparked the idea for this book, we thank our contributors for their amazing activities, their unwavering patience, and, most of all, for being our partners in sharing G.I.F.T.S. on a larger scale. We are also grateful to the folks at Bedford/St. Martin's for making this book part of their professional development series, and particularly, Erika Gutierrez for her willingness to listen carefully to our ideas and for catching our vision for this book; Catherine Burgess for her grace while responding to loads of pestering questions; and Jesse Hassenger for his dedication and sagacity, especially down the home stretch.

We're all three hopelessly indebted to our community at Utah State University and elsewhere. To our students, thank you for motivating, teaching, and tolerating us. To our communication colleagues, past and present (you know who you are!), thank you for making our community a place where learning thrives and people are happy. How did we get so lucky? To our teachers who inspired us to join their profession: for John: Miss Gordon, Pat Ganer, Patricia Parmelee, Bob Gass, Joyce Flocken, Tom Hollihan, Lynn Miller, and Michael Cody; for Jen: Martha Cooper, Sean O'Rourke, John Bettolo, Ann Staton, Mrs. Patrick, Mrs. Lubbers, and Mrs. Thomas; and for Matt: Scott Hammond, Bryan Taylor, Wayne Boss, April Trees, and Mike Zizzi. And finally, unending thanks to our families for their support, patience, and sustenance through this project. To John's wife, Debora; Jen's husband, Charles, and Matt's wife, Julie.

Finally, John and Matt appreciate Jen's legendary ability to always be right while giving credit to everyone else. John and Jen suggest that Matt epitomizes the phrase "To know me is to love me." And we do. Jen and Matt are thankful that John never made them live up to his superhuman work ethic and instead used his sense of humor to make each and every interaction fun.

**John S. Seiter**
Department of Languages, Philosophy, and Communication Studies
Utah State University
john.seiter@usu.edu

**Jennifer Peeples**
Department of Languages, Philosophy, and Communication Studies
Utah State University
jennifer.peeples@usu.edu

**Matthew L. Sanders**
Department of Languages, Philosophy, and Communication Studies
Utah State University
matt.sanders@usu.edu

## REFERENCES

Craig, R. T. (1989). Communication as a practical discipline. In: B. Dervin, L. Grossberg, B. O'Keefe, & E. Wartella (Eds.), Rethinking communication: Vol. 1. Paradigm issues (pp. 97–122). Newbury Park, CA: Sage.

Kolb, D. A. (2015). *Experiential learning: Experience as the source of learning and development* (2nd ed.). Upper Saddle River, NJ: Pearson.

Meyers, C., & Jones, T. B. (1993). *Promoting active learning: Strategies for the college classroom.* San Francisco, CA: Jossey-Bass Publishers.

Wurdinger, S. D., & Carlson, J. A. (2010). *Teaching for experiential learning: Five approaches that work.* Lanham, MD: Rowman & Littlefield.

# Communication in the Classroom:
## A Collection of G.I.F.T.S.

# I

## Public Speaking

# Audience Analysis and Adaptation

# 1

## Creating Community Time Capsules: A Creative Approach to Analyzing Audiences

*Lisa K. Hanasono, Ph.D.*
*Department of Communication*
*Bowling Green State University*
*LisaKH@bgsu.edu*

**History:** This activity was presented at the annual meeting of the National Communication Association, November 2012, in Orlando, Florida.

**Primary courses in which this activity might be used:** Public Speaking, Culture and Communication, Organizational Communication

**Concepts illustrated:** Psychological Audience Analysis, Demographic Audience Analysis, Audience Adaptation, Persuasion

### PURPOSE

In an increasingly diverse society, students need to be able to effectively analyze and adapt to different audiences. Audience adaptation is a core communication competency (Lucas, 2007; Morreale et al., 2007; National Communication Association's Core Communication Competencies Task Force, 2014; Schreiber, Paul, & Shibley, 2012). Most introductory public speaking courses focus on three types of audience analysis: demographic, situational, and psychological (Beebe & Beebe, 2015; Lucas, 2015; Zarefsky, 2011). *Demographic* audience analyses examine recipients' social identities (e.g., their age, gender, socioeconomic status, race, nationality, religion, and group memberships). *Situational* audience analyses focus on the communication environment's physical setting. *Psychological* audience analyses investigate recipients' attitudes, beliefs, and values. Collectively, these analyses provide valuable information to speakers and can help them communicate more effectively with different groups of people (Morgan, 2009).

Demographic audience analyses provide speakers with heuristic information about their audiences, but their emphasis on broad social categories (e.g., gender, race, age) can promote stereotypical thinking and surface-level understanding (Ross, 2013). Therefore, students must also conduct psychological audience analyses. Understanding and adapting to audience members' values, attitudes, customs, and beliefs are extremely important skills that can reduce the likelihood of stereotyping audience members. However, successfully accomplishing these tasks can be challenging. This teaching activity helps students strengthen their psychological audience analysis skills and learn more about their local community.

This activity challenges students to conduct psychological audience analyses and think critically about cultural artifacts. By completing this activity, students should be able to (a) utilize their critical thinking skills to analyze audience members; (b) conduct psychological audience analyses by identifying their audience members' values, beliefs, and attitudes; and (c) tailor oral presentations to different groups of people.

## EXPLANATION OF ACTIVITY

### Preparing for the Activity

Before the activity's class meeting, instructors should inform their students that they are going to create a community time capsule. First, instructors should ask their students to think carefully about their local community and brainstorm a list of objects that would represent their community's values, interests, and concerns. For example, students who live in a rural community where agriculture is important might consider fresh produce from the farmers' market. Second, instructors should ask each student to bring an item to donate to a community time capsule to their next class meeting.

### Part One: Conducting an Audience Analysis (Twenty-five minutes)

Instructors should review the three major types of audience analysis (i.e., demographic, psychological, and situational). Then instructors should tell students that they will be completing a psychological audience analysis of their local community by creating a time capsule. Ask students to place their time capsule items on their desks. Next, organize students into small groups. Instruct each student to explain how their items reveal information about the local community's values, beliefs, attitudes, values, and behaviors. In other words, how do their time capsule items represent their community? Encourage students to go beyond surface-level knowledge. After students have had the opportunity to discuss their items in small groups, bring the class together and invite one spokesperson from each group to succinctly highlight key findings about their group members' time capsule items and analyses. Once all groups have shared their findings, ask students to summarize key themes from the group presentations and characteristics of the local community. To document and track the class discussion, the instructor can write down the students' key themes and perceived community characteristics on a whiteboard or chalkboard.

Remind students that conducting an audience analysis is important, but it is not sufficient in most communication contexts. Rather, students *also* need to be able to adapt their verbal and nonverbal messages to their audience. The second part of this activity challenges students to use their time capsule analyses to present audience-centered messages.

## Part Two: Audience Adaptation (Forty minutes)

Instructors should divide their class into approximately five groups. Each group will need to prepare a four-minute persuasive presentation using a problem-solution format. However, students will need to imagine that they are giving their persuasive presentation to members of their local community (instead of their classmates). They will need to use the information from their psychological audience analyses to successfully develop and deliver their presentations.

Give each group a different topic. I recommend selecting interesting topics that persuade audience members to enact a particular behavior (see Table 1). To structure their persuasive presentations, students may wish to utilize

**TABLE 1** A List of Recommended Group Presentation Topics

| Proposed Topic |
| --- |
| 1. Persuade the community to bring a local celebrity to town for a speaking engagement. (Students can use their psychological audience analysis skills to pick the celebrity, or you can come up with an interesting person.) |
| 2. Persuade the community to honor one of its members with a special monument. |
| 3. Persuade the community to change the speed limit of a local highway from 55 to 40 mph (or from 55 to 75 mph). |
| 4. Persuade the community to declare a local holiday. (Students should use their psychological audience analysis skills to pick the specific day and the reason to declare it a holiday.) |
| 5. Persuade the community to buy a new gadget or fashion item. |
| 6. Persuade the community to hold a wacky sports tournament. (Students can use their psychological audience analysis skills to select the sport, or you can come up with an interesting one. In past semesters, students have advocated for a synchronized shake weight tournament and a paper airplane throwing contest.) |
| 7. Persuade the community to change the local high school's mascot. |
| 8. Persuade the community to start a creative and new program that will help save the local environment. |
| 9. Persuade the community to vote in favor for a new law or ordinance. |

Monroe's Motivated Sequence (McKerrow, Monroe, Ehninger, & Gronbeck, 2003; Morgan & Natt, 2012; Seiter & Gass, 2007), or organize their speeches in a problem-solution format. After giving students ten minutes to prepare, each group should give a short persuasive presentation in class. Before each group gives its persuasive pitch, encourage students to carefully observe how the speakers adapted their verbal and nonverbal messages to the local community's attitudes, beliefs, behaviors, and values. After each group's presentation, ask the rest of your students to share their observations.

## DEBRIEF (Ten minutes)

Once all groups have presented their persuasive speeches, instructors can debrief the activity through a discussion session. First, instructors can ask student presenters how they adapted their presentations to the local community's values, attitudes, beliefs, and interests. In other words, what specific persuasive appeals, evidence, nonverbal behaviors, and arguments were designed to connect with the community's characteristics? To promote critical thinking, instructors can challenge students to evaluate their peers' presentations and provide constructive feedback. For example, instructors may ask student audience members to identify what positive and negative assumptions the speakers made about their community. Instructors could ask students how they could improve their presentation's content and delivery to more effectively adapt to their audience. Instructors can also challenge students to explain how they might adapt their group presentations to different audience groups, such as a classroom of first graders or a team of corporate executives.

Students enjoy this activity because it is unique, educational, and creative. This activity challenges students to think more critically about everyday household items (e.g., the newspaper, a local restaurant's menu), instead of taking them for granted. In addition, there are a variety of ways to adapt this activity to other courses and topics.

This activity can be adapted to improve students' communication skills in a wide variety of college courses. For example, instructors who teach classes on communication and culture could assign each group to bring in artifacts that are symbolically important to a specific culture. Students can analyze their artifacts and inform their classmates about different cultures. Alternatively, students can create real time capsules by running this activity at the beginning of the semester with nonperishable items and keeping the items until the last week of classes. When pursuing this option, instructors should inform their students that they will not be able to have their time capsule items until the end of the semester. At the end of the semester, instructors should bring the items to class and ask students to analyze them a second time. To what extent do these items still represent their community? Some items, such as toys, clothing, and technology, may be outdated as fashion trends and popular toys often rotate each season. Other items, however, may continue to have significant meaning to the community. Students can discuss how their perceptions of the community have changed since the beginning of the semester and how they would adapt their presentations to more diverse audiences.

## REFERENCES

Beebe, S. A., & Beebe, S. J. (2015). *Public speaking: An audience-centered approach* (9th ed.). Boston, MA: Pearson.

Lucas, S. E. (2007). *Instructor's manual to accompany the art of public speaking* (9th ed.). New York: McGraw-Hill.

Lucas, S. E. (2015). *The art of public speaking* (12th ed.). New York: McGraw-Hill.

McKerrow, R., Gronbeck, B. E., Ehninger, D., & Monroe, A. H. (2003). *Principles and types of speech communication* (15th ed.). Boston, MA: Allyn & Bacon.

Morgan, M. (2009). *Presentational speaking: Theory and practice* (7th ed.). New York: McGraw Hill.

Morgan, M., & Natt, J. (2012). *Effective presentations* (2nd ed.). Mason, OH: Cengage Learning.

Morreale, S. P., Moore, M. R., Surges-Tatum, D., & Webster, L. (2007). "The competent speaker" speech evaluation form (2nd ed.). Washington, DC: National Communication Association. Retrieved from http://www.natcom.org/uploadedFiles/Teaching_and_Learning/Assessment_Resources/PDF-Competent_Speaker_Speech_Evaluation_Form_2ndEd.pdf

National Communication Association's Core Communication Competencies Task Force. (2014). Core Competencies for Introductory Communication Courses. Retrieved from https://www.natcom.org/uploadedFiles/Teaching_and_Learning/Core%20Competencies%20Handout,%20April%202014(1).pdf

Ross, D. G. (2013). Deep audience analysis: A proposed method for analyzing audiences for environment-related communication. *Technical Communication, 60(2)*, 94–117.

Shreiber, Lisa M., Paul, G. D., & Shibley, L. R. (2012). The development and test of the public speaking competence rubric. *Communication Education, 61(3)*, 205–233. doi: 10.180/0363452.3.2012.670709

Seiter, J. S., & Gass, R. H. (2007). Teaching social influence: Resources and exercises from the field of communication. *Social Influence, 2*, 197–210. doi: 10.1080/15534510701396625

Zarefsky, D. (2011). *Public speaking: Strategies for success* (6th ed.). Upper Saddle River, NJ: Pearson.

# 2

# "I Totally Missed That!": Using Twitter to Teach Critical Listening

*Megan M. Wood*
*Department of Communication*
*University of North Carolina at Chapel Hill*
*megan.wood.gillette@unc.edu*

**History:** This activity was presented at the annual meeting of the National Communication Association, November 2015, in Las Vegas, Nevada.

**Primary courses in which this activity might be used:** Public Speaking, Introduction to Media, Media Literacy, Interpersonal Communication, Rhetorical Criticism

**Primary concepts illustrated:** Critical Listening, Active Listening, Passive Listening, Hearing, Listening Behaviors

## PURPOSE

Being an active, engaged, critical *public listener* is as important as learning the skills of public speaking. Most public speaking instructors conceptually differentiate between hearing and passive, active, and critical listening for their students (e.g., Keith & Lundberg, 2014), but to what extent do we guide the actual practice and self-assessment of these skills outside of the public speaking classroom? This activity uses Twitter, the social networking platform, to teach students about listening through experiential learning (Kolb, 1984). Experiential learning involves an independent experience had by the student, followed by in-class reflection, analysis, and application. Following a live-tweeting experiment at a speech event (or events) in the community, students share, compare, and contrast their own tweets with those of their classmates and discuss observations that can be made about their listening behaviors during public speaking events.

Social media sites like Twitter not only increasingly prove to be successful tools for accomplishing experiential learning objectives (Rinaldo, Tapp, & Laverie, 2011; Shilpa, 2014), but are also incredibly relevant to students' lives.

The Harvard Institute of Politics (2016) reports that 47 percent of US college student social-media users tweet on a daily basis. Therefore, most students are familiar with how Twitter works, and many of them will already have had live-tweeting experience. The opportunity for students to incorporate a popular tool they or their friends use on a daily basis for entertainment into a learning experience is appealing. The relevancy embedded in this activity is a key pedagogical tool; as Frymier (2002) explains, the more relevant the content, the more motivated students are to learn. From this activity, students will learn to 1) define and articulate the concepts of hearing, passive and active listening, and critical listening; 2) demonstrate the ability to see how tweets/collections of tweets demonstrate various listening behaviors; 3) assess their own listening behaviors through reflection on their experience in comparison with others; 4) devise strategies to be better critical listeners; 5) feel more connected to fellow classmates through shared experiential learning.

## EXPLANATION OF ACTIVITY

Provide your students with one or two options to attend public speaking events on campus or in a nearby community venue. Have students sign up for a Twitter account on their phones or tablet devices. They can create an anonymous/"fake" account if necessary and delete it afterward, if privacy is of concern for them. Mobile devices are typically available to borrow in university libraries if the students do not have a smartphone or tablet—I recommend seeking out and providing this information to your students when presenting the assignment.

Ask your students to live-tweet the public speaking event they select. Do not provide further instructions on what to tweet, since the goal is to assess what they choose to tweet as indicative of their personal listening behaviors—some might only tweet the main points of the speech, others will comment on delivery, others will talk about the setting or audience, and others will tweet their opinions, thoughts, or unrelated ideas (all excellent discussion fodder). I recommend indicating a minimum number of tweets they should write, depending on the length of the event—for a one-hour talk, about fifteen to twenty tweets should be the minimum; in my experience, students tend to exceed this number. You may choose to provide a connecting class hashtag so students can see what others are tweeting in real-time, or you may choose to forgo this option so students have a more solo listening experience to compare with others during discussion. After the event, have your students go to "Settings" in Twitter and download their tweet archive, which will be emailed to them as an Excel file. Alternatively, they can screenshot or copy and paste individual tweets into a Word document.

Have all students bring a paper copy of their tweets to class, as well as email you a copy ahead of time so you can select a few contrasting examples for illustration. To start class, review major listening concepts (see above). Then, ask the students to compare and contrast the content of their tweet collections in small groups. They should be looking for similarities and differences in the nature of the tweets (Frequency? Detail? Breadth vs. Depth?) and the focus of the tweets (Environment? Argument? Delivery? Audience?). From these observations, they can discuss how different pieces of information tweeted during the same speech illustrate how we listen subjectively. Have them also find tweets in their groups' collections that they think exemplify passive listening, active listening, and critical listening.

## DEBRIEF

Coming back together as a class, debrief your students by helping them summarize the differences between hearing and passive, active, and critical listening using select tweets as representative listening feedback. Have each group share their observations from discussion. Project some contrasting examples you selected before class on a screen, and perhaps some exemplars that the students chose themselves. Discuss these in terms of passive, active, and critical listening, and then help them to point out how comments about the speaker, setting, and audience add to or detract from critical listening. Have them speculate on what the activity of tweeting contributes to or detracts from the listening process. (You should get varied perspectives.)

You should especially hone in on the difference between *active* (gleaning the purpose and relevance of a speech) and *critical* listening (evaluating the effectiveness of the speech content in context), as this distinction often proves the most arduous for public speaking students. Remind them of the subjective nature of listening—a refrain I heard several times during this activity was "I totally missed that!," as students examined the content of each other's tweets. I also found this activity to be a good jumping-off point for discussing various media literacy principles: how publicly disseminated feedback (tweets) during speaking events are themselves speech acts, how tweeting can both enhance and detract from personal engagement with a speaking event, and what tweeting can and cannot accomplish as a form of public participation. Last, you can work to devise and record strategies for better critical listening as a group based on your discussion (e.g., one student in my class mentioned that tweeting main points and evidence before evaluating a speaker's claim gives useful context to those following your tweets, and demonstrates that you are, indeed, critically listening as you live-tweet).

In addition to its relevancy to students and their everyday media use, this activity provides for a lot of flexibility in discussion. How the discussion about listening goes will depend upon the observations the students make about the tweet collections. This means that the lesson will feel new every time it is taught by the instructor, and will feel personalized and novel for the students. Students have some autonomy over the learning process in this activity by selecting the event to attend, deciding what to tweet, and having the opportunity to self-assess. Through this experiential learning activity, students will feel like they have more to contribute to discussion, will take responsibility for the subject matter, and will feel more connected to the class (Boud, 2012).

## REFERENCES

Boud, D. (1988). *Developing student autonomy in learning* (2nd). Milton Park: Taylor & Francis.

Frymier, A. B. (2002). Making content relevant to students. In J.L. Chesebro & J.C. McCroskey (Eds.), *Communication for teachers* (pp. 83–92). Boston, MA: Allyn and Bacon.

Harvard Institute of Politics. (2016). Use of social networking technology: Facebook remains the dominant platform, but education, race, and political party play role in social network preferences. Retrieved July 22, 2016, from http://iop.harvard.edu/use-social-networking-technology

Keith, W. & Lundberg, C. O. (2014). *Public speaking: Choices and responsibility*. Boston: Wadsworth.

Kolb, D. A. (1984). *Experiential learning: Experience as the source of learning and development.* Englewood Cliffs, NJ: Prentice-Hall.

Shilpa, J. (2014). New media technology in education: A genre of outreach learning. *Global Media Journal: Indian Edition 5*(1), 1–10.

Rinaldo, S., Tapp, S., & Laverie, D. (2011). Learning by tweeting: Using twitter as a pedagogical tool. *Journal of Marketing Education 33*(2), 193–203.

# 3

# Argument Framing Based on Audience Disposition

*Katie L. Turkiewicz, Ph.D.*
*Department of Communication*
*University of Wisconsin Green Bay*
*turkiewk@uwgb.edu*

**History:** This activity was presented at the annual meeting of the Central States Communication Association, April 2015, in Madison, Wisconsin.

**Primary courses in which this activity might be used:** Public Speaking, Persuasion, Organizational Communication, Human Communication, Rhetorical Criticism

**Concepts illustrated:** Persuasion, Argument Framing, Competence, Social Judgment Theory, Audience Adaptation

## PURPOSE

The role of the audience in persuasive argument development is a crucial element in instructing methods of persuasion. When tasked with developing their first persuasive speech in an introductory-level public speaking course, many students identify topics they are interested in and seek to engage the audience's interest and concern in that topic. The notion that these audience members would be enthusiastically opposed to their topic is often not a factor they consider during persuasive speech development and delivery. This activity targets the concepts of audience disposition and latitudes of acceptance and rejection in an effort to expose students to the impact supportive, unsupportive, and neutral audiences can have on persuasive argument development. My goal in designing this activity was to get students to confront situations in which the audience is potentially hostile and challenge them to demonstrate critical thinking and flexibility in how they approach these audiences with persuasion remaining the primary goal.

## EXPLANATION OF ACTIVITY

This activity takes approximately twenty-five to thirty-five minutes to complete. It requires either the use of handouts or a projection screen with a scenario(s) and instructions for the students.

In preparation, the students should understand the following concepts related to persuasive speech development: (a) audience dispositions (i.e., hostile, sympathetic, and neutral), (b) the impact of audience disposition on main point development, (c) latitudes of acceptance and rejection, (d) the boomerang effect, and (e) social judgment theory (Fraleigh & Tuman, 2011; O'Keefe, 1990; Sherif & Hovland, 1961).

Once the above topics are covered in a lecture, the class can be broken down into dyads or small groups. The students are handed (or shown) a persuasive speech topic (e.g., "Turning a public beach on Lake Michigan into a 'dog-friendly' beach") and a list of three different audiences (e.g., local dog-owners, town council members, and a special interest group directly opposed to their efforts that is trying to get that exact same beach turned into a public recreation area for intramural sports teams). The students are instructed to do the following:

(1) Identify the disposition for each of the three audiences (hostile, sympathetic, or neutral).
(2) Develop three main points that would accommodate each disposition (nine points in total).
(3) For the hostile audience, identify which of the three main points that you think would fall into their latitude of acceptance and/or latitude or rejection, and explain why.

Depending upon the size of the class, you can ask a representative from each dyad or group to present their responses to the entire class.

## DEBRIEF

After students have presented their responses to the class, the following prompts and questions can be utilized to guide discussion:

- As a pair or group, how did you determine the disposition for each of the three audiences provided?
- Which of the three audiences took you the most time to develop main points for? Why do you think that is?
- Which of the three audiences took you the least time to develop main points for? Why do you think that is?
- Explain your group process for approaching the same topic in multiple ways to account for different audience dispositions. What sorts of challenges came up, and how did you handle them?
- Now that you have heard from your fellow classmates, what main points had the potential to produce a boomerang effect with the hostile audience?

- How can this exercise help you as you embark on developing your own persuasive speeches?

A major point of emphasis that instructors should take care to highlight during this debrief discussion is that this activity challenges students to make educated guesses about the different audiences they are addressing. These educated guesses must remain flexible so that the speaker can adjust in the moment based on audience feedback.

After several years of doing this exercise in my public speaking courses, I have found that students really enjoy it and capitalize on the opportunity to critically think about audience disposition in persuasive speech development. Furthermore, I have found that applying the lecture material in this manner promotes retention for subsequent exams or quizzes.

This activity requires students to think critically and demonstrate flexibility in their approach to various types of audiences. It oftentimes alerts students to the large variety of approaches they can take when making a persuasive argument and reinforces the importance of audience tailoring in a manner that is applied and practical.

## REFERENCES

Fraleigh, D. M., & Tuman, J. S. (2011). *Speak up!: An illustrated guide to public speaking* (2nd ed.). Boston: Bedford/St. Martin's.

O'Keefe, D. K. (1990). *Persuasion: Theory and research.* Newbury Park, CA: Sage.

Sherif, M., & Hovland, C. I. (1961). *Social judgment, assimilation, and contrast effects in communication and attitude change.* New Haven: Yale University Press.

# 4

# Middle School Service-Learning Informative Speech

*Joshua F. Hoops*
*Department of Communication & Theatre*
*William Jewell College*
*hoopsj@william.jewell.edu*

**History:** This activity was presented at the annual meeting of the National Communication Association, November 2016, in Philadelphia, Pennsylvania. **Primary courses in which this activity might be used:** Public Speaking **Concepts illustrated:** Audience Analysis and Adaptation

## PURPOSE

After teaching public speaking for a number of years, I had become dissatisfied with the way in which I was approaching the class. Part of this discontentment can be traced to how unnatural some of the major assignments felt. For example, in what context would someone actually give a speech about gun control, rubber (a real topic!), legalization of marijuana, and so on, to a captive audience of his/her peers? Thus, this assignment developed out of my desire to provide my students with a real audience with a very clear and tangible objective, as well as to increase student ownership/engagement and serve the community. To consummate my vision, I developed a partnership with the Kansas City school district, and began working with middle school teachers who offer college preparation classes. Each semester I work with a different middle school.

## EXPLANATION OF ACTIVITY

During the second week of the semester, you should introduce students to audience analysis at length. The class will then take a field trip to a partnering middle school to get acquainted with the interests and personalities of the students, as well as the social dynamics of the specific class. The field trip can be divided into two parts: 1) icebreaker(s) and 2) small-group discussions. The students should be given responsibility for selecting and leading the icebreaker(s) and facilitating the small-group discussions. The icebreakers are intended to begin establishing rapport between your students and the middle school students, hopefully leading to richer and more open small group discussions.

After the field trip, students should complete audience analysis forms, which ask them to record their observations, including demographics (e.g., ethnicity and socioeconomic class) and psychographics (e.g., ambitions, attitudes, curiosities, and hobbies). These insights then become focal points for subsequent class discussions on speech organization, visual aids, and delivery, in preparation for the first major assignment, which is an informative speech about college.

Your students will probably have some generalized thoughts on what a middle school student would be like and what they should know about college, but you should challenge them to be very intentional in framing their speech to the specific audience your class has visited. That audience should inform aspects of their speech such as thesis statement development, evidence selection, and use of jargon. In my two-and-a-half years doing this assignment, I have been fascinated by the diversity of middle school students with whom my classes have worked. For example, one class had a number of students who just wanted to know about the majors that would make the most money. A second group had a number of students who felt marginalized at their schools. Other classes have had students who do not see college as a realistic pursuit. My students are also routinely surprised by the questions they are asked, such as "Do you have a curfew?" These epiphany moments have influenced insightful student topics such as the benefits and perils of collegial freedom.

Toward the end of the semester, the middle school students should visit your campus. Divide the speakers into smaller groups to be sensitive to middle school attention spans. Following the speeches, you may find it beneficial to have your students take the youth on campus tours—not to recruit for your college, but to provide the middle school students with information that will help launch them on a trajectory toward their desired outcome(s).

Upon returning to their school, the middle school students should complete an assessment created by your students. The instructions I provide my students for the assessment are a) how will you know if your speeches were successful? and b) what would you like to know from the middle-school students afterward? Your students will then get audience feedback from the kids, which my students have often found to be very encouraging.

## DEBRIEF

After the day of speeches, debrief with the students about how they felt the day went, how they perceived the students responded to their speeches, and the questions they were asked during the tours. Ask them to reflect on how the field trip, specifically the things they learned about the students through observation and interviewing, informed their oratorical and rhetorical choices they made regarding the components of public speaking, such as introductions, vocal variety, and language. Were there certain examples or words that they emphasized? Avoided? For example, one of my students assumed that the middle school students would all be familiar with the movie *The Lion King*, only to learn during the field trip that this was not the case. Finally, ask them to watch videos of their speeches and to identify specific examples of audience adaptation.

There is an opportunity for students to be really intentional about how they frame their messages for their specific audiences. Admittedly, not every student will take advantage of this opportunity (e.g., "I am going to talk about being a student athlete," despite knowing that none of the middle school students are interested in sports), but overall I have been very encouraged by the initiative my students have taken in trying to make a difference in the lives of the middle school students. This assignment has helped me to make the class more relevant for students, who regularly state that they have enjoyed the assignment and that their communication apprehension (another class concept) had been reduced as well.

# 5

# Analyzing Diverse Audiences to Recruit Students to Your College

*Nathan G. Webb, Ph.D.*
*Department of Communication Studies*
*Belmont University*
*nathan.webb@belmont.edu*

**History:** This activity was presented at the annual meeting of the National Communication Association, November 2013, in Washington, D.C.
**Primary courses in which this activity might be used:** Public Speaking, Introduction to Communication, Persuasion
**Concepts illustrated:** Audience Analysis, Diversity, Persuasion, Audience-Centered Communication

## PURPOSE

Audience analysis is central to effective communication. Because of the importance of analyzing one's audience to best construct messages, the subject is widely discussed in communication textbooks and courses like public speaking. Warner (2011) states that "Audience [analysis] ... is an absolute necessity when one is giving a persuasive speech. It is the overarching principle that guides persuasion" (p. 50). Due to the prevalence and importance of both audience analysis and persuasion in communication courses, this activity provides students with the opportunity to draw from their personal experiences as college students to practice analyzing and persuading differing fictional audiences.

A common way speakers evaluate their audience is doing a demographic audience analysis. Miller (2012) asserts that the demographic makeup of families is rapidly changing in the United States. When discussing the differences between today's families and American families of past decades, Golden (2009) claims that children today "come from a variety of home situations including blended, single-parent, dual-career, grandparent-headed, and gay and lesbian families" (p. 1). A comparison of the television shows *Leave it to Beaver* and *Modern Family* illustrates how popular media representations of familial demographics have changed in recent decades. *Leave it to Beaver*, a popular television show in the 1950s and 1960s, idealizes a picture of the traditional, homogenous, nuclear family (Golden, 2009). *Modern Family*, a current popular television show, paints a very different picture of how families are represented on television, and, according to Allen (2012) more accurately represents a new reality of family life in America. Among the three households portrayed on *Modern Family*, there is diversity in age, race, ethnicity, sexual orientation, and parenting styles.

## EXPLANATION OF ACTIVITY

After lecturing on and/or assigning readings on audience analysis and persuasion (e.g., Beebe & Beebe, 2014) students are given the task of evaluating the families from *Leave it Beaver* and *Modern Family* and constructing persuasive messages to recruit college-age family members to attend the student's college or university. This activity takes approximately thirty minutes. Following are suggested step-by-step directions on how to organize the activity:

1. Divide students into groups of three to four.
2. Review course material on the importance of audience analysis and persuasion, specifically focusing on demographic analysis and being audience-centered when giving a speech.
3. Discuss specific ways the demographics of American families have changed in recent decades. (A good source of information on this topic is Galvin, Braithwaite, & Bylund, 2015.)
4. Tell students they will analyze two fictional television families who are very different from one another. They will analyze the Cleaver family from *Leave it to Beaver* and the Dunphy family from *Modern Family*, in order to best persuade members from each family to attend their college or university. Students will act as admissions personnel speaking to each family after completing a campus tour in order to recruit Haley Dunphy from *Modern Family* and Wally Cleaver from *Leave it to Beaver*. If needed, provide a synopsis of both shows.
5. Show students a brief (two- to three-minute) clip from each show that serves as a representative of a typical interaction with the family. Representative clips from each show can be found on youtube.com (search "Leave it to Beaver Clips" and "Modern Family Trailer") and additional *Modern Family* clips can be found on abc.com. Instruct students to pay special attention to the demographic makeup of the families and how the families communicate with one another in order to gain the best analysis.
6. Ask each group to discuss the families and prepare an outline of an audience-centered persuasive speech recruiting Haley and/or Wally to attend their school.
7. You can choose to ask your students to focus on different aspects of persuasion, depending on the needs of your class. Example topics could include persuasive organizational patterns; appealing to an audience's ethos, pathos, and logos; and motivating an audience.

8. After approximately fifteen minutes of small-group discussion, instruct each group to report the findings of their audience analysis and to also explain how they would persuade the student(s) to their school. This happens in two steps:
   a. Students are asked to explain their analysis (i.e., what they learned and/or know about each character/family).
   b. In light of their analysis, students are then asked to act out how they would pitch the college/university to Haley, Wally, and their families.
9. Finish the activity by debriefing the class.

## DEBRIEF

I debrief the class by making connections between the activity, their own experience as college students, and course content. The class is asked to discuss differences between typical Haley and Wally messages. Students regularly point out significant differences between the two persuasive messages. In addition, students often point out how persuasive appeals to family members might differ from appeals to Haley and Wally. I ask the class to discuss how this activity relates to their own experiences going through the recruitment process with higher education institutions. Students often share examples of how they were effectively recruited to attend their university. I also remind the class about different types of audience analysis (e.g., demographic analysis) that they can utilize when crafting a persuasive argument. When debriefing on demographic audience analysis, it is also important to discuss how we must not base our persuasive arguments on stereotypes, but must strive to understand the complexities of each audience. To wrap up the debrief, we discuss how this activity and audience analysis can help prepare them for persuasive speeches in the course and for persuasive appeals in any scenario.

In summary, student responses to the activity have been overwhelmingly positive. First, because all college students, to varying degrees, have experienced both family life and some level of recruitment to higher education institutions, they can easily relate to the activity. Second, by comparing two different families, students report the activity helps them better understand how families have changed in recent years and ultimately how diverse audiences can affect constructing persuasive messages. Third, student effort has consistently been high for this activity. I have challenged groups to come up with the best persuasive message for the fictional students/families, and students have consistently risen to the occasion. Since all students in a particular class have a shared experience of attending the same higher education institution, there are usually rich discussions both at the small-group level and at the classroom level.

## REFERENCES

Allen, J. R., Jr. (2012). Estate planning for the modern family. *Journal of Financial Service Professionals, 66*, 40–46.

Beebe, S.A. & Beebe, S.J. (2014). *A concise public speaking handbook* (4th ed.). Boston, MA: Pearson.

Galvin, K.M., Braithwaite, D.O., & Bylund, C.L. (2015). *Family communication: Cohesion and change* (9th ed.). Boston, MA: Pearson.

Golden, L. (2009). Counseling children: Working with families. *Counseling and Human Development, 41*, 1–12.

Miller, K. (2012). *Organizational communication: Approaches and processes* (6th ed.). Boston, MA: Wadsworth.

Warner, B. (2011). Building persuasion into public speaking. In M.B. Asbury, B.J. Craig, & K. Bruss (Eds.), *Speaker-Audience communication* (pp. 50–53). Boston, MA: Pearson.

# 6

# Myers-Briggs Communication Exercise

*Patrick Breslin*

*Department of Humanities and Foreign Languages*

*Santa Fe College*

*patrick.breslin@sfcollege.edu*

**History:** This activity was created in 2010 and has been shared online with instructors worldwide. It was presented during a G.I.F.T.S. forum at the Central States Communication Association conference in Madison, Wisconsin, on April 19, 2015.

**Primary courses in which this might be used:** Communication Theory, Group Communication, Interpersonal Communication, Interpersonal Psychology, Social Psychology

**Concepts illustrated:** Audience Adaptation, Personality, Persuasion, Psychology

## PURPOSE

Students' understanding of communication and persuasion may be enhanced by the awareness that different people prefer to receive messages in different ways. The message receiver's innate personality style as defined with the Myers-Briggs Type Indicator offers insight into message construction. For example, outgoing and interactive people—extroverts—thrive on input from multiple sources and individuals, while loners—introverts—comfortably communicate one-on-one. Sensors prefer to be given facts, while intuitives prefer to be told about possibilities. Thinkers appreciate messages delivered with directness, while feelers like to exchange pleasantries beforehand. Judgers prefer factual data provided in an organized manner, while perceivers function best when receiving free-flowing and spontaneous information (Lawrence & Martin, 2001). Understanding that each of these differences is a valid approach to communication can support the exchange of messages with individuals different from oneself. This exercise was created to promote the understanding of how to communicate with different types of people.

## EXPLANATION OF ACTIVITY

This activity may be completed in a fifty or seventy-five-minute class period, with a class of eighteen to thirty students. It begins with students filling out a customized version of the Myers-Briggs Type Indicator instrument. (The official questionnaire published by the MBTI organization may also be used if circumstances and the department budget allow; various free online versions may also be employed prior to class; my own version, along with a link to online support, is available upon request.)

I begin by telling the students a parable highlighting the difference between communicating a message according to the preferences of the speaker (the Golden Rule) versus the preferences of the receiver (the Platinum Rule). Then I provide a brief history of the creation of the MBTI by Isabel Briggs Myers and her mother Katherine Cook Briggs, and the influence of Carl Jung in the system's formulation (Saunders, 1991; Myers and Myers, 1980). There follows a detailed description of the differences between the various types, accompanied by PowerPoint slides that provide visual reinforcement of the concepts. I explain that everyone is able to exhibit behaviors common to all personality types, and that we frequently need to do so in our everyday lives, but every individual has one set of behavioral preferences with which they are most comfortable: That is their type.

Students are then told to stand up, come to the whiteboards in front of the classroom, and based on the results of their assessment, divide themselves into perceivers and judgers. They are told to design a party that they would like to attend, and given five minutes to create on the board a poster to advertise it, one that specifically addresses the preferences of the *other* group so that the latter will want to show up. I remind the judgers that the perceivers want flexible activities, unplanned fun, and open-ended events, and I tell the perceivers that the judgers want things to start and stop on time, with organized events and a smooth flow of activities. Upon completing the poster design, members of each group discuss the reasons why they crafted the poster as they did.

Students then divide into groups of thinkers or feelers. They are told that they are the management team of a fictitious store, the Romance Emporium, and that they must design a poster (again, within five minutes) advertising romantic items that the other group will want to buy for their significant others. They are reminded that thinkers focus on goals to achieve, details and data, and pros and cons. Conversely, the feelers focus on other people's feelings because they desire harmony and happiness for everybody. Afterward, each group discusses their rationale for the items they advertised and the way these were depicted.

Following this, students divide into extroverts and introverts. They are told that the other group consists of high school students who should be convinced to enroll at our college. I instruct them to quickly put together a presentation and to choose one of their members to present it. I remind them that extroverts want interaction, sociability, action, variety, and an understanding of what is expected of them. Introverts want peaceful surroundings, solo time to focus, and a chance to adjust to new things at their own pace. Each group jointly creates a message and one individual delivers it as a sales pitch to the other group.

Finally, students divide into sensors and intuitives. They are told to create a sixty-second radio commercial, complete with a musical jingle, to convince the other group to visit all the theme parks and attractions in Orlando (our college is in north Florida, so most of the students have visited these attractions before). They are reminded that sensors want facts, numbers, and concrete information, whereas intuitives want the big picture, fantasy, imagination, and experiences.

In the years that I've administered this exercise, I've never yet encountered an unworkable imbalance in the numbers of types for each section—say, two versus twenty; the numbers tend to even out.

## DEBRIEF

After students return to their seats, I discuss the importance of structuring a message so that the receiver may best understand and appreciate it. I explain to the students that in general they will seldom address specific personality types but rather a blend of all the types, and that it is beneficial to structure a message that accommodates the communication preferences of everyone. I then turn on the computer projector and randomly ask individual students for their four-letter personality profile. A few of these are typed into a search engine, and websites appear that provide more extensive explanations of the personality types.

Parenthetically, in searching online for the four-letter types, the program auto-fills corollary search options, one of which is "career." I usually click on the topmost website that appears, PersonalityPage.com. It provides a list of personality descriptors along with examples of the types of careers that such individuals often choose. I then tell the students, "The fact that these careers are shown for your personality type doesn't mean that you need to do one of these jobs for a living. Every personality type is represented in every profession. But if you were to administer this assessment to people working in these fields, a large percentage of them would have the same type as you."

At the end of every semester, I poll my students, asking what they liked most about the class and what they liked least. The answer to the latter is almost always "Exams!," though an occasional wise guy will say, "Speeches!" But in regard to what they liked the most, they always and without exception mention this Myers-Briggs exercise as the most enjoyable educational activity in the course.

## REFERENCES

Lawrence, G., and Martin, C. (2001). *Building people, building programs*. Gainesville, FL: Center for Applications of Psychological Type.

Myers, I., and Myers, B. (1980). *Gifts differing*. Palo Alto, CA: Consulting Psychologists Press.

Saunders, F. (1991). *Katharine and Isabel: Mother's light, daughter's journey*. Palo Alto, CA: Consulting Psychologists Press.

# 7

# Take a Stand for Persuasion: Teaching Audience Analysis for Persuasion and Beyond

*Jenny Tatsak*

*Department of Business Communication*
*Walsh College*
*jtatsak@walshcollege.edu*

**History:** This activity was presented at the annual meeting of the National Communication Association, November 2009, in Chicago, Illinois. It was a top-ranked submission.
**Primary courses in which this activity might be used:** Public Speaking, Persuasion, and Organizational Communication
**Concepts illustrated:** Audience Analysis, Demographic Audience Analysis, Psychological Audience Analysis, Situational Audience Analysis, and Persuasion

## PURPOSE

Audience analysis is addressed from day one of any communication course, especially public speaking; however, by the time persuasive speeches occur (typically near the end of the course), students often assume they already know their audience. Overconfidence can lead to hasty audience assumptions, idealistic solutions, and unrealistic calls for action. The purpose of "Take a Stand" is to help students analyze their audience in preparation for a persuasive speech as well as to emphasize the importance of audience analysis to communication. In addition to speech courses, this assignment can be used in any course with a persuasive writing or speaking assignment with few or no changes to the directions.

Comparisons are a tool routinely used to better understand an audience and implicit in the audience analysis process. Our public speaking textbooks even categorize audiences into three opposing types: interested-uninterested, favorable-unfavorable, and captive-voluntary (Beebe & Beebe, 2005). Kenneth Burke (1989) explains the power of comparison lies in these oppositions, which intrinsically join phenomena as the standard by which the other is compared.

For instance, understanding of the always vague, somewhat indescribable "good" is made more accessible when contrasted to the equally vague and indescribable "evil." Burke (1953) recommends blending opposites to blur the lines of opposing perspectives, which will create the gray area where persuasive change occurs and exceptions are made for the tidy categories used to box beliefs.

"Take a Stand" exposes the gray areas in students' persuasive stances. Students identify general audience trends and specific arguments in support and opposition of their individual speech topics. They can emphasize those topical aspects the audience supports and refute areas of contention. Most important, they can target those audience members in the fence-sitting middle.

## EXPLANATION OF ACTIVITY

The instructor will collect each student's central idea before the designated class period. The central ideas should be very specific (e.g., "the legal age to purchase cigarettes should be raised to twenty-one" instead of a general topic, "smoking cigarettes"). This specificity enables the reader to more fully understand the speaker's specific purpose, which will increase the predictive value of the activity.

Once the central ideas are collected, the instructor will group similar topics together or to make PowerPoint slides with each central idea for easy viewing by the entire class. A few minutes before class starts, the instructor will set up the room by simply drawing a line in the middle of the board to divide the class into two. On one side, the instructor will write "Agree," on the other side, "Disagree." If the room allows, the instructor can ask students to push the individual desks off to the side to clear the space so that students have to stand; otherwise, they can just sit in the appropriate side of the room.

At the start of class, the instructor will remind students about the different types of audience analysis learned earlier in the semester. Typically, public speaking texts stress demographic, psychological, and situational audience analysis. The instructor will briefly highlight the need to conduct thorough audience analysis *before* writing the speech and constructing specific persuasive arguments. The instructor will briefly highlight the components of psychological audience analysis, which includes audience attitudes toward the speaker and the topic. The importance of this type of audience analysis should be emphasized because of the propensity of audience attitudes, beliefs, and values to predict responses to the presentation. Finally, the instructor will invite the audience to "Take a Stand."

After the preparation, the instructor will begin the activity by reading or projecting a central idea. Students will move to the appropriate location based on their opinion of the presented central idea. Students should bring paper or a device to record arguments for and against their central idea, as well as other observations about classroom trends. Once everyone has taken a stand, the instructor will begin the discussion with the "Disagree" side. Students should offer only a brief reason for their disagreement to enable contributions from as many students as possible. A one-minute time limit works well; however, more time may be given for longer class periods. Next, the instructor will invite the "Agree" side to offer their reasons for agreement. Equal time for the "Agree" side should be given to discuss the reasons for support. Finally, the "Disagree" side will offer a rebuttal to the arguments in support of the central idea. A shorter rebuttal time is sufficient.

The instructor should set ground rules to facilitate the activity. Students are not allowed to speak when their central idea is discussed. The speakers' job is to listen and the actual presentation is the opportunity to share their perspective. Students will be tempted to speak when their topic is offered; however, the instructor should remind them of the rare opportunity this activity provides to listen and learn arguments for and against their topic. Some students will be insistent not to take a stand; however, they should be discouraged from straddling the fence, although a middle line on the board can provide a space for undecided students.

## DEBRIEF

Reflection is critical to the success of "Take a Stand." Reflection begins with an understanding of persuasion as a process instead of just another speech to write and deliver. The process involves each student considering not only the audience's perspective on their topic and central idea, but extending the process to assess the overall trends of the class (e.g., conservative, liberals, apathetic) and trends specific to types of topics (e.g., fiscally-conservative, socially-liberal). While the students will capitalize on the audience's agreements with their central idea, a broader understanding of audience trends and tendencies will help the speaker minimize both voiced disagreements and anticipate potential unvoiced disagreements. The instructor should explain ways these trends may impact the audience's reception of specific topics and central ideas. A speaker, persuading the audience to support raising the age to consume cigarettes to twenty-one, should assess the audience's reception of other speech topics involving government involvement, personal freedoms, and smoking. Audience's resistant to government interventions, especially with personal freedoms like smoking, drinking, and food, will be less likely to support raising the smoking age to twenty-one. The instructor should encourage the class to discuss ways to incorporate these broader insights and trends to understand all the potential ways an audience may respond to their specific central idea. The instructor can also identify ways speakers can conduct thorough audience analysis in the absence of classroom activities by considering the demographic, psychological, and situational characteristics of any audience.

As part of the debrief, the instructor should point out the important role succinct communication and listening skills played in the activity, which serve as the secondary learning objective. The time limitation can be compared to the time limits for speeches and similar to the constraints of any speaking situation; whereas the critical listening required of the activity is common in persuasion as well as most facets of our daily lives.

## REFERENCES

Beebe, S.A., & Beebe, S.J. (2005). *Public speaking: An audience-centered approach* (4th ed.). Boston, MA: Allyn & Bacon.

Burke, K. (1953). *Counter-Statement* (2nd ed.). Los Altos, CA: Hermes.

Burke, K. (1989). *On symbols and society.* J.R. Gusfield (Ed.). Chicago, IL: University of Chicago Press.

# 8

## Worst Case Scenario: Public Speaking Edition

*Laura Beth Daws*
*School of Communication & Media*
*Kennesaw State University*
*ldaws@kennesaw.edu*

**History:** This G.I.F.T.S. activity was originally presented at the annual meeting of the Kentucky Communication Association, September 2006, in Cumberland Springs, Kentucky.
**Primary courses in which this activity might be used:** Public Speaking, Human Communication
**Concepts illustrated:** Public Speaking Anxiety, Communication Apprehension

### PURPOSE

Communication apprehension is a common stumbling block for many students enrolled in public speaking courses. Learning to manage public speaking fears is also a critical topic in many basic communication courses (Bodie, 2010). This activity helps students pinpoint their specific fears about giving a speech. After completing the activity, students realize that often, with enough practice and preparation, what they think of as the "worst-case scenario" when giving a speech can be prevented. Also, students are reassured that they are not alone in their most common fears, as through a class discussion, they realize many of their classmates share the same fears.

### EXPLANATION OF ACTIVITY

This activity, which can easily be incorporated in a fifty- or seventy-five-minute class session, works best if conducted during a unit on speech anxiety. Covering the basics of communication apprehension either in a prior class session or at the beginning of the class session in which the activity will take place provides helpful context for understanding the principles covered here. Students should be familiar with the different types of public speaking anxiety, and the ways in which communication apprehension manifests itself before doing the activity. It is also helpful to offer students the chance to complete the Personal Report of Public Speaking Anxiety, or PRPSA (McCroskey, 1970) to determine their individual level of anxiety.

Before the activity, the instructor should make copies of the PRPSA to give to all students to complete. It is available at http://www.jamescmccroskey.com /measures/prpsa.htm. Completion of this measure and score tabulation take roughly fifteen minutes, so depending on the amount of time an instructor has, the PRPSA can be offered in a prior class session or in the same class session in which the activity will take place. The PRPSA is a useful tool that has been used widely across the country and internationally (Hunter, Westwick & Haleta, 2014). Administering this test will get students to think through what specifically about public speaking makes them fearful, serving as a good introduction to the activity.

To begin the activity, the instructor divides the class up into small groups of three to five students each. Next, the instructor tells the students to spend ten minutes coming up with a list of the worst possible things that could happen when they give their speeches in class. Each group should designate one note-taker who will be responsible for compiling the list developed by the group. Students are encouraged to be honest, creative, and not worry about how irrational their fears may sound. Remind students that both highly realistic and unrealistic scenarios are allowed at this stage of the activity. Brainstorming for ideas is the key.

Then the instructor asks each group to share with the class their top three fears, and the instructor writes them on the board, creating a "worst-case scenario" list. If time permits, allow students to continue to share the remainder of their lists. Instructors will likely hear a range of fears, and it's important not to trivialize or edit the fears as the groups announce them. For example, in my classes, I routinely have students say things like a zombie apocalypse or a spontaneous building fire would be the worst thing that could happen. I laugh along with the class as I list these irrational and unlikely fears on the board. I also make sure to encourage the suggestion of more realistic fears, such as stuttering, experiencing a visual aid malfunction, or forgetting what they wanted to say.

After the instructor has listed all the "worst-case scenarios" on the board, a discussion follows about which of the fears are actually likely to come true (i.e., a visual aid malfunctioning or forgetting notecards are more likely scenarios than zombies attacking the classroom). Cross off any item on the board that could be classified as unrealistic or highly unlikely. This should result in a much shorter list of fears that can likely be grouped into two categories: things that are within the students' control and things that are not.

Discuss ways to prepare for the worst case scenarios that are within students' control and can likely be prevented, such as ensuring students have a backup visual aid in case technology is not functioning on the day of their speech, or preparing a backup copy of notes to keep with them at all times leading up to the speech. Then talk about things that are outside of the students' control, such as losing one's voice or having a panic attack on speech days. This provides the instructor the opportunity to let students know of policies on speech makeups, and to reassure students that the number of things that could happen to ruin a speech that are outside the student's control are very few and still unlikely to happen.

## DEBRIEF

At the conclusion of the activity, instructors should ask students to comment on how their PRPSA scores may have influenced the list of items they feared most in public speaking. Discussions may reveal that higher scores result in more things to fear, or that the intensity of the fears they have may be more severe than classmates with lower scores. Though it is not recommended to have students share their PRPSA scores with the class, a general discussion in which it is apparent that nearly everyone in the class experiences PRPSA to some degree makes students feel less isolated and reminds them that speech anxiety is common. Instructors may also ask students whether they see ways to improve their PRPSA scores as a result of the activity and the completion of the speeches they will deliver in class. Generally, coming face-to-face with one's public speaking fears and thinking through ways to minimize the threat of those fears materializing is a helpful way to improve one's confidence when delivering a speech.

Students generally appreciate this interactive activity, and most feel better about delivering a speech after the activity is over. In many of my classes, we have referred back to it later in the semester because it is so memorable. Most of the time, the class discovers that the "worst-case scenario" isn't really as bad as it sounds, and that most of their fears can be minimized with enough practice and preparation. The small group interaction is usually enjoyable to the students, and it makes students feel better to hear that they are not alone in their common fears. After completing this exercise, students are also more likely to recognize the need to prepare for those situations that may derail a speech yet are within their control.

## REFERENCES

Bodie, G. D. (2010). A racing heart, rattling knees, and ruminative thoughts: Defining, explaining, and treating public speaking anxiety. *Communication Education, 59*(1), 70–105. doi:10.1080/03634520903443849

Hunter, K. M., Westwick, J. N. & Haleta, L. L. (2014). Assessing success: The impacts of a fundamentals of speech course on decreasing public speaking anxiety. *Communication Education, 63*(2), 124–135. doi:10.1080/03634523.2013.875213

McCroskey, J. C. (1970). Measures of communication-bound anxiety. *Speech Monographs, 37*(4), 269–277.

# 9

# Which Do You Prefer?: Understanding Communication Anxiety

*Andrea L. Meluch*
*Communication Studies Department*
*Indiana University South Bend*
*ameluch@iusb.edu*

**History:** This activity was presented at the 2016 Central State Communication Association Annual Conference in Grand Rapids, Michigan.
**Primary courses in which this activity might be used:** Introduction to Public Speaking; Basic Course; Advanced Public Speaking, Interpersonal Communication
**Concepts illustrated:** Communication Anxiety, Communication Apprehension

## PURPOSE

Public speaking consistently ranks at the top of the list when people are asked what they fear most, and in general, most people experience some level of fear related to public speaking (Brewer, 2001; Richmond & McCroskey, 1992). As communication educators, we are commonly presented with the task of helping our students overcome their anxieties and apprehension related to public speaking and other communication activities. The purpose of this activity is to encourage students to share their feelings about public speaking anxiety, give them an opportunity to see that most people have similar anxieties about communicating in public (Beatty, 1988), and help them consider ways to manage public speaking anxiety. Over the course of the activity, students learn that they should not feel isolated in their fears and realize that almost everyone is going through similar communication challenges.

## EXPLANATION OF ACTIVITY

This activity can be completed within ten to fifteen minutes of class time and requires prepared slides or a handout. Before starting the activity, the instructor should cover communication anxiety in-depth with the class, so that students have an understanding of the concept and its prevalence. For example, the instructor should discuss definitions of public speaking anxiety and its causes (Hamilton & Creel, 2011).

Popular books and board games inspire this activity—*Would You Rather?* (e.g., Horn, Horn, Brailler, & Chabert, 2001; Spin Master Games, 2014). *Would You Rather?* books and games present individuals with two equally difficult situations, and asks them to choose the situation that they would prefer to face. For the purposes of this activity, have each scenario presented in a comparison format on a slide or handout for the class. As a class, students should examine each prompt and consider the two options side-by-side. Have students indicate their choices by raising their hands or using interactive software, which can be used for more anonymity or for larger class sizes.

### Which Do You Prefer? Prompts

- Which do you prefer from these options?: Presenting a five-minute speech in class that is evaluated by five classmates, or writing a two-page paper that is evaluated by the instructor?
- Which do you prefer from these options?: Delivering a short speech on your college campus informing students about a new health campaign, or recording a short video to post on your college's website to inform students about a new health campaign?
- Which do you prefer from these options?: Presenting a persuasive speech to a small audience of individuals who have opposing views, or presenting a persuasive speech to a large audience of individuals who share your viewpoint?
- Which do you prefer from these options?: Delivering a short presentation to work colleagues during regular business hours, or working late into the evenings for a week to create a handout for colleagues?
- Which do you prefer from these options?: Presenting a project proposal to a boardroom filled with your colleagues, or presenting a project proposal to a boardroom filled with executives from a different organization?
- Which do you prefer from these options?: Being the best man/maid of honor (what have you) at your best friend's/sibling's wedding and give a toast in front of five hundred people, or not being asked to be the best man/maid of honor?

## DEBRIEF

After the activity is complete, again summarize the prevalence of public speaking anxiety and the concept itself. As a class or in small groups, have students share why their chose one scenario over another and discuss whether they were surprised with their classmates' answers to the prompts. Further, as a class or in small groups, students should consider (a) why they were more likely to choose alternative activities (e.g., writing a paper, creating a handout) to public speaking, (b) what types of audiences they were most apprehensive to speak in front of (e.g., colleagues or executives), and (c) if there were specific scenarios (e.g., speaking at a best friend's wedding) that counteracted their public speaking anxieties.

After the class has assessed their responses to the activity, have students share ideas for managing their anxiety related to public speaking. The instructor can also take this time to cover public speaking anxiety management strategies (e.g., deep breathing, practicing, positive imagery; Hamilton & Creel, 2011).

Over the course of this activity, students are challenged to think about their comfort level with public speaking, where they stand in relation to their peers, and how they can overcome their communication anxieties related to speaking in public. This activity is limited by its focus on public speaking issues related to communication anxiety; however, it may be adapted to other communication anxiety scenarios.

## REFERENCES

Beatty, M. J. (1988). Situation and predispositional correlates of public speaking anxiety. *Communication Education, 37*, 28–39. doi:10.1080/03634528809378701

Brewer, G. (2001, March). Snakes top list of Americans' fears. Gallup News Service. Accessed at http://www.gallup.com/poll/1891/snakes-top-list-americans-fears.aspx.

Hamilton, C., & Creel, B. (2011). *Communicating for success*. New York: Pearson Education, Inc.

Horn, R., Horn, D., Brallier, J., & Chabert, S. (2001). *Would you rather? The outrageous book of bizarre choices*. New York, NY: Workman Publishing Company, Inc.

Richmond, V. P., & McCroskey, J. C. (1992). *Communication: Apprehension, avoidance, and effectiveness* (3rd ed.). Scottsdale, Arizona: Gorsuch Scarisbrick, Publishers.

Spin Master Games. (2014). *Would you rather? Board game*. Toronto, Ontario: Spin Master Ltd.

# 10

## Ten-Second Stand Up or Scribble: Build Community and Reduce Communication Apprehension

*Rachel C. Murdock*

*Department of English, Speech Communication Program*
*Iowa State University*
*rmurdock@iastate.edu*

**History:** This activity was presented at the annual meeting of the Central States Communication Conference, April 2015, in Madison, Wisconsin.

**Primary courses in which it might be used:** Public Speaking, Hybrid Communication Courses, Interpersonal Communication, Business Communication

**Concepts illustrated:** Communication Apprehension, Self-disclosure, Repeated Exposure, Audience Awareness

### PURPOSE

Many students taking the basic oral communication or public speaking course dread the experience. They often suffer from speech anxiety, and nearly always suffer from "I hate that I have to take this class because it is required" syndrome. One of the many reasons such a course is required, of course, is the positive correlation of repeated exposure to an audience and a reduction in speech anxiety (see Finn, Sawyer & Schrodt, 2009, for one of several studies showing this correlation). However, in a basic course a student may give only three to four speeches in front of the class; in a hybrid course, a student generally gives only two speeches (one informative and one persuasive). Such a small number of speeches significantly reduces the benefit of exposure therapy (Gray & McNaughton, 2000).

The "Ten-Second Stand Up or Scribble" activity counters this problem by providing students with multiple opportunities to stand and speak in front of an audience each semester while simultaneously offering a safe opportunity for appropriate self-disclosure. As noted by scholars such as Reis and Patrick (1996), appropriate self-disclosure can increase feelings of closeness and comfort. Additionally, speech anxiety is reduced when students feel more comfortable in their class and with their classmates. This activity encourages appropriate self-disclosure, with students choosing how much or how little to disclose, thereby providing an atmosphere that can encourage bonding and empathy among the members of the class. In such an environment, students are often less apprehensive about delivering their full-length speeches.

## EXPLANATION OF ACTIVITY

This activity takes place first thing almost each day class meets. I introduce the activity to students on the first day of class, explaining both the logistics of how it takes place and the purposes for the activity, including community building and decreasing anxiety. I let students know that we will complete either a "Ten-Second Stand Up" (a quick, oral response to a fun or thought-provoking prompt) or a "Ten-Second Scribble" (a brief, written response to a similar prompt) each day beginning on the second day of class. I also give them examples of prompts that they might encounter (see Appendix on p. 38 for some examples of prompts you could use).

To carry out this activity, I take the following steps:

- I write a prompt for the day on the board or have it on a PowerPoint slide that is posted a few minutes before class starts so that students have time to think of a response.
- At the time class is scheduled to start, I announce the name of the person who will respond to the prompt first. I choose this either by using a random number generator or by starting with the first person on the alphabetical list the first day, the second person the second day, etc.
- After the first person speaks, we go around the room from that person. This ensures that there is a different speaking order each day.
- On speech or presentation days (or other days, if you'd like), we complete a "Ten-Second Scribble." The prompt still goes on the board, but I write "Scribble" instead of "Stand Up."
- Students write a few sentences on a piece of paper to respond to the prompt for the day, then they put the answers in the folder I pass out. I've found that it helps to have blank scratch paper in the folder for those who don't have paper or who don't want to waste a whole sheet for the short scribble. Remind students to write their name on the paper if you are using it as an attendance marker. There may be times that you want your students to have the option of remaining anonymous. Just be sure to mark roll separately on those days, and let students know their answers are anonymous.

I also choose to use this activity as a "tardy" marker. If someone gets to class after the "Ten-Second Stand Up" is finished, then they're tardy. If they get there while we're still presenting, I don't mark them tardy. The name of the activity helps explain that their answers should be brief. If someone takes a little long (it only happens rarely) I just give them the gentle reminder, "This is a Ten-Second Stand Up, not a Ten-Minute one."

## DEBRIEF

For the "Ten-Second Stand Up," I typically only hold a short debriefing. If a prompt is meant primarily to build community in the class and is often not intended to prompt further discussion, I will typically comment on how similar or different people's experiences are, or I will briefly relate the results to class topics (such as noting how someone mentioned a "sudden death" statement that led to a conflict or so on). To make the transition between the activity and the beginning of class, I will either comment on one of the responses or answer the question myself, before moving on with the subject matter for the day. Some prompts lead directly into the topic of discussion for the day, and that makes for an easy transition, as I can segue the discussion from one of the responses and into the topic for the day.

On days that we have a "Ten-Second Scribble" (generally speech or presentation days), the prompts are about topics that are of interest to me as an instructor. There are many times that I will discuss their comments on the next day we meet, and I have often made adjustments to class delivery either in that semester or in future semesters based on the input I receive from the Scribbles. If students recommend changes or give insights that directly affect the class (such as a change of due dates for a particular assignment or troubles with Blackboard), I will ask for input about the issue from the rest of the class in a subsequent class period before making changes.

This activity is often mentioned on my course evaluations and in reflection papers as being one of the students' favorite aspects of the class. Students tell me that these mini-speeches not only build camaraderie and classroom community, but also help them be more comfortable when it is time to give their more formal speeches, as can be expected based on cited research. Despite the time it takes each day (usually about seven to ten minutes), this activity is a valuable tool for both my students and me, increasing both the efficacy of the class and the enjoyment we get from learning together.

## REFERENCES

Daly, J. A., McCroskey, J. C., Ayres, J., Hopf, T., & Ayres, D. M. (Eds.). ( 2004 ). *Avoiding communication: Shyness, reticence, and communication apprehension* (3rd ed.). Cresskill, NJ: Hampton Press.

Finn, A. N., Sawyer, C.R., and Schrodt, P. (2009). Examining the effect of exposure therapy on public speaking state anxiety. *Communication Education, 58*(1), 92–109.

Gray, J. A., & McNaughton, N. (2000). *The neuropsychology of anxiety* (2nd ed). New York: Oxford University Press.

McCroskey, J. C., & Richmond, V. P. (1987). Willingness to communicate. In J. C. McCroskey & J. A. Daly (Eds.). *Personality and interpersonal communication* (pp. 129–156). Beverly Hills, C A: Sage.

Reis, H. T., & Patrick, B. C. (1996). Attachment and intimacy: Component processes. In E. T. Higgins, & A. W. Kruglanski (Eds.). *Social psychology: Handbook of basic principles* (pp. 523–563). New York: Guilford Press.

## APPENDIX

## POSSIBLE PROMPTS

*General:*

1. What was the last movie you saw in a theater? Did you like it? Why or why not?
2. What is an embarrassing thing that happened to you?
3. What is something you got in trouble for as a child?
4. What is your favorite board game?
5. What is your favorite vacation spot and why?
6. What ghost (person who has died) do you wish you could meet and why?
7. If you could be an animal for a day, what animal would you choose?
8. Who is the best superhero: Batman, Superman, Spiderman, or any other, and why?
9. Love is a choice: Yes or No, and why?
10. What's your beef? (Something that is irritating you today)
11. What TV or movie character or plot is most like you or your life?
12. What is one stupid mistake you have made?
13. What is the best/worst book you have read?
14. If you had the power of time travel for the day, how would you use it?
15. What is your favorite holiday and why?
16. What is a goal you have for the upcoming month?
17. Reality shows: Love 'em or leave 'em? Which is the best/worst?
18. When you were a kid, what did you want to be when you grew up? Has it changed?
19. What is the best pet and why?
20. How many selfies have you posted this week? How many Snapchats?
21. Is honesty always the best policy?
22. What is your favorite dessert?
23. What is your favorite Olympic event?
24. If you could take any class at college just for fun, what would it be?

*Communication Specific:*

1. What is a way that you were persuaded today?
2. Think of the last conflict you had. What kind of conflict resolution strategy did you use?
3. Have you ever had an experience with pseudo-listening? What was it?
4. What is a family story that your family tells?
5. What is a time when you were aware of going through one of the stages of relationship building or disintegration?
6. What is a personal idiom used in one of your relationships?

*Ten-Second Scribble:*

1. What is one thing you like best about the class so far? What is one thing you would change?

2. Did you read my comments about your working outline on Blackboard and make adjustments? Did you have any trouble finding the comments on Blackboard?

3. If Arnold Schwarzenegger (or whoever) were to give an instructional speech in our class, what topic should he choose?

4. What is one thing you have learned from informative speeches so far?

5. What is one thing we should have spent more time on preparing for the informative speech?

6. What was the most helpful thing we did in class to prepare for persuasive speeches?

7. What is the most helpful thing you did on your own to prepare for persuasive speeches?

8. What could we have spent more time on in class when preparing for persuasive speeches?

9. What is something you have been persuaded to think about or do differently as a result of listening to your classmates' persuasive speeches?

10. Have you ever had the opportunity to give a special occasion speech in your life outside of class?

11. What will you do differently if/when you are asked to give a(nother) special occasion speech than you might have done without this course?

# 11

# Even Dwight Schrute Suffers from Public Speaking Anxiety

*Kelly Soczka Steidinger*
*General Education Department*
*Mid-State Technical College*
*kelly.steidinger@mstc.edu*

**History:** This activity was presented at the annual meeting of the National Communication Association, November 2013, in Washington, D.C.

**Primary courses in which this activity might be used:** Public Speaking, Introduction to Communication Studies, Business and Professional Communication

**Concepts illustrated:** Public Speaking Anxiety, Delivery, Gestures, Vocal Variety

## PURPOSE

Students enrolled in communication courses will typically enter the classroom with varying levels of public speaking anxiety and addressing the subject early on in the semester is warranted. Introductory public speaking courses, in particular, should strive to train students to utilize anxiety-reducing techniques to help them constructively cope with public speaking anxiety. Bodie (2010) defines Public Speaking Anxiety (PSA) as a "situation-specific social anxiety that arises from real or anticipated enactment of an oral presentation" (p. 72). Educators should address the anxiety that students experience while giving an oral presentation, but often neglect to discuss the potential anticipatory anxiety students can experience before the speech even begins. A study by Sawyer and Behnke (1999) found that "self-reported anticipatory anxiety was significantly higher than anxiety for any other period of speaking" (as cited in Bodie, 2010). If educators address anticipatory anxiety in the beginning of a public speaking course, then instructors will experience increased retention and successful course completion.

The purpose of this learning exercise is to engage students, using a comedic spin, in relevant course material and to assist in lowering their public speaking anxiety before their first graded presentation. This exercise focuses on a fictional sitcom character that struggles with public speaking anxiety: Dwight Schrute. In the second season of *The Office*, in episode 17 titled "Dwight's Speech," his colleagues give him poor advice, yet he still conquers his fears and delivers a successful speech in spite of his severe anxiety. This learning activity illustrates and solidifies several course concepts, including the types and symptoms of PSA, effective speech delivery techniques, and methods for relieving the symptoms associated with public speaking anxiety (O'Hair, Stewart & Rubenstein, 2015). This visual demonstration of these types of anxiety helps students make the connection between PSA and their own past, present, and future speaking experiences.

## EXPLANATION OF ACTIVITY

The first twenty minutes of class should be spent introducing the four types of public speaking anxiety (pre-preparation, preparation, pre-performance, performance), discussing where these fears originate from, the symptoms of the anxiety speakers experience, and the various techniques used to alleviate PSA (O'Hair, Stewart, & Rubenstein, 2015). During the next twenty to twenty-five minutes, the instructor and students will watch selected scenes of *The Office* episode 17, "Dwight's Speech." The second season of *The Office* is available on DVD and to subscribers of Netflix. The minute and second notations in the instructions below correspond to the DVD recording. In addition to locating the video, the instructor will need access to a computer, a projector, and audio speakers to execute the exercise.

### Part 1: Lecturing on PSA

1. Start the lecture by asking students where they believe their fears of public speaking originate. Typical responses should include lack of previous experience, having a previous negative experience, feeling different from audience members, and uneasiness with being the center of attention (O'Hair, Stewart, & Rubenstein, 2015). Fill in any responses that students missed.

2. Explain to students that O'Hair, Stewart, and Rubenstein (2015) assert that PSA consists of four types of anxiety: pre-preparation, preparation, pre-performance, and performance anxiety. While writing the four types of PSA on the board, ask students to record this information for future reference during the activity.

   a. Pre-preparation anxiety sufferers experience fear when they initially discover the requirement to engage in a public speaking situation. This anxiety may cause students to "consider active avoidance strategies such as skipping the assignment or dropping the course" (Behnke & Sawyer, 1999, p. 167).

    b. Next, preparation anxiety can initiate a cycle of "stress, procrastination, and outright avoidance" during the topic selection, research, and writing of a speech (O'Hair, Stewart, & Rubenstein, 2015, p. 45). Sufferers may feel overwhelmed by the amount of preparation time that is required to construct a speech.

    c. The third type of PSA is pre-performance anxiety, which occurs during speech rehearsal and may cause sufferers to stop practicing his or her performance.

    d. Finally, performance anxiety typically materializes in the introduction of a speech, when speakers become aware of the audience's attention (O'Hair, Stewart, & Rubenstein, 2015). Symptoms of PSA include physiological arousal, negative self-focused cognitions, and/or behavioral concomitants (Daly, Vengelisti, & Weber, 1995; Bodie, 2010). Consequently, students may experience an increased heart rate, self-doubt, and trembling during the delivery of an oral presentation.

3. Discuss and connect strategies to elevate each type of PSA that O'Hair, Stewart, and Rubenstein (2015) identify. For instance, effective PSA reducing techniques include building confidence through preparation and practice, modifying thoughts and behaviors, using positive visualization, using positive self-talk, and various relaxation exercises including stress-control breathing.

**Part 2: *The Office* Activity**

1. To provide some context of the plot of the episode, allow students to watch from 2:00–2:40.

2. Show the video from 3:20–5:14. At 3:40, pause the video on Dwight's shocked face. Ask students what type of PSA Dwight is experiencing. Once Dwight discovers that he has to give a speech, he begins to experience pre-preparation anxiety.

3. At 4:18, pause the video and ask the class which type of anxiety Dwight is experiencing. He is experiencing preparation anxiety because he is trying to prepare his thoughts about what he plans to say during his speech.

4. At 4:36, pause the video.

    a. First, ask students where Dwight's fear is coming from. His anxiety is coming from a previous bad experience. Take a moment to emphasize to students the need to use positive self-talk, to surround oneself with positive influences, and to explain Robert Merton's Theory of the Self-Fulfilling Prophecy (Merton, 1948). Lucas (2015) suggests that for each negative thought, a person should counter with a minimum of five positive thoughts.

    b. Next, ask students what Dwight can do to reduce his fear and anxiety. Students should identify the techniques previously discussed.

5. Begin the video again and pause at 5:14. In this scene Dwight's mentor, Michael Scott, uses language that hurts Dwight's self-esteem. Discuss with students what they can do and say to one another to help lower a speaker's anxiety. Ask students to identify types of verbal and nonverbal communication behaviors that support a speaker and which do not.

6. View the video from 9:39–14:28. At 10:25, pause the video and ask the class which type of anxiety Dwight is experiencing. In this scene, he is experiencing pre-performance anxiety while attempting to practice his speech in front of his peers. Instead of practicing his speech in its entirety, he quickly gives up. Discuss the need for students to practice their speech in its entirety and successful methods for practicing speeches.

7. At 13:16, pause the video and ask students what type of PSA Dwight is experiencing. Remind students that he is suffering from an extreme case of performance anxiety and that his symptoms are exaggerated for comedic affect.

8. At 14:20, pause the video and ask students why they think Michael Scott's speech is failing with the audience. It is failing because he does not have a purpose for speaking, and is unprepared and rambling.

9. Watch the final clip from 15:20–18:51. Before starting the final clip, instruct students to pay attention to Dwight's speech delivery and the overall message of his speech. Specifically, students should pay attention to his voice, including volume, pitch, and rate. In addition, students should focus on observing his eye contact, hand gestures, and body movements.

## DEBRIEF

After watching the video clips mentioned in the prior section, lead a ten-minute discussion using the questions listed in the Appendix on p. 44. Since incorporating this activity, students have had an easier time identifying triggers and origins of anxiety. Students can clearly distinguish the type of speech anxiety and take more accurate measures to relieve their symptoms. Consequently, presenting this activity early in the semester fosters a more supportive speaking environment in the classroom throughout the entire semester.

## REFERENCES

Bodie, G. (2010). A racing heart, rattling knees, and ruminative thoughts: Defining, explaining, and treating public speaking anxiety. *Communication Education, 59*(1), 70–105. doi: 10.1080/03634520903443849

Daly, J.A., Vengelisti, A. L., & Webster, D.J. (1995). Speech anxiety affects how people prepare speeches: A protocol analysis of the preparation process of speakers. *Communication Monographs, 62*, 383–397.

Lieberstein, P. (Writer), & McDougall, C. (Director). (2006). Dwight's speech. [Television series episode.] In *The Office*. Universal City, CA: Universal Studios Home Entertainment.

Lucas, S. (2015). *The art of public speaking.* (12th ed.). New York: McGraw-Hill.

Merton, R. (1948). The self-fulfilling prophecy. *The Antioch Review, 8*(2), 193–210. Retrieved from http://www.jstor.org/stable/4609267

O'Hair, D., Stewart, R. & Rubenstein, H. (2015). *A speaker's guidebook: Text and reference.* (6th ed.). New York: Bedford/St. Martin's.

Behnke, R. & Sawyer, C. (1999). Milestones of anticipatory public speaking anxiety. *Communication Education, 48*(2), 165–172. doi:10.1080/03634529909379164

Sawyer, C. & Behnke, R. (1999). State anxiety patterns for public speaking and the behavior inhibition system. *Communication Reports, 12*(2), 84–94.

## APPENDIX

## DISCUSSION QUESTIONS FOR THE DEBRIEF OF THE ACTIVITY

1. Do you think Dwight did well when delivering his speech? What does he need to improve upon?
2. Did his delivery improve from the beginning to the end of the speech? How? Why?
3. What did you think about Dwight's use of language? Which words do you think were politically incorrect? Why?
4. In the beginning of the speech, the audience did not seem enthusiastic about Dwight's speech. Why do you think the audience became enthralled with his speech the longer his speech continued? (Dwight used identification with the audience, and he also gained confidence during the speech, which improved his delivery.)
5. Did this speech seem appropriate to the speaking occasion? Why or why not?
6. Given what you know, what should Dwight have said or done when accepting the award?
7. Which techniques discussed today do you think could help Dwight lower his speech anxiety?

# Arrangement

# 12

## An Organizational Pattern for Narrative-based Ceremonial Speeches

*Eddie Glenn*
*Tulsa Community College*
*reglenn2@gmail.com*

**History:** This activity was presented at the 2013 Central States Communication Association annual conference in Kansas City, Missouri.
**Primary courses in which this activity might be used:** Public Speaking, Business & Professional Communication
**Concepts illustrated:** Narrative as a Facilitator of Information Retention, Narrative as Supporting Material, Appeals to Values

### PURPOSE

While most public speaking textbooks provide organizational patterns for persuasive speeches, no such pattern is provided for ceremonial speeches, although texts do provide goals and purposes for ceremonial speaking (see Lucas, 2015, Chapter 18 for a representative example). This is a curious omission, since in many basic courses, students are in their late teens or early twenties and are quite likely to be attending weddings and other ceremonial contexts in which the ability to create and deliver an impromptu speech can be a valuable skill. I first became aware of this paucity in rhetorical pedagogy when a student in my public speaking course informed me that, while she had given a speech and toast at her sister's wedding the summer before, she didn't think she had done a very good job. She wondered why there was no pattern for such speeches presented in our text, as there were for problem/solution and Monroe's Motivated Sequence persuasive speeches. I could relate to her frustration. In the past, I have been asked *at* a funeral to give the eulogy and asked *at* an awards ceremony to present an award. Such impromptu situations do not provide a great deal of time to prepare a speech! A simple organizational pattern would at least provide an outline for such impromptu speaking situations.

Inspired by Walter Fisher's (1984) argument that humans are the story-telling beings who recount and account for events "to establish a meaningful life-world" (p. 6), I devised the organizational pattern presented below. The pattern is designed to give students an easily remembered template for fulfilling all the requirements of a ceremonial speech—primarily the appeal to particular context-based values—without having to spend a great deal of time during the invention stage of speech preparation. This classroom exercise gives students experience with creating and presenting an impromptu ceremonial speech, and demonstrates the use of narrative as a form of supporting material in speeches. In short, this activity introduces a pattern for an organized, value-based ceremonial speech.

## EXPLANATION OF ACTIVITY

As ceremonial speeches tend to be the last category of oratory studied in a public speaking course, this activity provides an augmentation to the study of ceremonial speaking that students can apply immediately. In implementing this exercise, I first lecture on the importance of evoking values in ceremonial presentations, and provide a brief explanation of the importance of narrative (Fisher, 1984, p. 6). At the end of the class period, I present the three-step ceremonial speaking organizational pattern as described below:

1. Determine a value that is pertinent to the ceremony at hand.
2. Make a claim that the person or persons being honored personify that value.
3. Use real-life examples in narrative form to support the claim made in the second step.

I write this pattern on the dry-erase board and then present the assignment: *Give a two- to three-minute hypothetical wedding speech or toast for a close friend and new spouse using this organizational pattern during the next class period.*

After presenting the assignment, I remind students that the narrative they choose to present should serve as supporting material for the claim that the honoree(s) personify the value being evoked in the speech. For example, if the claim is made in the second step that the honoree is the most dependable person the speaker has ever known, a narrative in the third step that recounts an episode where the honoree slept for three days after a night of binge-drinking is likely not the best choice.

During the following class session, it takes about fifty minutes for approximately twenty students to complete the exercise.

## DEBRIEF

After the students have presented their speeches, I spend approximately twenty minutes of the next class period discussing their experiences of implementing the organizational pattern. Typically, I ask the following questions:

- What are the most memorable parts of some of your classmates' speeches that you heard?
- How does telling a story help evoke values in a speech?
- What are some other ceremonial contexts, besides wedding speeches, where this pattern could be utilized?
- Would you feel comfortable preparing one right now? Why or why not?

I have found that this activity is quite effective in demonstrating the power of narrative in supporting a claim, and in helping audience members retain information from a speech. Students often respond to the first debriefing question by pointing out that another student's narrative reminded them of events in their own lives. This recognition of shared values and common narratives often facilitates more nuanced answers to the second debriefing question. The fourth debriefing question often catches students a bit off-guard, but as they consider other ceremonial contexts, they are able to almost immediately outline a speech, thus demonstrating *to themselves* the utility of the pattern in organizing impromptu speeches. Finally, this activity gives both students and instructors a relatively low-stress and even fun activity at the end of a semester, which is when ceremonial speaking is typically taught in a public speaking course.

## REFERENCES

Fisher, W. R. (1984). Narration as a human communication paradigm: The case of public moral argument. *Communication Monographs, 51,* 1–23.

Lucas, S. E. (2015). *The art of public speaking* (12th ed.). University of Wisconsin Press: Madison.

# 13

## *Apples to Apples*: Connecting Disconnected Ideas

### Nicholas T. Tatum

College of Communication and Information

University of Kentucky

Nick.Tatum@uky.edu

### Anna-Carrie Beck

College of Communication and Information

University of Kentucky

anniebeck@uky.edu

**History:** This activity was presented at the annual meeting of the Central States Communication Association, April 2016, in Grand Rapids, Michigan.

**Primary courses in which this activity might be used:** Basic Course, Public Speaking, Advanced Public Speaking, Argumentation and Debate

**Concepts illustrated:** Transitions, Outlining, Public Speaking

### PURPOSE

Even the most skillful speakers may struggle to transition between main ideas in a natural, smooth way. Zarefsky (2014) explains that a *transition* is "a connection, or bridge, between the main elements of the speech and between the main ideas within the body of the speech" (p. 255). Transitions are especially effective when made up of three distinct elements: internal summary, link, and preview. By *summarizing* what has been said, connecting one idea to the next by *linking* them together, and *previewing* what is about to be said, a speaker can effectively take the audience from one concept to another in a smooth and predictable manner.

Thus the purposes of this activity are threefold. First, by the end of this activity, students should be able to effectively construct three-part transitions. Second, students should be able to identify effective and ineffective transitions. Third, students should make progress in reducing public speaking anxiety.

Incorporating this vital public speaking concept into an engaging classroom game helps facilitate increased cognitive learning and deceased communication apprehension (Girard, Ecalle, & Magnan, 2013).

## EXPLANATION OF ACTIVITY

This activity utilizes *Apples to Apples®*, a popular family board game, to help students practice transitioning between main ideas when speaking. Begin the activity by dividing students into groups of four to five. Then, distribute the red *Apples to Apples®* cards, each printed with a unique noun, equally among the groups. Instruct each student to randomly select two cards from the pile; the chosen cards will inevitably be disconnected and humorous (*e.g., televangelists, Anne Frank, friction, witches, dating, Mexico, zippers*). Give each student one minute to construct a three-part transition to connect the two nouns. After time is up, have each student verbally share their completed transition one at a time to the others in their group. Each transition should last about fifteen to thirty seconds. The outrageous and ridiculous nature of these examples will help bring energy and interest to an otherwise dull topic (e.g., "After exploring the various forms of regalia worn by *witches* during the Middle Ages, it is important to highlight one commonality amongst their wardrobes. While seemingly unique, each type of robe incorporated a *zipper* for fastening"). After each student has completed sharing his or her transition, pose the following questions for each group to discuss amongst themselves for several minutes: (a) What was the most effective transition in your group? Why? (b) Which transition was the most natural? Why? (c) What was the most difficult transition to make? Why?

After completing this brief discussion, have students place their cards back into their pile. Continue having students draw two new cards, complete a transition, and discuss with their group until each has completed about five transitions. Finally, have every group compile their cards into a single deck at the front of the room. Then instruct each group to elect a representative to compete in a final, class-wide competition. Have each selected student go through the same procedure as before and share their transitions with the class. After each student has presented, let the class vote on who made the most effective transition.

## DEBRIEF

Debrief with your students by connecting the game with speeches they will complete during the course of the semester. First, pose the following question: What is the most difficult part about developing transitions? Responses typically focus on the difficulty of *connecting disconnected ideas*. When developing a speech, transitions are more smooth and predictable when you choose main ideas that are naturally connected. Ask students to respond to the following question: What makes the link important when speaking? Students often come to the conclusion that the link is how speakers justify the way ideas are organized and connected. Finally, pose the following summative question: What makes an effective transition? As an instructor, emphasize that effective transitions are smooth and effortless. As a speaker, your goal is to take the audience from one point to another with fluidity.

The activity and subsequent discussion typically results in positive affective reactions, increased ability in implementing transitions, and progress toward reducing public speaking anxiety. While this activity is designed to take place in a face-to-face classroom, it could also be easily implemented in an online learning environment. Assign students several pairs of red cards via email or learning management system. Then, have students post a video of their best transition on a class blog. This also serves as excellent way to familiarize students with posting videos and speaking virtually in front of their peers.

## REFERENCES

Girard, C., Ecalle, J., & Magnan, A. (2013). Serious games as new educational tools: How effective are they? A meta-analysis of recent studies. *Journal of Computer Assisted Learning, 29,* 207–219. doi:10.1111/j.1365-2729.2012.00489.x

Zarefsky, D. (2014). *Public speaking: Strategies for success.* (7th ed.) Saddle River, NJ: Pearson Education, Inc.

# 14

# Transitioning from Essay Writing to Speechwriting: Using Post-It Notes for Invention

*Susan M. Ward, Ph.D.*
*Department of Communication Studies*
*Delaware County Community College*
*sward@dccc.edu*

**History:** This activity was presented at the annual meeting of the Eastern Communication Association, April 2012, in Cambridge, Massachusetts.

**Primary courses in which this activity might be used:** Public Speaking, Speechwriting, or any course with a speechwriting component
**Concepts illustrated:** Aristotle's Canons of Rhetoric (invention and arrangement)

## PURPOSE

Many students enter classes with a fair amount of knowledge about outlining from their prior coursework in composition. While many students understand the importance of outlining, many readily admit that they often do not outline an essay and/or speech before they begin writing. Furthermore, the brainstorming process for speech content can be short-circuited by the instructor's or student's expectation of how many points a speech should include, such as the classic three-point speech or essay. In fact, students can become somewhat fixated on structure at the expense of considering the most engaging content. This activity is designed to help students understand the importance of outlining for both the audience and the speaker by focusing on two of Aristotle's canons of rhetoric—invention and arrangement. It creates room for greater creative engagement in these processes via the use of a visual tool.

As a foundational rhetorical theory about the speechmaking process, Aristotle's canons of rhetoric provide the speechwriter with guidance regarding developing speech content. In particular, for Aristotle, rhetoric is primarily an activity of invention as the speaker works to discover the available means of persuasion. This discovery process inherently involves idea generation and argu-ably, to be most effective, should encourage creativity as a means of generating as many content choices as possible. Such a breadth of choices affords the speaker the opportunity to harness the best available means of persuasion.

The goal of the activity is threefold. The first is to help students to under-stand the importance of outlining in the speechmaking process. Second, stu-dents transfer prior knowledge about writing essays to the context of writing an outline for a speech. Third, students use a creative approach to developing and organizing speech content.

## EXPLANATION OF ACTIVITY

This activity has three parts: before class, during class, and after class.

### Before Class

Note: This step assumes that students have already chosen a speech topic and have been taught about credibility of sources. Although the latter could easily be taught later, using the articles students bring to class.

1. Students are asked to read material about outlining. Chapters about outlining included in most introductory public speaking texts suffice for the activity. An open-source option includes The Public Speaking Project (2011).
2. Students are asked to research their speech topic with the goal of find-ing two articles to bring to class. These articles should follow the credi-bility guidelines discussed previously.
3. Students are asked to read the articles and highlight the idea(s) that they'd like to consider including in their speech.

### During Class

1. Have students write their speech topic at the top of a blank sheet of paper. Give them three minutes to write down all of the ideas that come to mind that they could include in their speech. Encourage them that there's no right or wrong here—they should write down whatever ideas result from brainstorming.
2. Using the articles they located, give them a couple of minutes to add any ideas to their list that they do not already have listed.
3. Next, have them place a star next to the ideas that they think would work well as main points for the speech. Emphasize here that there is no specific number of main points you are looking for at this stage. The goal here is to encourage them not to short-circuit the brainstorming process because they think they only need two points and thus stop con-sidering other valuable points.

4. Give each student several large Post-it notes (4×6 or larger) and have them write down their main point ideas on the top of separate Post-it notes (i.e., one large Post-it note per main idea).

5. Give each student several small Post-it notes (2×2). Using the rest of the ideas from their brainstorming list and/or additional ideas they think of along the way, write sub-point ideas on separate small Post-it notes (i.e., one small post-it note per sub-point idea). Note: it works best if the large Post-it notes are different colors than the small Post-it notes.

6. Next, have the students place the small Post-it notes on top of the large Post-it note with the main idea that they think it pairs with the best. If there are any sub-point ideas that do not match with main point ideas, students can set them aside for later consideration.

7. Now ask students to identify the strongest main point ideas. This process includes discussing whether some of their ideas can be combined, whether or not a sub-point would work better as a main point, ...and so on. During this step, students should be encouraged to move the Post-it notes around as needed.

8. Once they've have identified the strongest main points, they can begin to arrange the sub-point Post-it notes in a logical order on top of the corresponding main point Post-it note.

9. Finally, students are directed to consider the amount of time they have for the speech and how that influences the number of main points they wish to address in the speech. They are directed to make any obvious changes to the content choices they've made so far (e.g., they've identified five rather lengthy main points for a five-minute speech), and to continue to revise as they practice the timing of the speech in the coming days.

## After Class

1. Students are asked to make any necessary revisions to the arrangement and content of the main ideas and sub-points.

2. Using the revisions, they are asked to construct a rough draft of a keyword outline for the speech and to bring it with them to the next class. Recommended resources for constructing the outline include the textbook and supplemental course material, such as an example outline.

3. The revision process continues as students practice the speech on their own and/or during in-class practice sessions.

## DEBRIEF

The activity provides a context within which students can not only engage in the process of invention in a visual format meant to stimulate the discovery process but also to use the visualize format to assist with arrangement. Debrief with your students by using two discussion prompts: How does approaching outlining using this method differ from what they've done in the past and what is the usefulness of this approach? The prompts are designed to process the experience more so than to get at a right answer. Additionally, lead them in a discussion about how invention and arrangement are dynamic processes much like moving around the Post-it notes to find the organizational pattern and ideas that best suited the message and audience. This discussion prepares students for the next steps in the speechmaking process, including practicing the content in order to determine how much time it will take for them to move through it. Follow-up class sessions can include a focus on determining how to decide which content to keep and which content to remove from the speech outline based on audience and speaker needs.

The typical results of this activity are tripartite in form. First, students report that they enjoy using the Post-it notes because they don't have to keep erasing or scratching out ideas from a brainstorming list. Second, students report that the visualization process of using Post-it notes helps them to think of a lot of ideas beyond the more obvious ones, because they are able to visualize how the parts of the speech connect with one with another. In addition, they more readily identify what explanations or supporting materials are needed to connect ideas more firmly with one another. Third, students are able to gain valuable experience about how the creative process using Post-it notes can help them develop stronger speech content because the brainstorming process isn't short-circuited by stopping at whatever required number of main points may be assigned and/or the number students think suffices.

## REFERENCES

Engleberg, Isa N., and John A. Daly. Chapter 9: Organizing and Outlining. *THINK: Public speaking*. 1st ed. New York: Pearson, 2012. N. pag. Print.

The Public Speaking Project (2016, July 29). Organizing and outlining. Retrieved from http://publicspeakingproject.org/outlining.html

# 15

## Talk Story: Developing Thematic Narratives

*Rose Helens-Hart, Ph.D.*
*Fort Hays State University*
*rhhelenshart@fhsu.edu*

**History:** This activity was presented at the annual meeting of the Central States Communication Association Conference, April, 2014, in Minneapolis, Minnesota.
**Primary courses in which this activity might be used:** Public Speaking, Oral Interpretation, Speech Writing, Introduction to Rhetorical Theory
**Concepts illustrated:** Impromptu/extemporaneous speaking, narratives/storytelling, nonverbal presentation skills, rhetorical themes/values, vivid language

### PURPOSE

Communication serves an important function in perpetuating, changing, and sharing culture by reinforcing and challenging traditional beliefs and values. One of the ways beliefs and values are shared is through storytelling (Hancox, 2011) because they are "memorable, easy to understand, and establish a common ground with others that create credibility" (Barker & Gower, 2010, p. 299). Humans have been described as innate storytellers (Cragan & Shields, 1998). Even when stories are fiction, they can teach us about what others value and believe, and can be used for developing memorable thematic threads in speeches.

A cultural tradition in the Hawaiian Islands referred to as *talk story* serves as inspiration for this activity. Talk story is an informal conversation and the practice of gathering to share stories and cultural knowledge, which can bring individuals closer together as a community. By having students tell their own stories, this activity assists them in identifying and showcasing values and themes within narratives, which can reflect their cultural memberships. Students gain a greater understanding of each other, which may facilitate bonding in the classroom community. Also, through storytelling, students experiment with nonverbal elements of public presentation involving the use of their voice, body, and language. They also have to opportunity to practice impromptu and extemporaneous speaking.

## EXPLANATION OF ACTIVITY

The activity is ideally done after students have reviewed concepts related to using vivid language, elements of nonverbal communication (Engleberg & Daly, 2008), and the basics of storytelling (Karia, 2013a; Karia, 2013b). Reserve approximately forty-five minutes for preparation and presentations in a class of twenty-five students and ten to twenty minutes for debriefing. After describing the activity and potentially telling a story of your own, distribute slips of paper that contain three themes from which students can choose (see Appendix, p. 57). You may make the themes available to students twenty-four hours before the exercise to reduce the set up and preparation time if attempting to complete this activity in a fifty-minute class period. Students will select one of the themes they wish to develop in a story. Stories may reflect real events or be fabricated in class during a short (ten minute) preparation period. Stories should be approximately three minutes long. You may use a timer and bell to help students keep to the time limit.

After prep time as passed, students should be placed into groups of three to four and take turns telling their stories to their group members. All groups will be working simultaneously so that at any time, up to seven students could be speaking. Once all the stories have been told in the small group, students will write on a slip of paper the student's name who they believed exemplified the best storytelling technique as outlined on the activity instructions slip (clear connection between theme and story; vivid, interesting, and specific language; clear and easy to follow organization). Students will then rotate to form new groups with others they have not worked with before two to three more times, voting for the top storyteller after each round. At the end of the rounds, the instructor will collect votes and determine the top three to four storytellers, who will then present in front of the entire class.

## DEBRIEF

This activity helps students connect the common practice of storytelling with public speaking. It facilitates the integration of their personal experiences, knowledge, and values in the classroom, and connects coursework to their everyday lives. Students' work will likely vary from highly original to the retelling of fairy tales. With each round, stories become more refined. This exercise also gives students practice in limited-prep speaking without the pressure of a grade. I typically use this activity near the end of a semester during the unit on ceremonial speaking and as an opportunity to receive extra credit on a sliding scale that connects to the number of votes received. This activity could also be used earlier in the semester as an icebreaker and to reduce speaking anxiety. Students get to know each other as they hear about the values and beliefs shared in the stories. The small group also provides a comforting setting to practice their storytelling skills.

Debriefing questions that begin conversations on the practice and value of storytelling may include:

- What were the themes and values present in these stories?
- How did the values help you understand the storyteller's cultural background?
- How did the speaker's use of language/organization/delivery contribute to the development of these themes and the communication of values?
- What storytelling techniques help make these stories memorable?
- In what speaking occasions might you use thematic narratives?

Students generally enjoy this activity because many use humor and personal stories to develop themes. In an ideal situation, students will recall a story they can develop rather quickly. I have seen a couple of students develop "writers block," but by the third round they have produced a complete story. I usually demonstrate a short impromptu story to set the standard of detail and length expected. The most complicated part of this activity is sorting students into groups after each round of storytelling. If attendance is predictable, the instructor may want to preset small groups to reduce the likelihood that students will hear repeat stories.

## REFERENCES

Barker, R. T. & Gower, K. (2010). Strategic application of storytelling in organizations: Toward effective communication in a diverse world. *Journal of Business Communication* 47(3), pp. 285–312. doi: 10.1177/0021943610369782

Cragan, J. F., & Shields, D. C. (1998). *Understanding communication theory: The communicative forces for human action.* Needham Heights, MA: Allyn & Bacon.

Engleberg, I. & Daly, J. (2008). *Presentations in everyday life* (3rd Edition). New York, NY: Pearson.

Hancox, D. (2011). Stories with impact: The potential of storytelling to contribute to cultural research and social inclusion. *M/C Journal, 14*(6).

Karia, A. (2013a). *Storytelling for electrifying presentations* [Kindle Edition]. Retrieved from Amazon.com

Karia, A. (2013b). *TED Talks storytelling techniques: Master the one thing all great TED Talks have in common* [Kindle Edition]. Retrieved from Amazon.com

## APPENDIX

### SAMPLE ACTIVITY INSTRUCTION SLIP

You will tell a story that exemplifies **one** of the following themes listed below. This story should take about **three minutes** to tell. Peers judge the stories. Top-ranked stories should demonstrate:

- A clear connection between theme and story
- Vivid, interesting, and specific language
- A clear and easy to follow organization

Themes: friendship, bravery, embarrassment

**Other sample theme sets:**

- Theme set 1: pride, dignity, devotion
- Theme set 2: generosity, love, gratitude
- Theme set 3: friendship, bravery, embarrassment
- Theme set 4: sadness, desperation, perseverance

# 16

## Hot Potato Extreme: An Exercise to Enhance Presentations, Problem Solving, and Personal Relationships

*Colleen Packer*
*Department of Communication*
*Weber State University*
*cpacker@weber.edu*

**History:** This activity was presented at the annual meeting of the National Communication Association, November 2005, in Boston, Massachusetts. This activity was selected as a top ten submission.

**Primary courses in which this activity might be used:** Public Speaking, Small Group Communication, Interpersonal Communication, or any course that utilizes individual or group presentations

**Concepts illustrated:** Presentational Skills, Narrowing Topics, Organization, Figurative Analogies, Goal Setting, Team Building, Cooperation, Cohesiveness and Creative Problem Solving. This exercise can also be used as a formative or summative assessment tool to determine student learning about basic principles of public speaking.

### PURPOSE

Many instructors utilize individual and group presentations as instructional strategies and/or assignments in their courses. Many students in these courses demonstrate unorganized, unfocused, and uninteresting presentations. "Hot Potato Extreme" (adapted from Project Adventure, 1995) facilitates student identification and utilization of factors related to planning and presenting more effective presentations. Using kinesthetic modes of learning, which are often absent from many university classrooms, this activity provides students with an opportunity to engage in goal setting, collaboration, creative problem solving, and critical thinking skills. Finally, this exercise creates active student involvement and engagement with course material, cohesiveness, camaraderie, and a sense of accomplishment as students work together toward a common goal.

"Hot Potato Extreme" is best suited to introduce general concepts associated with developing and giving effective speeches. It can be used as a standalone activity at the beginning of a course, or at the point in the semester when students begin to focus on the process of speech development.

## EXPLANATION OF ACTIVITY

Start the activity by giving each eight to twelve person team one hot potato (a Koosh ball or similar object) that can be easily thrown among team members without causing harm. Each team forms a circle and establishes a pattern of throwing the hot potato to one another. To determine whether someone has caught the hot potato, have all students start with their hands in front of them. After they have caught and thrown the hot potato to another person, have them put their hands down. The hot potato must be thrown to a different person each time. The last person to catch the hot potato throws it back to the person who started the pattern. In short, the hot potato should start and stop with the same person. The goal of this portion of the activity is to have students remember the pattern they followed when throwing the hot potato. Note that the teams will be performing the activity at the same time, so the timer needs to move back and forth between the teams. Once students realize they are in a friendly competition with themselves or other teams in the class, interest and engagement are high.

After the teams have established their patterns, time them to see how quickly they can throw the hot potato around the circle. The hot potato must be thrown to and caught by each person in the proper order. When the person who started the pattern catches the hot potato, stop timing. Give the teams their official times. Usually, students complete the task in twenty to twenty-five seconds. Encourage teams to get through the pattern even faster. Let team members collaborate within their teams to determine how they can reduce their original times. Time subsequent attempts to see how quickly students can throw the hot potato around the circle (students usually reduce their times to ten seconds or less at this point). Remind students that the only rule to the game is that the hot potato needs to touch and pass through the same order of people. Off-the-wall ideas are welcome!

An effective "Hot Potato Extreme" solution involves a paradigm shift. Students must rearrange themselves to be in the order that they receive the hot potato. Sometimes this involves trading places in the circle, or forming a straight line. Times drastically decrease when students figure this out. Another time-reducing strategy involves the team members putting their hands together and forming a ramp for the hot potato to roll down. This strategy can cut the time to one second or less. Often, team members use only their fingers (cutting the surface area to about one-fifth), which results in times so fast that the timer can't start and stop the watch quickly enough. Teams may determine different solutions and be perfectly happy with a five-second time—which may be the most extreme hot potato experience for that group.

## DEBRIEF

After the students are finished cheering for their team's accomplishments, debrief the activity, applying observations from the exercise to concepts associated with principles of effective presentations. Observations include a plethora of ideas including, but not limited to, having a specific goal to work toward in order to be effective, decreasing time by rearranging and/or deleting extra space, being actively engaged in the exercise, and practicing with different approaches to enhance effectiveness.

Next, ask students how these observations apply to effective presentations. For example, knowing the specific purpose or goal of a speech can help a speaker be more effective in the process of creating and giving a speech. Much like students had to rearrange themselves in different ways to reach extreme times, there are numerous ways to organize information (canon of arrangement) for a presentation with some patterns more effective than others. Students might have to revise the organizational pattern of their presentations to make them flow more smoothly. Minimizing extra space in the activity relates to narrowing a topic and recognizing that not every piece of supporting material can be used in a presentation. To that end, students need to cut irrelevant information and use only the most salient evidence to develop main points. Active engagement in this activity is likened to audience analysis in that involving the audience at the beginning of a presentation can be a good attention-getting and rapport-building strategy. The audience will enjoy and be more engaged with the presentation. Finally, effective presentations require practice. Students may have to practice using different approaches, and when they find one that works, they practice it to become more proficient. In sum, planning a presentation is a dynamic process that requires continual revision.

It may also be useful to discuss how the exercise might *not* apply to effective presentations. Be certain that students don't confuse speed with efficiency and effectiveness. For example, a rapid verbal delivery might detract from the speech itself, regardless of the quality of content (see Marshall, 2013). Sometimes, pauses in presentations can gain audience attention, add drama, emphasize main ideas, create emotion, or provide time for the audience to reflect on what has been said.

## REFERENCES

Marshall, L.B. (2013). *Smart talk: The public speaker's guide to success in every situation.* New York: St. Martin's Press.

Project Adventure. (1995). *Youth leadership in action: A guide to cooperative games and group activities written by and for youth leaders.* Dubuque, IA: Kendall Hunt Publishing.

# 17

# Can They Survive the *Shark Tank?*: Identifying and Evaluating Monroe's Motivated Sequence in Persuasive Appeals

*Sarah VanSlette*
*Department of Applied Communication Studies*
*Southern Illinois University Edwardsville*
*svansle@siue.edu*

**History:** This activity was presented at the annual meeting of the National Communication Association, November 2015, in Las Vegas, Nevada.

**Primary courses in which this activity might be used:** Public Speaking, Persuasion, Business Communication, Entrepreneurship

**Concepts illustrated:** Persuasion, Monroe's Motivated Sequence, Bloom's Taxonomy, Public speaking, Nonverbal communication

## PURPOSE

In the 1930s, Alan Monroe developed the persuasive speech structure now called Monroe's Motivated Sequence (MMS). MMS consists of five steps: attention, need, satisfaction, visualization, and action (Grice & Skinner, 2013). MMS is used to move audiences to action. While people use persuasive appeals to motivate people to act for many reasons and in many occupations, this teaching activity focuses on the use of MMS in persuasive business pitches. Specifically, your students will watch and analyze entrepreneurs' persuasive appeals to a panel of potential investors on the popular TV show *Shark Tank*.

In this activity, students identify each step of Monroe's Motivated Sequence in a clip of *Shark Tank*, and then assess the persuasive power of the entrepreneur's pitch to investors based upon the strength of each step. Based upon their assessments of the persuasive appeal, students guess whether the entrepreneur received an offer from one of the sharks (investors). In the end, this activity takes students through the higher order thinking skills identified in Bloom's Taxonomy (i.e., Application, Analysis, Synthesis, and Evaluation).

## EXPLANATION OF ACTIVITY

Before class, choose a clip of a *Shark Tank* episode to use in class. Each episode of *Shark Tank* consists of three entrepreneurs pitching their business ideas to a panel of investors. On this show, some entrepreneurs get bids from one or more of the "Sharks," while other investors walk away hearing all the investors say "I'm out" (i.e., they are not interested in investing). Students will watch just one of those pitches (approximately five minutes in length) to identify and evaluate the use of MMS. The website Hulu.com streams the latest episode of *Shark Tank* for subscribers, and abc.go.com also streams both single pitches and entire episodes for free. You may be tempted to find a larger selection of *Shark Tank* clips on YouTube, but the vast majority of those videos are uploaded by YouTube users without the permission of the copyright holders.

The day of the activity, start by breaking the class into pairs or groups of three (if your class is under twenty students in size, pairs may be best). You should have already lectured and students should have read about Monroe's Motivated Sequence (MMS) and speaking to actuate (influencing listeners' behavior). Chapter 17 of Grice and Skinner's *Mastering Public Speaking* (2015) gives a thorough overview of MMS. Before the activity begins, you should review the five steps of attention, need, satisfaction, visualization, and action. Remind them that while they may not be pitching their business ideas to investors anytime soon, these same MMS steps are used regularly to motivate them to buy products, to vote for candidates, and to support causes. Then set up the clip of *Shark Tank*. Describe the show's concept (entrepreneurs come and ask the men and women on the panel to invest in their business), then generally describe the pitch they are about to watch.

The students may get excited about watching a popular TV show in class, but focus their attention on the tasks at hand. Tell the students they are expected to watch the clip and try to identify each step of MMS in the pitch. Encourage them to each write down the phrases or arguments they see that accompany each step. Let them know that the next step of the activity will be to evaluate the strength of each step of the persuasive appeal, but ask them to focus first on identifying what the entrepreneur said to establish attention, need, satisfaction, visualization, and action.

Show the clip, but stop it before the entrepreneur accepts any offers, or stop the clip before the last one or two "Sharks" say, "I'm out." Have the pairs or groups take five minutes to discuss how they identified each of the five steps.

As a class, briefly discuss how the speaker in the clip used the five steps of MMS. After you've identified the five steps as a class, tell the class that you will watch the clip again, but this time assessing the strength of each step and the impact each step seemed to have on the panel of investors. Ask them to take notes when they see a particularly weak or strong step in MMS.

Show the clip again and stop at the same point you stopped the clip before. Give them five to ten minutes to discuss the strengths and weaknesses they identified. Discuss the strengths and weaknesses as a class. Ask: What made that step weak? What made that step strong? Was the overall persuasive appeal weak or strong? Do you think they will get/accept an offer from one of the sharks? Show the last few seconds of the clip so the class can see where the entrepreneur's pitch is either accepted or rejected.

## DEBRIEFING

Remind the class of the importance of each step, on its own, as well as the overall strength of a call to action that utilizes each step well. They need to be able to assess the appeals they hear so they can make good decisions. Remind students that they also can use MMS to motivate people they know to act in specific ways (get mom and dad to buy you a car, motivate your sorority chapter to vote in the upcoming election, motivate classmates to give to your favorite charity, persuade your boss to give you a promotion, etc.). If appropriate, discuss if external factors played a part in the final outcome of the clip (e.g., if the product was terrible or the product was exceptionally novel, the delivery or speaking skills of the entrepreneur were weak or very engaging, or the speaker or sharks seemed hostile and not willing to negotiate fairly).

This activity has many benefits. First, many students watch *Shark Tank* already, so they find the clips engaging and enjoyable. This leads students to understanding how the MMS steps of attention, need, satisfaction, visualization, and action are used in high stakes, real world persuasive situations. The students then are able to assess the strength of each step of MMS individually, before evaluating the entire pitch (as a whole) to guess whether it was a persuasive failure or success. Congratulate the students on their ability to take a theoretical concept, identify it in a real life situation, and evaluate its use.

## REFERENCES

Bloom, B. S. (1956). *Taxonomy of educational objectives book I: The cognitive domain.* New York: Longmans.

Grice, G. & Skinner, J. (2015). *Mastering public speaking* (9th ed.). Pearson Higher Education.

# 18

## John Oliver's Long Rants: Teaching the Modes of Persuasion in an Online Public Speaking Class

*George F. (Guy) McHendry, Jr.*
*Department of Communication Studies*
*Creighton University*
*gmchendry@creighton.edu*

*Erika L. Kirby, Ph.D.*
*Department of Communication Studies*
*Creighton University*
*ERIKAKIRBY@creighton.edu*

*James L. Leighter, Ph.D.*
*Department of Communication Studies*
*Creighton University*
*leighter@creighton.edu*

**History:** This activity was presented at the annual meeting of the National Communication Association, November 2015, in Las Vegas, Nevada.

**Primary courses in which this activity might be used:** Public Speaking, Introduction to Communication Studies, Argumentation, Debate, Persuasion

**Concepts illustrated:** Modes of Persuasion, Ethos, Pathos, Logos, Mythos

### PURPOSE

John Oliver's long rants on *Last Week Tonight* gain notoriety for taking poignant and urgent stands on pressing social issues amidst humor and entertainment. In ten- to twenty-minute monologues, Oliver works to hail his audience to think, believe, and at times take action; this results in funny, sad, and/or complex examples of persuasion. These rants provide relevant examples of the modes of persuasion in action, and when shown to students the rants can be used to make abstract appeals (ethos, pathos, logos, mythos) identifiable and understandable. We use these rants to help teach the modes of persuasion in our basic communication studies course—a one-credit online course that is, in part, designed to ask students to think about theories of speaking and persuasion. The purpose of this activity is to engage students in the study of the modes of persuasion through the use of John Oliver's long rants.

## EXPLANATION OF ACTIVITY

This is an online activity where students are broken into discussion groups of five, although it can be adapted to small groups in a face-to-face class setting. The discussion takes place as a class activity over one week and consists of two discrete course activities: a discussion post and replies to group members. To prepare for the activity, select one of John Oliver's long rants from *Last Week Tonight* and embed the video on the online discussion board. It is important to access or create a transcript of the video for students who are hearing impaired. One video we use is Oliver's rant on the state of prisons in the United States of America. This clip can be located by searching YouTube.com for "Oliver, Rant, and Prisons." Other long rants from John Oliver will also work for this assignment. In subsequent semesters, we have used Oliver's rant on Net Neutrality. This video can be located by searching "Oliver, Rant, and Net Neutrality." Almost any of Oliver's rants can work for this assignment; however, we strongly recommend that you screen each rant for content. Oliver's show is on HBO and often contains adult themes and language. In the discussion, students are given the following prompt:

> As this chapter discussed, messages are more effective when they draw from multiple, and ideally all, forms of persuasive proof (ethos, logos, pathos, and mythos). For this discussion, watch the following John Oliver video on the state of prisons in the United States of America: https://www.youtube.com/watch?v=_Pz3syET3DY. Whether you agree with Oliver or not, there is no doubt his comedic bit was also intended to be persuasive. In your post, provide *one* example of each of the four persuasive proofs. Display quotes and/or screen shots of Oliver's bit for each. Explain how you think your examples illustrate each of the four artistic proofs.

Students are given five days (in our class the discussion opens on Sunday and is due on Thursday) to watch the video, find examples of ethos, pathos, logos, and mythos, and post and explain their examples with quotes and screen shots.

After students have posted their answer to the prompts above, they are asked to interact and assess the proofs their peers found. Students are given three additional days (in our class this occurs Friday to Sunday) to read the examples their peers found and to argue which they find most persuasive. In seeing that different proofs and examples were persuasive to different group members we can emphasize how diverse audiences may respond differently to a speech. Students are given the following prompt:

> In your replies to two group members, have a discussion about which type of artistic proof seems most effective for Oliver's purpose and which type of artistic proof seems least effective.

Alternatively, with smaller groups, students could be required to respond to all peers.

In their replies, students then lobby for appeals as the most and least effective, arguing why they found a specific appeal to be moving and persuasive (e.g., Oliver's use of pathos around the low-quality food service prisoners receive). Because the initial discussion required the use of quotations or screen captures, student replies should be clear and specific.

## DEBRIEF

After students engage in this discussion it is important to offer both informal and formal evaluation. Informally, since students can only see the comments within their own group (or in face-to-face, hear the comments of their own group), to debrief the assignment instructors should point out (a) the variety of the examples in the discussion posts and (b) which appeals were ranked most and least effective across the class. Instructors can choose to upload a video (or write a message) to students that discusses salient examples. The instructor's discussion should emphasize why so many different examples were found to be either persuasive or unpersuasive, emphasizing that different audience members respond to different proofs. It is also important to underscore that the ways the proofs are used depends on genre (here a comedy show) and the audience (HBO subscribers are generally affluent). When illustrating the variety of examples in the class, instructors can link this variety to the importance of adapting to audiences in speaking and persuasion. It is crucial to reinforce for students that speaking requires audience adaptation, and that means diversifying rhetorical appeals.

Second, instructors should provide formal assessment of each student's work. We use a grading rubric that assesses the quality of the students' examples and their replies. We ask: Did they correctly identify an example of ethos, pathos, logos, and mythos? In their replies did they indicate the most and least persuasive example in the group and provide reasoning for their choices? We use these questions to grade the assignment. Instructors can also provide positive and constructive feedback to help students understand concepts that they may have struggled to locate in the video. Overall, students should receive global recorded or written feedback, as well as individual feedback on their individual work.

## REFERENCES

Aristotle. (2007). *On rhetoric*. (G. A. Kennedy, Trans.). New York: Oxford University Press.

Birkholt, M. (2015). *Oral communication and critical issues: Com 101*, 2nd ed. Plymouth, MI: Hayden-McNeil Publishing.

Griffin, G. (2006). *Invitation to public speaking*, 2nd ed. Belmont, CA: Thomson Wadsworth.

# 19

## *Shark Tank*: Connecting Ingenuity, Interpersonal Influence, and the Entrepreneurial Spirit in Communication Classes

*Lisa K. Hanasono, Ph.D.*
*Department of Communication*
*Bowling Green State University*
*LisaKH@bgsu.edu*

**History:** This competitively selected activity was presented at the annual meeting of the National Communication Association, November 2013, in Washington, D.C.

**Primary course in which this activity might be used:** The Basic Course on Public Speaking, Business Communication, Small Group Communication, Argumentation and Debate, and Persuasion

**Concepts illustrated:** Persuasion, Negotiating, Public speaking, Impression Management, and Monroe's Motivated Sequence

### PURPOSE

Inspired by the popular reality television show *Shark Tank*, this teaching activity challenges students to embrace their entrepreneurial spirit. Working in small groups, students will develop an innovative and profitable product and use Monroe's Motivated Sequence (e.g., Morgan & Natt, 2012; Seiter & Gass, 2007) to deliver a persuasive pitch to a panel of investors (i.e., "Sharks"). Finally, students will utilize their interpersonal influence and negotiation skills to attempt to secure the terms of a business partnership with one of the "Sharks."

By completing this activity, students should be able to (a) utilize small group communication skills to create a new product, (b) develop and deliver a persuasive presentation, (c) manage a question and answer session, and (d) negotiate a business deal with a panel of investors.

## EXPLANATION OF ACTIVITY

### Introduce the Activity

To begin, tell your students that they will be given an opportunity to think like an entrepreneur and utilize their persuasive and negotiation skills. Inform students that they will get to pretend they are candidates on ABC's *Shark Tank* and that a few students will get an opportunity to play the role of the investors (i.e., the "Sharks"). To clarify the concept of the show—and to get students excited about the activity—instructors could show a short video clip from the show (ABC, 2016).

### Preparation

First, instructors should divide students into small groups consisting of five to six students. Each group needs to create a brand-new product that addresses a relevant and timely problem. The product must be safe, ethical, and profitable. (To prevent potential issues, I do not allow my students to create products that are intended to be ingested, and I remind students that "no living creature should be harmed in the development of their product.") If the development of a product is too ambitious, instructors could invite students to conceptualize a new product (but not actually create it). For example, they might describe an app that allows people to participate in three-dimensional video conferencing. However, they would not need to actually design the app. It is important to give students a sufficient amount of time to brainstorm and create their products, so I recommend assigning this project near the middle of the semester and allowing students to present their pitches near the end of the term.

Second, each group should develop a speech outline for a three- to five-minute persuasive pitch. Each group member is required to speak during his or her presentation. Following the organizational structure of Monroe's Motivated Sequence, each group's persuasive outline and presentation should contain the following elements:

   a. **Attention:** Introduce the group members, identify your investment request, and gain the Sharks' attention.
   b. **Need:** Identify a relevant and pervasive problem.
   c. **Solution:** Present your product and provide a short demonstration or present the proposed product and describe how it would work.
   d. **Visualization:** Explain how consumers will benefit from your product and identify the dangers of failing to invest in it.
   e. **Call to Action:** Reiterate your request and invite the Sharks to invest in your product/you.

Third, each group will need to craft a budget and negotiation plan. How much money do they want from investors? How much money do they need? How much of their company (0 to 99%) are they willing to give in exchange for the investors' money? To help students gage the size and scope of their requests, instructors might want to recommend a range of reasonable financial request for this assignment (e.g., $20,000 to $500,000). For information about negotiating business deals and persuading difficult audience members, see texts written by Baber and Fletcher-Chen (2015) as well as Cash and Stewart (2013).

Finally, students will need to be prepared to answer the "Sharks'" questions and negotiate a deal (five to seven minutes). Ultimately, their goal is to secure a mutually satisfying partnership with one of the "Sharks." However, both parties have the right to reject each other's offers and walk away from the deal.

### Select the Panel of Sharks

To strengthen students' critical thinking skills and add a new level of intrigue to the activity, instructors should select five students to play the role of the "Sharks." (I recommend picking one student from each group.) Each "Shark" has a profile that contains public and private information (see Appendix, p. 72–74). The public information will be shared with the entire class; the private information will not be revealed until after the activity is over.

### Presentations

Give students time to develop their products and persuasive pitches, and then run the Shark Tank activity. On "Shark Tank Day," students should arrive to class with their products and prepared presentations. Instructors should position the "Sharks" at the back of the classroom. One by one, each group should give their persuasive pitches to the "Sharks" and attempt to negotiate a deal. Instructors will ensure that the groups' presentations and negotiation sessions do not go over the advised time limits. Finally, instructors should debrief the activity.

### DEBRIEF

After each group completes its persuasive pitch and negotiation session, instructors can facilitate a discussion session to help students critically reflect on the activity. The following are some sample questions:

1. What persuasive strategies did the presenters use? Which one was most effective, and why? How could the presenters improve their persuasive pitch?
2. Considering the proposed product, describe the group's target audience. How could the group improve their marketing strategy to cater to their target audience?
3. What negotiation strategies did the entrepreneurs use? What negotiation strategies did the "Sharks" use? Which negotiation strategies were most effective? Least effective? Why?

4. If you were a "Shark," what elements of your classmates' pitch convinced you to invest (or not invest) in the product?

### Adding a Twist: Ways to Adapt this Teaching Activity

There are several ways to vary this activity. To raise the stakes, instructors can select a panel of external judges to serve as the "Sharks" for the class period. Instructors could invite local business owners or graduate teaching assistants to listen to students' persuasive pitches and make hypothetical (or real) investment offers. Alternatively, instructors could make this activity more competitive by selecting one central problem (e.g., texting while driving, studying for final exams, or improving one's time management skills), and challenging each group to create a product that addresses that issue.

## REFERENCES

ABC (2016). *Shark tank*. Retrieved from http://abc.go.com/shows/shark-tank

Baber, W. W., & Fletcher-Chen, C. C. (2015). *Practical business negotiation*. New York: Routledge.

Cash, W., & Stewart, C. (2013). *Interviewing: Principles and practices* (14th ed.). Boston, MA: McGraw-Hill.

Morgan, M., & Natt, J. (2012). *Effective presentations* (2nd ed.). Mason, OH: Cengage Learning.

Seiter, J. S., & Gass, R. H. (2007). Teaching social influence: Resources and exercises from the field of communication. *Social Influence, 2*, 197–210. doi: 10.1080/15534510701396625

## APPENDIX

### SHARK PROFILES

| SHARK #1 | |
| --- | --- |
| **Public Profile** | **Private Profile** |
| You are a seasoned investor who isn't afraid to ask tough questions. | You have a decent budget. |
| Over the years, you have made a variety of successful investments. Currently, you have investments in the restaurant industry, educational software, and video game industry. | Your business is worth 2.5 billion dollars. Today, you are willing to invest up to $500,000 dollars. |
| | Despite your large purse strings, you don't like to make a bad investment (as it damages your reputation). |

| SHARK #2 | |
| --- | --- |
| **Public Profile** | **Private Profile** |
| You are a well-known investor. | You have a surprisingly small budget! |
| Your main industry is in media and sports. However, you are willing to invest in products beyond your home turf. | Today, you are willing to invest up to $50,000.

Not many people know this, but you strongly dislike Shark #1, because s/he swindled you out of a great deal in the past. Today, you'd like to beat Shark #1 by out-negotiating him/her. |

| SHARK #3 | |
| --- | --- |
| **Public Profile** | **Private Profile** |
| You are a new investor. The rest of the Sharks and presenters see you as a wild card, because they do not know much about you, your budget, or your negotiating style. | You have a surprisingly large budget! Today, you are willing to invest up to $1,000,000. |
| Your main industry is in retail/fashion. However, you are willing to branch out to different markets. | Even though you have a large budget, you LOVE to negotiate with entrepreneurs for a better deal. Start making some tough offers! |

| SHARK #4 | |
| --- | --- |
| **Public Profile** | **Private Profile** |
| Over the years, you have cultivated a reputation as the Nice Shark. | An ex-employee is currently suing you. Your lawyer is VERY good, but she is VERY expensive. |
| Although you are known for launching the careers of people who promote their products on infomercials and the home shopping network, you are always happy to consider a good deal. | Sadly, your budget is very small. You are willing to invest up to $25,000 today.

To help you negotiate a winning deal, you might want to make a partnered offer with another shark. (e.g., imagine that an entrepreneur requests $40,000 for 25 percent of his/her company. Given your small budget, you might offer to invest $20,000 in a product—as long as Shark #2 agrees to chip in an extra $20,000. Then Shark #2 and you could share the company's 25 percent.) |

| SHARK #5 | |
| --- | --- |
| **Public Profile** | **Private Profile** |
| You are a respected investor. | You have a decent budget of $500,000. |
| Your main industry is technology, but you've been known to invest in promising products in other industries. | It is important to note that you really like and respect Shark #1. During today's class meeting, try to partner with Shark #1 and help him/her make a successful deal. |

# 20

## From Politics to Zombie Survival: Teaching Gestures in Presentational Speaking

*Erin F. Doss, Ph.D.*

*Assistant Professor of Communication, Honors Program Director*
*Indiana University Kokomo*
*efdoss@iuk.edu*

**History:** This activity was presented at the annual meeting of the National Communication Association, November 2014, in Chicago, Illinois.

**Primary courses in which this activity might be used:** Presentational Speaking, Communicating in Public, Business Communication, Persuasion, Argumentation & Debate

**Concepts illustrated:** Presentational Speaking Gestures, Nonverbal Communication, Eye Contact, Manuscript Speaking, Persuasion

### PURPOSE

Nonverbal communication is an important component of presentational speaking (Lucas, 2011; Morgan & Natt, 2012). With this in mind, teaching students to practice using nonverbal communication techniques, such as gestures, is an important if not always easy task. Students often struggle with what type of gestures to use, how large to make gestures, and how to incorporate them fluently into their presentations. This activity allows students to practice using gestures and helps them recognize when gestures are and are not appropriate. The activity can be used to help students both rehearse purposeful movement and recognize ways they might overuse or misuse gestures. Students always seem to enjoy this activity. It serves to both draw the class together through shared laughter and experience and encourage students to continue using stronger gestures and nonverbal communication in future speaking assignments.

## EXPLANATION OF ACTIVITY

To prepare for this activity, copy the mini-presentation scripts included in the Appendix on p. 77, or create your own presentations following the samples. Next, tape/glue the scripts onto index cards for students to hold while they deliver their presentations. Make two copies of each presentation so students can work in pairs.

Before beginning the activity, be sure students have read and reviewed information about gestures, including why gestures are important, the types of gestures used in presentational speaking (emphatic, descriptive, locative, transitional, comparing/contrasting, etc.), gestures to avoid, and how to incorporate gestures into presentations more easily (Beebe & Beebe, 2014; Minnick, 1983; Templeton, 2010; Zannes & Goldhaber, 1983).

To begin, ask students to find a partner and give each pair a set of index cards containing one of the mini-presentations. Provide students ten minutes to practice reading the card to each other, using a gesture to accompany every underlined word on the card. Ask students to stand up while practicing their presentations so they become more comfortable using large gestures above elbow height. Encourage students to be creative with their gestures and to have fun with the presentation. It may be helpful to demonstrate the types of gestures students can use to give them more ideas.

Once students are comfortable with their mini-presentations, ask each pair to present to the class one at a time. Although both partners will give the same presentation, they often have different gestures, demonstrating that there is more than one way to use gestures and providing material for debriefing after the activity.

## DEBRIEF

Immediately following the activity, have students discuss their experience with the activity, focusing on what types of gestures were used and not used, and how comfortable or uncomfortable the experience was for them. As a class, determine which types of gestures worked well in the mini-presentations and which ones needed work, keeping the discussion at a general level rather than singling out individual students. Talk about the ways those gestures added to the presentation. Ask what happened when different students presented the same presentation with alternate gestures—did both interpretations of gestures work equally well, or was one better? Why? Have students discuss the ways gestures can be overused or used to emphasize the wrong words. How does the overuse or misuse of gestures impact the presentation? Finally, make the connection to larger course objectives by asking students to discuss how they can use the gestures they practiced during the activity to improve their use of gestures in future presentations.

## REFERENCES

Beebe, S. A. & Beebe, S. J. (2014). *Public speaking: An audience-centered approach* (9th ed.). New York: Pearson.

Lucas, S. E. (2014). *The art of public speaking* (12th ed.). Columbus, OH: McGraw-Hill Education.

Minnick, W. C. (1983). *Public speaking* (2nd ed.). Boston: Houghton Mifflin Company.

Morgan, M. & Natt, J. (2012). *Effective presentations* (2nd ed.). New York: Cengage.

Templeton, M. (2010). *Public speaking and presentations demystified.* New York: McGraw-Hill Professional.

Zannes, E. & Goldhaber, G. (1983). *Stand up, speak out: An introduction to public speaking* (2nd ed.). Reading, MA: Addison-Wesley Publishing Company.

## APPENDIX

## SAMPLE MINI-PRESENTATIONS

### Politician

Hi! I'm _____. Today I'm going to give you <u>three</u> good reasons to vote for <u>me</u>. <u>First</u>, I have <u>more</u> experience than my <u>opponent</u>, who is only <u>beginning</u> her political career. <u>Second</u>, I have a <u>powerful</u> program to <u>increase</u> business and create at least two hundred new jobs for Gotham City within the next <u>two</u> years. <u>Most important</u>, vote for me because I will <u>cut</u> taxes by <u>5</u> percent and give <u>taxpayers like you</u> your hard-earned money back.

### Tour guide at a museum

<u>Welcome</u> to the museum! Today we are going to visit <u>three</u> exhibits: <u>the Egyptian mummy</u>, <u>the sunken treasure</u>, and <u>the prehistoric dinosaurs</u>. We'll <u>start</u> our tour by heading through <u>this</u> door to the <u>left</u>. If at any time you need to leave the tour, please look for one of the <u>red "Exit" signs</u> located in each room of the building along the <u>south walls</u>. <u>Come on</u>, let's get started—we are going to have a <u>great</u> tour!

### Zombie survival lecture

The <u>single</u> most important thing to remember about fighting zombies is to <u>never</u> assume they are dead. The <u>double-tap</u> is your best weapon. <u>Shoot</u> them in the head <u>once</u>, then shoot them <u>again</u> to be sure they don't get up. <u>Don't</u> worry about wasting that <u>second</u> shell. It's worth the extra ammunition to be sure the dead <u>don't rise again</u>. Be <u>safe</u> out there friends.

### Circus announcer

<u>Welcome,</u> ladies and gentlemen, to the <u>greatest</u> show on earth! Today we have <u>three</u> amazing acts for you. <u>First</u>, <u>step</u> right up close and see the <u>death-defying</u>

feats of the Flying Fontains, a family of <u>four</u> who <u>take to the skies</u> on the trapeze. <u>Next</u>, be awed by the lion taming duo of Her and Him, and their <u>fantastically</u> trained lions and mice. <u>Finally</u>, <u>hold on to your hats</u>, ladies and gentlemen, because you are going to see the Amazing Andy today in a <u>once-in-a-lifetime</u> act featuring his famous penguins! <u>Grab</u> your tickets and <u>let's get started</u>!

## Children's show personality

<u>Hello</u> friends! Today we are <u>going</u> to go to the <u>zoo</u>! Do <u>you</u> know what are at the <u>zoo</u>? <u>All</u> of the animals! We are going to see <u>lions</u>, and <u>tigers</u>, and <u>bears</u>—oh <u>my</u>! It's <u>so much</u> fun to see the animals. What is <u>your</u> favorite animal? (Pause.) <u>I</u> love the <u>monkeys</u>! They <u>swing</u> in the trees and talk to each other using monkey language, like this: <u>*Eee—ooo—eee*</u>! Do <u>you</u> want to see the monkeys? (Pause.) <u>Let's go</u> visit them <u>now</u>!

## Chef

Today I am going to show you how to make an omelet in <u>five</u> easy steps. <u>First</u>, <u>chop</u> up the onions, tomatoes, green peppers, and any other vegetables <u>you</u> want to put in your omelet—the <u>choice</u> is <u>yours</u>! <u>Second</u>, <u>crack</u> three eggs, place them in a bowl and <u>whisk</u> them together. <u>Third</u>, <u>pour</u> the eggs in a skillet over medium heat. <u>Fourth</u>, <u>add</u> chopped veggies, meat, and cheese to <u>one half</u> of the cooking eggs. <u>Finally</u>, <u>fold</u> the eggs over to enclose the fillings. Time to <u>eat</u>!

## Presenter at business meeting

So, as you can see from <u>these</u> charts, the company is doing very well this quarter in three areas, including <u>lug nut</u> sales, <u>wing nut</u> sales, and <u>bolt cutter</u> sales. <u>First</u>, lug nuts are doing very well thanks to <u>increases</u> in tire rotations. Sales are <u>up</u> 50 percent <u>this quarter</u> alone. <u>Second</u>, although wing nut sales <u>do not</u> <u>match</u> lug nut rates, they are also <u>on the rise</u>, thanks to a <u>greater than normal</u> demand. <u>Finally</u>, bolt cutters have become popular this quarter, <u>rising</u> in proportion to lug nut sales. <u>Overall</u>, the company is doing very well.

## Diamond salesman

<u>Good morning</u>! I want to tell you about a fabulous, <u>once-in-a-lifetime</u> opportunity to purchase the diamond of your fiancé's <u>dreams</u> at <u>half</u> the regular cost. <u>Visualize</u> her reaction to this sparkling, <u>four-carat</u> diamond, sure to make her <u>fall in love</u> with you <u>all over again</u>. Now you may get the <u>same</u> diamond from the <u>other</u> guys <u>across the way</u>, but not for the incredible price <u>I'm</u> offering <u>today</u>. Why don't you <u>come on over here</u> and <u>let's</u> do some paperwork!

# 21

## Acting Out: An Interactive Activity for Reducing Ineffective Public Speaking Behaviors

*Narissra Maria Punyanunt-Carter*
Department of Communication Studies
Texas Tech University
n.punyanunt@ttu.edu

*Vladimir Santiago Arias*
Department of Communication Studies
Texas Tech University
vladimir.s.arias@ttu.edu

**History:** This activity was presented at the annual meeting of the Central States Communication Association, April 2016, in Grand Rapids, Michigan.

**Primary courses in which this activity might be used:** Public Speaking; Business & Professional Communication

**Concepts illustrated:** Delivery, Nonverbal and Verbal Behaviors, Communication Competence, Perception, Audience Adaptation

### PURPOSE

Public speaking courses are typically required for undergraduate students across the nation. For instructors teaching such courses, two important goals include enhancing students' awareness of their own communication (Allen, Willmington, & Sprague, 1991) while lessening students' speech anxiety, which is prevalent (Dwyer, 2000). With that in mind, the purpose of our activity is twofold. First, it increases students' awareness by helping them identify ineffective delivery behaviors. Second, it is a fun, interactive, and collaborative activity that can help decrease students' public speaking anxiety.

Public speaking is a complex skill because it requires students to develop the cognitive and behavioral expertise to tune their nonverbal and verbal behavior, while freeing themselves from their anxiety. Unfortunately, several students lack this ability. My ongoing research interest in communication apprehension shows that finding innovative class activities to face this challenge is paramount. Doing so would help students to pass the course, increase their self-esteem, and impact their future professional success. This activity is aimed at achieving those goals.

## Description of the Activity

This activity can be completed in a fifty-minute class period. Before class, print out the following list and cut out each phrase:

1. Using *ums* again and again
2. Swaying from side to side
3. Bad posture or slouching
4. No eye contact
5. Talking too softly
6. Talking too slowly
7. Using repetitive annoying gestures over and over
8. Looking at only one person
9. Saying "You know" over and over
10. Using the same transition over and over (*For example ...*)
11. Too many pauses
12. Talking too loud
13. No enthusiasm at all
14. Mispronouncing words
15. Emphasizing mistakes
16. Crossed arms
17. Jingling coins or keys in pockets or hands constantly
18. Rubbing or picking at body or clothes
19. Playing with hair and/or jewelry
20. Gripping on to the podium with no gestures
21. Chewing on objects, cuticles, fingernails, lips
22. Constant throat clearing
23. Rocking back and forth
24. Pacing back and forth like a typewriter
25. Rambling and apologizing constantly

Shuffle the slips of paper and pass them out to your students at random. Ask each student to give an impromptu speech on topics such as your favorite movie, a desirable superpower, a favorite cartoon character, or someone you would like to meet. At the same time, they have to emphasize what is on their slip of paper. Before your students present, ask them to look for ineffective examples of delivery that their classmates are using. After each student presents, talk about why that delivery style was appropriate or not appropriate, and what can speakers do to improve their delivery style.

## DEBRIEF

This activity illustrates the importance of delivery and its effect on audiences. To help students recognize inappropriate and appropriate speech practices, the instructor should lead a discussion after each speech, and in doing so, make students aware of the ways in which inappropriate delivery influences an audience's perceptions of competence, credibility, intelligence, and preparedness. Instructors are encouraged to talk to students about credibility, competence, and other variables that are judged by the audience. While most of the delivery styles in this activity are not considered desirable for public speaking, it is the audience that makes the final judgment in terms of efficacy. Certain situations, such as a humorous or entertaining speech, might use several of the speaking behaviors in this activity to have a positive outcome. Thus, it is important to discuss audience adaptation as well as speech type (e.g., entertaining versus persuasive).

This activity has always been a fun and beneficial exercise. Students seem to enjoy acting out the bad delivery styles, and the performances lead to meaningful and insightful discussions about how to improve speech delivery styles. It also helps students to increase their motivation to speak in public, and to ameliorate their anxieties about doing so, because it gives them more public speaking experience. Because all the students will be participating, it gives students a safe environment to be evaluated on their public speaking behaviors. Finally, this activity helps students to realize that public speaking is a set of skills that can be internalized for their own benefit rather than just a class to pass.

## REFERENCES

Doca-Morgan, T. & Schmidt, T. (2012). Reducing public speaking anxiety for native and non-native English speakers: The value of systematic desensitization, cognitive restructuring, and skills training. *Cross-Cultural Communication, 8*(5), 16–19.

Dwyer, K. K. (2000). The multidimensional model: Teaching students to self-manage high communication apprehension by self-selecting treatments. *Communication Education, 49*(1), 72–81.

Liao, H. (2014). Examining the role of collaborative learning in a public speaking course. *College Teaching, 62*, 47–54. doi: 10.1080/87567555.2013.855891.

# 22

# Animation and Attention Exercise: Helping Your Students to Become More Dynamic Speakers

*Carole Bennett*
*Communication Discipline*
*Oakland Community College-Orchard Ridge*
*cabennet@oaklandcc.edu*

**History:** This activity was presented at the annual meeting of the Eastern Communication Association Conference, April 2009, in Philadelphia, Pennsylvania.

**Primary courses in which this activity might be used:** Fundamentals of Speech, Business Communication, Performance Studies, Practicum in Forensics

**Concepts illustrated:** Impromptu Speaking, Delivery Skills, Listening Skills, and Supportive Feedback

## PURPOSE

After doing an assessment in the public speaking class, I realized that my students were learning how to outline, introduce topics, use effective support material, and improve their speeches in a number of important ways, but their delivery wasn't changing radically. Most students, especially the very shy ones, were still trying to use manuscripts or memorize their speeches. With both approaches, their delivery lacked spontaneity, energy, and emphasis. Having worked with competitive speech programs, I decided to try a version of what we call "distraction" exercises in the classroom. However, this time rather than having individual students giving speeches and coaching them in the moment, I had multiple students speaking at the same time. The resulting exercise helped students to break their stiff delivery style and move toward a more expressive delivery.

## EXPLANATION OF ACTIVITY

There are two steps to set-up this assignment. In the first part, you give the students a general overview of impromptu speaking and allow them to prepare a speech, and in the second part, you introduce the idea of competition.

First, explain the assignment by saying something like, "It's important to learn impromptu speaking skills, and the next exercise will help you do that. Remember in impromptu speaking, you state your thesis, and then support it with two or more types of support material. In a minute, you'll pick an index card and prepare a roughly one- to two-minute speech. Everyone with the same card will come to the front of the classroom at the same time. When I say *go*, the three or four of you with the same topic will begin speaking at the same time." There is usually some disbelief and laughter from the students, and you may have to let them know that you understand this is rude behavior. However, it is necessary for the class exercise.

The energy level in your room will likely immediately go up too. Then read the speech topics to the class. The following are my topics: the weather, your favorite vacation, your most or least favorite class, Girl Scout cookies, needing money, your favorite food, high school, your pet peeve(s). Beforehand, write the topics on index cards and have four index cards for each topic. On the day of the exercise, count the number of students and cut the cards so there are only as many cards as there are students. If you have a smaller class, you can use three index cards for each topic or delete one or more of the topics. Then invite the students to come up and claim their topic by picking up the index card.

Students should then be given two to ten minutes to prepare a speech about their topic, and then the *rest* of the activity is explained to them. Only after students have prepared a speech do I tell them this is a competition and not only will they be speaking at the same time as the other students with the same topic, but they will be competing for the attention of the audience.

As an instructor, you know your most shy students will be terrified, and it is important to get them up first. The competition tends to build, and having quiet students sit for a long time will probably drive up their anxiety. So quickly ask which topics belong to whom and privately decide on the order the topics will be covered. I recommend that you also announce to students that everyone has to *try* the exercise.

When you call up your first group, have speakers introduce themselves by name. That allows for better discussion afterward. A "Ready? Go!" works to get everyone speaking at the same time. There are three items to note:

1. Although students have prepared for a longer speech, keeping the actual competition time to twenty to thirty seconds works best. Calling time sooner also decreases the dropout rate.
2. After the first group has spoken, you can add coaching prompts written on different index cards. I pass one coaching card to one individual in each group. The cards help to encourage specific behaviors, and I usually start with the easier cards. My cards say the following: Make strong

eye contact, use larger gestures, increase your volume, walk forward, ask one person in the audience a direct question, call on someone by name, walk INTO the audience rows, walk in front of another speaker, use a visual.

3. When you call time, ask the audience who they watched most and why. Repeat this cycle until everyone has spoken.

## DEBRIEF

It is *very* important that no student feel like a failure for this exercise, so after the first set of students has spoken, not only do I ask who pulled more of the attention of the audience, but I also have the audience talk about the strong elements of *each person's* delivery. After all, the attention of the audience will bounce around, so be sure to let people know what is working for each person's delivery. Comments from the audience often include things like, "He seemed so friendly," "She looked right at me," or "Your topic was so interesting." Sometimes I don't ask about who pulled the most attention, and instead ask, "For those of you who watched more than one person, what made you shift your focus?"

After everyone has gotten at least one compliment, you might continue the debriefing by asking questions like:

1. What types of things do speakers sometimes compete against? (e.g., other speakers, cell phones, audience members, etc.)
2. Who seemed to be authentically passionate about their speech, and what are the specific behaviors that made you believe that?
3. What behaviors make a speaker move from dynamic to comical?
4. In presidential and other debates, when a speaker uses some of these approaches, when is a speaker holding his or her ground, and when do they cross a line into rude or unethical behavior?
5. If the person you are debating is saying something you totally disagree with, how should you respond?

As you wrap things up, encourage students to identify one or two specific delivery elements that they will incorporate into their next speech. This activity helps to break students out of their shells, and if the instructor is careful about how feedback is given to all the participants (not just the winners), *all* the students can feel like winners.

# 23

## Stylish Speech Day: A Fun Way to Learn Schemes and Tropes

*Lorelle B. Jabs*

*Communication, Journalism and Film Department*
*Seattle Pacific University*
*ljabs@spu.edu*

**History:** This activity was presented at the annual meeting of the National Communication Association, November 2011, in New Orleans, Louisiana.

**Primary courses in which this activity might be used:** Public Speaking, Argumentation, Oral Interpretation, Persuasion, Rhetoric

**Concepts illustrated:** Figures of Speech, Schemes, Tropes

### PURPOSE

By creating a contest that requires both the use and identification of schemes (a change in the usual order of words) and tropes (a change in the usual meaning of a word), students gain not only another public speaking opportunity, but also the chance to hear their classmates' imaginative ideas and experience how much fun it is to use language in interesting ways. Through this activity, students learn to use language creatively by specifically incorporating schemes and tropes to make their speeches more engaging and compelling. The overall goal is to help students appreciate, enjoy, and *use* schemes and tropes in their speeches and interactions.

### EXPLANATION OF ACTIVITY

By creating a friendly competition between two teams, students are motivated to study and make use of schemes and tropes in a semi-impromptu (one- to two-minute) speech delivered to the class. Their team receives one point for each different scheme or trope used and identified by their team. The fun that students experience in this class period motivates them to continue to use schemes and tropes in the remainder of their speeches throughout the term.

I typically take part of the previous class to give a brief introduction to the style cannon of rhetoric. We discuss how to adapt language to the particular audience and how to keep language interesting through the use of figures of speech. We specifically talk through ten schemes and fifteen tropes in class. I have used the MODCOM Speech Preparation Pamphlet by John Campbell (1981) for this purpose, but any list of schemes and tropes with examples of each figure of speech would work well. To talk through the figures of speech, we sit in a circle and I offer an explanation of each one, then the next student in the circle chooses an example from the two or three examples provided in MODCOM (1981) and reads that example aloud. I encourage each student to use good delivery techniques as they are reading their examples, and have them do it again if they simply read the example without appropriate emphasis and volume.

For example, asyndeton (a scheme) is formed when words or phrases are piled on top of each other without intervening conjunctions. An ad for an ABC News *20/20* advertisement went "Every Thursday night you will be stimulated, motivated, excited, intrigued, exasperated, educated, shocked, rocked, provoked, inspired, moved, amused, enlightened, and entertained" (MODCOM, 1981, p. 36). An example of a trope might be anthimeria, in which one part of speech is substituted for another as in "they returned from the wedding unsingled" (MODCOM, 1981, p. 38).

We talk through appropriate usage of schemes and tropes, so that while the exercise encourages them to use as many as possible for "Stylish Speech Day," they use discernment regarding an appropriate number of figures of speech for their speeches throughout the rest of the term.

At the end of the first class, I hand out the assignment shown in the Appendix (see p. 87) with instructions that they are to come prepared with their stylish speech for the next class period. If the class is not already divided into teams, then I suggest dividing them into Team A and Team B at this point, so they know their teammates for the competition. At the beginning of the "Stylish Speech Day" class period, I have the students divide into their respective teams so Team A is sitting together on one side of the room and Team B on the other side. I ask for one volunteer from each team to keep the time and score for their opponents. I get a score keeper and time keeper from Team B for Team A. I then sit in the back of the room between the teams and arbitrate any disputes or clarify any scorekeeping, but the students themselves run the class for the day in terms of keeping score and time on the whiteboard at the front of the classroom.

I let the students know at the beginning of the class what the prize for the winning team will be, usually either treats or five points on the next quiz. (It amazes me how much competition can be generated by a few points, usually 10 percent or less, on one quiz!) The speeches that students create for this class period are often hilarious because of their creativity along with overusing figures of speech. The students are engaged in the competition, and the class period is filled with laughter, smiles, and excitement.

## DEBRIEF

To debrief this activity, you can talk about where the students have heard schemes and tropes in their everyday lives. You may also want to bring in some recent examples from newspaper ads, YouTube shows, recent political speeches, etc. Ask the students to recall where they have heard figures of speech in their own conversations, or where they have read or used them in their homework assignments. Discuss why one would want to use figures of speech (e.g., make words memorable, sound intelligent, delight listeners or readers), and what one might need to be careful of when using figures of speech.

Specifically, we consider when figures of speech can be distracting and detract from one's message versus enhance it. One fun way to get the students to think about the appropriate usage of schemes and tropes is to have them come up with examples of other things that can be overused. Then you can create similes or metaphors for the appropriate use of figures of speech. For example, like fine spices, figures of speech should be sprinkled throughout a message just enough to catch the interest of the listener without overpowering the flavor of the message itself.

If there is time, you may want to show examples of famous or current speeches and discuss the use of schemes and tropes in those speeches. Martin Luther King's "I Have a Dream" speech works well for this purpose. President Obama's inaugural address also works well as a more recent example. If you don't have time to view and discuss these speeches in class, you may want to give the students the text for one of these current or famous speeches and have them specifically identify the schemes and tropes used by underlining the figure of speech and writing in the name of it in the margin. These can be turned in the following class period as an assignment or as extra credit. My experience has been that students usually enjoy the Stylish Speech Day and include schemes and tropes appropriately in their remaining speeches throughout the term.

## REFERENCES

Campbell, J. A. (1981). Speech Preparation. In R. L. Applebaum & R. P Hart (Eds.), *Modules in speech communication* (pp. 1–53). New York, NY: Macmillan Publishing Company.

## APPENDIX

### "STYLISH SPEECH DAY" ASSIGNMENT

The core concern of this contest is to get practice in incorporating schemes and tropes into your speeches. Just as cream cheese frosting enhances the flavor of a mouthwatering carrot cake, so schemes and tropes provide the finishing touch to sensational speeches. The outstandingly clever and incredibly competent members of Team A will compete against the wonderful, remarkable, intelligent, interesting, amazing members of team B.

Each of you will prepare a one- to two-minute (semi-impromptu) speech on a topic of your choice. The object is to artfully use schemes and tropes in your speech; you will get one point for your team for each scheme or trope that the speaker uses and your team correctly identifies. Please note that your speech should be a surprise to the entire class on "Stylish Speech Day" (i.e., please don't show your speech to your teammates before class).

On "Stylish Speech Day," each speaker will give an impromptu speech. The speaker's team will be taking notes on the schemes and tropes used, and after the speech, they will have one minute to call out the name (or the form, e.g., "the one where words or phrases are piled up without conjunctions") of the scheme or trope, along with the specific example of its use in the speech. That team will get one point for each different figure of speech that was used and correctly identified by team members. (Please note that the speaker may not coach the team on the schemes and tropes used in the speech.)

**Summary:**

- You will have one to two minutes for delivering your stylish speech to the class.
- Your team will have one minute to identify and recall the examples of the different schemes and tropes used.
- You get points only for schemes and tropes used by speakers from your team.
- You get one point for each *different* scheme or trope.
- The audience must identify the scheme or trope with *specific examples* (i.e., not "he used alliteration," but "he used alliteration when he said 'purple-padded panthers'").
- Winning team members will receive prizes!

# 24

# Seussically Speaking: An Elocution Activity

*Stephanie Kelly*
*School of Business & Economics*
*North Carolina A&T State University*
*sekelly@ncat.edu*

**History:** This activity was presented at the annual meeting of the Eastern Communication Association, April 2013, in Pittsburgh, Pennsylvania.

**Primary courses in which this activity may be used:** Business Communication & Public Speaking

**Concepts illustrated:** Elocution, Listening, Self-Improvement

## PURPOSE

The purpose of this activity is to teach students how to control their elocution through reading Dr. Seuss books aloud. This exercise was designed to help students hear the difference in what they *mean* to say and what they are *actually* saying. For example, a student may silently read the full sound of *-ing* at the end of an active verb, but actually read *-in'* aloud. Thus this activity was devised to help students become more aware of words that they have grown up pronouncing in ways that are linguistically correct for their subculture, but not appropriate for all settings.

## EXPLANATION OF ACTIVITY

Before using the activity for the first time, the instructor should explain the purpose of the activity as described above. The steps are then as follows:

1) The instructor encourages the class to enunciate carefully and then, with intentional vocal dynamics to encourage fun, reads the first two pages of a Dr. Seuss book.
2) The instructor then hands the book to the closest student who reads a page.
3) That student then passes the book to a neighbor who reads a page, and so forth until every student has read at least one page. Most books can be passed around a class of twenty-five students twice.

Books that work especially well for this activity include:

- *How the Grinch Stole Christmas*
- *Green Eggs and Ham*
- *The Sneeches and Other Stories*
- *There's a Wocket in My Pocket*
- *Oh Say Can You Say*
- *Oh, the Places You'll Go!*

Once every student has had a chance to read, the teacher finishes the story. Although using the activity once is helpful, it is recommended that instructors conduct this brief activity every other week in class, as not all students are likely to acquire their own collection of books to continue their progress. The last ten minutes of class time is ideal.

After many semesters of trial and error, Dr. Seuss books were identified as ideal for this activity for two reasons. First, Dr. Seuss stories are a great equalizer. Students cannot possibly sound *cool* when they explain that they have "a Wocket in [their] pocket" or "will not eat green eggs and ham." The content of the books makes the entire class laugh, so students are not embarrassed when they realize that they have made a pronunciation error. After all, many of the words are nonsensical.

The nonsensical nature of the words constitutes the second reason that Dr. Seuss books are ideal for this activity. These books are written as poetry, so students must often identify the pronunciation of Dr. Seuss' nonsensical words based on the end of the preceding stanzas and phonetics. When the phonetic pronunciation of the nonsensical word does not match the word that it was intended to rhyme with, students realize that they are mispronouncing particular sounds. Again, students do not feel embarrassed because the realization that there was a mispronunciation of a real word typically does not occur until the nonsensical word had been read which is supposed to induce audience laughter.

## DEBRIEF

This activity does not require a long debriefing, but it is important that students understand when it is especially important to be aware of their elocution. The purpose of this activity is not to practice away students' linguistic heritage, but rather to give them a communicative tool in preparation for entering the global business world. The current generation of college students are entering a more globalized workforce than any before them (Fall, Kelly, MacDonald, Primm, & Holmes, 2013). Clear speech is always an aid in clear communication, but it is critical when communicating to individuals who do not speak English as a first language and have trained their ears to identify precise pronunciation (Levis, 2005). Therefore, being aware of and in control of their elocution is important for students who are preparing to work in the global business environment.

## REFERENCES

Fall, L. T., Kelly, S., MacDonald, P., Primm, C., & Holmes, W. (2013). Intercultural communication apprehension and emotional intelligence in higher education: Preparing business students for career success. *Business Communication Quarterly, 76*, 412–426. doi: 1080569913501861.

Levis, J. M. (2005). Changing contexts and shifting paradigms in pronunciation teaching. *TESOL Quarterly, 39*, 369–377. doi: 10.2307/3588485.

# 25

# Knowing Jack: Comprehending Stylistic Choices

## Vanessa A. Condon
Department of Communication Studies
Clemson University
vcondon@clemson.edu

## Joshua N. Westwick
Department of Communication Studies and Theatre
South Dakota State University
joshua.westwick@sdstate.edu

**History:** This activity was presented at the National Communication Association annual meeting, November 2015, in Las Vegas, Nevada.
**Primary courses in which this activity may be used:** Basic Public Speaking, Advanced Public Speaking, Public Discourse, Language, and Persuasion
**Concepts illustrated:** Style, Register, Language, and Communication Accommodation

## PURPOSE

The stylistic flair of language remains an integral component of communicative instruction (Biber & Conrad, 2009). According to Sorlin (2014), "teaching stylistics encourages students to 'navigate' within language ... rather than have a static relationship with it" (p. 13). With strong influence from our prodigious communication philosophers Cicero, Quintilian, and Aristotle, the use of style, in addition to the other rhetorical elements, remains an important foundation for effective discourse (Floyd, 2015). According to Gee (2008), "teaching language in a stylistic perspective is thus to introduce students to use different registers, genres and styles" (p. 155). First, this exercise specifically focuses on the canon of style and is designed to exercise student analysis of these three interconnected stylistics components: style, register, and genre (Biber & Conrad, 2009). First, the activity operates using Charlesworth's

(2010) definition, which frames style as "selecting linguistic devices (such as metaphor) to make the message more appealing" (p. 122). Second, Wagner, Greene-Havas, and Gillespie (2010) defined register as "a variety of linguistic styles ... that vary according to social context and social relationships" (p. 1678). Sorlin (2014) elaborated that in comparison to style, "register is more 'functional' as it is directly influenced by the communicative situation" (p. 11). Finally, the instructor should also explain genre, or "the culturally expected way of constructing texts" (Biber & Conrad, 2009, p. 16). By having students witness the difference between two distinct forms of register and utilize style's key principles, this activity ensures the achievement of the following student learning outcomes:

- To increase students' awareness and use of style as a rhetorical tool for presentations
- To analyze key principles and features of style (appropriate, clear, concise, concrete, simple, and vivid language) in public performance
- To illustrate the difference between formal and casual register

## EXPLANATION OF ACTIVITY

This exercise requires access to YouTube, the discussion questions outlined in this manuscript, and the attached worksheet in the Appendix (see p. 95). Depending on the depth of discussion, this can be completed in twenty to twenty-five minutes. This activity has four phases: 1) students presenting informal register; 2) analysis of informal versus formal communication through a YouTube video and short discussion; 3) application of this knowledge through the presenters converting their casual register prompt response into formal register; and 4) debriefing.

The instructor should begin with a review of the rhetorical canon of style. Style describes how a speaker uses language to convey ideas (Haleta, 2013). The educator should highlight principles of language and style and their use within a public speaking context. Next, two volunteers will share a personal experience with the class. Each volunteer should be provided a prompt such as, "Tell the class about one of the most interesting moments of your life," and given approximately one minute of time to prepare. Each speech should be about two minutes. While the students prepare their impromptu speeches, the audience should formulate one question to ask the speaker if the student freezes mid-speech. The volunteers should be encouraged to speak as naturally as possible in order to provide an example of casual register. While each student speaks, the remainder of the class should record stylistics components the volunteers used naturally in an informal, impromptu setting (Appendix—Part I, p. 95).

Next, the instructor should introduce Rita Pierson's video "What about Jack," which can be found on YouTube (search "Rita Pierson What About Jack" on YouTube). Feel free to begin with Pierson's example of casual register, which starts at 1:00. This video was selected because Pierson utilizes entertaining and exaggerated language. Her pairing of a complex narrative juxtaposed against an example of clear, concise language offers a relatable illustration of the expected transformation in the students' register. Moreover, Pierson exemplifies what the students unknowingly demonstrated in their personal experiences by neglecting clarity and emphasizing a conversational tone. At the conclusion of Pierson's informal narrative and follow up question (7:00), the instructor should pause the video and ask the following questions:

1. What is the beginning of that story?
2. Why is it difficult to remember the plot?
3. What are some of the stylistic choices Pierson uses in her narrative? (e.g., repetition, imagery)
4. In what way did these choices overlap with your classmates' style? (e.g., abstract language)

Upon completion of the discussion, the instructor should review register and genre, particularly accentuating formal and informal registers. Providing an adequate background prompts students to better analyze the upcoming use of formal register. The instructor can then play Pierson's second version of the same narrative (begins at 7:15). Students should record examples of how Pierson used language and style on their activity worksheet (see Appendix—Part II, p. 96). Following the video, the instructor should ask each of the volunteers to repeat their personal experience to the class using formal register. The speakers should be given one minute of time to prepare a thirty-second to one-minute long contribution. During the preparation time, the audience should form an additional, different question to prompt the volunteer if they freeze. While the student speaks, the remainder of the class should again record examples of how the speakers use language on their activity worksheet (see Appendix—Part III, p. 96).

## DEBRIEF

The activity concludes with an opportunity to debrief the exercise. Possible questions to ask include:

1. What were the major differences between the informal and formal stories? Which style do you prefer?
2. How would you classify our genre in this classroom?
3. What register do you think is effective for this course?
4. Have your beliefs on the influence of style changed after this activity? In what ways?
5. How can you apply stylistic differences to improve public discourse? To improve your next speech?

An overwhelming majority of participants indicated that this activity was highly beneficial to their understanding of style. Multiple students sought out the instructor to discuss their communicative choices, specifically articulating that they had not recognized the differences, disadvantages, or advantages of informal and formal register before taking part in this activity. They indicated that they were ready to apply these ideas to their next speech. Overall, Pierson's use of style intertwined with immediate student application ensured that this was a memorable activity beneficial to student learning.

## REFERENCES

Biber, D., & Conrad, S. (2009). *Register, genre, and style.* Cambridge: Cambridge University Press.

Charlesworth, D. (2010). Re-presenting subversive songs: Applying strategies for invention and arrangement to nontraditional speech texts. *Communication Teacher, 24,* 122–126. doi:10.1080/17404622.2010.489192

Floyd, K. (2015). *Public speaking matters.* New York: McGraw-Hill.

Gee, J. P. (2008). *Social linguistics and literacies* (3rd ed.). London, New York: Routledge.

Haleta, L. L. (2013). *Public speaking: Strategic choices* (7th ed.). Englewood, CO.

Sorlin, S. (2014). The 'indisciplinarity' of stylistics. *Topics in Linguistics, 14,* 9–15. doi:10.2478/toppling-2014-0008

Wagner, L., Greene-Havas, M., & Gillespie, R. (2010). Development in children's comprehension of linguistic register. *Child Development, 81,* 1678–1686. doi:10.1111/j.1467-8624.2010.01502.x

## APPENDIX

## ACTIVITY WORKSHEET

**Part 1:** In the spaces provided, provide specific examples of the volunteer speakers' casual stylistic choices.

| Volunteer 1 |
|---|
| Volunteer 2 |

**Part 2:** In the spaces provided, provide specific examples of Rita Pierson's stylistic choices for both "Casual Register" and "Formal Register."

| You Don't Know Jack: Casual Register |
|---|
| You Don't Know Jack: Formal Register |

**Part 3:** In the spaces provided, provide specific examples of the volunteer speakers' formal stylistic choices.

| Volunteer 1 |
|---|
| Volunteer 2 |

# 26

# Historic Speech Assignment

*Jacob Metz*

*Department of Communication*

*Tennessee Technological University*

*jmetz@tntech.edu*

**History:** This activity was presented at the annual meeting of the Southern States Communication Association, April 2013, in Louisville, Kentucky.

**Primary courses in which this activity might be used:** Introduction to Speech Communication, Introduction to Public Speaking, Advanced Public Speaking

**Concepts illustrated:** Speech Delivery Skills, Kinesics, Oculesics, Paralanguage, Listening to Provide Feedback

## PURPOSE

Proper delivery skills are one of the many things that a student is supposed to learn within a speech class. However, speeches often require students to focus at the same time on learning to write a speech as well as on how to deliver it. As a result, students must divide their attention between the two learning goals and may not learn either goal as effectively as possible. Psychological research notes that continuous tasks being performed simultaneously results in either a delay in completing the secondary tasks or a less-than-perfect completion in the tasks overall (Pashler, 1994, pp. 235–237). Research also indicates that familiar tasks are easier to simultaneously utilize and create less problems when multitasking (Schneider & Shiffrin, 1977, pp. 51–53). This assignment is designed to allow students to focus solely on delivery skills without the distraction of learning how to plan, organize, write, and cite material in a speech. Once delivery skills are more familiar to the students, they can then more effectively develop and deliver later speeches. The activity also benefits students through practicing effective listening skills by providing feedback to their peers, developing critical thinking skills as they analyze the presentations of their peers, and enhances their knowledge of historic figures and events.

## EXPLANATION OF ACTIVITY

Before beginning this assignment, a class discussion regarding speech delivery skills should be held and should cover the topics of paralanguage, filler words, gestures, body language, eye contact, and proper attire. Once students are acquainted with the aforementioned concepts, they are given the historic speech assignment and are asked to pick a historically significant speech to present. This can be done on the same day as the class discussion on delivery skills or during the following class period. The historic speeches that students select may be picked from a library of speeches that the instructor has, or may be chosen through outside research by the student after gaining approval from the instructor.

These speeches will be delivered in a manuscript method due to the difficulty of memorizing or extemporaneously presenting such a speech. Historically significant speeches may also be found on The American Rhetoric website's top 100 Speeches (Eidenmuller, 2016) or The History Place website's Great Speeches Collection (Gavin, 2015). Regardless of the overall length of the text of the speech, a maximum speaking time of five minutes should be imposed for the presentation of the speech. This should allow the instructor enough time to evaluate the different aspects of delivery without causing the speeches to drag on for too long.

Practice has shown that the speeches can be completed across two to three presentation days depending on the length of the class period. Instructors could opt to have a slightly lower maximum speaking time if they so choose, but they must be careful not to lower it so far that they are unable to observe the effectiveness of all of the criteria to be graded within a speech. Once students reach the maximum speaking time, they will be asked to finish their sentence and end the speech. While there is no minimum time limit for the speech, the instructor should ensure that all historic speeches chosen for this assignment will allow the student enough time to properly demonstrate their understanding of effective delivery skills.

It is generally recommended that students be allowed between two and a half to three weeks to practice and develop their delivery skills before they are required to formally present the speech. Students should be instructed that they will be graded on the following categories: filler words, varied and effective vocal pitch, varied and effective vocal rate, varied and effective speaking volume, providing consistent and frequent eye contact, providing natural and meaningful gestures, maintaining proper body usage, maintaining clear articulation, and having attire that promotes ethos.

Students are given verbal instructions regarding the grading and are also provided with the rubric and scoring guide for the assignment (provided in Appendix A and Appendix B pp. 100–103) when the assignment begins. In particular, this project has a focus on helping students to develop proper gestures within a speech. Students are asked to plan and utilize a minimum of fifteen gestures in the speech. Students will be asked to make a copy of their manuscript, highlight the words or phrases where they plan on using these fifteen gestures, and turn in the manuscript one class period before the speech is presented. As students present, the instructor will review the highlighted manuscript to see if students are utilizing gestures effectively in the highlighted places on the manuscript.

While students should certainly practice this speech outside of class, the instructor can help guide the students to more effectively utilize the different elements of delivery by designating a portion of class time to practicing the speech. This can be done by splitting the students into pairs so they can practice both their speech and giving constructive criticism. Before practice begins each class period, the instructor gives verbal instructions regarding which aspects of delivery students should focus their critiques on for the day. Students are instructed to focus on practicing one or two of the items from the speech rubric each day (see Appendix A, p. 100). After each speaker finishes, time is allowed for students to give verbal feedback. Meanwhile, the instructor is free to move about the classroom, giving advice to different pairs of students as needed.

In addition to receiving feedback from peers during practice, students should also critique each other's formal presentations. To facilitate such critiques, place students in groups of five to seven, and provide them with a peer evaluation form (provided in Appendix C, p. 104) and guidelines for giving constructive feedback. Beyond simply reinforcing the verbal peer critiques from the practice sessions, this set of peer evaluations allows the speaker to get written feedback that they can continue to reference as they work on other speeches within the course and provides additional perspectives on the speech than just that of the instructor. It also allows the audience to continue to practice and develop their listening and critical thinking skills.

## DEBRIEF

After presentations have been completed, students should be debriefed by discussing their application of delivery skills in light of the concepts that were discussed in the course textbook. Students should also discuss how delivery affects the process of making a speech. Did the students grow in their ability to present a speech in a natural and meaningful manner? What aspects of delivery caused students the most difficulty? What helped students to work past those difficulties? Did students see a change in how an audience responded to improved delivery skills? How do students think the delivery of a speech may have affected how memorable the speech was? How was the students' understanding of public speaking changed by giving a famous speech, rather than by presenting a speech of their own? Finally, beyond discussing the effect that nonverbal communication has within the context of a speech, the instructor can take this opportunity to discuss how the same nonverbal communication concepts that were utilized in a speech are utilized in everyday life.

Student response to this assignment is typically very positive. Students often comment that it lowers their speech anxiety in regards to later speeches in the course. They also often note that they are able to better focus on the organization and content of later speeches because they are more comfortable in their delivery skills due to this assignment. They typically enjoy having the opportunity to take a famous speech and make it their own.

## REFERENCES

Eidenmuller, M. E. (2016, January 10). *Top 100 Speeches*. Retrieved from http://www.americanrhetoric.com/top100speechesall.html

Gavin, P. (2015, December 31). *Great Speeches Collection*. Retrieved from http://www.historyplace.com/speeches/previous.htm

Pashler, H. (1994). Dual-task interference in simple tasks: Data and theory. *Psychological Bulletin, 116*(2), 220–244. doi:10.1037/0033-2909.116.2.220

Schneider, W., & Shiffrin, R. M. (1977). Controlled and automatic human information processing: I. detection, search, and attention. *Psychological Review, 84*(1), 1–66. doi:10.1037/0033-295X.84.1.1

## APPENDIX A

### HISTORIC SPEECH  Name_____  Grade_____

| Presentation 60 Points | Excellent | Good | Meets Minimum Standards | Unacceptable |
|---|---|---|---|---|
| Filler Words—*Um* | 5 | 4 | 3 | 2 1 |
| Projected Voice | 5 | 4 | 3 | 2 1 |
| Varied Pitch | 5 | 4 | 3 | 2 1 |
| Varied Rate | 5 | 4 | 3 | 2 1 |
| Eye Contact | 10 | 9 8 | 7 6 | 5 4 3 2 1 |
| Gestures Reinforce Message | 15 | 14 13 12 11 | 10 9 8 7 6 | 5 4 3 2 1 |
| Appropriate Body Usage | 5 | 4 | 3 | 2 1 |
| Clear Articulation | 5 | 4 | 3 | 2 1 |
| Attire Promotes Ethos | 5 | 4 | 3 | 2 1 |

Comments:

**APPENDIX B**

| | HISTORIC SPEECH SCORING GUIDELINES | | | |
|---|---|---|---|---|
| **Skills (60 Points)** | **Excellent** | **Good** | **Average** | **Unacceptable** |
| Filler Words— *Um* | Filler words occur a maximum of four times in the speech. | Filler words occur between five and eight times in the speech. | Filler words occur between nine and twelve times in the speech. | Filler words occur more than twelve times in the speech. |
| Projected and Varied Volume | The speaker's volume is easy to hear and they provide variance in their volume to accentuate important points in the speech and to keep audience interest. | The speaker's volume is easy to hear and they provide variance in their volume in most of the speech to accentuate important points and to keep audience interest. | The speaker's volume is occasionally too soft or too loud and/or the speaker provides little variance in volume to accentuate important or to keep audience interest. | The speaker's volume is too soft or too loud through most of the speech and/ or little to no variance in volume is provided in the speech. |
| Varied and Appropriate Pitch | The speaker's pitch is easy and pleasing to hear and they provide variance in their pitch to accentuate important points and to keep audience interest. | The speaker's pitch is easy and pleasing to hear and they provide variance in their pitch in most of the speech to accentuate important points and to keep audience interest. | The speaker has several points in the speech in which their pitch does not vary and creates a monotone sound. | The speaker provides little variation in their pitch throughout the speech and creates a monotone sound as a result. |

*(Continued)*

| Skills (60 Points) | Excellent | Good | Average | Unacceptable |
|---|---|---|---|---|
| | | HISTORIC SPEECH SCORING GUIDELINES *(Continued)* | | |
| Varied and Appropriate Rate | The speaker's rate is easy to follow and they provide variance in their rate to accentuate important points and keep audience interest. | The speaker's rate is mostly easy to follow and they provide variance in their rate in most of the speech to accentuate important points and keep audience interest. | The speaker has several points in the speech in which their rate is hard to follow and/or in which they don't vary their rate appropriately. | The speaker's rate is hard to follow throughout the entire speech and/or they provide little to no variation in their rate. |
| Eye Contact | Speaker is making lengthy eye contact with all audience members throughout the entirety of the speech. | Speaker is making lengthy eye contact with most audience members through most of the speech. | Speaker is making lengthy eye contact with audience members in parts of the speech, but there are some longer blocks of time where eye contact is not made with the audience or there is continual eye contact made with audience, but much of it is by simply glancing up at audience members. | Speaker makes very little eye contact with audience members and/or all eye contact made is by quickly glancing at the audience and then looking away. |

| | | | | |
|---|---|---|---|---|
| Gestures Reinforce Message | Gestures are made in appropriate places during the speech, all fifteen planned gestures are made, look natural, and are within the gesture zone. | Gestures are in appropriate places during the speech. Gestures mostly look natural and are mostly within the gesture zone and/or a few planned gestures were skipped. | Several gestures that are made look unnatural and/or are not within the gesture zone and/or the speaker missed several planned gestures in the speech. | Most or all gestures are made in a manner which looks unnatural and/or are not within the gesture zone and/or the speaker missed most or all of the planned gestures in the speech. |
| Appropriate Body Usage | The speaker keeps a proper posture throughout the speech and any movement is purposeful and appears natural. | The speaker keeps a proper posture through most of the speech and any movement is purposeful and appears natural. | The speaker has several points in the speech in which they have improper posture and/or most movement in the speech is purposeful and appears natural. | The speaker has improper posture through most of the speech and/or most or all movement in the speech appears to have no purpose and/or appears unnatural. |
| Clear Articulation | Words and syllables within the speech are distinct and are easy to understand. | Words and syllables within the speech are mostly distinct and easy to understand. | Several words and syllables within the speech run together and are harder to understand. | Words and syllables throughout the entire speech run together and are hard to understand. |
| Attire Promotes Ethos | The speaker is dressed as professionally as they are able. | The speaker is not dressed as professionally as the instructor knows that they are able to (example: The speaker has dressed in a more professional manner for a previous speech). | The speaker is not dressed in a professional manner in one way (example: Wearing a hat, shorts, or a T-shirt with a logo or a design). | The speaker is not dressed in a professional manner in multiple ways (example: wearing a hat, shorts, or T-shirt with a logo or design). |

## APPENDIX C

## HISTORIC SPEECH

Peer Evaluation

Speaker: _____

Evaluator: _____

Filler Words (*um*):
Numerous _____|_____ None or Minimal

Projected Voice:
Hard to Hear _____|_____ Engaging & Varied

Varied Pitch:
Monotone/Distracting _____|_____ Engaging & Varied

Varied Rate:
Hard to Follow _____|_____ Engaging & Varied

Eye Contact:
Lacking/Distracting _____|_____ Direct/Effective

Gestures:
Lacking/Distracting _____|_____ Expressive/Purposeful

Appropriate Body Usage:
Awkward/Distracting _____|_____ Poised

Articulation:
Words Are Mumbled _____|_____ Words Are Distinct

Attire:
Inappropriate _____|_____ Professional

The Speech Overall Was:
Poor _____|_____ Outstanding

What I liked best:

The best way to improve this speech would be to:

Other comments:

# 27

## Stop Talking to PowerPoint!

*Tara M. Franks, Ph.D.*
*The Hugh Downs School of Human Communication*
*Arizona State University*
*tara.franks@asu.edu*

**History:** This G.I.F.T.S. activity was presented at the National Communication Association Conference in 2012 in Orlando, Florida, and was awarded a "Top 9" submission by the division.
**Primary courses in which this activity might be used:** Public Speaking, Business Communication/Professional Skills Training, Group Communication
**Concepts and skills illustrated:** Eye Contact, Speech Practice and Preparation, Visual Aids and Presentation Tools, Impromptu-Style Speaking, Speaker Credibility, Delivery Skills

### PURPOSE

As a public speaking instructor, one of the recurrent challenges I have seen students face is understanding how to effectively integrate visual aids, namely PowerPoint presentations as well as alternative digital media platforms (e.g., Keynote, Prezi, YouTube), into their speech presentations. More often than not, it is quite clear that students underestimate the time and practice required from a speaker in order to build adequate familiarity with their visual aid content. Without the proper preparation, PowerPoint presentations, as well as Keynote, Prezi, and/or other digital visual aids, may serve as a distraction to the *presenter* herself. In such cases, students are tempted to rely on their presentation slides as organizational tools (i.e., visual outlines of their speeches) rather than visual enhancements or supplementary aids to speech content. As a result, I have witnessed several students give speeches *to* their PowerPoint slides, rather than maintaining eye contact with their intended audience. This classroom activity requires students to work with unfamiliar PowerPoint slide images as a practice in turning away from their slides, and toward their audience. The activity reinforces the need for adequate visual aid preparation, practice with all speech materials (digital and otherwise), as well as making eye contact with audience members.

## EXPLANATION OF ACTIVITY

To begin, each student is given a thirty-second preview of a PowerPoint slide that contains two arbitrary and unrelated images. These images are selected at random by the instructor from an online database (e.g., Google Images, Shutterstock Photos) and have no apparent connection to one another or the course concepts. For example, one of the slides I use includes a picture of a bunny wearing a holiday hat alongside a photograph of Chuck Norris in a karate uniform. During the thirty-second slide preview, students are encouraged to take as many notes as possible about the contents of their assigned slide. After thirty seconds, students are then asked to come to the front of the room and present a one-minute impromptu speech linking the images together in a creative narrative presentation format.

Here is the catch: The instructor explains to the students that they are not allowed to look at (i.e., turn back toward) the slide during their one-minute impromptu speech, but instead, must maintain eye contact with their audience for the duration of the activity. Because the images on the slides are unfamiliar to the students and appear seemingly unrelated, students are often tempted to turn back toward the slide in order to refer to its content as they attempt to come up with a story that connects the images. However, if the student turns and looks at the slide, they must begin anew. The activity continues until all students have completed a one-minute impromptu speech.

## DEBRIEF

To debrief, students are asked *if* and *why* they were tempted to look back toward their slides. Often, students mention that their general unfamiliarity with the content, or the overall *strangeness* of the images is what tempted them to break eye contact with their eye contact with the audience. Together, the class may then discuss helpful strategies that speakers can employ in order to avoid speaking *to* their visual aids (e.g., practice, preparation), as well as the potential outcomes, consequences, and/or influence (on credibility) this practice may have on future audiences. The discussion provides an opportunity to address topics such as maintaining eye contact, speaker credibility, adequate preparation with visual aids, and familiarity with digital presentation content. The debrief may be done in pairs, groups, or as a class, depending on class size.

# 28

## See What I Mean: An Applied Approach to Teaching About Visual Aids

*Mary K. High*
*Department of Communication Studies*
*The University of Iowa*
*Mary-high@uiowa.edu*

**History:** This activity was presented at the annual meeting of the National Communication Association, November 2013, in Washington, D.C.

**Primary courses in which this activity might be used:** Public Speaking, Business and Professional Communication, Group Communication

**Concepts illustrated:** Types of Visual Aids, Effective Design of Visual Aids, Effective Use of Visual Aids

### PURPOSE

This activity uses a hands-on approach to teach students how to use visual aids effectively. The exercise applies active-learning strategies that help students remember more information than they would through lecture-based teaching (e.g., see Archer & Miller, 2011; Freeman et al., 2014). Students gain awareness of commonly used types of visual aids, discover ways in which each type may be used effectively, and learn to identify and avoid common visual aid errors (for a review of the effective use of visual aids and the advantages and disadvantages of PowerPoint, see Cyphert, 2007; Stoner, 2007; and Levasseur & Sawyer, 2006). These outcomes are valuable, because well-used visual aids improve public presentations. Audiences understand and remember information better when it is presented both audibly and visually, compared to only audibly (Patterson, Dansereau, & Newbern, 1992). In addition, effective use of visual aids can enhance a speaker's credibility (Schrodt & Witt, 2006) and make a presentation more interesting and enjoyable (Susskind, 2005; Szabo & Hastings, 2000). After completing the activity, students are prepared to make good use of visual support in the classroom and beyond.

This exercise also offers supplemental benefits. As students complete the assignment, they begin to:

- Develop effective group communication skills
- Improve their public speaking abilities
- Feel more confident speaking in front of the class
- Build a collaborative classroom environment
- Engage in meaningful peer evaluation

## EXPLANATION OF ACTIVITY

This exercise of approximately forty to fifty minutes is geared toward undergraduate students who are enrolled in small- to medium-sized (i.e., about twenty to forty students) public speaking, business and professional communication, or group communication classes. It is intended for use after students have completed an out-of-class reading about principles for using visual support effectively in public presentations. Most public speaking and business communication textbooks include a discussion of this topic.

To conduct the activity, divide the class into small groups (approximately three to seven students per group). The exercise works best when each group has access to a computer that can be used to create visual aids. The classroom should have a projector that students can use to display their visual aids. The assignment also can be adapted for use with a chalk/whiteboard, flipchart, or other classroom visual aid materials.

### Step 1

Instruct each group to play the role of a team of visual aid experts that is visiting class to discuss effective visual aid use. Assign each group a specific type(s) of visual aid that was discussed in the assigned reading. Examples of visual aid types include objects and models; photographs; diagrams; tables; pie, bar, and column charts; graphs; pictograms; video; chalk/whiteboards; flipcharts; presentation software (e.g., PowerPoint, Prezi, Keynote, and so on). Invite teams to plan a brief (about two- to three-minute) presentation in which they describe effective implementation of the visual aid type(s) and point out strengths and challenges or downsides to its use. Tell students that their presentation must include two or three visual aids.

### Step 2

As students begin planning their presentations, assign each team a common visual aid problem that you have noticed in students' speeches or that was discussed in the assigned reading. Ask students to keep their assigned visual aid problem a secret; tell them not to share it with other groups (see Appendix, p. 111, for examples of visual aid problems). Instruct each team to perform their assigned mistake during the presentation. For example, if a team was assigned the problem of placing too much text on PowerPoint slides, that team should use at least one overly wordy PowerPoint slide in its presentation.

## Step 3

Allow each team to deliver its presentation in front of the class. Encourage all members to participate. After the presentation, ask the audience to name the common visual aid error that they saw the team enact.

During the discussion of each presentation, audience members often will identify problems that were not assigned to the presenting team. For instance, students might note that the presenters created visuals that appeared cluttered or too busy, but the team may have been asked to demonstrate the problem of making eye contact with your visual aid rather than your audience. When such discrepancies occur, presenters are made aware of problems with their delivery or use of visual support that they can aim to correct.

## DEBRIEF

Debrief the activity by asking students what they learned about visual aids, public speaking, or working in teams. You might, for example, ask students what surprised them about the feedback they received from the audience or invite them to talk about the challenges they experienced while designing visual aids or working with others to plan their presentation. Encourage students to consider how they could overcome the difficulties they had creating and using their slides, speaking in front of the class, and working with others. Ask them what they will do to avoid the types of visual aid problems made during the presentations (see Appendix, p. 111).

As you close the activity, point out aspects of students' visual aids or delivery that were done particularly well, and note any problems that were not addressed. If your course includes peer evaluation, ask students how they felt about giving and receiving feedback. Although students can be reluctant to criticize their peers, in this exercise, they do so freely because they know that each group is consciously making a mistake. Ask questions such as the following: How can you provide helpful feedback? How can you become more open to receiving feedback from others? With appropriate debriefing questions, the exercise helps to create a classroom environment in which students feel comfortable openly critiquing and discussing others' work.

Finally, provide a summary of students' concluding comments. Remind them what they told you they learned and emphasize the improvements they hope to make as they move forward in your course. Offer genuine words of encouragement, set a challenge for the class, and/or sincerely thank students for their participation and willingness to make and learn from mistakes.

## REFERENCES

Archer, C.C. and Miller, M.K. (2001). Prioritizing active learning: An exploration of Gateway courses in political science. *The Teacher, 44*(2), 429–434.

Cyphert, D. (2007). Presentation technology in the age of electronic eloquence: From visual aid to visual rhetoric. *Communication Education, 56*(2), 168–192.

Freeman, S., Eddy, S.L., McDonough, M., Smith, M.K., Okoroafor, N., Jordt, H., and Wenderoth, M.P. (2014). Active learning increases student performance in science, engineering, and mathematics. *PNAS, 111*(23), 8410–8415.

Patterson, M.E., D.F. Dansereau, D.F., & Newbern, D. (1992). Effects of communication aids and strategies on cooperative teaching. *Journal of Educational Psychology, 84*(4), 453–461.

Schrodt, P. and Witt, P. (2006). Students' attributions of instructor credibility as a function of students' expectations of instructional technology use and nonverbal immediacy. *Communication Education, 55*(1), 1–20.

Stoner, M.R. (2007). PowerPoint in a new key. *Communication Education, 56*(3), 354–381.

Susskind, J. (2005). PowerPoint's power in the classroom: Enhancing students' self-efficacy and attitudes. *Computers & Education, 45*(2), 203–215.

Szabo, A. and Hastings, N. (2000). Using IT in the undergraduate classroom: Should we replace the blackboard with PowerPoint? *Computers & Education, 35*, 175–187.

## APPENDIX

## EXAMPLES OF VISUAL AID PROBLEMS

- Using long blocks of text
- Using a slide or slides cluttered with too many words and images
- Using a visual aid that appears unprofessional or unplanned (e.g., messy writing on a chalkboard)
- Using a font size or image too small to see clearly
- Using a font style or styles difficult to read
- Using a color or colors difficult to see
- Using a chart or graph too complex or cluttered to be easily understood
- Using distracting animation or sound
- Using a visual aid not purposeful or relevant
- Using a slide or slides with spelling and/or grammatical errors
- Using an inconsistent visual theme (e.g., mix various font types, colors, and slide designs)
- Overusing all capital letters
- Passing an object or single handout around the audience while you are speaking
- Making eye contact with the visual aid, rather than the audience
- Reading text to your audience without elaborating or clarifying information
- Displaying a graph or chart without explaining it (e.g., "Here are our sales figures.")
- Changing slides at inappropriate times (e.g., moving to the next slide before you finish explaining the previous one)
- Presenting slides that are out of order (i.e., advancing the slides forward then backward while speaking)

# 29

# Your Life in One Hundred Words or Less: A PowerPoint Activity for the Basic Course

*Tim Rumbough*
*Department of Communication Studies*
*Bloomsburg University*
*trumboug@bloomu.edu*

**History:** This activity was presented at the annual meeting of the Eastern Communication Association Convention, April 2013, in Pittsburgh, Pennsylvania.

**Primary courses in which this activity might be used:** Public Speaking, Fundamentals of Oral Communication

**Concepts illustrated:** Visual Aids, Impromptu Speaking, Speech Organization, Speech Delivery

## PURPOSE

In many public speaking courses, beginning speakers have a tendency to use too many words on visual aids. This often leads speakers to either (a) read the visual aid word-for-word to the audience, (b) not explain what is on the visual aid, or (c) continue on with their speech while the audience focuses on the visual aid, rather than the speaker. In order to address these common problems, this activity helps students create and present effective visual aids while using limited notes. The activity also encourages students to think on their feet and deliver speeches with confidence and enthusiasm.

## EXPLANATION OF ACTIVITY

This activity works best in the middle of a semester, after the students have completed their first graded speech. This allows them to apply what they have learned about delivery, speech organization, and other key ideas. In addition, before assigning this activity, it is best that the instructor discuss how to effectively use visual aids in a presentation.

Students are asked to create and present PowerPoint slides about their life. They will not create the slides during class time. Instead, class time is used to organize their main points and write out the content of their PowerPoint slides. To assist them, a printed handout with eight blank PowerPoint slides is provided. Please see the example handout in the Appendix on p. 114.

Students are told to develop two to three main points about their life. Suggested main points include hobbies/interests, family, friends, pets, and interesting facts. Another method of organization that is suggested includes dividing their life into chronological order (e.g., early years, recent years, the future).

Once students understand their task, they are told that when they create their PowerPoint slides, they may use pictures, but they may only use a total of one hundred words or less on a maximum of eight PowerPoint slides. The students then use class time to develop a hand-written draft of the PowerPoint slides on the handout provided. Students are then told that they will create their actual PowerPoint slides as homework.

The following class day, each student presents his or her PowerPoint slides to the class. In addition, students are informed that they may not bring any notes to the front of the room to present their speech, and that the only notes they may use are the PowerPoint slides that they have created. Students may use as many words as they like to elaborate on the PowerPoint slides. The speeches/ PowerPoint slides are not graded, however, students earn participation points by completing the activity. After each speech, students are praised for what they do well, and gently reminded if there is something they could do to enhance future presentations (have more eye contact, enlarge a photo, etc.).

If the size of the class is too large and class time is limited, there can be many variations of the activity. These include:

- One-day option A: Students complete the "One hundred words or less" handout in class, and do not actually create a real PowerPoint presentation nor present their speech to the class.
- One-day option B: Students complete the "One hundred words or less" handout in class, then the class is divided into small groups, and students simultaneously talk about their lives to their small group, while showing them their completed handout.
- Two-day option A: Students complete the "One hundred words or less" handout in class, then they create and print out their PowerPoint slides as homework. In the following class, only a few volunteers present their speech to the class. If there are not enough volunteers, then a small amount of extra credit can be offered to encourage students to volunteer. The printed version is then collected from students who do not present in class.
- Two-day option B: Students complete the "One hundred words or less" handout in class, then they create and print out five copies of their PowerPoint slides as homework. In the following class, students are divided into small groups and students simultaneously talk about their lives to their small group while providing each group member a print-out of their slides.

- Topic Change option: Since some professors already use a self-introduction speech, the topic of the "One hundred words or less" activity could easily be changed to any common impromptu topic, such as "my favorite form of entertainment."

## DEBRIEF

After students present their life in one hundred words or less, they are debriefed by reminding them about the importance of using limited words in future visual aids. Students are also reminded that an effective speech can be delivered without writing out the entire speech word-for-word. Since many students use photographs for the activity, it is important to discuss how the photographs can serve as a visual clue to help them keep organized and stay on track while they are delivering the speech. Additional debriefing questions that could be asked of students include the following: How do you feel this presentation would be different if the speech was written out word-for-word? Did the speakers have more a conversational delivery style since they did not write out the entire speech? Were the visual aids effective? Why or why not?

Students say that they enjoy this activity because it helps them apply what they learned in the semester, it helps them think on their feet, and that it's fun! Since the activity is easy to set up, is enjoyable, and gets the students involved, students often describe this activity as one of their most memorable experiences of the semester.

## APPENDIX

### EXAMPLE STUDENT HANDOUT

**Name:** _____

### Your Life in One Hundred Words or Less: PowerPoint Activity

**Goal:** To give you experience in creating visual aids without using too many words.

**Directions:** Your task is to create a draft of a PowerPoint presentation about the topic of your life. Use class time to organize your main points and write out the content of your PowerPoint slides on this handout. For your PowerPoint slides, you are limited to *one hundred words or less* on the eight PowerPoint slides, so you should only write key words and phrases on the slides.

You should develop two to three main points about your life. Suggested main points include: hobbies/interests, family, friends, pets, and interesting facts. Another method of organization could be to divide your life into chronological order (i.e., early years, recent years, the future).

**Hand in:** Your completed handout for participation points.

**Total words used for all 8 slides =** _____

# 30

# Building Informers through Team-Teaching

*Katherine Beich-Forkner*

*Department of Communication Arts and Literature Teaching*

*Winona State University*

*kforkner@winona.edu*

**History:** This activity was presented at the annual meeting of the Central States Communication Association, April 2016, in Grand Rapids, Michigan.

**Primary courses in which this activity might be used:** Public Speaking, Foundations of Communication, Interpersonal Communication

**Concepts illustrated:** Informative Speaking, Description, Operational Definition, Definition by Negation, Definition by Example, Definition by Synonym, Definition by Etymology, Comparison and Contrast, Literal and Figurative Language, Narration, Demonstration

## PURPOSE

With this activity, students gain a broader understanding of informative speaking and practice various methods of informing. Educational institutions are often criticized for losing their real-world application and turning too often to "death by PowerPoint" lectures and cumulative, multiple-choice testing. Therefore, with each lesson I strive to show students the big picture that can be gleaned beyond the term's final exam. I seek students' understanding on how to educate audiences and not merely how to pass the six- to eight-minute classroom informative speech. This activity stretches students' understanding of informing by showing a variety of ways to convey information. It allows students to explore their creative freedom and to enjoy, often to their surprise, informative speaking. It affords students on-the-spot skill development through the final impromptu presentation. Finally, during debriefing, students learn the importance of using a variety of supporting material types. At the foundational level, it is the difference between a speech being assigned and speaking being learned.

## EXPLANATION OF ACTIVITY

This activity was originally designed for a fifty-minute class period, although it can be modified to fit other time needs. Prior to this class period, students should understand that informative speaking requires the speaker to be (or become) knowledgeable on a subject and share that knowledge with others. Students should understand that there are several methods that can be used to inform—or to teach—content, such as describing, defining, comparing and contrasting, narrating, and demonstrating (Verderber, Sellnow, & Verderber, 2015). These methods can be adapted to the titles that better mirror the text you use in your classes or can be taught in a lecture if no class text is used.

When students arrive to class, they are told they will be informative speakers on that day, and that they will have to use different methods to teach the class about the same topic (I typically give an abstract concept to all groups: *freedom* and *love* have both been successful choices in my classes). This way, the class will be able to see how we inform in different ways and in turn learn diverse things about the same topic.

Students are then divided into five groups: the Description group, the Definition group, the Comparison and Contrast group, the Narration group, and the Demonstration group. Each group is given a sheet of instructions (see Appendix on p. 118) particular to that group. (In my classes, students also have their class textbook to use as a resource guide.) The class then has twenty minutes to work in groups to prepare brief informative speeches about the topic, to be presented impromptu. Please refer to the group instructions handout in the Appendix on p. 118 to see the steps groups complete at this time.

Following the twenty minutes of work time, groups present their informative speeches to the whole class. Before each presentation, I introduce the groups and what they will be presenting (e.g., "This group is going to show us what LOVE is by defining it for us. Remember there are several ways one can define a term."), and I cue the class to particular things to look for ("If they do this well, you should hear a moral behind their narrative, connecting us back to their main point about LOVE. Let's see if we can identify that in their presentation now.")

## DEBRIEF

After all of the group presentations are complete, debrief by asking the class the following questions:

- How do each of these methods of informing bring to light different aspects of the topic?
  - You may also choose to get more focused on each specific method, such as: What did we learn about this concept from Group 1, who merely described a symbol of it for us?

- From your perspective, which method of informing seemed to present the most accurate information? The most biased? Note: This often leads into a discussion of denotative versus connotative language, and how language is used by a speaker to appeal to an audience (i.e., pathos), such as with the speaker's perspective communicated in narratives or the adjectives used in descriptions.
  - What insight can we gain from your answer to this question and how can we apply this to our upcoming formal informative speeches and the supporting material that we gather?
- From your perspective in the audience, which method of informing was the most interesting to listen to? The least interesting?
  - What insight can we gain from your answer to this question and how can we apply this to our upcoming formal informative speeches and the supporting material that we deliver?
- What if we only had one method of informing at our disposal? Imagine what we would be missing!

Students enjoy the active learning and practicing that comes with this class session. I require all students to have a speaking part in the group presentation and reward participation points to those who follow those guidelines. For an extension, give each group a large piece of poster paper and some markers and require at least one visual aid; I have also trialed computer-generated presentation aids. This is especially useful for the description and comparison and contrast groups who are likely to display a photo and explain their Venn diagram, respectfully. I accept skits as an alternative, but caution students that if they choose this option, the end result must be both functional and educational. This activity can be adapted into an online or hybrid public speaking classroom by having individuals or groups post videos of their final presentation.

## REFERENCES

O'Hair, D., Stewart, R., & Rubenstein, H. (2012). *A speaker's guidebook: Text and reference* (5th ed.). Boston, MA: Bedford/St. Martin's.

Verderber, K. S., Sellnow, D. D., & Verderber, R. F. (2015). *COMM 3*. Stamford, CT: Cengage Learning.

## APPENDIX

## GROUP INSTRUCTIONS HANDOUT

Cut the below instructions into slips and hand one to each of the five informative groups.

### Group 1: Describe

What is *freedom*? Inform us about FREEDOM by choosing an "object, geographic feature, setting, event, person, or image" (Verderber et al., 2015, p. 247) to describe that relates to this concept (e.g. Statue of Liberty, American flag, bald eagle, etc.). Give a detailed description, including such things as "its size, shape, weight, color, composition, age, condition, and spatial organization" (Verderber et al., 2015, p. 248).

### Group 2: Define

What is *freedom*? Inform us about FREEDOM by defining the term. Use each of the five types of definitions: operational definition, definition by negation, definition by example, definition by synonym, and definition by etymology (O'Hair, Stewart, & Rubenstein, 2012). (Note: I allow students to use a laptop or smartphone to look up the word's etymology.)

### Group 3: Compare / Contrast

What is *love*? Inform us about LOVE by comparing and contrasting it to something related (e.g., love vs. infatuation). Use both literal and figurative language (e.g., similes, metaphors, analogies, as well as direct comparisons) to explain your concept. You have laptops, smartphones, and other technology at your disposal; this will also require some brain work.

### Group 4: Narration

What is *love*? Show us LOVE, using the narration method of informing. Be sure to include all parts of a typical narrative: the exposition (e.g., setting, characters), rising action (e.g., sequence of events leading to the complication or problem), climax (e.g., height of the drama), and resolution (how the problem was solved). To do this well, you will also need to invent some sort of *moral to the story*, such as "Love takes time," "Love conquers all things," or "Love is a choice, not a feeling." You may choose to use first-, second-, or third-person voice in your narrative.

### Group 5: Demonstration

Inform us about the abstract concept of LOVE through a demonstration. Demonstrations are used to "show how something is done, display the stages of a process, or depict how something works" (Verderber et al., 2015, p. 249). You will need to be very creative in your *specific* topic selection within this category (e.g., the process of forgiveness, the listening steps, Knapp's model of relational development, etc.). Be sure to organize the steps chronologically or sequentially (from first to last) and *show* the audience the process. Your audience should also be able to identify and repeat your thesis when you are done presenting.

# 31

# Gizmos and Gadgets: A Small Group Impromptu Public Speaking Experience

*Harriet Sharlow Benavidez*
*Department of Communication Studies*
*Rowan University*
*benavidez@rowan.edu*

**History:** This activity was presented at the annual meeting of the Eastern Communication Association, April 2015, in Philadelphia, Pennsylvania.

**Primary courses in which this activity might be used:** Public Speaking, Small Group, Interpersonal Communication, Intercultural Communication, Persuasion

**Concepts illustrated:** Communication Apprehension, Persuasion, Audience Adaptation, Language, Leadership

## PURPOSE

Public speaking is often a required course for certain majors at the college level. It is well documented that students exhibit anxiety in public speaking situations. This activity is designed to reduce speech anxiety by fostering a relaxed classroom environment with increased student interaction through the use of creativity and humor in a low-stress situation.

## EXPLANATION OF ACTIVITY

### Directions Prior to the Day of the Activity

Announce to students that there will be an informal small group (three students) impromptu speech activity the next class session. Everyone who participates will be given credit. Before class you, the instructor, will need to come up with a hypothetical, yet humorous, scenario of a very bad day to which students can easily relate. For example, a very bad day for students could start with oversleeping for class, discovering that they have no food for breakfast, tripping over their belongings on the way out the door, and finally arriving to class late only to realize they forgot their homework, and missed a pop quiz. Be prepared to relate this scenario, or a similar one, on the day of the activity.

Gather the needed equipment:

- Ten objects whose individual purpose may not be readily known to most students. For example: kitchen items such as a coiled wire whisk, pastry blender, honey dipper, apple slicer/corer, pickle picker, egg slicer, back-in-pie lifter, old fashioned hand juicer ... and so on
- A numbered list of the above items.
- Paper bag large enough to contain all items.
- Index cards, one for each student.
- Timing device.

Place the gathered objects in the paper bag, and bring bag, numbered list, index cards, and timing device to class.

## Day of the Activity

Introduce the activity by asking, "Has anyone ever had a bad day?" Continue with the preplanned hypothetical example of a very bad day. End with, "But I have a fix for you!" then pull an item from the bag, such as the coiled wire whisk, and state, "Here it is ... your own personal atom rearranger!" Demonstrate how circling it over your head can rearrange all those atoms with their negatively charged particles into a pattern of calm and peacefulness. Exaggerate the solution.

Then tell students that it is their turn. Have them get into groups of three. Let them know that you have additional items in the bag. Go to each group and have one person say a number from one to ten, and then you reach into the bag and give the group the corresponding object. Also distribute an index card to each student.

Announce that you will set the timer for five minutes. During this time, each group will need to come up with at least three very creative uses for the item. The more preposterous their ideas, the better! Each student can use the index card to jot down any notes needed. For a public speaking class, remind the group that they need to have an introduction (gain attention, reveal the item, answer the question of why we should care, and give a short preview).

The introduction needs to be followed by three main points composing the body of the speech that will usually relate to creative uses. Remind them not to forget to use transitions to move from one creative use to the next. Finally, a conclusion is needed to wrap up the speech. For a non-public speaking class, or a class that has not yet covered these topics in detail, you may provide additional detail by way of lesson, notes on a handout, or other such means. I leave it open as to whether the group wants to try to get the audience to buy the item (infomercial style) or just inform us of its uses.

Set the timer and tell students to let their creativity run wild. At the end of five minutes, call the groups up to the front of the class to present one at a time. All students are encouraged, but not required, to speak.

## DEBRIEF

Typically, students love this activity. It works well with any mix of students. Because of the outlandishness of the uses, the classroom is usually filled with laughter, and students become much more relaxed. Some of the creative examples that have been used in the past are the "levitation device" which was a bake-in-pie lifter, a "musical instrument" which was a wired egg slicer, and a "language translator" which was an old fashioned hand juicer. After the activity, I purposely busy myself with rearranging papers and/or checking the computer to give the students a few minutes of unstructured time together. It is interesting to note that reticent students will often stay involved with the continuing conversations as opposed to disengaging.

For a public speaking class: You can debrief students by asking questions about how the presentations differed in terms of various speech elements such as gaining attention in the introduction, presenting main points and using transitions in the body, and summarizing and ending the speech in the conclusion. Other elements of effective public speaking can be addressed such as delivery, eye contact, and nonverbal behavior and how each of these elements can be used to enhance their regular speeches. Guide the discussion to end on a positive note about overcoming speech anxiety. This can be done by thanking and complimenting students for their participation and for creating an accepting and welcoming environment for further participation.

For small group, interpersonal, intercultural, persuasion: You can debrief by asking questions related to individual course content such as how group members worked together in preparation for the presentation; what behaviors were noted in regards to listening, assertiveness, differences of opinions; what techniques were used to persuade classmates to purchase the items (if applicable); and other concepts/skills/behaviors in the specific course being taught.

For all students: Emphasize that learning may involve stepping out of one's comfort zone, but as this activity shows, the result can actually be fun!

# Interpersonal Communication

# 32

## Adapting the "A–B–Scene" to Communication Classrooms: An Exercise for Understanding the Role of Context, Empathy, Perceptions, and Message Dimensions

*Christian R. Seiter*
*Department of Medical Humanities and Bioethics*
*University of Rochester*
*christian.seiter@yahoo.com*

*John S. Seiter*
*Department of Languages, Philosophy, and Communication Studies*
*Utah State University*
*john.seiter@usu.edu*

**History:** This activity was presented at the annual meeting of the New York State Communication Association, October 2016, in Callicoon, New York.

**Primary courses in which this activity might be used:** Interpersonal Communication, Intercultural Communication, Communication Theory

**Concepts illustrated:** The Role of Context in Communication, Perception, Message Dimensions, Verbal and Nonverbal Communication

### PURPOSE

In theater contexts, an "A–B Scene" involves a script with nothing more than dialogue between two characters (Tayler, Kowal, Wells, 2015). For example:

**Character A:** Are you out of your mind?
**Character B:** What's it look like?
**Character A:** I'll get you for this.

Because these scenes provide little information about context, they invite a variety of interpretations. For example, reread the conversation above while imagining that Character A is a wife, who is angry at Character B, her husband, who has just arrived late for a funeral. Try again, this time imagining that Character A is delighted to have shown up at a surprise birthday party, which is being thrown by Character B. While A–B Scenes are powerful tools for instructing actors, communication students can benefit from them as well. Indeed, this activity is designed to help students understand four concepts that are commonly encountered in communication classrooms: the role of context, empathy, perception, and message characteristics in the process of communication. Because students get involved in performing and interpreting the scenes, this activity is both engaging and fun.

## EXPLANATION OF ACTIVITY

The activity lasts about forty-five minutes and works best with smaller classes (twenty-five students or less). The materials include scripts for two separate scenes (see Appendix A, p. 127), and several circumstances that provide context for those scenes (see Appendix B, p. 128). To prepare, copy one script for each student (half get Scene 1, and half Scene 2). Next, write or print the circumstances on 4x6 cards, one circumstance per card.

After lecturing on the topics of interest (i.e., context, empathy, perception, and/or messages characteristics), divide your students into two groups (i.e., "Script 1 Group" and "Script 2 Group"), and ask them to find one partner *within their own group*. Next, each *pair* of students is given one $4 \times 6$ circumstance card. Explain that their goal is not to memorize or adlib lines, but rather to perform their scene for the rest of the class using the given circumstance to guide how they relate to their partner and surroundings. It is important that only the actors know the circumstance of the scene. Allow ten minutes for rehearsal and let the fun begin, asking each pair of students to perform its scene. If time is an issue, or there are students with stage fright, you can adapt the exercise. Specifically, each pair of students can perform for just one other pair and then some (but not all) pairs can volunteer to perform for the entire class. In addition, you can shorten the scripts.

After each performance, ask the audience to share guesses about the circumstances for each scene. Who were the characters? How are they related? What were their intentions? How did they respond to what was going on? Why did audience members form these impressions? Ask the actors to read their scenarios to the class. Was anyone surprised by the scenario? Why or why not?

## DEBRIEF

After the performances, debrief your students by connecting the activity to concepts covered in class. Most models and definitions of communication, for example, highlight the importance of context. Did context play a role in this exercise? How? Does contextual awareness affect empathy? Without context, is it difficult to be empathetic? You might also apply this activity to the process of perception. Why did students' attributions and interpretations of the same performances differ? Do such differences matter? What types of behaviors most affected perceptions? What specific aspects of the scene led to different perspectives? Why did students pay particular attention to certain aspects of the scene?

Finally, you might relate this exercise to the notion of content (i.e., what is said) versus relational (i.e., how it is said) dimensions of messages. What most affected students' guesses about what was happening in the scenes? What information was used most to understand the relationship between the characters? What do these observations tell us about verbal and nonverbal communication?

In our experience, students have fun participating in this activity and learn a lot in the process. Expect applause and laughter, especially when students experience how drastically the actors' verbal and nonverbal behavior changes from scenario to scenario. The exercise has proven to be an effective way to *show* rather than *tell* students how context impacts communication, empathy, and perceptions.

## REFERENCE

Tayler, H., Kowal, M. R., & Wells, D. (2015, Sept. 20). *Writing Excuses 10.38: How does context shape dialog?* [Audio podcast]. Retrieved from www.writingexcuses.com/2015/09/20/writing-excuses-10-38-how-does-context-shape-dialog/

## APPENDIX A

## SCRIPTS FOR TWO DIFFERENT SCENES

Script for Scene 1

Character A: How do you feel about this?
Character B: Look at me. What do you think?
Character A: It's pretty obvious.
Character B: So, what's next?
Character A: Like I said, pretty obvious.
Character B: Easy for you to say.
Character A: You got any better ideas?
Character B: You don't want to know.
Character A: Try me.
Character B. I don't know what to say.

Character A. Why's that?
Character B. You really want to know?
Character A. It's getting interesting.
Character B: I don't believe you.

## Script for Scene 2

Character A: I can't believe this.
Character B: It's not like I planned it.
Character A: So what did you expect?
Character B: Not this.
Character A: I don't know what to say.
Character B: Then don't say anything.
Character A: I have to, don't I?
Character B: You've already said enough.
Character A: So what now?
Character B: That's up to you, I guess.
Character A: Should I?
Character B: Probably.
Character A: Should we?
Character B: Definitely.

## APPENDIX B

### CIRCUMSTANCES

1. Character A has been waiting all night for his/her teenage child, Character B, to come home. At six in the morning, Character B walks through the door.
2. Character B just made a comment implying that his/her significant other, Character A, could stand to lose some weight.
3. After fifteen years, Character A just encountered Character B, a long-lost buddy from the Army.
4. Character B, a new chef, has accidentally served raw chicken to Character A, a food critic with a reputation for being ruthless.
5. Character A convinced Character B to go on the highest rollercoaster at an amusement park. Character B is terrified of heights. It's too late to turn back now.
6. Character A just proposed to Character B while both were featured on the jumbotron at a baseball game. Character B said no, but the camera is lingering on them.
7. Character B just admitted to Character A that he/she has been unfaithful in their relationship.
8. Character A and Character B are in love with the same person. For the sake of their friendship, both have agreed not see this person anymore. While out on the town, Character A caught Character B on a date with this person.

9. Character B, a doctor, just shared the news that Character A's cancer is in remission and he/she will be able to attend his/her sister's wedding.

10. Character A, a superhero, has been captured by his arch-nemesis, Character B.

11. Character B, an employee, has been called into the office of Character A, the boss. Character A just informed Character B that he/she knows Character B has been stealing from the company.

12. Character A, a recovering alcoholic has bumped into Character B, his/her sponsor, at a party. Both are drinking alcohol and neither wants to cause a scene.

13. Character B wakes up in a strange room with Character A watching. Character B recognizes Character A from a news reports as the serial killer the FBI has been looking for.

14. Character A works in the customer complaints department, and Character B is a disgruntled customer who wishes to return a faulty product.

15. Character A and Character B are two teenagers who just vandalized (with toilet paper) their teacher's house. A light in the house goes on. Character A and Character B scramble under the porch to hide.

# 33

## Alex and Sarah: Experiencing Emotions through Role-Playing

*Mark D. Cruea*
*Department of Communication and Media Studies*
*Ohio Northern University*
*m-cruea@onu.edu*

**History:** This activity was presented at the annual meeting of the National Communication Association, November 2014, in Chicago, Illinois.

**Primary courses in which this activity might be used:** Interpersonal Communication, Organizational Communication

**Concepts illustrated:** Appraisal Model of Emotions, Gibb's Categories of Supportive and Defensive Climates, Emotional IQ, Communication Apprehension, Emotional Vocabulary

### PURPOSE

The purpose of this activity is for students to evaluate a scenario involving two characters and the emotions these characters experience. For the role-play, students are encouraged to think about what they might say, how they would say it, and how their body language and facial expressions signal the emotions. Students subsequently identify the emotions they personally experience while role-playing in front of their classmates and work to expand their emotional vocabulary.

### EXPLANATION OF ACTIVITY

At the beginning of the activity, students are provided with a scenario (see Appendix, p. 132) that describes a workplace situation involving two characters—Alex and Sarah. Several issues exist between these two characters. Half of the students are assigned the role of Alex and the other half are assigned the role of Sarah. After reading the scenario, students who are assigned the role of Alex must identify the issues that Alex has with Sarah, and students assigned the role of Sarah must identify the issues that Sarah has with Alex.

Subsequently, students must determine the emotions that might be experienced when Alex and Sarah meet to discuss their issues including the content, manner, and delivery of their concerns.

Next, choose four to six students from the Alex group and four to six students from the Sarah group, and ask them to line up opposite one another in front of the class. They should bring their list of issues with them. One pair at a time, have one student start a conversation by naming one of the issues on his or her list. The other student then responds to the chosen issue and the conversation continues for a few exchanges or until the conversation dies. Students can ad lib as much as they wish, and are encouraged to get into their roles by reacting in very supportive or defensive ways (Gibb, 1961). After one pair is finished, the next pair in line starts a new conversation based on a new issue on the list. This process is repeated until all pairs have performed their roles. Once the first group has completed the role-play, another group takes their place until all students have completed the process.

## DEBRIEF

After everyone is seated, engage the class in a discussion about the experience. Ask them what they did to convey the emotion. Students will often discuss making an angry face or using a harsh tone of voice. Further questions may be required in order to address all four components of emotion including physiological responses, nonverbal reactions, cognitive interpretations, and verbal expression (Genov, 2001; Gentsch, Grandjean, & Scherer, 2014). For example, the instructor may need to ask students what words were chosen to express the characters' frustrations with one another, or how students used posture in passive and aggressive manners. Then ask students to discuss their own emotional responses when they figured out that they were required to stand up in front of the class to role-play (McCroskey, 2009). Once students identify these emotions, they will easily pick up how they felt physically. Common responses include queasy stomach, sweaty palms, and increased heart rate (Chang, Chang, Zheng, & Chung, 2013; Rochman & Diamond, 2008). They will also find it easy to identify the facial expressions and nervous gestures displayed by themselves and others. Generally, a prompt such as "How did you know that you or someone else was nervous?" is enough to start the discussion.

Next, encourage students to consider how a small change in scenario will change their emotional response. For example, if students had been allowed to role-play while in their seats and not in front of the class, they may have felt less pressure but more awkward. At this point, students learn how their cognitive interpretations affect the emotional response they experience. Finally, ask students to describe those emotions. Responses generally include nervous to fine. Follow up by asking students to think of other words that are more descriptive. At times it is necessary to prompt the students with suggestions. Did she or he feel inadequate or afraid of rejection instead of just nervous? Did she or he feel confident or secure instead of fine? As an option, students can meet in small groups or pairs to explore different word choices (Lieberman et al., 2007). The goal is for students to expand their emotional vocabulary.

## REFERENCES

Chang, C., Chang, C., Zheng, J., & Chung, P. (2013). Physiological emotion analysis using support vector regression. *Neurocomputing: An International Journal, 122,* 79–87.

Genov, A. B. (2001). Autonomic and situational determinants of the subjective experience of emotion: An individual differences approach. *Dissertation Abstracts International: Section B. The Sciences and Engineering, 61*(9-B), 5043.

Gentsch, K., Grandjean, D., & Scherer, K. R. (2014). Coherence explored between emotion components: Evidence from event-related potentials and facial electromyography. *Biological Psychology, 98,* 70–81.

Gibb, J. R. (1961). Defensive communication. *Journal of Communication, 11*(3), 141–148.

Lieberman, M. D., Eisenberger, N. I., Crockett, M. J., Tom, S., Pfeifer, J. H., & Way, B. M. (2007). Putting feelings into words: Affect labeling disrupts amygdala activity to affective stimuli. *Psychological Science, 18,* 421–428.

McCroskey, J. C. (2009). Communication apprehension: What have we learned in the last four decades. *Human Communication, 12,* 157–171.

Rochman, G. M., & Diamond, G. M. (2008). From unresolved anger to sadness: Identifying physiological correlates. *Journal of Counseling Psychology, 55,* 96–105.

## APPENDIX

### ALEX AND SARAH STUDENT HANDOUT

Sarah is a member of a steering committee whose job it is to oversee and advise the operations of several autonomous work teams in her company. The committee is not the "boss" of the teams but rather an advisory group to help team performance and to act as a liaison between the teams and upper management. Her committee of five employees is about to hold a monthly meeting with one of the teams: a five-member research and development team.

The research and development team normally does good work; the review process generally goes smoothly. However, there is one person on the team, Alex, with whom Sarah has difficulties. Alex's personality and style grate on Sarah. She believes that he is a poor listener and, at times, a domineering speaker who is overly defensive when questioned about his team's work, and is prone to interrupting people on the committee. To Sarah, he comes across as smug and abrupt; he always seems to have a ready answer, such that Sarah believes that he does not really hear messages from her committee. It is her belief that he influences other members of his team to pay less attention to feedback from her and her committee. At times, she has felt (and resisted) a strong urge to put him in his place. More than once, the reports he has provided have been incomplete or hazy in detail such that she has had difficulty figuring them out. Requests for follow-up information have been met in a sporadic fashion. Sarah has asked to have the reports two days ahead of time, but neither Alex nor others have yet responded to that request. At the same time, Alex and his team appear to get their jobs done to standards that are well above average.

Alex and others on his team have, at times, questioned the value of having to document and report all their progress to the steering committee. Alex finds Sarah in particular to be overly inquisitive and questioning of his team's work, with a tendency to pry into details, and too frequently for his taste, to question the accuracy of reports. He believes she has little confidence in the team's ability to complete projects on time, and that she offers advice without seeming to get what the team's actually doing and what its recommendations are. She rarely, if ever, acknowledges its accomplishments. Whereas other members of the steering committee appear to take an interest in individuals on the team, Sarah is all business from the moment she arrives. Her comments on the reports are mostly criticisms related to style and procedure, with an emphasis on details and deadlines. Alex does not mind it when things and events at the meetings seem to needle her or get under her skin. He would like to see her lighten up and show him and his group some of the respect he believes they deserve.

On the occasion of the meeting, Alex arrives fifteen minutes late, and is two copies short with the team's report that he has put together. Parts of the report are not immediately clear to Sarah, and she notes two errors that have to be clarified before the meeting can get down to business. Otherwise, the report summarizes what the team has been doing in the past month and includes general plans for the upcoming quarter. The meeting begins with Sarah inquiring into the details of two of the projects listed in the quarterly work projections that seem unclear to her. Alex's response alludes to the fact that the projects are still in a developmental stage and details have yet to be worked out.

# 34

# Alternatives to Self-Disclosure Activity

**History:** This activity was presented at the Central States Communication annual meeting, April 2014, in Minneapolis, Minnesota.
**Primary courses, in which this activity might be used:** Interpersonal Communication, Introduction to Communication
**Concepts illustrated;** Self-Disclosure, Lying, Equivocation, Silence, Hinting, Ethical Communication

## PURPOSE

Self-disclosure is an important topic in interpersonal communication classes. However, it is also important that students understand the alternatives to self-disclosure. If students chose *not* to honestly share information about themselves with others, they are faced with choosing whether to remain silent, lie, equivocate, or hint. This exercise challenges students to think about the effects of those choices and their ethical ramifications. Too often the white lie, hint, or evasion is used without consideration of the long-term implications. The activity is designed to increase students' understanding of the alternatives to self-disclosure, to examine the ethical implications of those alternatives, and to encourage informed choices about self-disclosing.

## EXPLANATION OF ACTIVITY

This activity may be completed in fifty minutes or less, depending on the number of teams. Prior to completing this activity, the students must understand self-disclosure and the four most common alternatives to self-disclosure: Silence, equivocating—ambiguous statement designed to mislead, hinting—indirect message to get a desired response, and lying—an untrue statement (Adler & Proctor, 2014; Bavales, Black, Chovil & Mullett, 2010).

The class should be divided into teams of two to five students. Each team will be given a handout (see Appendix, p. 135), assigned a different role-play situation from the handout, and asked to brainstorm possible responses that are either self-disclosure, equivocation, hints, or lies. Each team should spend time practicing the role-play scenario and different responses, and then examine the ethical implications of each choice. After about ten to fifteen minutes, each team will be asked to select two of the responses to role-play in front of the entire class. You may choose to have the teams disclose the types of responses they role-played or ask the class to guess them. Those team members not involved in the role-play will be asked to explain the situation and debrief the ethical implications of the choices made in the role-play performance.

## DEBRIEF

The student groups will do most of the debriefing as they explain the situation, the types of responses they selected, and the ethical implications of those choices. The debriefing questions are the same questions students will discuss in their preparation of the role-play and are included in the Appendix on p. 135. If the students do not fully answer the questions in their debriefing, the instructor can ask them as follow up questions. The instructor may also wish to ask the entire class the following questions: Were some types of responses easier to make? What responses do you prefer to receive from others? What responses do you least like others to give you?

This is a popular activity and generates laughter, discomfort, and a great deal of discussion. Students report being more conscious of the choices they make when responding to others.

## REFERENCES

Adler, R., & Proctor, R. (2014). *Looking out looking in*. Boston, MA: Wadsworth.
Bavelas, J. B., Black, A., Chovil, N., & Mullett, J. (2010). Truths, lies, and equivocations: The effects of conflicting goals on discourse. In M. L. Knapp & J. A. Daly (Eds.), *Interpersonal communication* (Vol. II, pp. 379–408). Thousand Oaks, CA: Sage.

## APPENDIX

### INSTRUCTIONS FOR ALTERNATIVES TO SELF-DISCLOSURE ACTIVITY

There are four alternatives to self-disclosure (silence, equivocating, hinting, and lying.) Your instructor will assign your team a situation from the list below. Discuss the situation in your team, brainstorm possible ways to respond and then answer the questions. After completing the questions, you will have two members of your team perform the role-play situation twice for the class using two different responses. The other members of your team will explain the situation, discuss the choices you made, and examine their ethical implications. All members of your team should be involved in presenting and discussing the role-play scenario with the class.

## Situations

   A. A coworker is much more interested in becoming friends than you are. She invites you to a party on Friday. You aren't doing anything, but you don't want to go. What would you say?
   B. Your boss asked you to complete a report and turn it in on Monday morning. You hope that this report will help you receive a promotion. Although you started the report, you got busy and forgot to complete it. When you arrive at work Monday, your boss asks you for the report. How do you respond?
   C. Your best friend spent $75 and an entire day preparing a special birthday meal for you. Unfortunately, you dislike both the taste and texture of the food. Your friend asks how you like your birthday meal. How do you respond?
   D. Your mom asks you what you think about her new dress. You think it is ugly and unattractive. What would you say?

## Questions

   1. What would you say in this situation? Write two different responses you might give.
   2. Are these responses self-disclosure, equivocating, hinting, or lying? Identify the type of response you used and explain why you used it.
   3. What conflicting interaction goals were you accomplishing in your responses? (e.g., saving face versus being honest.)
   4. What are the ethical implications of your choices? How do competent, ethical communicators deal with conflicting interaction goals?

# 35

# The Interpersonal Communication Playlist

*Mary Vaughn, Ph.D.*
*Department of Communication Studies*
*Belmont University*
*mary.vaughn@belmont.edu*

**History:** This activity was presented at the annual meeting of the National Communication Association, November 2015, in Las Vegas, Nevada.

**Primary courses in which this activity might be used:** Interpersonal Communication, Communication Theory

**Concepts illustrated:** Self-dislcosure, Listening, Conflict, and other topics from a typical Interpersonal or Communication Theory course

## PURPOSE

Public Speaking classes emphasize the importance of attention-gaining devices, and the interpersonal communication playlist can serve as the attention-gaining device for each class session of an interpersonal communication or communication theory course. Bain (2004) suggested that effective college teachers gain students' attention with provocative questions about topics the students know or *think* they know. This activity offers familiar texts students can consider through the lens of interpersonal communication theory. It also helps students organize theoretical constructs and recall them later on.

The interpersonal communication playlist can also help instructors whose apprehension makes it difficult to cultivate a warm and welcoming learning environment. Baiocchi-Wagner's (2011) study found that instructors with communication apprehension have difficulty initiating conversation with students prior to class. The ritualized nature of the interpersonal communication playlist absorbs some of that tension and creates a welcoming learning environment.

## EXPLANATION OF ACTIVITY

The primary learning outcome of the interpersonal communication playlist is for students to use constructs from interpersonal communication theory to analyze popular song lyrics. As students walk into each class session, they hear a song that will be associated in some way with the theories or constructs to be discussed that day. For example, in a class session on facework (e.g., Cupach & Metts, 1994), a simple lyric on a slide can serve as a quick test of students' understanding of facework strategies. Carly Rae Epsen's "Call Me Maybe" can help students think about how one might use a cognitive disclaimer ("I just met you and this is crazy") and a hedge ("maybe") to make a threat to negative face ("call me").

Alternatively, the song of the day may provoke a more general discussion. For example, "Brave" by Sara Bareilles proclaims that we should "say what we want to say," but social penetration theory and privacy management theory suggest good reasons why people are more intentional in the way they manage self-disclosure. *Saturday Night Live* parodied this song and imagined various interpersonal situations wherein people say exactly what is on their minds. The video and song provide a great launch point for discussion of disclosure and privacy management.

In addition to the two examples mentioned, a representative list of theories, their accompanying songs, and typical prompts follow:

- Introduction to the Course: "What Do You Mean?" (Justin Bieber)
  - Prompt: "Justin is frustrated with his inability to read the nonverbal signals of his beloved. What do you find frustrating about interpersonal communication? When do you experience misunderstanding?"
- Nonverbal Communication: "When You Say Nothing at All" (Alison Krauss)
  - Prompt: "What types of nonverbal communication does she reference?" (Smile on your face, truth in your eyes, touch of your hand.) "Is it possible to say 'nothing' at all?"
- Perception: "Tom's Diner" (Suzanne Vega)
  - Prompt: "What counter-schema stimuli does she encounter, and how does she revise or work the stimuli into her existing schema?" (e.g., When the waiter fills her coffee cup halfway, and when she sees the woman outside the window hitching up her skirt, she tries to make sense of this counter-schema stimuli. She concludes that the waiter is distracted by someone coming in the door, and that the woman sees her own reflection rather than seeing through the glass).
- Facework: "Call Me Maybe" (Carly Rae Epsen)
  - Prompt: "Analyze the facework you hear in the lyrics of this song" (e.g., cognitive disclaimer—"I just met you and this is crazy"; hedge—"maybe"; threat to negative face—"call me").
- Self-Disclosure: "Brave" (Sara Bareilles)
  - Prompt: "This song suggests that it is brave to say what we want to say. What does privacy management theory suggest about this?"

- Listening: "Listen" (Beyoncé)
  - Prompt: After we've discussed paraphrasing, students can practice paraphrasing a lyric:
    - "Oh, now I'm done believing you; You don't know what I'm feeling; I'm more than what you made of me; I followed the voice you think you gave to me; But now I've gotta find my own."
    - Paraphrase: "So you seem to be saying that I'm out of touch with who you are, and the potential you have. You feel that you are responsible for what you've become, and that I underestimate that. Is that right?"
- Constructivism: "My Stupid Mouth" (John Mayer)
  - Prompt: "Have you ever felt like the singer of this song? To what extent or in what contexts do you plan conversations before you engage in them?"
- Uncertainty Reduction Theory: "Comfortable" (John Mayer)
  - Prompt: "How do you hear this song through the filter of uncertainty reduction theory?" (Generally, students talk about how his comfort from the certainty of his former relationship is what he misses, and note his cognitive and behavioral questions about his new relationship—why she doesn't swear or understand jazz.)
- Social Information Processing/Hyperpersonal Perspective: "Online" (Brad Paisley)
  - Prompt: "How do you hear this song through the filter of the social information processing theory?" (Students note how this song illustrates the tendency to selectively present one's self online and create a hyper-personal connection.)
- Relational Dialectics: "Drive By" (Train)
  - Prompt: "How do you hear this song through the filter of the relational dialectics perspective?" (This song depicts someone who wants certainty and connection, but becomes scared of commitment and bails. He then regrets his extreme response to what students will recognize as relational dialectics.)
- Relational Dialectics: "Forever & Always" (Taylor Swift)
  - Prompt: "How do you hear this song through the filter of the relational dialectics perspective?" (Lyrics relate to openness/closedness: "Was I out of line? Did I say something way too honest? Made you run and hide like a scared little boy? I looked into your eyes / Thought I knew you for a minute, now I'm not so sure".)
- Functionalist Perspective: "Everything is Awesome" (Tegan & Sarah)
  - Prompt: This song is ironic and provokes good discussion on how teamwork doesn't necessarily mean thinking and acting the same. There is a fitting scene in *The Lego Movie* that depicts individual master builders attempting to work together to solve a problem that goes along with the song.
- Conflict: "One More Night" (Maroon 5)
  - Prompt: "What type of conflict styles and behaviors does this song depict? Do you think this behavior is normal?" (Lyrics depict aggressive and destructive conflict behaviors, as well as avoidance.)

Most of the songs are available on YouTube, and many include lyrics on the screen for karaoke. I typically take suggestions from students at the end of each semester to keep my interpersonal communication playlist relevant. I time the song to play twice and end just as class is starting. After a few class sessions, I find that the room automatically gets quiet when the song ends. The songs serve as a ritual to signal the start of class. If I'm using PowerPoint, I typically include a picture of the artist and the song lyric for analysis.

## DEBRIEF

At the end of the semester, I have a discussion with students about the interpersonal communication playlist as a learning tool. I ask them the extent to which they think popular music describes and prescribes interpersonal communication behavior. They generally conclude that it does both, and they always say that they think about song lyrics more critically. They make comments like, "I can't listen to music now without thinking about the interpersonal communication message," and make frequent recommendations for future semesters. I've also tested the learning outcomes of the interpersonal communication playlist systematically. One semester, I offered students extra credit on the exam if they could use a theoretical perspective to reflect on the lyrics of any song I had played. The majority of the students received extra credit, and many could very competently make theoretical connections. Anecdotally, I've noted that the music serves as a positive ritual to begin each class. I've noticed many students humming along to the song, watching the video, or discussing the song or artist with a classmate. In summary, the interpersonal communication playlist is a great way to cultivate an energetic and inviting classroom culture, and it provides students with a tool to organize and recall course concepts.

## REFERENCES

Baiocchi-Wagner, E. (2011). "Facing threats": Understanding communication apprehensive instructors' face loss and face restoration in the classroom. *Communication Quarterly, 59(2)*, pp. 221–238.
Bain, K. (2004). *What the best college teachers do.* Cambridge, MA: Harvard University Press.
Cupach, W. R., & Metts, S. (1994). *Facework.* Thousand Oaks, CA: Sage.

# 36

## Teaching the Communication Process with a Grab Bag

*Jennifer B. Gray*
*Department of Communication*
*Appalachian State University*
*grayjb@appstate.edu*

**History:** The activity was presented at the annual meeting of the National Communication Association, November 2008, in San Diego, California.

**Primary courses in which this activity might be used:** Public Speaking, Interpersonal Communication

**Concepts illustrated:** Transactional Communication, Communicator/ Relationship, Content and Relational Dimensions, Communication Process, Message Types, Channel, Setting, Noise

### PURPOSE

The communication process is often taught in basic courses. It is essential for understanding the nature of communication, but can be perceived as quite abstract. This activity aims to explain the transactional nature of the communication process through an engaging and interactive process. The activity involves a discussion of the communication process and then an activity involving a grab bag (or a basket or bowl) of paper slips with different examples of components in the communication process, including channel, communicator, noise, environment, and message. For instance, channel components may include text messaging, telephone, cell phone, face-to-face, and email. By interchanging the elements of the process at random, the elements of the process are explained and the multi-faceted influence of the various components in everyday interaction is illustrated. This explanation of elements includes a central tenet, the transactional nature of communication.

### EXPLANATION OF ACTIVITY

Prepare five grab bags, each containing several examples of the components of the communication process; there should be grab bags for channel, communicator, noise, environment, and message. The examples for each component are up to the instructor but suggestions are provided below.

**TABLE 1.** Suggestions for Grab Bag Slips

| Channel | Communicator Relationship | Noise | Message | Environment |
|---|---|---|---|---|
| Text message | Romantic partners | Silence | Breaking up | Park bench |
| Phone | Friends | Child crying | Clean up | Apartment |
| Cell phone | Co-Workers | Cell phone ring | Angry words | Coffee shop |
| Face-to-face | Boss and subordinate | Traffic | Bad hair | Office |
| Email | Acquaintances | Previous argument | "You're wearing that?" | Hair salon |

Also prepare to discuss the communication process during class prior to the activity; students should also be asked to read about the process prior to the class in which the activity will occur.

In class, discuss the communication process by using a model drawn on a whiteboard or project one with a PowerPoint slide. A simple, visually appealing one is easily found in several textbooks (e.g., Adler, Rosenfeld, & Proctor, 2007). Review the components of the communication process, including channel, communicators (relationship), noise, environment, and message. Ask the students to get into groups and ask each group to draw a component from each grab bag.

Once the students have drawn their components, ask them to reveal their picks and then to perform the situation given these picks. For instance, if students pick romantic partners (communicators), loud music (noise), text message (channel), breaking up (message), and environment (park bench), the students must meet briefly and create an impromptu scenario incorporating these elements.

After each group performance is completed, a discussion may be led by asking about the contribution of each element to meaning and what occurs in the scenario. This may be done after each group performs, or may be done after all groups have performed.

## DEBRIEF

The performances may also lead into a more general discussion of the communication process model, exploring what the model reveals about sending and receiving, meaning, channels, environment, noise, and the transactional nature of communication. Questions to guide such discussion may include:

- How did the particular channel contribute to each communicator's messages? How did it contribute to interpretation of each message?
- How did the type of noise, the environment, and the message content contribute to message delivery and interpretation?
- How did the relationship of the communicators contribute to the interaction?
- How did each communicator contribute to the message? Did both of them contribute?
- Did one of the performances make you think about the communication process differently? How?

You then may sum up with a review of the model posed at the beginning of the lesson and a reference back to one or more of the scenarios to offer examples of each component of the model. Students thoroughly enjoy this activity and tend to remember the various scenes performed when we discuss components of the communication process throughout the semester.

## REFERENCES

Adler, R.B., Rosenfeld, L. B., & Proctor, R. F., II (2007). *Interplay: The process of interpersonal communication.* (10th ed.) New York: Oxford University Press.
Lucas, S.E. (2007). *The art of public speaking.* (9th ed.) Boston: McGraw-Hill.

# 37

## Defining Communication with Legos: Building an Understanding of the Constructivist Approach

*Lindy Grief Davidson, Ph.D.*
*Honors College*
*University of South Florida*
*lindyd@mail.usf.edu*

**History:** This activity was presented at the 2015 annual conference of the National Communication Association, November 2015, in Las Vegas, Nevada. It was ranked as a top submission.
**Primary courses in which this activity might be used:** Communication Theory, Health Communication, Public Speaking, Interpersonal Communication, Organizational Communication
**Concept illustrated:** Constructivist/constitutive approach to communication

### PURPOSE

The constructivist (constitutive) model of communication is one of the most difficult concepts for beginning communication students to grasp. Students frequently fall back on a transmission model, looking at communication as a simple information exchange (Craig, 1999). This reliance on the transmission model exposes students' inability to apply the constructivist model of communication. The concrete act of creating Lego structures offers students a visual representation of this important communication concept. Additionally, once the lesson is complete, students remember the activity in future discussions and will begin to use the constructivist model to describe communication in a variety of contexts. Since this activity teaches a foundational communication concept, it may be used in a variety of communication courses.

### EXPLANATION OF ACTIVITY

For classes of twenty or fewer, students will need eight to ten Lego blocks each, but for larger classes, two to three blocks per person is best. Hand out an assortment of Lego blocks to students and say, "Build something." (I often place the Legos in individual sandwich bags for quick distribution, but students may also select blocks out of a large box or bag.) After students have created their structures, tell them to find a partner and join their structures together. Once those structures are joined, have groups continue to join their structures until there are only two structures. Bring the two structures to the front of the room.

*Ask*: What is communication? (Depending on students' previous experiences in communication studies, they may offer a variety of definitions, but the transmission definition will likely come out.) Talk briefly about the transmission model and its limitations. Guide students by asking: How is communication more than a transmission of information? Imagine a couple with communication problems. What would happen if they attempted to resolve their disputes using only the transmission model of communication?

*Explain*: For this course, we will use a constructivist model of communication, meaning that "each conversation is embedded within, will become a part of, will be influenced by, and will influence myriad other past and future conversations" (Bartesaghi & Cissna, 2009, p. 131).

*Ask*: How does our Lego activity illustrate this idea of communication? You may need to guide students by asking more specific questions such as:

- Look at the building of your Lego structure as communication. When you merge it with another person's structure, what are you doing? (As you work together, you are negotiating back and forth. This is like conversing.)
- Are you exchanging information? (Help them to see that they are making something or building something.)
- When your Lego structure left your hands, were you still participating in the conversation? (Yes, your structure continues to exist in the larger structure others put together.)
- How is this like communication?

*For Example:* Think of a romantic relationship. Does a transmission model of communication capture what's happening when two people are falling in love? Are their interactions simply information exchanges?

*Ask*: How do people "construct" a romantic relationship through communication? How do past relationships impact this construction? (Each person is building on what already exists from previous interactions and experiences.) How are other relationships similarly constructed?

Ask two students to come to the front of the room to work with the two Lego structures created at the beginning of the lesson.

*Say*: Let's assume these two people are getting to know one another, what might their individual Lego structures represent? (Past relationships, desires, hopes, norms, values, expectations, etc.)

Give the two students more Lego blocks and ask them to use the new blocks to join the two pieces. As they work, point out that each person is adding to the structure but also taking into account the existing structures. It is constantly changing, shifting, morphing into something new. This is a constructivist approach to communication.

## DEBRIEF

The structure of this activity lends to discussion and explanation within the activity itself (as indicated with the questions above); however, in previous uses of this exercise, participants referred back to the idea in future lessons and interactions. For example, in Health Communication, students talked about the different Lego structures doctors and patients bring into a medical exam, showing that each has a unique set of experiences the other does not necessarily understand but will influence the interaction significantly. Since the activity illustrates a foundational communication concept, it is best used toward the beginning of a semester so it can be referenced throughout the course.

## REFERENCES

Bartesaghi, M. & Cissna, K. N. (2009). Social construction. In W. F. Eadie (Ed.), *21st century communication: A reference handbook* (pp. 128–136). Newbury Park, CA: Sage.

Craig, R. T. (1999). Communication theory as a field. *Communication Theory, 9*(2), 119–161.

# 38

## "Do You Remember That Time When…?": Modeling StoryCorps Interviews to Teach Family Storytelling

*Kristina A. Wenzel Egan*

*Communication Discipline, Collegium of Creative Arts*

*Eckerd College*

*Wenzelka@eckerd.edu*

**History:** This activity was presented at the annual meeting of the Southern States Communication Association, April 2015, in Tampa, Florida. **Primary courses in which this activity might be used:** Family Communication, Interpersonal Communication, Relational Communication **Concepts illustrated:** Shared Joint Storytelling, Family Identity, Narrative, Relational Culture, Turn-Taking, Perspective-Taking

### PURPOSE

Family narratives and storytelling have significant implications for family satisfaction, cohesion, and adaptability (Koenig Kellas, 2005). The content of family stories (re)produce family norms, values, and goals, and serve to socialize new family members to the family culture (Stone, 2004). While the *content* of family stories matter, interpersonal communication during the narrative event can influence how family members make sense of their lives and impact overall well-being (Kranstuber Horstman et al., 2016). As Langellier and Peterson (2004) noted, we rarely stop to reflect upon and critically assess the stories that narrate our lives. By examining shared joint family storytelling, students can begin to understand how family stories influence their family identity and critically examine their interpersonal communication with their family members. The present article summarizes a class activity and assignment designed to: (1) show students how family identity is (re)produced in the act of family storytelling; (2) develop students' ability to analyze how families engage in shared joint storytelling; and (3) help students reflect on personal family stories as told in joint interaction.

## EXPLANATION OF ACTIVITY AND ASSIGNMENT

A central component of the present class activity is listening to audio clips of families participating in shared joint storytelling that are published online by the non-profit organization StoryCorps. The organization is funded by the Corporation for Public Broadcasting and partnered with National Public Radio and The American Folklife Center. The purpose of StoryCorps "is to provide people of all backgrounds and beliefs with the opportunity to record, share and preserve the stories of our lives" (StoryCorps, 2013). StoryCorps has collected and preserved more than sixty thousand interviews and shares select stories with millions of listeners on NPR's Morning Edition and the organization's website (http://storycorps.org). The collection of stories affords instructors a tremendous opportunity to exemplify a variety of diverse experiences. The website categorizes the published stories by themes, which include Family, Friendship, LGBTQ, Hurricane Katrina, Struggle, Identity, Romance, Teachers, and Military.

For the present activity and assignment, instructors utilize StoryCorps stories to exemplify families who have participated in the performative act of storytelling. Students then model StoryCorps interviews by recording and analyzing a personal family story retold with a family member. By listening to and modeling StoryCorps interviews, students increase their understanding of the communicative construction of family identity and ultimately work toward understanding how family is constituted in communication.

The lecture is guided by key family communication and storytelling concepts, such as family rules, norms, identity, turn-taking, story coherence, and perspective-taking. Instructors may encourage interesting small-group discussions about the functions of family storytelling (e.g., to remember, to develop family culture), and other family communication concepts (e.g., relational culture, family secrets). After discussing family storytelling, instructors exemplify jointly told family stories by playing a few three-minute StoryCorps interviews from storycorps.org. Stories can be found by clicking "Listen" and selecting "Family" under "Browse Themes" on the StoryCorps website. Instructors should listen to and select stories prior to the class session because some stories demonstrate narrative and family concepts better than others. Examples of stories:

1. *Jackie and Scott Miller*
   A mother and son discuss adoption and coming out as gay. Demonstrates family secrets, turn-taking, perspective-taking, and relational culture. Search StoryCorps website for "Me & You."
2. *Samuel Black and Edda Fields-Black*
   A husband shares stories of his hard-working father with his wife. Demonstrates perspective-taking, family values, family norms, and family culture. Search StoryCorps website for "A Family Man."
3. *Tasha, Willa, and Brad Guidi*
   Parents tell their daughter how they met and their family reactions to their interracial relationship. Demonstrates turn-taking, family

definitions, and family identity. Search StoryCorps website for "Tasha Guth with her parents Willa and Brad Guidi."
4. *Hector and Leopoldina Vega*
Husband and wife tell the story of Hector's return from Iraq. Demonstrates perspective-taking, turn-taking, and relational culture. Search StoryCorps website for "Hector Vega and his wife Leopoldina."
5. *Danny and Annie Perasa*
Husband and wife discuss their relationship. Demonstrates family rituals, relational culture, and perspective-taking. Search StoryCorps website for "Danny & Annie."

Instructors should guide students' listening of the stories with discussion questions. Depending on the number of students in class, instructors may choose to discuss the stories as a class, in small groups, or in student pairs. Examples of discussion questions:

1. What is the overall message or theme of the story?
2. What family values or beliefs are underlying the story?
3. What was the emotional tone of the family members while telling the story?
4. What do you think it means to be a member of their family?
5. Do the family members confirm each other's perspectives during the narrative event?
6. How do the family members enact behaviors such as engagement with the story, turn-taking, and perspective-taking?
7. Where do you think these families tell these stories when they are not in a StoryCorps interview booth?
8. How do you see their familial and relational identity being materialized in the story?

After lecture and discussing the questions above, instructors should explain the family story assignment and analysis paper. The assignment requires students to retell a significant family story with at least one family member. Students are required to record and analyze the storytelling event. Instructors may consider requiring students to transcribe the event. The graded component of the assignment is a two- to three-page analysis paper, which requires students to examine the story by analyzing elements, such as how the content of the story reinforces family rules, norms, and values. Students should also examine how the story was told by analyzing the performative aspects of the storytelling event such as turn-taking and perspective-taking. Finally, instructors may require a personal reflection on what was eye-opening about their family or this story. Students are awarded points based on (1) a submission of the audio file containing the family storytelling event (and/or the completeness of the transcript), and (2) their ability to connect family storytelling concepts to the storytelling event in their analysis paper.

## DEBRIEF

After students have submitted their analysis paper, you can debrief by asking students to share their family storytelling experience with a partner in the class. The following discussion questions can assist with class discussion:

1. What was eye-opening from analyzing a family story?
2. Were there any family rules regulating what was revealed or concealed during the storytelling event?
3. How might you improve your interpersonal communication with this family member? Are there any examples of areas you could improve upon in the storytelling event?

## REFERENCES

Koenig Kellas, J. (2005). Family ties: Communicating identity through jointly told family stories. *Communication Monographs, 72*, 365–389. doi: 10.1080/03637750500322453

Kranstuber Horstman, H., Maliski, R., Hays, A., Cox, J., Enderle, A., & Nelson, L. R. (2016). Unfolding narrative meaning over time: The contributions of mother–daughter conversations of difficulty on daughter narrative sense-making and well-being. *Communication Monographs, 83*, 326–348. doi: 10.1080/03637751.2015.1068945

Langellier, K. M. (2002). Performing family stories, forming cultural identity: Franco American Memere stories. *Communication Studies, 53*, 56–73. doi: 10.1080/10510970209388574

Langellier, K. M., & Peterson, E. E. (2004). *Storytelling in daily life: Performing narrative.* Philadelphia: Temple University Press.

Stone, E. (2004). *Black sheep and kissing cousins: How our family stories shape us.* New Brunswick, NJ: Transaction Publishers.

StoryCorps. (2013). *StoryCorps 2013 annual report.* Retrieved from http://cdn.storycorps.org/wordpress/wp-content/uploads/2013_Annual-Report.pdf

# 39

# One Truth and Two Lies: A Game That Reinforces Narrative Paradigm

*Yifeng Hu*
*Department of Communication Studies*
*The College of New Jersey*
*hu@tcnj.edu*

**History:** This activity was presented at the annual meeting of the National Communication Association, November 2014, in Chicago, Illinois.

**Primary courses in which this activity might be used:** Communication Theory, Human Communication, Interpersonal Communication, Persuasion

**Concepts illustrated:** Fisher's Narrative Paradigm, Narrative Rationality, Coherence, Fidelity, Persuasion

## PURPOSE

According to Walter Fisher's narrative paradigm (1985), humans are storytellers, and we are more persuaded by a good story than a good argument. The effectiveness of a story depends on whether it has narrative rationality, a standard for judging which stories to believe and which to disregard. Narrative rationality operates on the basis of two principles: coherence and fidelity. Coherence refers to the internal consistency of a story, which includes structural coherence (the flow of the story), material coherence (the congruence between one story and other related stories), and characterological coherence (the believability of the characters in the story). Fidelity refers to the credibility of a story, or "good reasons," a set of values for accepting the story as true and worthy of acceptance.

The purpose of this class activity is to enhance students' understanding of the narrative paradigm by engaging and exciting them with an adapted popular icebreaker game. In the original game, "Two Truths and a Lie," players come up with two truths and one lie about themselves and tell them to their partners. Their partners, meanwhile, try to guess which is the lie, and vice versa. The goal is to trick others into not being able to figure out which is the lie! This class activity puts a twist on the game by incorporating the narrative paradigm. Specifically, students are asked to apply the major principles of narrative rationality while making and evaluating stories relevant to their own lives. For example, a well-constructed lie may not be easily detected. This may prove that mythos (a traditional or recurring narrative) is more convincing than logos (arguments). However, if the story around the lie lacks coherence and/or fidelity, listeners may quickly reject it. This will teach students the importance of considering narrative rationality when creating and judging a story.

## EXPLANATION OF ACTIVITY

This game is best played after the class has learned the theory (i.e., the different types of coherence and fidelity), giving them the opportunity to put the theory into practice. First, students are asked to prepare their stories before coming to the class meeting. Here is a brief instruction: "Find one truth and make up two lies about yourself. Write a story around each truth and lie. For one lie, the story must lack coherence and/or fidelity in some way, and the other must utilize coherence and fidelity as much as possible. Don't go too wild, such as 'I once saw a dinosaur!' and do not share your stories with anyone in the class yet!"

During the class meeting, form groups of two to three (depending on class size). In the first round of the game, each student takes turns sharing their one truth and two lies with the group. Stick with straight facts. Let the group guess which is the truth and which is the lie. But do not reveal which is which yet! Play a second round in which students form stories around their one truth and two lies and share them with the group. Again, the group will evaluate the stories. After both rounds have been played, each student may reveal the mystery. Students should then discuss with one another how they were tricked or not tricked by the story, and what aspects of the story made the lie seem more or less believable. The instructor may even ask a few volunteers to share their stories with the whole class, or have the class vote for the best lie.

## DEBRIEF

Students are asked to reflect on their experiences and relate them to the theory. Further, they are asked to think about whether this activity helps reinforce what they have learned. In the past, students who have tried this game found it very "interesting and relevant," and extremely "helpful" in deepening their understanding of the theory. Students reported that they had really applied the theory during the game. One student said: "I really found myself trying to locate the different types of inconsistencies in their stories." Another said: "It forced me to use coherence and fidelity to judge my partner's stories." A positive by-product of this game may be that it helps students learn more about their classmates.

There are several scenarios as a result of this game. A well-told story around a truth (met the criteria of coherence and fidelity) is usually believed. A lie that is not well told (e.g., lacks structural coherence) is easily detected. However, there are two tricky situations. One: When a story around a lie is well told, it becomes harder to detect. The instructor can thus challenge the students: Why is a lie believed? By doing so, students are learning the powerful and convincing nature of a good narrative. Two: A truth is not believed. For example, a student shared a true story in great detail about how she was badly bitten by her own dog on the face when she was a kindergartener. A brief roadmap of her story is as follows:

"My dog was outside → I tried to get him back in the house by wrapping my arms around its neck and pulling → he turned back and bit me → my cheek was hanging off → my mom immediately took me and dragged me into the car → I got 16 stitches."

Her story contained structural (full of details) and characterological coherence (typical kid's behavior). However, almost all her classmates did not believe the story mainly because there was no evidence to back it up (lack of material coherence). The first thing everyone asked about (or looked for) was a scar on her face, which did not exist. But if one knows that facial wounds and scars are easier to treat with young kids, as their skin still possess high elasticity and their tissues are growing faster, one will accept the story. This example presents a good opportunity to critique the theory: how persuasive (believable) a story is also depends on the listener's life experience and knowledge.

In summary, here is a series of questions to debrief this activity:

- Why is a truth usually believed but not always? Students will focus on whether the story around the truth has used all three elements of the narrative paradigm.
- Why is it relatively easier to pick out the lie during the first round, but after hearing a well-constructed story about the lie, it suddenly becomes harder? By discussing this question, students will further recognize the power of narratives and storytelling.
- Are there ethical concerns about learning what makes a good lie? By now students have learned that narrative paradigm is a double-edged sword. Students may discuss when it is acceptable to tell a good lie and when it is not. For example, one may argue that it is OK to use a lie to get people (especially kids) to change unhealthy behaviors, but most agree it is highly unethical to use a lie, however good it is, for one's own benefit.

### REFERENCES

Fisher, W. R. (1985). The narrative paradigm: An elaboration. *Communication Monographs, 52,* 347–367.

# 40

# Barbie, Lego, and Play-Doh: Exploring Communication Theory Through Childhood Experiences

*Nancy Bressler*
*Department of Communications and Composition*
*Wheeling Jesuit University*
*nbressler@wju.edu*

**History:** This activity was presented at the annual meeting of the International Communication Association, May 2014, in Seattle, Washington.

**Primary courses in which this activity might be used:** Communication Theory, Introduction to Communication, Gender and Communication, Culture and Communication, Interpersonal Communication

**Concepts illustrated:** Gender Theory, Interpersonal Theory, Social Learning Theory, Cognitive Development Theory, Symbolic Interactionism, Standpoint Theory

## PURPOSE

This activity has two main goals: the identification and application of communication theories, and the implementation of critically examining those theories. Through this activity, students recognize and relate communication and gender theories to real-life scenarios. This activity uses biological, interpersonal, psychological, cultural, and critical theories of gender and communication to present an extensive overview of how communication theorists study gender. Childhood toys, games, and activities cultivate distinctions in how children communicate (Wood, 2011). Young boys' activities often emphasize individualism, problem-solving skills, and competition; for young girls, their activities accentuate relational, responsive, and supportive communication (Wood, 2011). Thus by applying their own childhood experiences, students engage directly with these gender and communication theories; this approach encourages students to be active learners and critical thinkers in the classroom.

Moreover, when students apply these course concepts to their own childhood memories, their individual voices and perspectives enter the classroom conversation. Rather than the teacher's voice being authoritative, students engage in dialogue about how these communication theories resonate with their own lived experiences. This embraces Freire's "problem-posing education" whereby students are reflexive in their pursuit of knowledge and make connections between what they learn and their own personal knowledge. Students assess to what extent gender is a perceived cultural concept in their interpretations about gender and their own identity construction through this activity. Through critical thinking and the application of theory to their own lives, students are also more likely to examine how culture influences gender and communication.

## EXPLANATION OF ACTIVITY

Prior to the class, students read about the prevalent theories of communication and gender. I recommend chapter two from Julia Wood's (2011) book *Gendered Lives: Communication, Gender, and Culture*. Once class begins, ask students to name three of their favorite toys, games, and/or hobbies from their childhood. Once they have their list, have students pick one favorite that they are willing to share with the class. Next, pose questions such as:

1) Why was this toy, game, or hobby your favorite?
2) What childhood memory/memories does this toy, game, or hobby invoke?
3) What people, places, or things do you associate with this toy, game, or hobby?

After they address these questions, discuss the common theories of gender, including biological, interpersonal (psychodynamic), psychological (social learning theory and cognitive development theory), cultural (symbolic interactionism), and critical theory (standpoint). Facilitate a discussion on how gender is socially and culturally constructed through our relationship with family, friends, formal institutions (such as schools), and the mass media. Break the students into smaller groups of three to five students (depending on the class size). Ask each smaller group to answer the following questions:

- Recall when you first observed gender similarities and/or differences within your family. What was the situation and how did your experience relate to gender?
- Recall when you first observed gender similarities and/or differences with your friends or in school. What was the situation and how did your experience relate to gender?
- What were some of your favorite television shows and/or movies? What ideas about gender do you recall observing?

Then gather the class together and discuss the students' observations as a group. Further connect the activity to course content by asking students what theories they now believe influenced their earliest perceptions about gender.

Ask students to return to the list of their favorite childhood activities and select one theory about gender that best relates to their earlier analysis of their preferred toy, game, or hobby. In other words, students should have already selected a reason for their favorite childhood activity, but now they will assess which theory best explains that observation. Once they have chosen a theory, ask them to share and explain their choice with a partner. For example, students have revealed that playing Barbie with their mother and/or sisters was a ritualistic occasion; because this was one of the earliest relationships they developed, these students realized how interpersonal theory explained how they first understood gender roles. Other students have also expressed that commercials featuring Lego sets and/or Play-Doh persuaded them to want these toys. These students thus identified that the happy children in the commercials demonstrated social learning theory because it socialized them that if they had the product they would be as delighted as the children in the commercials.

After allowing some time for partner discussion, bring the class together as a whole. Have volunteers present their childhood activity and the theory of communication and gender that they selected. Facilitate a discussion on the class's overall interpretations about how their lived experiences now connect with these gender theories.

## DEBRIEF

Because they are engaging with their own backgrounds and childhood memories, students really enjoy this interactive activity. After discussing which theories students perceive impacted their childhood memories, the teacher should poll the students to see which theories resonated with them the most and the least. In previous classes, I have found that interpersonal and psychological theories are the most prevalent theories. Students interpret that their relationships with their family and friends play a major role in their gender construction. The teacher may also pose questions about how these relationships influenced student perceptions about other social norms. Or the teacher could ask students how their role models influenced their assumptions about gender. In contrast, cultural theories are often the least frequently used theories. Even though gender is a culturally based construct, students often do not perceive it as having an impression on their gender construction. Teachers could continue the discussion by asking students to contextualize their interpretation of culture and contemplate what attributes and characteristics within their culture also affect their gender perceptions. Once students start to consider their cultural assumptions, a robust discussion about why they thought culture was least likely to influence them can begin. Consequently, through this activity, students engage in the transformative learning process (Merriam, Caffarella, & Baumgartner, 2007). Students critically reflect on the trends they observed through this activity; therefore, the activity moves from their individual lived experiences into a broader discussion about social and cultural norms that can affect gender perceptions.

## REFERENCES

Freire, P. (1996). *Pedagogy of the oppressed.* London: Penguin Books Ltd.

Merriam, S. B., Caffarella, R. S., & Baumgartner, L. M. (2007). *Learning in adulthood: A comprehensive guide.* San Francisco, CA: Jossey-Bass.

Wood, J. (2011). *Gendered lives: Communication, gender, and culture* (9th ed.). Boston, MA: Wadsworth Publishing.

# 41

# "Did You Just See That?": Using Critical Communication Pedagogy and Observation to Teach about Identity and Social Norms

*Kristina Ruiz-Mesa*
*Department of Communication Studies*
*California State University, Los Angeles*
*Kruizme@calstatela.edu*

**History:** This G.I.F.T.S. learning activity was presented at the International Communication Association annual meeting, May 2015, in San Juan, Puerto Rico.
**Primary courses for this activity:** Communication Theory, Communication Education, Sex and Gender in Communication, Feminism in Communication and other courses involving identity and communication
**Concepts illustrated:** Communicative Practices, Critical Pedagogy, Normative Discourses, Materiality of Identities, Qualitative Research Methods

## PURPOSE

As a "practical discipline" (Craig, 1989, p. 97), communication offers opportunities to learn about theory through everyday observations and interactions. Through observations at regularly visited locations, students are able to learn: 1) more about each other; 2) critical communication pedagogy (Fassett & Warren, 2007); 3) how to critically examine hegemonic discourses on gender and other identities; 4) to evaluate the communicative processes and normative assumptions present in observations; 5) qualitative research practices; 6) about creating and presenting research posters.

## EXPLANATION OF ACTIVITY

Begin the activity by asking the students to share a favorite place they frequently visit in the surrounding college area where there are many people present to observe. Next, have the students explain to their peers why they enjoy the location. While each student speaks, the rest of the class takes notes about the location and its appeal to the speaker. Afterward, if students in the class have visited any of the places mentioned by the speakers, ask them to rank those places from most to least favorite. Next, invite the class to create groups of four to five students each based on their favorite places. Typically, students pick locations like the campus gym, a local restaurant, a bookstore, a shopping center, or local amusement attraction.

Once students have self-selected into groups, ask each group to visit their selected location twice in the coming month: (1) visiting as they would regularly and (2) as a group. In both visits to the location, students should take observational, qualitative notes about: 1) the multiple ways they see gender, sexuality, race, and other intersectional identities being expressed, pressured, marked, and adapted based on location; 2) images, advertisements, music, and other discourses that could impact behaviors; 3) what is interesting, surprising, and what they are seeing for the first time; 4) how their observations support or challenge previous course readings and discussions.

As the individuals and groups complete their observations, have students compile their notes and begin to look for common themes, practices, and behaviors, and tie these observations to readings and class discussions. Ask students to reflect on how their own life experiences confirm or conflict with what they observed and how cultural norms and expectations create a lens for their observations. Next, have students search academic literature and locate sources that help explicate their observations. Using communication theories and research in conjunction with gender, race, and identity research in other disciplines, ask students to offer a critical analysis of their observations and provide an argument based in theory and on previous class readings and lessons to discuss the hegemonic and counter-hegemonic discourses present as well as the ways that oppressive discourses can be disrupted. When framing the research project for students, discuss how cultural and social norms and practices inform how we see, create expectations for, and critique those around us. Explain how power, privilege, and oppression function to normalize experiences and identities, and discuss how normalization guides communication practices.

Using location images, group observations, critical reflections, media clips and graphics, each group creates a virtual poster presentation detailing their research experience. The virtual posters are created in PowerPoint, Prezi, or in PDF form, and are visually displayed for the class, typically using the classroom projector, while the group presents an eight- to ten-minute research presentation about their project. The virtual poster format provides students with the experience of giving a poster presentation without incurring any printing costs. Virtual posters can easily be shared with other groups prior to the presentation on the learning management system for peer review and feedback. After the group poster presentation, student peers then pose questions to the group about the observation and research process, and provide written feedback to each group using a rubric sheet handed out at the beginning of the class. The peer evaluation sheet asks students to assess the cohesiveness, clarity, and organization of the presentation, and provides space for students to share critical and positive feedback to group members they may not feel comfortable giving in front of the class.

## DEBRIEF

The debrief process for this assignment is conducted in class between student presentations. This process allows for students to engage topics and questions with each other in a safe classroom space. Additional and less formalized debriefing occurs with student groups following data collection. As students begin to analyze their data, provide the students with class time for groups to work on their projects and to meet with the instructor to ensure that all students understand the data analysis process.

To debrief this activity during group presentations, first ask students what observation most surprised them. Incorporating various student responses, start to unpack *why* these observations were surprising. Ask about normative communicative practices and behaviors, and how what they observed violated their expectations for interaction. Using communication theories such as Expectancy Violations (Burgoon, 1978; Burgoon & Jones, 1976), explore how dominant discourses and framings guide everyday interactions and communication expectations. Ask how normative communicative practices are informed by gendered, raced, and classed communication expectations. Invite student experiences and reactions to these observations into the debriefing conversation.

This project has been well received in several undergraduate Sex and Gender courses and in an upper-division Feminism in Communication course. Students enjoy the opportunity to go out as a group and be part of a project. This project can be particularly useful in building social support, student accountability, and classroom community on campuses where the majority of students are commuters or first-time students with few connections on campus. By offering student groups the opportunity to engage in diverse literatures and make connections between what they observe and what is being published in academic journals, undergraduate students become familiar with a range of academic resources, learn how to conduct academic literature searches, and gain experience reading and reviewing academic journal articles. Student comments on the project in classes were overwhelmingly positive. The major benefits of the exercise from student feedback included building peer community, being introduced to research, incorporating their voices and experiences into the class, and using places they are already familiar with in their community as potential research sites.

## REFERENCES

Burgoon, J. K. (1978). A communication model of personal space violations: Explication and an initial test. *Human Communication Research, 4,* 129–142. doi: 10.1111/j.1468-2958.1978.tb00603.x

Burgoon, J. K., & Jones, S. B. (1976). Toward a theory of personal space expectations and their violations. *Human Communication Research, 2,* 131–146. doi: 10.1111/j.1468-2958.1976.tb00706.x.

Craig, R. T. (1989). Communication as a practical discipline. *Rethinking communication, 1,* 97–122.

Fassett, D.L & Warren, J.T. (2007). *Critical communication pedagogy.* Thousand Oaks, CA: SAGE.

# 42

# Do Clothes Make the Student?; Makeover Day "Selfie" Project

*Terri Toles Patkin*

*Eastern Connecticut State University*

*Department of Communication*

*patkin@easternct.edu*

**History:** This activity was presented at the annual meeting of the National Communication Association, November 2015, in Las Vegas, Nevada.

**Primary courses:** Interpersonal Communication, Nonverbal Communication, Public Speaking, Persuasion, Organizational Communication

**Concepts illustrated:** Person Perception, Impression Management, Identity, Nonverbal Communication, Appearance and Adornment, Rhetorical Choices

### PURPOSE

Makeover Day harnesses the power of the "selfie" as a means to demonstrate rhetorical concepts in everyday life. This activity asks students to engage with perception theory and implicit personality theory, and to apply concepts pragmatically in their own lives. Students must first consciously recognize the rhetorical choices they convey with their everyday appearance and adornment and then identify ways in which they might shape those messages.

Human interaction incorporates both discourse and dialogic functions, which in tandem influence the processes of person perception and impression formation. The attribution and assignment of identity forms a central component of impression management, which consists of strategies to enhance our credibility, excuse our failures, influence others, secure help, hide our faults, and confirm our self-image (DeVito, 2013). Contemporary conceptualizations of identity often emerge from Goffman's view that all interaction is a performance, which helps define the situation and helps others know how best to act. The performer's conduct, appearance, and manner combine to form a *front* that permits the audience member to appropriately interpret the expressions the performer *gives* (the verbal channel) as well as the expressions the performer *gives off* (the nonverbal channel) (Goffman, 1959). Hecht (1993) notes that identity is inherently a process of communication and may be conceptualized through four frames: personal (one's self-concept), enactment (that which emerges via social interaction), relationship (a mutually constructed coexistence), and communal (in which identity contributes to group cohesion). Student reflections on these frames of identity dovetail nicely with this activity. For the online or blended class, the elasticity of identity in the online context, already flexible in the face-to-face world, provides rich opportunities for examination (Turkle, 2011).

## EXPLANATION OF ACTIVITY

Students are provided with the instruction: "We are often creatures of habit. Our clothing, hairstyle, and personal artifacts often work together to form a personal style that is consistent from day to day. Figure out what your *typical* personal style is ... athletic? Casual? Formal? Sexy? Professional? Now change it—noticeably—for a day. If you usually come to class in jeans and sneakers, pull out your Sunday best. If you wear a lot of makeup and dress professionally, show up in old sweatpants. Wear that outfit you really liked back in high school but wouldn't be caught dead in ever again. Pull out the bridesmaid dress you thought you'd never wear again. Now, go through a normal day in abnormal clothing. Don't forget to alter your hairstyle and accessories, too!"

It is important to encourage participants to be really dramatic in their Makeover Day choices. While one student did choose to wear a prom dress to class, sometimes students change something so subtle that others who don't know them well may not notice. One male student who exchanged his usual athletic shorts and tee shirt for a polo shirt and khaki pants felt that he had changed his appearance significantly, while observers did not find his presentation of self to be markedly different. The potential disconnect between external and internal perceptions of self can form the foundation for valuable discussion.

Deliverables include a short reflection paper describing student results with links to appropriate theoretical concepts, along with *before* and *after* photographs. The photographs are key, both to document completion and to facilitate instructor understanding of the approach taken. Technologically, asking students to email their photos to the instructor or print them out is easily accomplished, as a majority of students own either a smart phone or digital camera. Even if a particular student doesn't personally own either device, it is likely that s/he knows someone who can assist. I always offer alternatives in the event that the student cannot comply with the photo requirement, but no one has ever requested this option.

This three-page paper allows students to place their lived experience within theoretical frames discussed in class. In addition, students are asked to reflect on their own emotional response to taking risks with their self-presentation. For example, a female student who put on makeup and wore a dress and heels to class (instead of her usual yoga pants, comfortable top, and flip flops) explored the ways in which her makeover influenced not only others' perceptions of her, but her own emotional responses as she interacted throughout the day, finding that she was perceived as being more professional and that she felt more competent. Assessment of the paper relies not on the quality of the student's makeover choices or the success of their attempt, but rather their ability to draw connections between those choices and previously identified concepts.

## DEBRIEF

The photos become the foundation for class discussion about relevant self-presentation concepts. Sharing the photos in a small-group context creates a comfortable environment for students to explore both the specifics of the experience and the larger theoretical context within which it falls. Often, students can be guided to identify concepts such as communication apprehension, impression management, or embodied cognition in their evaluation of their project. Discussion groups can be rearranged throughout the class period, either randomly or by some demographic or activity-related variable (e.g., males/females, those who dressed up/down, those who wore a uniform). Depending on time constraints and pedagogical preference, the photos could be shared with the entire class, or only with the instructor.

Typically, students report that the people they encounter treat them differently during the day. Professors may ask if a well-dressed student is going to a job interview or classmates may express concern for the health of a dressed-down peer. Students are often surprised to discover that the largest difference is the one they themselves experience as they mindfully engage in interactions throughout the day. Some students are excited to try this activity, while others express a degree of apprehension. Simply acknowledging that the activity may take them out of their comfort zone and allowing students to choose when and where to complete the activity (within a specific window) relieves stress. Ultimately, even reluctant participants describe the experience as enjoyable (or at least interesting), and the activity has a side effect of increasing the sense of cohesion among class members.

Variations of Makeover Day could be utilized in media-focused classes such as Mass Communication, Media Effects, or Political Communication, where the student activity would serve as the foundation for a broader discussion of presentation of self in the mediated environment (e.g., the JFK-Nixon debates or the sartorial choices of newscasters.) Similarly, this activity could easily be incorporated into an online or blended class, and could assist in building interpersonal connections among class members.

## REFERENCES

DeVito, J. A. (2013). *The interpersonal communication book* (13th ed.). Boston, MA: Pearson.

Goffman, E. (1959). *The presentation of self in everyday life.* Garden City, NY: Doubleday

Hecht, M. L. (1993). 2002—A research odyssey: Toward the development of a communication theory of identity. *Communication Monographs, 60,* 76–81.

Turkle, S. (2011). *Alone together: Why we expect more from technology and less from each other.* New York: Basic Books.

# 43

## "I Am . . .": An Exercise in Self-Concept

*Deleasa Randall-Griffiths, Ph.D.*
*Department of Communication Studies*
*Ashland University*
*drandall@ashland.edu*

**History:** This activity was presented at the annual meeting of the Central States Communication Association, April 2014, in Minneapolis, Minnesota.

**Primary courses in which this activity might be used:** Introductory communication courses or upper level interpersonal communication courses

**Concepts illustrated:** Self-Identity, Self-Concept, Self-Image, and Self-Schema

### PURPOSE

The objective of this activity is to explore the multifaceted ways in which students describe themselves as a way to unpack the multifaceted nature of identity. Textbook chapters on identity and self-concept cover some of the most abstract material in the field of communication. Whereas many topics, such as nonverbal communication or conflict, have concrete examples students can analyze, qualities of identity are more ephemeral and harder to pinpoint. This exercise helps students connect the theories and concepts to their own lived experience. It also allows for discussion of individual perceptions of identity and how we highlight certain aspects of "who we are in the world" based on different perspectives.

### EXPLANATION OF ACTIVITY

At the beginning of class hand each student a sheet of paper with "I am _____" written twenty times down the page. Ask students to fill out all twenty lines. Tell them that as long as it makes sense in the English language and it is true, it counts. Give them about three to five minutes to fill out the sheet. Since most students struggle with this exercise, it helps to roam around the room looking at their papers, encouraging them, challenging them, and praising the first few students who make it halfway or finally complete the list. It helps to be playful in your encouragement, saying things like, "How can you possibly be stumped by this exercise? Who knows you better than you?" Really try to get them all to complete all twenty lines. Sometimes you will need to move on when it feels like a few stragglers will never quite make it to the finish line. The assignment is deceptively simple. Since no one ever asks us to describe ourselves in this manner, many students draw a blank when asked to fill out the sheet. The potential for an enriching discussion based on this exercise makes it worth the effort and encouragement.

## DEBRIEF

Begin the discussion by acknowledging the difficulty of the task. Ask them to explain why it was so difficult. Students give a range of responses, including their dependence on others to help define them. The most common reasons center on the lack of experience articulating who they are. From there, ask for examples of things they had on the list. Let the examples come out very freely for a while. Since anything was fair game, sometimes students may offer unusual (e.g., I am persnickety) or funny (e.g., I am annoying) responses. Mostly the items appearing on the sheets stem from four basic categories.

> **Temporal descriptors:** I am hungry, I am tired, etc.
> **Physical descriptors:** I am tall, I am blonde, etc.
> **Role-based descriptors:** I am a student, I am a football player, I am a coach, etc.
> **Personality descriptors:** I am stubborn, I am artistic, etc.

The discussion of this exercise can continue in many ways. Talk about proportion by asking students to estimate how many of the twenty items fell into each of the four categories. Ask students to look for patterns or discuss why some aspects get highlighted while others are ignored. Point out the basic answers that many students may have forgotten to put on their list. Ask them if they included items such as name, age, a student, a son/daughter. Focus just on family roles and point out the four to five items that almost everyone could have listed (i.e., son/daughter, grandson/granddaughter, sibling/only child, niece/nephew, cousin).

The overall lesson to convey is that individuals focus their attention on different aspects of their identity depending on the situation. Ask students to reflect on the fluidity of identity. This is easy to see with regard to the Temporal descriptors, but it is equally true of Role-based categories. Ask students about how their roles have changed in the past year. This discussion moves easily into material on how our self-concept is formed. This initial discussion helps students understand how their family, peers, and society in general have contributed to their perception of identity. From there, discussion may branch into how one's communication choices are influences by particular facets of identity.

## REFERENCES

Adler, R. B. & Proctor, R. F. (2014). *Looking out looking in* (14th ed.). Boston, MA: Wadsworth.

Adler, R. B. & Rodman, G. (2011). Perceiving the self. In Kathleen Galvin (Ed.) *Making connections: Readings in relational communication* (5th ed). (pp. 101–106). New York: Oxford University Press.

Braithwaite, D. O. & Wood, J. T. (2000). *Case studies in interpersonal communication: Processes and problems.* Boston: Wadsworth.

Floyd, K. (2009). *Interpersonal communication: The whole story.* New York: McGraw Hill.

McCornack, S. (2016). *Reflect & relate: An introduction to interpersonal communication* (4th ed.) Boston, MA: Bedford/St. Martin.

Trenholm, S. & Jensen, A. (2013). *Interpersonal communication* (7th ed). New York: Oxford University Press.

Wood: J. T. (2013). *Interpersonal communication: Everyday encounters* (7th ed). Boston, MA: Wadsworth.

# 44

# Music in the Communication Classroom: Using Music to Teach about Stereotypes and Expectations

*Dr. William Mullen*
*Communication Arts Department*
*Shorter University*
*bmullen@shorter.edu*

*Dr. Faith Mullen*
*Division of Humanities*
*Georgia Highlands College*
*fmullen@highlands.edu*

**History:** This activity was presented at the annual meeting of the National Communication Association, November 2015, in Las Vegas, Nevada.

**Primary courses in which this activity might be used:** Basic Course, Small Group, Intercultural, Persuasion, Nonverbal, Organizational

**Concepts illustrated:** Stereotyping, Perception, Attribution, Labels, Audience Adaptation, Generalizations, First Impressions, Identification, Cultural Differences

## PURPOSE

The word *stereotype* has been defined as a general "belief about a group of individuals" (Kanahara, 2006, p. 306). Typically, stereotypes carry negative connotations because they are often overgeneralized, superficial, incorrect, exaggerated, or rigid (Kanahara, 2006). Students often believe that other individuals who use stereotyping are prejudiced, while they themselves are immune to such practices because they are "open-minded." The purpose of this activity is to teach students that they do indeed engage in stereotyping—especially in small, everyday life practices. As students experience this issue firsthand, they realize that they judge, critique, and have expectations of the people around them. Through this activity students begin to understand the importance and prevalence of stereotyping in their own communication practices. This exercise is a great way to teach three concepts: First, students learn about ascribed characteristics. Second, students learn how easy it is to stereotype. And third, students learn how their communication with specific groups of people is influenced by their expectations and stereotyping. Instructors can easily use the activity any time during the semester without a great deal of organizing and preparing prior to class. Because students enjoy music and sharing their ideas, they find this activity very enjoyable. Admittedly, this activity is about having fun and enjoying class, but it also helps students to understand important concepts that are so important to human communication.

## EXPLANATION OF ACTIVITY

Give each student a handout that has five separate rows labeled *Clip 1, Clip 2, Clip 3, Clip 4, and Clip 5*. Make sure the rows are wide enough for the students to write brief descriptions or terms. Or you can simply ask the students to get their own paper and divide it into five sections. Explain that you will be playing five different types of music, and that when they hear the music clip they need to describe the person who would listen to that particular style of music. Next you should play one style of music. Classical music is always a good style to begin with. After having the student listen to the music, tell them to write down in the first category a description of the person who would listen to that style of music and to include as much detail as possible. Then move onto the next style of music, repeating the process until the students have heard five distinct music genres and have described five different groups of people. You can access music on the Internet (by searching music genres or specific musical artists) and easily play the clips in a smart classroom. Music clips from the following genres work especially well: classical, hip-hop, jazz, country, and pop. However, you can choose music from any genre and even music from various cultures.

## DEBRIEF

The activity should conclude with a thorough debriefing. Ask the students to describe the individuals who listen to classical music and work through listener descriptions of each style of music. Ask the following questions as part of the debriefing session: Why did you describe specific (e.g., classical/hip-hop/country) music listeners in the manner you did? What led you to the various descriptions? Are all music listeners (e.g., classical/hip-hop/country) like you? Is it stereotyping to ascribe characteristics to a specific group of music listeners? How would stereotyping various music listeners into categories change your communication with that individual? Is it possible to not stereotype?

Should we try? When does stereotyping become a problem? How can we try to avoid the issues that can come with stereotyping?

Typically, students are surprised to learn that they stereotype so quickly and easily. They generally are quick to provide other examples of stereotyping in their daily lives and relationships. Students say they describe music listeners in certain ways because they have "observed" the people who listen to specific types of music and seem convinced that their beliefs are correct. However, as they realize they are ascribing characteristics to groups of people the light comes on, and they realize they are stereotyping. As teachers, we make an effort to point out that stereotyping is a normal part of everyday thinking. In fact, we demonstrate that people use stereotyping as a defense mechanism for avoiding dangerous situations. But we also discuss the pitfalls of stereotyping. Acknowledging the fact that they do stereotype usually opens a frank discussion about how inaccurate, negative, and often hurtful stereotyping can be and how it can be curtailed.

Students tend to enjoy this activity because they love to listen to music. The activity requires about fifteen to twenty minutes, depending on the length of your debriefing session. It is a relatively quick exercise, very portable, and easy to use. The activity involves students in class discussion and it helps them to apply the class material to real life.

## REFERENCES

Harris, T. E., and J. C. Sherblom (2002). *Small group and team communication* (2nd ed). Boston, MA: Allyn and Bacon.

Hirokawa, R. Y., R. S. Cathcart, L. A. Samovar, and L. D. Henman (2003). *Small group communication theory and practice: An anthology* (8th ed.). Los Angeles, CA: Roxbury Publishing Company.

Kanahara, S. (2006). A review of the definitions of stereotype and a proposal for a progressional model. *Individual Differences Research, 4*(5), 306–321.

# 45

# Experiential Learning and Perception: Cutting Through the Assumptions (The Knife Exercise)

## Lou Davidson Tillson
*Department of Organizational Communication*
*Murray State University*
*ltillson@murraystate.edu*

## Marilyn D. Hunt
*Department of Communication and Journalism*
*Missouri Western State University*
*huntmd@missouriwestern.edu*

**History:** This activity was presented at the annual meeting of the National Communication Association, November 2006, in San Antonio, Texas. It was designated as a Top 10 GIFTS submission.
**Primary courses in which this activity might be used:** Interpersonal Communication, Organizational Communication, Public Speaking, Persuasion, Small Group, Intercultural, Leadership
**Concept illustrated:** Perception

## PURPOSE

Perception is the process by which we assign meaning to what we experience in the world around us. Those meanings create our individual realities and lead us to communicate with others according to our unique interpretations. Misunderstandings commonly occur because we assume others share our view of reality when we communicate with them. More than five hundred years ago, Leonardo da Vinci highlighted the importance of this foundational element of communication when he stated, "All our knowledge is the offspring of our perceptions" (Da Vinci, trans. 1906, p. 13). Today, many interpersonal communication textbooks emphasize its significance with an entire chapter dedicated to its study, typically employing two-dimensional optical illusions, word plays, and alphabetical/numerical examples.

Although simple to execute, the Knife Exercise requires more cognitively complex thinking and may more effectively emphasize the active, individualized, and complex nature of perception. The purposes of this exercise are to engage students in the multistep process of perception (selecting, organizing, interpreting), to help them recognize that people can perceive the same phenomenon in very different ways, and to demonstrate the impact those differences can have on the quality and effectiveness of our interactions with others.

## EXPLANATION OF ACTIVITY

Use this activity as an introduction to your unit or lecture on perception. Ask students to get up and gather around you so all can see you manipulate five plastic knives (or forks or spoons) on the top of a desk or table. If class size or layout precludes student mobility or visibility, you might record the demonstration in advance or project it live onto a large screen so all students can easily participate in the exercise. Carefully announce to the students: "I will be creating a pattern on the desk or table and your job is to identify that pattern using the numbers 0, 1, 2, 3, 4, or 5." Be sure to say *a pattern*, without actually referencing the knives. Next, slowly and deliberately arrange the plastic knives in any formation (e.g., | | | | |, \\|//, < | >) near the center of the desktop. After arranging the knives, very subtly rest 0, 1, 2, 3, 4, or 5 of your fingertips nearby on top of the edge of the desk or table.

Next, ask the students to verbally identify the appropriate number for the pattern you've created, but caution them not to reveal their reason for choosing that number to their classmates. After fielding their guesses, identify the correct number for them. The correct answer will be the number of fingertips you left visible on top of the desk or table. Repeat the process eight to ten times or more as you rearrange the plastic knives and alter the number of fingertips you rest on the desk or table. You might form the Roman numeral for three (III) or four (IV) with the knives yet place an unrelated number of fingertips on the desktop or even leave the knife arrangement the same, but switch the number of fingertips you place on the edge of the desk or table.

The students will likely select the positioning of the knives as the relevant stimulus in the activity, organize their thoughts according to what they already know about patterns (e.g., IV = four), and interpret the display of plastic knives accordingly. As frustration levels escalate due to their misperceptions, begin creating arrow patterns (—>) with the knives that actually point toward your fingertips.

If some students still don't interpret the pattern correctly, become more deliberate or dramatic in placing your fingertips on the desktop, even drumming them to attract attention, thus making the relevant pattern with your fingertips blatantly obvious as the stimulus they need to select in order to share your perception. Additionally, you might leave the knife arrangement the same, but switch the number of fingertips you display several times while verbally stating the correct number. By this time, all students should be able to successfully identify the appropriate number. If any still remain in the dark, you can briefly clarify that you were creating the pattern with your fingertips before asking the students to return to their seats to fully process the activity.

## DEBRIEF

This exercise quickly yet dramatically illustrates the multistep and complex nature of perception (i.e., selecting, organizing, and interpreting stimuli), and its connection to communication (i.e., creating or failing to create shared meaning). First, students are directed to select the stimuli: *a pattern on top of the desk (or table)*. Most initially select the placement of the plastic knives because of the novelty of their presence in the classroom or because they erroneously interpreted the verbal instructions as directing them to do so. You will need to remind them that your instructions did not ask them to actually focus on the plastic knives. As a result of selecting the wrong stimuli, they were unable to organize and correctly interpret the *relevant* pattern on the desktop: the instructor's fingertips. Subsequently, they likely engaged in perception-checking behaviors, such as comparing their answers to their peers and instructor, asking to repeat the activity, relying on multiple senses (e.g., seeing, hearing), challenging their assumptions, and so forth. As you performed subtle movements or more dramatic behaviors (e.g., creating arrows, tapping fingers), students shifted their attention to the more pertinent stimuli and organized and interpreted it. By the end of the activity, it should have become readily evident that if we are to communicate effectively, we must strive to create shared meaning and a shared reality. We must be aware that, for a variety of reasons, others can easily select, organize, and interpret our messages in myriad ways other than what we intended. Perception and therefore communication are truly complex acts.

To debrief the exercise with your students, utilize the *What, So What, Now What* approach. This reflective-thinking model is based on Kolb's (1984) experiential learning cycle, which explores how individuals make sense of and learn from their concrete experiences. Briefly, Kolb's cycle includes having a learning experience, reflecting on the experience (*What*), drawing conclusions about the experience (*So What*), and applying those conclusions in a meaningful way to other situations or contexts (*Now What*). The debriefing can be conducted as a group discussion, reflection paper, or both (preferred option) that systematically poses the following types of questions, which you can easily modify to suit your individual classroom needs:

- *What*: Ask the students to objectively describe their individual experience of what happened during the activity without evaluating the process.
  *Sample Questions*: What were the instructor's directions? What did the instructor do? What did you perceive (i.e., see, hear)? What did you do? What did your peers do? Where did you focus your attention? What thought processes did you go through as you tried to determine the correct number?

- *So What*: Ask the students to draw conclusions about the experience.
  *Sample Questions*: Why did you focus your attention on the movement and positioning of the knives instead of your instructor's fingertips? How did you feel as you and your classmates discovered, or failed to discover, the pattern? What do you think your peers felt as they discovered, or failed to discover, the pattern? More broadly, how can you check the accuracy of your perceptions against others' perceptions of the same phenomenon or event?
- *Now What*: Ask the students to apply their key takeaways from the activity to other situations.
  *Sample Questions*: During a conversation, have you ever intentionally led someone to focus on one thing instead of something else? If so, what tactic/s did you employ? When might that type of manipulation be ethical vs. unethical? What are additional examples of miscommunication that might occur because of errors in the perception process? (Most students can easily identify misunderstandings they have experienced with texting or emailing.) How could those misunderstandings have been prevented? As a public speaker, friend, intercultural communicator, group leader, or other role related to your course, what can you do to increase the likelihood that your audience members (friends, listeners, team members, etc.) will share your perceptions when you communicate with them?

As students reflect on this experiential learning activity during the debriefing, four common themes typically emerge:

- *Frustration*: because some students failed to figure out the pattern as quickly as others.
- *Smugness*: because some students figured out the pattern more easily than others.
- *Appreciation*: because students enjoyed a fun, experiential learning activity.
- *Understanding*: because eventually all of the students realized that individuals may select, organize, and interpret the same stimuli in very different ways resulting in very different communication experiences and outcomes.

Overall, the Knife Exercise is a relatively short and engaging activity, which enables students to understand and appreciate how complex perception (and hence, communication) is and that they, as active agents in the process, must work to create shared meaning.

## REFERENCES

Da Vinci, L. (1906). *Thoughts on art and life*. (M. Baring, Trans.). Boston, MA: The Merrymount Press. (No original publication date.)

Kolb, D. (1984). *Experiential learning: Experience as the source of learning and development*. Englewood Cliffs, NJ: Prentice Hall.

# 46

## How Do You See Me?: Understanding the Perception Process

*Mark D. Cruea*

*Department of Communication and Media Studies*

*Ohio Northern University*

*m-cruea@onu.edu*

**History:** This activity was presented at the annual meeting of the Central States Communication Association, April 2012, in Cleveland, Ohio.
**Primary courses in which this activity might be used:** Interpersonal Communication, Public Speaking, Persuasion
**Concepts illustrated:** Perception Process, Common Tendencies in Perception, Influences on Perception, Perceptual Schema, Self-Disclosure, and Stereotyping

### PURPOSE

The purpose of this activity is to actively take students through a question-and-answer session that relies on their perceptions of the instructor. In order to answer a series of questions, students must depend on their limited knowledge of the instructor and in the process, perceptual tendencies, and other factors influence their perception of the instructor. Through discussion, students learn what tendencies and influences have impacted their perception as well as how each went through the perception process including attention, organization, interpretation, and negotiation.

### ACTIVITY

For this activity, prepare a series of questions similar to the following that students will answer about you. You can get as personal as you wish, depending on your comfort level. One at a time, ask a question and allow students a few moments to record their responses on a sheet of paper. After you have run through all of the prepared questions, review those questions as well as the answers one at a time onscreen. This process keeps students from moving ahead too quickly. Sample questions include:

- What is my favorite color?
- What kind of vehicle do I drive?
- What is my favorite food?
- What are my hobbies?
- What pets do I own?
- Did I play sports in high school? If so, which sports?
- How many times have I been married?
- Where are my ancestors from?
- Am I a Republican or a Democrat?
- How old am I?
- What kind of music do I listen to?
- Do I have any tattoos? If so, how many and where?

Students typically respond with quizzical looks as they attempt to determine the answer. The teacher can even joke about these looks, and say something like, "And some students believe that if they look at me long enough, they will know my favorite food!" Keeping the tone lighted-hearted will create a positive environment. It is also useful to use self-deprecating humor in order to maintain that tone. Occasionally, it is helpful to prompt students to be more specific, such as with the vehicle, where a student may answer a car or truck, instead of a more specific style or even make and model.

## DEBRIEF

After asking all questions, go back to the beginning and review the questions one at a time. Reread the question, ask students to respond with their answers, and ask them to provide a reason for their perceptions. Their answers then become the basis for a discussion of the relevant concepts. For example, with the *favorite color* question, students will commonly respond with blue or green. The instructor can ask "Why blue?" and "Why green?" Students often indicate that blue, green, or any other color is their favorite color. At the most basic level, the exercise leads students through the perception process—attention, organization, interpretation, and negotiation—but it also provides grounds for discussing perceptual tendencies including that we assume others are like us or that we are influenced by the obvious (Coon, 2009; Freeman & Ambady, 2011; Macrae & Bodenhausen, 2001). Moreover, students will be influenced by their experiences with the instructor, their access—or lack thereof—to information about the instructor, and their cultural backgrounds (Adler, Rosenfeld, and Proctor II, 2015). Last, answers may lead to a discussion of perceptual schema including physical, role, interaction, and psychological constructs (Andersen, 1999; Freeman & Ambady, 2011). In addition, the activity helps students understand how discovering new information leads to changes in perception (Macrae & Bodenhausen, 2001). For example, when students learn that I dislike something that they like they may perceive me in a different/negative way. While there is no formal mechanism for assessment, the activity works well for generating a discussion on perception and self-disclosure. Students can self-score and award themselves one point for each correct answer. And candy or some other reward can be given to the student(s) with the highest point total(s).

## REFERENCES

Adler, R. B., Rosenfeld, L. B., & Proctor II, R. F. (2015). *Interplay: The process of interpersonal communication* (13th ed.). New York, NY: Oxford University Press.

Andersen, P. A. (1999). *Nonverbal communication: Forms and functions.* Palo Alto, CA: Mayfield.

Coon, D. (2009). *Psychology: A modular approach to mind and behavior* (11th ed.). Boston, MA: Cengage.

Freeman, J. B., & Ambady, N. (2011). A dynamic interactive theory of person construal. *Psychological Review, 118,* 247–279.

Macrae, C. N., & Bodenhausen, G. V. (2001). Social cognition: Categorical person perception. *British Journal of Psychology, 92,* 239–256.

# 47

## The Shopping List: An Exercise in Perception and Symbolic Interactionism

*Laura A. O'Connell*
*Communications Department*
*Nassau Community College*
*laura.oconnell@ncc.edu*

**History:** This activity was presented at the annual meeting of the Eastern Communication Association, April 2010, in Baltimore, Maryland.
**Primary courses in which this activity might be used:** Interpersonal Communication, Nonverbal Communication, Intercultural Communication, Small Group Communication, and Organizational Communication
**Concepts illustrated:** Symbolic Interactionism, The Perception Process

### PURPOSE

The purpose of this activity is to help students understand symbolic interactionism and the perception process by asking them to consider a picture of a stranger and then create a list of items they would purchase for this stranger. These purchased items become indicative of the perceptions that students developed of the person in the picture. This exercise can also be adapted for lessons on nonverbal communication or culture.

### EXPLANATION OF ACTIVITY

The activity is implemented after a discussion of the theory of symbolic interactionism, in which Blumer and Leeds-Hurwitz argue that the meaning of words results from social interaction (as cited in Verderber, Verderber, & Berryman-Fink, 2010). I help students understand how they have learned the meaning of things, focusing specifically on the notion of socially influenced connotations. In doing so, we highlight examples that illustrate the ways in which meaning is socially constructed through interactions with our families, teachers, friends, etc. According to Verderber, Verderber, and Berryman-Fink

(2010), the theory of symbolic interactionism is based on three premises including the notion that "humans have their own personal meanings for words" and "meaning arises through the process of interaction with others, so meaning is a social product" (p. 93). When we draw the conclusion that when observing other people's actions, we are not simply reacting to them, but rather we are interpreting them. In other words, as the third premise states, "based on their interactions, humans, through self-talk, interpret what an interaction or word means" (p. 93).

To prepare for the activity, I find several pictures of people on the Internet (one picture per group of three to five students). When choosing the pictures (royalty-free images), I avoid photographs of famous people or anybody that the students may know because preconceived notions and perceptions may exist. The guidelines I personally use for selecting images are that they are diverse in terms of culture, race, ethnicity, gender, body physique, and age. In the past I've used stereotypical pictures including, but not limited to, a model, a muscular/fit man, an elderly woman, children, and a crazed sports fan.

To conduct the activity, I put students into groups of three to five and provide each group with one of the pictures in addition to the following scenario: "Imagine that you are outside taking a walk (or any scenario you would like to use) when the person in your picture approaches you. This person hands you money and a grocery list that reads: milk, gum, cereal, soda, and cookies (bread, crackers, snacks, and drinks are others I have used). The person then runs away. You must buy these items for this person with no opportunity to ask any follow-up questions." I then ask students to discuss this as a group and report back what brand, type, flavor, and so on of each item they would buy the person in their picture. I give students about five to seven minutes to complete the exercise.

Students respond very well to the directions in this activity. Sometimes they joke that they would never go shopping for a stranger. I request that they pretend they would do it. The activity is received in a fun, honest, open-minded way. In my classes, students have asked each other questions if they think someone personally relates to any of the pictured individuals. For example, once I used a picture of a seemingly muscular, physically fit male. There was a male in the class who exercised often and students were asking him questions about his regimen, diet, etc. Students have also shared anecdotes about family members and friends, which makes for great classroom discussion and can be used later to debrief students about symbolic interactionism and perception.

## DEBRIEF

As groups report their shopping decisions to the class, I ask them to apply what they have learned about symbolic interactionism. Specifically, I guide them through this step by helping them to break down the theory and asking how they arrived at their answers. This helps them discover where they learned that somebody who looks like the pictured person would eat or drink the chosen type or brand of item. It inevitably shows the students what meaning they have placed on this individual and where they learned that meaning over the course of their lives. At times I focus more specifically on the labels that students have placed on these pictures (e.g., model, muscle man, child, etc.), and help them discover how their previous social interactions might have influenced the meaning they place on these words today. One example of this is a picture I use of a woman wearing a bikini. Many students have referred to her as "a model" with their list containing fat-free milk, Special K cereal, seltzer or diet soda, one hundred-calorie pack cookies, and sugar-free gum. When applying symbolic interactionism, students often connect back to messages from commercials and the media that claim a woman with this type of physique must eat certain items. Others may have a friend or family member with a similar appearance who eats these items, leading students to use personal experiences to develop their lists. In all cases, it prompts enriching classroom discussion and an understanding of symbolic interactionism.

After the exercise is done, we thoroughly review the three steps of the perception process: attention and selection, organization, and interpretation. Students once again have an opportunity to apply the activity to the process in an effort to understand it. As we go through each step, I reference the students' lists from the exercise.

By this point, students have effectively put both symbolic interactionism and the perception process into action. This helps to explain and clarify concepts, as well as create an enriching classroom atmosphere.

## REFERENCES

Blumer, H. (1986). *Symbolic Interactionism: Perspective and Method.* Berkeley, CA: University of California Press.

Leeds-Hurwitz, W. (Ed.). (1995). *Social Approaches to Communication.* New York: Guilford Press.

Verderber, K. & Verderber, R., & Berryman-Fink, C. (2010). *Inter-Act.* (12th ed.). New York: Oxford University Press.

# 48

## "Tell Me a Little About Yourself": Nonverbal Communication and Interviewing

*Jennifer Peeples*

*Department of Languages, Philosophy, and Communication Studies*

*Utah State University*

*jennifer.peeples@usu.edu*

*Matthew L. Sanders*

*Department of Languages, Philosophy, and Communication Studies*

*matt.sanders@usu.edu*

*John S. Seiter*

*Department of Languages, Philosophy, and Communication Studies*

*Utah State University*

*john.seiter@usu.edu*

**History:** This activity was presented at the annual meeting of the National Communication Association, 2016, in Philadelphia, Pennsylvania, where it was a top-ranked submission.

**Primary courses in which this activity might be used:** Interpersonal Communication, Interviewing, Technical and Professional Communication, and Business Communication

**Concepts illustrated:** Nonverbal communication and interviewing skills

### PURPOSE

Cami felt more than ready for her first interview! To prepare, she researched the company, practiced answers to common questions, and purchased a new suit. Yet when the big day arrived, she mumbled her introduction, tapped her foot, struggled to make eye contact, and hunched over her résumé. Although confident that she was perfect for the organization, Cami failed to communicate it to her interviewer. As a result, she did not get the job. Many students find themselves in similar situations as they approach interviews. While expecting questions about the job, they are less aware of how closely their nonverbal communication will be scrutinized, potentially removing themselves from the applicant pool before uttering a single word.

Countless articles from a variety of disciplines and professions emphasize the importance of nonverbal communication during interviews (e.g., engineering, Rathmann, 2011; business, Stafford, 2012; nursing, Becze, 2007), even breaking down the handshake into seven steps (Handshaking 101, 2006). Moreover, literature indicates that first impressions are often based on such seemingly trivial cues (see Burgoon, Buller, & Woodall, 1996). Even students who understand the importance of such behaviors may not recognize all the different types of nonverbal communication that require attention in order to interview successfully. With that in mind, we created this interview activity, which could be used in a variety of courses, including interpersonal communication, interviewing, technical and professional communication, and business communication.

The goals of this activity are to help students 1) understand and enact different types of nonverbal communication; 2) practice critical analysis and constructive feedback; and 3) recognize how various types of nonverbal communication come into play during interviews.

## EXPLANATION OF ACTIVITY

Conduct this activity after your students have been introduced (through reading and/or lectures) to the various types of nonverbal communication. The activity can be run in a seventy-five-minute class period with a lecture on nonverbal cues or a fifty-minute class period without one. To prepare, make copies of the two handouts discussed below (see Appendix, p. 186).

Begin the exercise by telling your students they will be interviewing for a server position at a local restaurant. While not a professional role, restaurants are comfortable contexts for students, allowing the instructor to bypasses what we have found to be time-consuming and sometimes confusing descriptions of positions and organizations that are necessary for more professional interview settings.

Split your class into two groups—interviewees and managers—and ask the interviewees to wait in the hall. Next, distribute two handouts to the interviewers (the restaurant managers), who remain in the classroom. The first handout is a list of job interview questions (about six), which you can find online by searching "common restaurant interview questions." The second handout (adapted from Wood, 2016) lists types of nonverbal communication and provides a place for managers to write notes (see Appendix, p. 186). Instruct managers that, as the interview is taking place, instead of noting the content of interviewees' answers, they will be taking notes on the interviewees' use of nonverbal communication. Give them a few minutes to review the handouts and ask questions, then ask them to spread their chairs around the room and provide an open seat near them for an interviewee. Invite the interviewees back into the room, asking them to find an open seat near a manager. Each interview must begin with a handshake.

Once the interviews have ended (usually less than ten minutes), allow interviewers a few minutes to fill out the handout. Next, ask them to provide constructive critiques of their interviewees' nonverbal communication—at least three things the person did well and three things to work on. We encourage the managers to point to specific behaviors. For instance, instead of saying the person had "good posture," note that the interviewee leaned forward, making it appear as if she was interested in the discussion. The completed handout can then be given to the interviewee or turned in for participation credit. The groups then switch; the managers heading to the hall and the interviewees taking the managers' place. You might consider distributing a different set of interview questions, so that the previous interviewers cannot anticipate what questions will be asked. The new interviewees are invited back into the room, asked to choose a new partner, and the same process of interview and critique as outlined above is repeated. After both sets of interviews are completed, the class forms a circle (if space allows) for discussion.

## DEBRIEF

The following questions can be addressed during the activity debrief. The debrief discussion can also be used to review concepts. For example, if a student said the interviewee played with a pen, ask what type of nonverbal communication is that? The students hopefully reply "kinesics."

Questions for students:

1. Now that we are done with the interviews, are any types of nonverbal communication still unclear to you? Can someone provide an explanation and example from the activity of that form of nonverbal communication?
2. Which was the most difficult aspect of nonverbal communication to control as an interviewee? Why do you think that is?
3. As the interviewer, what nonverbal communication stood out to you as a sign of nervousness?
4. What types of nonverbal communication showed confidence?
5. For the nonverbal communication that didn't reflect positively on the interviewees (e.g., difficult to control laughing or limited eye contact), what can be done to practice, control, or mask that type of nonverbal communication for a real interview?

6. How did your nonverbal communication change as you moved between manager and employee roles? Common responses are that the managers take up more room, initiate the handshake, and maintain stronger eye contact, which (if time allows) is a great transition into a discussion of nonverbal communication and power.
7. What is the difference between liking and responsiveness (Wood 2016)? How can a person appear responsive without seeming flirtatious? A consistent student response notes the amount of time certain nonverbal activities are held, for example too long of a handshake or too much eye contact can be seen as flirtatious when done by the interviewee. Touch outside of the handshake is also seen as liking.
8. Chronemics is not included on your handout. How might chronemics come into play in an interview? Discussions usually center on not being too early or too late for the interviews; also whether the interview felt rushed or leisurely. If time permits, a discussion of cultural impacts on perceptions of time is useful.
9. How would you change your physical appearance if this were a real job interview? What if it were for a professional organization? How would you know what is appropriate?

This activity provides a review and application of the types of nonverbal communication. As the activity is announced, nervous laughter is common. In the hall, we have also heard students making comments such as "How ridiculous! I'm totally nervous for a fake interview!," giving the activity some validity in assessing how the student might perform in an interview setting. Students often refer back to the activity during the course of the semester, and some report to the class that this activity changed how they prepared for interviews and commented on its positive impact on their ability to get hired.

## REFERENCES

Becze, E. (2007). Nonverbal communication can say a lot about you. *ONS Connect*, 22(4), 30.
Burgoon, J. K., Buller, D. B., & Woodall, W. G. (1996). *Nonverbal communication: The unspoken dialogue* (2nd ed.). New York, NY: McGraw-Hill Companies.
Handshaking 101. (2006). *Career World*, 35(1), 7.
Rathmann, V. (2011). Interview how-to: Non-verbal communications. *Power Engineering*, 115(4), 13.
Stafford, D. (2012). Beware of interview landmines. *Women in Business*, 64(1), 14–15.
Wood, J. (2016) *Interpersonal communication: Everyday encounters* (7th ed). Belmont, CA:Wadsworth.

## APPENDIX

## INTERVIEWING AND NONVERBAL COMMUNICATION

Interviewer name _____

Interviewee name _____

| Nonverbal communication: | Notes: |
|---|---|
| Kinesics | |
| Haptics | |
| Proxemics | |
| Paralinguistics | |
| Silence | |
| Environmental factors | |
| Artifacts | |

# 49

# Screaming for Your Attention Without Saying a Word: Finding Nonverbal Immediacy Cues in an Episode of ABC's *The Bachelor*

*John R. Katsion*

*Department of Communication and Mass Media*
*Northwest Missouri State University*
*johnkat@nwmissouri.edu*

**History:** This activity was presented at the annual meeting of the National Communication Association, November 2011, in New Orleans, Louisiana.

**Primary courses in which this activity might be used:** Nonverbal Communication, Interpersonal Communication

**Concepts illustrated:** Nonverbal Immediacy, Gender Communication, Nonverbal Communication (general)

## PURPOSE

Nonverbal immediacy is defined by Andersen (2007) as "messages that signal feelings of warmth, closeness, and involvement with others" (p. 214), and those who do well displaying immediacy in their social interactions tend to be seen as competent and pleasant (p. 193). I was looking for a class activity that allowed students to explore this concept. Also, in my classes students enjoy playing the role of nonverbal detective: they like to look for nonverbal cues while trying to guess each other's feelings, or if their partner was lying, or who is interested in whom based on nonverbal feedback. This activity asks students to use their detective skills to look for immediacy cues, thereby providing them a chance to apply concepts, and in turn, have a better understanding of how immediacy works in real life.

## EXPLANATION OF ACTIVITY

*The Bachelor* is a reality-television show where a man who is looking to find a wife is given thirty women to date and, in the end, to find one true love and

**187**

propose marriage. On the first episode, the Bachelor has to choose twenty women to keep out of the thirty presented to him. Each woman has one chance to make a good impression when first introduced to the Bachelor, and therefore their initial greeting should contain many nonverbal expressions of immediacy and provide a rich source of immediacy cues for analysis.

Before class, acquire the first episode of any year of ABC's *The Bachelor*. Watch the beginning of the episode where the women introduce themselves. Then make note of the ten women that were rejected after that first round. Next, make a handout that explains nonverbal immediacy, the premise of *The Bachelor*, and the coding activity. The handout should also include the numbers one through thirty so that students have space where they can make notes regarding their nonverbal cue. Feel free to use the handout included with this activity (see Appendix, p. 190) or to make one yourself. In class, cue up the first episode to where the women meet the Bachelor for the first time. Then break the class into groups of five to seven and have them choose which member will code for which nonverbal immediacy cue. Typically each student will code for one nonverbal cue in a group of seven, but with smaller groups of four or five, they may have to code for two or three cues. I ask them to mark down the frequency and duration of that nonverbal cue being displayed by the Bachelorette when interacting with the Bachelor. So for instance, the person who is looking for touch records how much touching they see between the Bachelor and the Bachelorette, and so on for each immediacy cue. I give them a sheet of paper numbered one through thirty on it, and room to make notes for their particular cue. The nonverbal immediacy cues I have them look for are the following:

- Facial expressions: expressive, non-expressive
- Smiles: how often?
- Eye Contact: how long is the gaze?
- Gestures: number and rate of gesturing
- Haptics: how often is touch used?
- Proxemics: close or kept distance
- Chronemics: how much time spent?

We then watch the first fifteen Bachelorettes introduce themselves with the sound off, and then the last fifteen with the sound on. Watching the women introduce themselves usually takes thirty to forty minutes. I then ask the groups to pick the ten women they thought would be rejected by the Bachelor. I stress that their decisions need to be based on the Bachelorette's skill and use of nonverbal immediacy cues in their interaction with the Bachelor. I ask each group to come to a consensus, which often leads to a lively discussion as many team members develop strong opinions about particular Bachelorettes. Before watching the introductions, I ask whether there are any avid fans of the show in the class. If so, I ask them not to reveal or say anything about any particular Bachelorette, but rather to let the group decide. I have found that even rabid fans of the show are willing to comply. After each group comes to a decision,

I then reveal the ten women that were rejected by the Bachelor and then find out which team was the most accurate in picking the rejected Bachelorettes.

## DEBRIEF

I then lead them in a discussion of the following questions:

1. Were the immediacy cues easy to spot? Why or why not? At first, students find it tough to locate their cue, but as the show moves forward, they begin to get the hang of it.
2. Which of the cues did you find hard to define or code? Why? It is a good demonstration of the way nonverbal cues appear and disappear very quickly, as well as the nature of coding and research. This activity helps them better understand and appreciate the nonverbal research they are reading for class.
3. Were any of the rejected Bachelorettes skillful in their use of nonverbal immediacy? Were you surprised that they were eliminated? I use this to point out that communication is much more than just nonverbal immediacy cues, and this leads to a better understanding of the impact of context, perception, and immediacy being in the eye of the beholder.
4. Was your task easier with the sound on or off? Why? Here we discuss the holistic nature of nonverbal communication and the difficulty in separating the nonverbal from verbal or paralinguistic cues.
5. Was there a Bachelorette who lacked of nonverbal immediacy skills? Look for the one or two Bachelorettes that every group chose and discuss the lack of immediacy skills they demonstrated.
6. Was there a Bachelorette that stood out because of her skillful use of immediacy cues? What did she do that worked well? This question can lead to a discussion about how nonverbal immediacy is a skill that everyone can develop.
7. How did the medium of television impact your perception of immediacy? This is a good question to get students to think about the way media shapes their perceptions. Lighting, framing, and camera shot selection are some of the concepts that could be discussed to help students understand the way that media shapes how they see reality and the nature of mediated reality.

My students have enjoyed this activity. They consistently talk about how they did not realize how much people judge other people based on nonverbal behaviors. Clearly, they liked and disliked various Bachelorettes because of the nonverbal messages they were sending, which makes them reflect upon the nonverbal messages they might be sending. Students also talk about the difficulty in separating and analyzing nonverbal codes, as they happen so fast. This activity helps them understand the way nonverbal communication works in concert with a host of other factors. It also gives them a sense of how coding works in nonverbal research and research in general. I also found it an excellent way to sum up and test to see if the students understand the concepts of non-verbal immediacy. Overall, students do not do well at predicting who will or will not be picked by the Bachelor, and this leads to a broader discussion about the difficulty in using nonverbal cues as a predictor of relational success.

## REFERENCES

Andersen, Peter, A. (2007) *Nonverbal communication: Forms and function* (2nd ed.). Long Grove, IL: Waveland Press.

Richmond, V. P., McCroskey, J. C., & Hickson, M. (2012). *Nonverbal behavior in interpersonal relation* (7th ed.). Boston, MA: Pearson/Allyn & Bacon.

## APPENDIX

### *THE BACHELOR:*
### NONVERBAL ASSIGNMENT

In the television show *The Bachelor,* a man meets thirty women who are whittled down every week by the Bachelor until he chooses one to be his future spouse.

On the first episode, the Bachelor must choose twenty women to keep out of the thirty presented to him. In their first encounter, the women try to make their best first impressions on the Bachelor. Therefore, this initial greeting should contain many nonverbal expressions of immediacy.

As we watch the women introduce themselves to the Bachelor, each member of your group should pick and keep track of one or two of the behavioral cues listed below. Specifically, as we go through each introduction, count the number and/or duration of nonverbal immediacy cues that you see for your behavior. When we are done watching, write down which of the women you think the Bachelor will choose and which ten he will let go. We will be watching with the sound off for the first fifteen women and then with the sound on for the last fifteen women.

The nonverbal expressions of immediacy that we should be keeping track of are:

- Facial expressions: expressive, non-expressive
- Smiles: how often?
- Eye Contact: how long and direct is the gaze?
- Gestures: number and rate of gesturing
- Haptics: how often is touch used, and where does touch occur?
- Proxemics: close or distant
- Chronemics: how much time spent with a woman as opposed to another woman he meets?

# 50

## Mark My Words: Using Etymology to Understand Words and Phrases

*Nakia Welch, PhD*

*English, Modern Languages, & Speech*

*San Jacinto Community College - South*

*nakia.welch@sjcd.edu*

**History:** This activity was presented at the annual meeting of the Southern States Communication Association, April 2012, in San Antonio, Texas.

**Applicable courses:** Introduction to Communication, Interpersonal Communication, Intercultural Communication

**Concepts illustrated:** Research, Language & Meaning, Connotative/ Denotative Meaning

### PURPOSE

Although communication courses typically address the relationship between language and meaning by covering topics such as connotation and denotation, abstract and concrete language, and cultural and demographic influences on language, an interesting but often overlooked aspect of language is etymology. This activity provides students the opportunity to learn both the etymological process of language and words as well as the process of how meaning is assigned to those words and phrases. Students are often exposed to language examples in textbooks, which often explain how the meaning of words is dependent upon those involved in the communication process. Moreover, these illustrations explain how words may be interpreted with multiple meanings to different audiences, oftentimes resulting in outcomes that are ambiguous, humorous, offensive, and/or result in a lack of successful communication. While textbook examples are helpful, they may not always be meaningful to today's students, as they often do not include idioms, regional vernacular, and/or age-related jargon that students can relate to and find interesting.

## EXPLANATION OF ACTIVITY

Students are instructed to research the origins of a word or phrase that they have heard used in everyday life. They are to apply the concept of connotative meaning, rather than denotative meaning, in selecting their words. Specifically, students should not choose a word whose definition is commonly understood and defined in standard dictionaries. Instead, words and phrases should be colloquial and/or cliché phrases, should be used in everyday conversation, and should have etymological origins that are not commonly known or understood. A phrase as common as the one used in the title of this activity, *Mark my words*, is a good example. What does this phrase mean? Why does it mean that? Where did the understood meaning come from? How did it come about? Was this a request to literally make a note in a transcript of conversation, as though our conversations are being transcribed somehow?

Students are instructed to find at least two different sources confirming the meaning of the word/phrase, print their findings, and prepare a short explanation of what they found to the class. Instructors may require students to turn in the hardcopy of these sources if they choose as evidence to support the verbal discussion in class. Instructors also may amend this assignment to require a written paper that explains the etymology of the chosen word/phrase, complete with in-text citations of the sources.

During the in-class discussion, students should address four criteria: (a) the word/phrase they chose, (b) the colloquial understanding of the word/phrase, (c) the origin of the meaning of the word/phrase, and (d) the sources verifying the meaning. For example, "Bite the bullet" is a commonly heard and often understood expression, but where did it originate? Kirkpatrick (1996) describes this phrase as an idiom cliché in which one must simply accept something that is otherwise distressing, unpleasant ... and so on, and just do it. An appropriate use of this phrase would be to explain to students that they will have to "bite the bullet and conduct some research to complete the assignment!"

Cresswell (2010) explains a commonly used explanation for the phrase in which wounded soldiers were provided a bullet to bite on in order to keep them from crying out in pain. However, she reports a lack of evidence to confirm this practice; most surgeons operating on soldiers carried leather straps to serve this purpose, not bullets.

Wilkes (2014) presents a suggested explanation of the cliché's common usage as stemming from the Indian Rebellion of 1857, where biting of a greased paper cartridge was necessary to fire their weapon. The paper cartridges contained a greasy substance on them, animal fat. Native Indian soldiers in the British army, the Sepoys, were not permitted to eat meat, fat, or sacred animals, thus the practice of biting the paper cartridges caused religious turmoil for these soldiers who were faced with ignoring their religious beliefs and biting the cartridge.

As Wynbrandt (2009) details the account, the British army gave the newly issued Enfield rifles to the Indian troops in January 1857, and instructed the soldiers to bite the tips of the cartridges before loading in preparation of firing. The Muslims believed the grease tasted like forbidden pork fat, while the Hindus thought the grease smelled like cattle, a sacred animal. Upon their refusal to "bite the bullet," these soldiers endured a very unpleasant punishment. They were stripped of their insignia, dismissed without pay, and forced to walk to their home villages, up to several hundred miles away in some cases.

According to Jones (2014), British writer Rudyard Kipling is thought to be the first to use the expression figuratively in his 1891 novel *The Light that Faded*, as part of the line: "bite on the bullet, old man, and don't let them think you're afraid." This may have contributed to the widespread introduction of the phrase into our cultural vernacular.

As many of the words/phrases may have a meaning that is relatively young, nonacademic websites are the most commonly used and accepted sources. Students should be encouraged to evaluate the credibility of these sources, however. Additionally, the requirement for two or more sources confirming the information serves to add to the reliability of the findings. The source requirement serves as an effective lesson/discussion on source credibility.

## DEBRIEF

Allow for volunteers to share their examples by explaining the four components mentioned above. Focus follow-up questions on how/why the student chose his/her word/phrase; this personalizes the chosen linguistic example. For example, ask the student the context in which they understood the word/phrase prior to their research, why they were interested in researching the origins of the word/phrase ...and so on. Discussion often revolves around determining the process involved in assigning meaning to the different words/phrases. By connecting the meaning of these words/phrases to their etymology, it provides students a better understanding of how language works. The instructor may also direct the discussion to identify how culture (e.g., age, region, ethnicity) influences/affects language and/or how some words/phrases cross cultural lines and the life cycle of words/phrases (e.g., how they are created, modified, and/or disappear).

There are several benefits to using this assignment as an instructional tool when teaching language and meaning in communication classes. First, students benefit from the opportunity to utilize research skills through the requirement of identifying at least two corroborating sources of explanation for the origin of the word/phrase. A second benefit is the application of culture and language as many words/phrases are dependent upon different cultural situations and experiences. Additionally, the activity is often cross-disciplinary, incorporating historical events as an aspect of understanding the etymology of the word/phrase. A final benefit is the pleasure that students gain from exposure to the origins and development of language used in everyday life. Researching and discussing how words and phrases have different meanings to different groups and how that assigned meaning came about contributes to improved critical thinking skills.

## REFERENCES

Cresswell, J. (2010). *Oxford dictionary of word origins.* Oxford: NY.

Jones, L. Y. (2014, April 18). Loaded language: The gun metaphors that pervade our everyday slang. *The Washington Post.* https://www.washingtonpost.com/opinions/ loaded-language-the-gun-metaphors-that-pervade-our-everyday-slang/2014/04/18/ 40c4053c-c3ed-11e3-b574-f8748871856a_story.html?utm_term=.cce656f6bfbf

Kirkpatrick, B. (1996). *Clichés: Over 1500 phrases explored and explained.* St. Martin's Griffin: NY.

Wilkes, J. (2014, August 20). Why we say: 'bite the bullet.' *Historyextra.com.* http://www .historyextra.com/facts/why-we-say-%E2%80%98bite-bullet%E2%80%99

Wynbrandt, J. (2009). *A brief history of Pakistan.* Facts On File/Infobase Publishing: NY.

# 51

## The Nonverbal Scavenger Hunt: Active Application of Concepts as They Occur!

*Nakia Welch, PhD*

*English, Modern Languages, & Speech*

*San Jacinto Community College - South*

*nakia.welch@sjcd.edu*

**History:** This activity was presented at the annual meeting of the Southern States Communication Association Convention, April 2015 in Tampa, Florida.

**Applicable courses:** Introduction to Communication, Interpersonal Communication, Nonverbal Communication

**Concepts illustrated:** Functions of Nonverbal Communication, Types of Nonverbal Communication: Kinesics, Oculesics, Haptics, Paralanguage, Adornment, Chronemics, Proxemics, Gestures, Territoriality

### PURPOSE

Students are often guided to learn concepts by memorizing terms with textbook and/or instructor provided examples as supplements to solidify understanding of the concept(s). A scavenger hunt is an activity in which individuals or teams must identify and/or locate as many items on a provided list within a specified period of time. Scavenger hunts can be used as an active learning exercise whereby students are tasked with finding exact objects. This scavenger hunt activity, however, encourages students to observe and identify naturally occurring real-life examples of nonverbal communication concepts. This activity helps students think beyond the textbook and demonstrate their understanding of concepts by providing opportunities to link specific discipline-based terminology to naturally occurring nonverbal behaviors.

### EXPLANATION OF ACTIVITY

There are several options for this activity, depending on how much class time is available. Specifically, students might (a) canvas the campus before they return to class to discuss their findings, (b) complete the checklist as homework to be discussed in the next class meeting, and/or (c) write a paper after completing the assignment, in which they explain how each checklist item was completed. I have experimented with all three options; the students seem to enjoy the first option (single class meeting) the most. The continued explanation below is based on the context of that assignment.

For classes meeting more than once per week, the instructor should plan for this activity to occur during one entire class meeting: Lecture one class meeting, and conduct the activity during the next class meeting. After the lecture on the types and functions of nonverbal communication is complete, distribute the scavenger hunt checklist (see Appendix, p. 197). Instruct the students to complete as many of the checklist items as possible. In my experience, students typically achieve approximately 50 to 75 percent of the items within about twenty minutes, which allows twenty to sixty minutes for the debrief/discussion portion of this assignment. If time allows, instructors may increase the scavenger hunt time to thirty minutes.

Students should take field notes on (a) what behavior(s) occurred, and (b) how/why it meets the definition of the categorical nonverbal behavior. Ask students to take descriptive notes, as they will need to adequately explain the situation and observation(s) to the class later. They should take notes immediately after completing a given task on the list to ensure they don't forget anything. These notes are not turned in or graded; they serve only to help students remember what occurred to prompt discussion. To ensure authenticity of the activity, explain to the students that it is important to not interact with other classmates who are also participating in the scavenger hunt and to avoid explaining what they are doing to those with whom they are interacting or observing prior to collecting field notes.

It is the instructor's discretion whether this activity is an individual effort or if students may team up. The team approach has yielded the best results in my experience, as students enjoy working with others, but only if the teams are limited in size to three to four classmates to ensure greater opportunity of participation by each student. In an effort to ensure greater opportunity for completion of all items on the list, the instructor may also break the list into smaller segments and assign different parts of the list to the different groups of the class.

## DEBRIEF

After students return to the classroom at the predetermined time, begin debriefing by addressing the students' thoughts about the activity; students are often excited to share their findings and this excitement will help break the ice for the actual discussion of the concepts. After a few minutes, move to address the specific items on the list, inviting students to share what they observed, and how it meets the selected scavenger hunt item. Inevitably, the examples of behaviors reported by students will differ from those provided in the textbook. This is beneficial as it helps students understand the terms and concepts because of the various examples provided.

As students (individually or as a group) share their observations with the class, others in the class are exposed to more and more examples, thereby reinforcing their knowledge and understanding of the concepts. Sometimes students incorrectly categorize nonverbal behaviors and the discussion is an excellent opportunity to provide corrective instruction. The instructor should identify any of the items that students struggled with during the activity to ensure adequate understanding of the concepts. The instructor should also manage the discussion to ensure coverage of all options available on the scavenger hunt list. Challenge students to continue applying concepts outside of the classroom environment in their everyday lives.

## APPENDIX

### NONVERBAL SCAVENGER HUNT

### Functions of nonverbal communication

- ☐ Observe or interact with someone who *repeats* their message to you.
- ☐ Observe or interact with someone who *compliments* their message to you.
- ☐ Observe or interact with someone who *substitutes* their message to you.
- ☐ Observe or interact with someone who *accents* their message to you.
- ☐ Observe or interact with someone who *regulates* their message to you.
- ☐ Observe or interact with someone who *contradicts* their message to you.

### Types of nonverbal communication

- ☐ Observe or interact with someone who uses *body orientation* or *posture* (kinesics) to communicate a message.
- ☐ Observe or interact with someone who uses their *face &/or eyes* (oculesics) to communicate a message.
- ☐ Observe or interact with someone who uses *vocalics* (paralanguage) to communicate a message.
- ☐ Observe someone who uses appearance/clothing (adornment) to communicate a message.
- ☐ Observe or interact with someone who uses *touch* (haptics) to communicate a message.
- ☐ Observe or interact with someone who uses *time* (chronemics) to communicate a message.
  - ○ Observe someone using *monochronic* time.
  - ○ Observe someone using *polychronic* time.
- ☐ Observe how the use of a color (chromadynamics) communicates a message.
- ☐ Observe the use of *physical environment* (territoriality) being used to communicate a message.
- ☐ Observe at least two people using *physical Space* (Proxemics).

- ○ Identify at least two people interacting according to Hall's *intimate* spatial zone.
- ○ Identify at least two people interacting according to Hall's *personal* spatial zone.
- ○ Identify at least two people interacting according to Hall's *social* spatial zone.
- ○ Identify at least two people interacting according to Hall's *public* spatial zone.
- ☐ Interact with someone who uses gestures during their communication with you.
  - ○ Interact with/observe someone who uses an *illustrator* in their message.
  - ○ Interact with/observe someone who uses an *emblem* in their message.
  - ○ Interact with/observe someone who uses an *adaptor* gesture in their message.
  - ○ Interact with/observe someone who uses a *manipulator* in their message.
  - ○ Interact with/observe someone who uses a *regulator* in their message.

# 52

## Explosion of Meaning: The Complexity of Context and Language

*Daniel Overton*
*Department of Communication Studies*
*University of Kansas*
*danielpoverton@ku.edu*

**History:** This activity was presented at the annual meeting of the National Communication Association, November 2015, in Las Vegas, Nevada.

**Primary courses in which this activity might be used:** Speaker-Audience Communication, Interpersonal Communication, Organizational Communication, Persuasion, Communication Theory

**Concepts illustrated:** Language, Connotation, Audience Adaptation, Transactional Model, Relativism

### PURPOSE

Most basic communication textbooks spend a great deal of time discussing the careful selection of language for specific contexts, yet the significance and complexity of language can be difficult for students to grasp. This activity is essentially a bundle of three short and related exercises. Used together, these exercises form a consonant lesson in connotation and language. The purpose of this enterprise is to help students comprehend the power and range of language and symbols using images, videos, and objects as demonstrations. Students will conjure and defend novel interpretations of various objects, highlighting the role of cultural location, experience, and education in shaping a worldview even at the most basic level.

### EXPLANATION OF ACTIVITY

This activity begins with an image and two short video clips. Ludwig Wittgenstein made famous a "duck-rabbit" sketch in his *Philosophical Investigations* (2009, p. 204); this simple illustration could be interpreted as a rabbit or as a duck. A quick Internet image search for "Wittgenstein duck rabbit" provides the instructor with several image options. The instructor should begin this activity by showing the class Wittgenstein's image and asking for a show of hands to determine who saw a duck and who saw a rabbit. Most students typically see a duck first, and it is helpful to trace or explain both angles. Which interpretation is correct? The instructor should spend a few moments asking students to imagine other ways that the duck-rabbit image could be interpreted.

As the students look at the duck-rabbit, how else might they describe the image aside from the two most obvious answers? If the duck-rabbit image were neither a duck nor a rabbit, what could it be? Can they defend, trace, or explain their newly proposed interpretations? This process facilitates a discussion of relativism and provides a way to address the concerns often accompanying that discussion. Other well-known ambiguous images or reversible forms might also be employed to illustrate this opening point, including *Rubin's Vase* and *My Wife and My Mother-in-Law* (Wimmer & Doherty, 2011, p. 2).

Next, the instructor will show two short video clips from the Disney classic, *The Little Mermaid*. Both clips may be available on YouTube. The instructor can locate the first clip by searching YouTube for "Ariel+dinglehopper," and the second clip by searching for "Ariel+fork." The first clip shows Ariel, the titular character, learning about a couple of human artifacts from a seasoned seagull. The bird informs her that the common fork is called a "dinglehopper" and is used for hair maintenance and that a tobacco pipe is actually a musical instrument. Ariel listens and learns with rapt attention, and later, the second clip shows Ariel among humans comically misusing a fork and a pipe based on the prior lessons learned. Ariel instantly interpreted forks as dinglehoppers without doubt, since that is what she had been taught. Everything is interpreted through history, experience, and presupposition, so individuals never see things "as they are" in some unmediated state. Instead, rhetors offer interpretations, never fully moving beyond the text (Smith, 2006; Derrida, 1976). Given the use of smoking pipe imagery, the instructor might consider invoking René Magritte's *Treachery of Images*, a painting which depicts a tobacco pipe over the caption: "This is not a pipe" (Zalman, 2015).

Having sufficiently piqued their interest in the coexistence of multiple meanings and social context of language, students will now practice outside-the-box thinking skills. The instructor will select an object and task the students with creatively interpreting the chosen object in a novel way. As an example, a staple remover could be interpreted as an ear piercer, a fingernail puller, a baby shark, a Venus Flytrap, a head scratcher, and so on, from the more literal to the more figurative. In other words—as with the earlier ambiguous images—if the object in question were something else, what would it be? Before letting students proffer their own interpretations, the instructor will likely need to provide a few examples using a sample object, perhaps interpreting a nearby pen as a javelin, a pogo stick, or drum stick. The three miniature activities outlined above can require less than twenty-five minutes, or the instructor might expand the discussion for a full class session.

## DEBRIEF

The instructor should debrief students by connecting the activities above to relevant theory and concepts in the specific course. The instructor might ask students to write down and share words that have particularly robust meanings. A discussion of connotation and the word "home" might be instructive. Aside from a dictionary meaning, "home" connotes specific places and powerful feelings in an audience. The instructor should challenge students to consider how diverse audiences will receive their choices of vocabulary and language for good or ill. The instructor might encourage the students to collectively brainstorm ways to practice and use inclusive language to account for its social context. Ariel interpreted her fork as a "dinglehopper" because of her past experiences, and in the same way, everyone interprets everything and word through various filters, mundane objects included. Finally, then, students might be asked about how everyday word choice can influence behavior or attitudes.

## REFERENCES

Derrida, J. (1976). *Of grammatology* (G. Spivak, Trans.). Baltimore, MD: Johns Hopkins University Press.

Smith, J. K. (2006). *Who's afraid of postmodernism*. Grand Rapids, MI: Baker Academic.

Wimmer, M., & Doherty, M. (2011). The development of ambiguous figure perception. *Monographs of the Society for Research in Child Development, 76*(1).

Wittgenstein, L. (2009). *Philosophical investigations* (G. E. Anscombe, P. M. Hacker, & J. Schulte, Trans.). Chichester, UK: Wiley-Blackwell.

Zalman, S. (2015). *Consuming surrealism in American culture: dissident modernism*. Surrey, UK: Ashgate Publishing.

# 53

# Increasing Our Understanding of Gendered Nonverbal Communication

*Rita Daniels*

*Department of Communication Studies,*

*Western Washington University*

*rita.daniels@wwu.edu*

**History:** This activity was presented at the annual meeting of the Eastern Communication Association, April 2015, in Philadelphia, Pennsylvania.

**Primary courses in which this activity might be used:** Gender and Communication, Interpersonal Communication, Intercultural Communication, Intergroup Communication, and Nonverbal Communication

**Concepts illustrated:** Gender Norms, Gender Expectations, and Proxemics and Appearance (Nonverbal Communication)

## PURPOSE

Nonverbal communication can be used to regulate, supplement, or convey the relational level of meaning (Knapp, Hall, & Horgan, 2014). Physical appearance is one of the concrete nonverbal forms through which men and women communicate their ideal gender. For instance, whereas girls and women may find themselves succumbing to the pressure to be thin and feminine, men may feel the pressure to live up to the standards of ideal masculinity by developing muscular bodies. The purpose of this activity is to further examine the gendered forms of nonverbal communication using real-life events as observed by students in their groups. The group work is designed to facilitate critical discussions among students.

## EXPLANATION OF ACTIVITY

Prior to this activity, the teacher should teach and discuss forms of nonverbal communication, and how men and women use nonverbal communication to express themselves as gendered people. A good resource that can be used for this lesson is Wood's (2013) chapter on gendered nonverbal communication. Students can be assigned to read this material prior to the class. They may also be asked to bring any scholarly material on the subject to class for discussion. This assignment can be given to students in groups; preferably not more than groups of five, to allow all students to participate in the group work. Each group should be given one prompt (see Appendix, p. 204).

These prompts are designed to enable students to examine gendered forms of nonverbal communication engrained in our everyday activities. Students should be given about thirty to forty minutes in class to devise their plan of action for carrying out their respective activities. Students can be given more time as deemed appropriate to plan their activity. The next class meeting should be used for these activities in a public area to allow for observations of diverse people. Examples of possible public areas are the shopping mall, grocery store, dining hall, and other common areas on campus. Let students know that they will present their findings in the next class after they have completed their activities. The teacher may provide a preferred format for presentation and or grading.

Finally, let students meet in their groups for about twenty minutes to compare notes/results and decide on how to present their findings while being as creative as they can. For instance, a group of students who worked with prompt two (see Appendix, p. 204) played a video recording of their group members performing their selected violation behaviors to give the class a good sense of exactly how these behaviors were performed. Allow ten to fifteen minutes for each group's presentation. The teacher can make these presentations formal and graded, but should provide students with a format for presentation and a rubric to help students meet the teacher's expectations.

Whether this presentation is formal or informal, students should provide details of the activity conducted as well as the setting in which the activity was conducted, their expectations prior to conducting the activity, results of the activity, and their analysis of the results (e.g., How do their results confirm what we already know about the subject? Are there any new findings? What lesson(s) have you learned from conducting the activity? Any recommendations?).

## DEBRIEF

In the next class meeting after students have completed their respective activity and prepared their presentations, give them about ten minutes to organize themselves for their presentation. If your class period is less than an hour, you may consider splitting students' presentation into two class periods to allow enough time for presentations and discussions. It will be ideal to have all group presentations done within a week to allow for continuity of the discussion. You should guide students to compare their findings with what is known from the literature on gendered nonverbal communication (you may want to review the previous lesson on gendered nonverbal communication as deemed necessary). Ask students whether their findings support the literature. For example, with reference to prompt four (see Appendix, p. 204), based on the group's findings regarding the physical ideals for men and women, would you say the ideals have changed? If yes, how and what are the implications of this change? To facilitate discussions, invite each group to ask a question during other groups' presentation.

## REFERENCES

Knapp, M. L., Hall, J. A., & Horgan, T. G. (2014). *Nonverbal communication in human interaction* (8th ed.). Boston, MA: Wadsworth.

Wood, J. T. (2013). *Gendered lives: Communication, gender, and culture* (11th ed.). Belmont, CA: Wadsworth

## APPENDIX

## ACTIVITY PROMPTS

Prompt 1: Visit ten different locations in your selected public area. What can you observe from the packaging of products marketed to men and women? Pay attention to name, size, price, image, positioning, color, and any other peculiar characteristics of the products that present gendered differences.

Prompt 2: Come up with five different gendered nonverbal behaviors and how to perform a violation of these behaviors in different sections of your selected public area. You should obtain your teacher's approval before completing the activity by confirming your selected behaviors and your plan for violating them. Upon approval, analyze people's nonverbal and verbal responses to your violation performances.

Prompt 3: As individuals in your group, observe men and women's use of nonverbal communication to signal a relational level of meaning. In your observation, for example, do women command more space than men or keep less eye contact than men? Share your individual findings and come up with a group report for presentation. Each individual should choose an area in order to be able to cover a wide area in your selected setting.

Prompt 4: Conduct an informal survey to ask thirty people to describe their physical ideal for men and women. Seek approval from your teacher for the survey questions before conducting the survey. Ask participants whether they feel they have the physical ideal for their gender. You should do this individually within your groups (divide the required number of participants amongst yourselves), and assign yourselves designated areas. Take note of the gender of respondents. Share your individual findings and come up with a group report for presentation.

# 54

## Crafting Competent Messages

*Katie L. Turkiewicz, Ph.D.*
*Department of Communication*
*University of Wisconsin Green Bay*
*katieturkiewicz@gmail.com*

**History:** This activity was presented at the annual meeting of the National Communication Association, November 2014, in Chicago, Illinois.

**Primary courses in which this activity might be used:** Interpersonal Communication, Persuasion, Organizational Communication, Human Communication

**Concepts illustrated:** Interpersonal Competence, Rhetorical Messaging, Reframing, Audience Analysis, Message Design

### PURPOSE

The undergraduate classroom is an ideal context for exploring issues of interpersonal incompetence. The opportunities to raise a students' personal awareness of their own communication skills are endless. One approach for helping students understand competence is to provide them with an understanding of a spectrum of different messages, ranging from less competent to more competent. For example, engaging students in a brief lecture on the construction and use of expressive, conventional, and rhetorical messages (see McCornack, 2010; O'Keefe, 1988; O'Keefe & Lambert, 1995) provides a foundation for understanding the various approaches people take when engaging with others. While expressive and conventional messages are often used in interpersonal interactions, they both sacrifice competence for emotional and instrumental goals. Rhetorical messages represent ideal message design because they successfully combine the three elements of competence—appropriateness, effectiveness, and ethics. Establishing an understanding of these types of messages through lecture and discussion is helpful, but does not provide adequate opportunities for students to engage in critical thinking, application, and personal reflection.

I designed this activity to address those gaps while simultaneously providing a small group context for students to comfortably engage with one another.

## EXPLANATION OF ACTIVITY

This activity takes approximately thirty to forty minutes and requires a handout (see Appendix, p. 207) detailing brief instructions to craft three different messages (expressive, conventional, and rhetorical), a scenario (ideally a different one for each small group), and an example scenario and corresponding responses for guidance. Instructors can create a large variety of scenarios as they see fit. An alternative is to ask the small groups to come up with their own scenarios to address. Appendix A on p. 207 can be used as both an instructor resource and an example handout for students to clarify instructions if necessary.

Before putting the students into small groups, they should have a basic understanding of (1) the role of appropriateness, effectiveness, and ethics in interpersonal competence; (2) what expressive messages are and how they are used; (3) what conventional messages are and how they are used; and (4) what rhetorical messages are, including the four distinctive components of a rhetorical message, and how they are used.

Using realistic scenarios that are likely to resonate with a majority of the students, I ask the small groups to design three messages to respond to the situation described on their handout. The expressive and conventional messages are more rapidly constructed and often times reflect how the students actually communicated in similar situations in the past. The construction of the rhetorical message involves more critical thinking, requiring the students to craft a message that corresponds to the four distinctive components of a rhetorical message—(1) the use of a neutral perspective, (2) expression of empathy, (3) offering specific solutions, and (4) leaving the door open to negotiation. It is common for some small groups to struggle with explaining all the components of the rhetorical message, so the sample outlined on the handout can provide useful guidance in this capacity. When the groups have completed their three messages, I engage in debriefing as a class and ask each small group to nominate one or several members to present their scenario and three response messages to the entire class.

## DEBRIEF

With this activity, I typically debrief after each group presents its messages. This allows me to engage their scenario very specifically and maintain the students' focus on one group at a time.

Small group prompts for students to address when presenting to the class:

- Explain your scenario briefly to the class.
- What is the (expressive, conventional, rhetorical) message your group came up with?

- Do you think the (expressive, conventional) message your group crafted corresponds to the interpersonal competence tenets of appropriateness, effectiveness, and ethics? Why or why not?
- Break down the rhetorical message for the class and explain how it is comprised of the four distinctive components outlined in the textbook.

Instructor questions for small groups after the presentation is completed:

- Has anyone in your group had a personal experience in the past that was similar to this? How did that inform your group discussion?
- Has this activity changed how you think you might approach similar situations like this in the future? Or has this activity caused you to reflect on how you handled a similar situation in the past? (If students are comfortable, probe further and ask how they handled the situation—what type of message did they use? Ask them how using a rhetorical message might have altered the relational outcome.)

Rhetorical message construction can be challenging for some groups. When debriefing, if a group misses some required components, you can use the opportunity to ask the entire class for suggestions on fine-tuning the message. Students really enjoy this activity because it provides a break from the instructor-led classroom, allows students to engage personally with their classmates, and puts theory into practice for those with similar personal experiences. I find that students are very engaged with this lesson and forthcoming about their own similar personal experiences, which leads to rich classroom discussion and enhanced learning outcomes.

## REFERENCES

McCornack, S. (2010). *Reflect and relate: An introduction to interpersonal communication* (2nd ed.). Boston, MA: Bedford/St. Martin's.

O'Keefe, B. J. (1988). The logic of message design. *Communication Monographs, 55,* 80–103.

O'Keefe, B. J., & Lambert, B. L. (1995). Managing the flow of ideas: A local management approach to message design. In B. R. Burleson (Ed.), *Communication yearbook 18* (pp. 54–82). Thousand Oaks, CA: Sage.

## APPENDIX

## INSTRUCTIONS

Design an expressive, conventional, and rhetorical message (three messages total) for the following situation. Please make sure that the rhetorical message has all four required components labeled clearly using the following numbers: (1) the use of a neutral perspective, (2) expression of empathy, (3) offering specific solutions, and (4) leaving the door open to negotiation:

**Your roommate owes you $100. It has been over two months since you lent them the money and if he/she doesn't pay you back, you will be unable to cover your portion of this month's rent.**

The following example scenario and responses demonstrate the approach you should take with this exercise:

**You caught your best friend's significant other in a very compromising situation with another person (i.e., they were clearly caught cheating). You are uncomfortable keeping this a secret and want them to come clean to your best friend about what they did.**

Expressive: "I saw you cheating the other night and you are such an unbelievable jerk! I am shocked at how stupid you are. I knew my friend never should have trusted you!"

Conventional: "You and I both know what I saw the other night cannot be explained any other way. I cannot and will not keep this information private. If you don't tell my friend about what you did, I will."

Rhetorical: "I do not pry into other people's relationships, but I witnessed you in a compromising position with someone else. (1) I am not a part of your relationship, so I do not know what is going on between you two; (2) Perhaps you are both going through a really challenging situation and because I care so much about my friend and his/her happiness; (3) I want to speak with you privately about what I witnessed; (4) Are you open and willing to talk with me about it?"

# 55

# Writing for *Dear Abby*: Analyzing Issues and Constructing Advice Using Interpersonal Communication Concepts

*Holly J. Payne*
*Department of Communication*
*Western Kentucky University*
*holly.payne@wku.edu*

**History:** This activity was presented at the annual meeting of the National Communication Association, November 2008, in San Diego, California.

**Primary courses in which this activity might be used:** Interpersonal Communication, Relational Communication, Introduction to Communication

**Concepts illustrated:** Conflict Management, Communication Climate, Relational Stage Models, Assertive Messages, Self-Concept, and Self-Monitoring

## PURPOSE

Interpersonal communication courses require students to analyze their own communication styles and those of others. While most textbooks provide sample statements and examples of positive and negative communication behaviors, they sometimes lack a variety of examples for efficient use during class time. Self-help advice columns provide a rich array of interpersonal dilemmas for communication students to analyze.

The purpose of this activity is to provide students in introductory interpersonal communication courses the opportunity to analyze communication issues presented by writers to the *Dear Abby* advice column and to construct responses using interpersonal communication concepts, theories, and models. This activity enhances understanding of course concepts, reinforces skill development particularly in designing competent messages, and prepares students for scenario-based exam questions. Instructors may choose to intersperse *Dear Abby* letters at the end of chapters or put them together collectively for review purposes.

## EXPLANATION OF ACTIVITY

Begin the activity by providing individual students or groups with the *Dear Abby* letters as listed in the Appendix on p. 213. Additional letters can be accessed in the *Dear Abby* archive located at http://www.uexpress.com/dear-abby/. Instructors can select letters based on specific interpersonal concepts they wish to apply. After students have read the letter, ask them to identify the most salient communication issues that should be addressed. Keep in mind that letters might address more than one communication theory or concept, and could be resolved with more than one communication technique.

After narrowing the possible problems, students should use their class notes and textbooks to define the issue and determine specific strategies for resolving the problem using relevant theories, concepts, or models. For example, if students are reading a letter about a developing relationship where the couple is struggling with a lack of independence and a need for time apart, students could use both a relational stages model and relational dialectics theory to explain the issues the couple is facing. Once the issues have been identified and defined, students should craft an advice letter, explaining the relational phenomenon and providing strategies for dealing with the issue. In the case above, students might focus on a specific relational maintenance strategy to alleviate the tension, but they might also develop a perception check as a way to communicate about the tension. Finally, student responses are discussed as a class. Dear Abby's response may be presented at the end of the discussion after students have analyzed the case and developed a solution.

An example *Dear Abby* case follows including the case analysis questions and possible solutions.

*DEAR ABBY: I recently let a friend borrow a bracelet of mine. I left it at her house and asked that she return it the next time we saw each other. That was Sunday morning, and I even called ahead of time to make sure she remembered. When we met, she told me she had forgotten to bring it.*

*A few days later I was at her house again. When she gave me the bracelet, it had been completely destroyed by her cat. She apologized and said she'd replace it. I said it was OK, and then asked if she would really buy me a new one. "No," she replied, "my cat did it, not me." I decided not to push the issue. The bracelet wasn't too expensive, but I feel I deserve some sort of payment because the cat didn't know any better. What should I do? – AT A LOSS IN MINNESOTA*

(*Dear Abby*, January 18, 2008)

1. **What are the specific communication issues addressed in the letter?**
   *Possible Responses*: The communication issues evident in this letter include perception checking, conflict and assertive messages. When "At A Loss In Minnesota" first perceived that something was amiss regarding her

friend not returning her bracelet, she could have conducted a perception check. Given that a perception check was not conducted, the writer
does take a direct approach in probing her friend's intention to buy her
a new bracelet. Once the friend retracts the offer, a conflict situation is
presented. It is at this point that "At A Loss In Minnesota" has a decision to make on how to respond.

2. **Describe and define any key terms relevant to the case. What skill or process should this person apply?**

*Possible Responses*: Even if the writer initially decided to respond with a
perception check, the conflict situation was still imminent. A perception check is a way of testing a perception we form based on contextual
and personal factors. The three parts to a perception check include a
description of the behavior, two interpretations of the behavior, and a
question to clarify the behavior (Adler, Rosenfeld, & Proctor, 2006). A
perception check may have led to the truth surfacing sooner.

Given that the truth ultimately came out and the friend did not
assume responsibility, "At A Loss In Minnesota" might choose to assert-
ively ask the friend to replace the bracelet. Similar to a perception check,
an assertive message contains five parts: a description of the behavior,
an interpretation of the behavior, the feelings that arise from the interpretation, the consequences of the information you have shared, and
the intention or request for what you hope to happen (Adler, Rosenfeld,
& Proctor, 2006). Assertive messages can help to diffuse conflict situations and ward off defensiveness. Ultimately, "At A Loss In Minnesota"
must evaluate how much the bracelet is worth to her and then gauge her
communication accordingly.

3. **Write a response to "At A Loss In Minnesota."**

*Possible Response:*

DEAR AT A LOSS IN MINNESOTA: There is no doubt that you have
a reason to be upset about your friend's avoidance of responsibility for
your ruined bracelet, as well as for her pseudo-promise to buy you a
new one. This incident requires you to construct an assertive message
that conveys your disappointment to your friend and persuades her to
replace the bracelet. It might sound something like this:

> "When your cat ruined my bracelet I really thought you would buy me a
> new one. Perhaps you thought that I wouldn't really care, but I'm upset
> about your decision because even though it is a cheap bracelet, it really
> meant a lot to me. Promising to buy a new bracelet and then taking
> back the offer made me question our friendship. I hope you'll reconsider
> because this friendship is important to me."

Hopefully, your friend will take this suggestion and replace the bracelet. If you try this and it doesn't work, then you have to decide how
important the bracelet is to you. Is it worth ending a friendship over? Our

recommendation is that your friend's insensitivity on this issue probably carries over into other parts of your relationship, so you might consider spending time with someone more respectful, but if you don't give her a chance to rectify the situation, you may needlessly lose a friend.

**Dear Abby's Official Response:**

*DEAR AT A LOSS: The bracelet may not have been "too expensive," but chalk this up as a valuable lesson. Your "friend" is irresponsible and not entirely truthful. Unless you're willing to risk losing what you lend her, refrain from making that mistake again.*

## DEBRIEF

The *Dear Abby* letters provide real world relational dilemmas that enable students to apply interpersonal communication theories and develop specific strategies for communicating competently. Students stay highly engaged in the activity as they openly discuss their assessments within groups and with the class. The instructor and class members can listen and evaluate the different response letters and might even choose which response was the best of the class. There is often laughter from students when they hear Dear Abby's actual response. The advice is typically brief and may not always follow the strategies taught in the interpersonal classroom, but it provides an opportunity to discuss the communicative options and the possible outcomes if the advice is followed. Students also come to realize that even following the most communicatively competent steps may not result in the intended outcome. This realization leads to further discussion of alternative strategies, relational quality, and personal communication styles and preferences. This activity promotes a thorough understanding of course content, and results in students performing well on open and close-ended application questions on exams and quizzes. The following questions could be used to debrief the activity:

1.) Was Dear Abby's advice communicatively competent? Why or why not?
2.) From the class, whose advice letter was the strongest and why? Is there anything you would add to strengthen the response? What pieces of information about the situation would have been helpful to know in drafting a response?
3.) What do you think would be the outcome if the reader followed the advice? Would things work out the way we intend? Why or why not? What specific personal or relational factors would affect the outcome?

## REFERENCES

Adler, R.B., Rosenfeld, L.B., & Proctor, R.F., II (2006). *Interplay: The process of interpersonal communication (10th Edition)*. New York: Oxford University Press.
Dear Abby (2008). Retrieved February 7, 2008, from http://www.uexpress.com/dearabby/

## ADDITIONAL DEAR ABBY LETTERS FOR ANALYSIS

| Topic | Dear Abby Letter | Dear Abby's Response |
|---|---|---|
| *Relational Stages* | DEAR ABBY: After giving my wife of 10 years a divorce at her request, she continues to contact me. She'll call about little things like what color to paint the house, things that are going on at work, or who she went dancing with. Why is she doing this? –ALREADY MOVED ON<br><br>(*Dear Abby*, January 20, 2008) | DEAR ALREADY MOVED ON: Because on some level, although she requested the divorce, she's unable to completely let go. Or, she fantasizes that you're actually interested in the things she's talking about. If her calls are an imposition, why don't you tell her so and put an end to the conversation? |
| *Cross-Sex Friendships & Jealousy* | DEAR ABBY: I am a stay-at-home mother with three young children. I have become friends with another stay-at-home parent. We share many things in common, and our children are great playmates. The problem is my friend is a man.<br><br>Even though both of us are happily married, sometimes we feel awkward spending time together. Our spouses are not thrilled about us hanging out together, but they haven't forbidden it because they trust us to be faithful.<br><br>Is it appropriate for a man and a woman to spend time together while their spouses are at work? –AT HOME WITH ANOTHER WOMAN'S HUSBAND<br><br>(*Dear Abby*, December 7, 2007) | DEAR AT HOME: It depends upon the individuals involved and whether there is a physical attraction. In your case, because you "sometimes feel awkward spending time together," I suggest you limit it—because what you're feeling may be sexual tension.<br><br>Has it occurred to you to include other stay-at-home parents in these visits? That might be a way to diffuse the situation without ending the friendship. |

*(Continued)*

| Topic | Dear Abby Letter | Dear Abby's Response |
|---|---|---|
| *Self-Concept* | DEAR ABBY: I am a very fair-skinned, natural blonde. The only way I can get a suntan is by getting burned first. I am attractive, and I have accepted the fact that in order to be healthy I must remain pale. However, people often make comments about my skin tone, and it's starting to hurt my feelings. Several people have called me "albino."<br><br>I know I should ignore them, but it's making me self-conscious. Tanning salons seem unhealthy, and self-tanners look unnatural. What can I say to these people that makes it clear they're out of line? –FAIREST OF THEM ALL IN D.C.<br><br>(*Dear Abby*, November 24, 2007) | DEAR FAIREST: Tanning salons ARE unhealthy, and you're wise to avoid them. You are also wise to forgo sunbathing because it is the foremost cause of premature aging of the skin—not to mention the danger of skin cancer.<br><br>When someone remarks about your complexion, you are within your rights to tell that person you don't appreciate that kind of personal comment and to knock it off. And if the person persists, you are also within your rights to avoid him or her—and that's what I advise you to do. |
| *Nonverbal Communication & Power* | DEAR ABBY: I have worked at my present job a little over a year. When I make a mistake, my supervisor comes over to my desk, leans very close to me and tells me loudly what I have done wrong.<br><br>The office is very large, and I find her behavior threatening. I feel like I am backed into a corner. My way of dealing with it is just to say anything to get her out of "my space." It's also embarrassing that everyone in the office can hear everything we say. I'm about ready to file a harassment suit.<br><br>How can I get her to back off a little or take it to a private office? – INTIMIDATED IN WICHITA, KAN.<br><br>(*Dear Abby*, December 15, 2007) | DEAR INTIMIDATED: Your supervisor's behavior is insensitive. Some people become so intimidated when they are publicly embarrassed or their space is invaded that they "blank out" and can't remember all the details of what happened—hardly an effective management technique.<br><br>At a time when both of you are calm, talk to her privately, in her office with the door closed (that's how she should be correcting you), and explain how her "corrective technique" affects you. If that doesn't work, then talk to her supervisor or your union rep. It appears your supervisor could use some coaching on effective management. |

*Conflict*

DEAR ABBY: Five years ago, prior to my grandmother's death, she gave my brothers and me her summer home. When we all went to see the place, we found an overgrown lot with a house in complete disrepair.

My brothers and their families wanted nothing to do with restoring it. They said they had neither the time nor the money to put into repairs, and "camping wasn't their thing." We all knew the only value in the place was the land, so we had a real estate company give us an appraisal. My husband and I decided we did want to rebuild the house, so we paid my brothers the full value of the property.

Five years and thousands of dollars later, the house has been rebuilt from the frame up. And now, here's the problem: My brothers and their wives say it is the "family" summer home and are demanding keys so they can come up and stay anytime. I had planned all along to hold family picnics and such, but not give out keys to the place.

My brothers are furious with me, and so is my mother. They say I'm "greedy" and don't know how to share. But Abby, we paid them off. We did all the work, and we pay all the bills each month, not to mention the taxes. The house is in my name only.

Now I wish Grandma had donated the land to the state park and kept us out of it. I know she wanted it to stay in the family, and so did I, but I don't think my family is being fair.

DEAR NO VACANCY: Selling the property wouldn't fix your problem because your relatives would then resent you for having done so. Instead, take a page out of your grandmother's book, thicken your skin, and—as you put it—stick to your guns.

You paid for the property fair and square, and your brothers willingly let it go. By inviting your relatives to enjoy it with you, you are being more than generous. Please don't allow yourself to be emotionally blackmailed into submission.

*(Continued)*

| Topic | Dear Abby Letter | Dear Abby's Response |
|---|---|---|
| | Grandma was also a hard worker, and she wasn't the type to let people walk all over her. Should I stick to my guns and welcome them to visit when we're here, or just sell the place (which would break my heart) and forget this ever happened? – SORRY, NO VACANCY, IN THE U.S.A.<br><br>(*Dear Abby*, November 2, 2007) | |
| *Communication Climate* | DEAR ABBY: I have a great job, get along with everyone I work with and go home at night happy, even when things get a little hectic. I love my job—except for one thing.<br><br>A woman who works here is a constant downer. She constantly talks about how fat she is (she's overweight, and so am I), how ugly she is (she's not), how horrible her marriage is, how she won't live past 38, how her son won't live to be 18, and other negative things. In fact, all she has to say are negative things.<br><br>Whenever I try to interject something positive, she finds a way to turn it into a negative. We work with the public a lot, and she has run so many customers off with her negativity that we are losing money. No one will fire her because there is no one to replace her in our small town, but everyone is at their wit's end. We have all tried talking to her about it. What else can we do? – READY TO EXPLODE IN WYOMING<br><br>(*Dear Abby*, November 28, 2007) | DEAR READY: Aside from slipping "happy pills" into her morning coffee, nothing. (Only joking!) People sometimes call themselves fat, ugly, etc., because they hope the person they're talking to will contradict them and say, "No, you're not." In this case, your co-worker appears to be very depressed—and with good reason.<br><br>I do have a suggestion, however, for the next time she makes a negative comment. Instead of trying to turn it around, agree with her. Say, "Yes, isn't it sad?" or "You're a saint," then change the subject. That may stop her. |

216

# 56

## "Will You Date Me?": Understanding the Importance of Creating Relatable Messages

*Mary Beth Asbury*

*Department of Communication Studies and Organizational Communication*

*Middle Tennessee State University*

*MaryBeth.Asbury@mtsu.edu*

*Nathan G. Webb*

*Department of Communication Studies*

*Belmont University*

*nathan.webb@belmont.edu*

**History:** This activity was presented at the annual meeting of the National Communication Association, November 2011, in New Orleans, Louisiana.

**Primary courses in which this activity might be used:** Public Speaking, Advanced Public Speaking, Persuasion, Interpersonal Communication

**Concepts illustrated:** Audience Analysis, Persuasion

### PURPOSE

Audience analysis is a skill taught in basic communication courses, yet students often fail to see its real-world application in other settings. This highlights three problems. First, it illustrates a lack of critical thinking skills. Second, students do not make connections between audience analysis skills regarding speech making and audience analysis skills in everyday encounters. Third, it results in poor performance in other courses as well as potential for poor interactions outside the classroom. If students could see how audience analysis is used in everyday situations, they could potentially understand why it is important in speechmaking. Thus, to help students understand this concept better, we ask them to apply audience analysis to a situation in which most of them are familiar—dating.

## EXPLANATION OF ACTIVITY

For this activity, we use online dating as the setting. Online dating is a common practice among adults in the United States (Madden & Lenhart, 2006). In fact, the number of American adults using online dating sites has doubled in the last 10 years. In 2015, approximately sixteen million American adults used an online dating website (Nuwer, 2015). By 2015, approximately thirty-two million American adults were registered with an online dating service (Nuwer, 2015). Online dating is also popular among young adults. Over one in five adults aged twenty-five to thirty-four and one in ten adults aged eighteen to twenty-four have utilized online dating sites (Smith & Anderson, 2015). In short, most college students are familiar with online dating.

After receiving a lecture on audience analysis and completing the required reading on the subject, students are given this activity to complete in class. For this assignment, instructors can create their own fictional profiles or can use free online dating sites as inspiration for their profiles. To get access to dating sites, including free sites, the instructor would likely have to sign up for the site and create a password. Therefore, we included some examples in the Appendix (see p. 220). Most profiles contain a picture, which we use Google Images for, and some general information, such as location, astrological sign, age, likes, and dislikes. In addition, we include a paragraph that sums up who the person is and what he or she is looking for in a romantic relationship. One thing to note is that the instructor may want to change the locations on the profiles to make them more local to students.

Students are placed into groups of three or four, and each group is given a fictional online dating profile to analyze. Based on the information in that profile and what they have learned about audience analysis, each group must write an email of at least a paragraph (five sentences) to that person with the intention of getting a date. After students have completed their emails, they summarize the dating profile and read their email aloud to the entire class. Students then explain to the class how they analyzed their profile, and why they wrote what they did. This activity can take ten to twenty minutes, depending on the amount of discussion generated.

## DEBRIEF

At the end of the activity, the instructor debriefs the class on the concepts of audience analysis, making note of how the skills they learned in the class carry over into other situations like dating. The instructor asks questions such as the following:

- When you read the profile, what were some things that stood out for you about this person?
- What are some of the assumptions you can make about this person from reading the profile?
- Why did you write your message that way?
- Why did you choose those words as opposed to others?
- If you were giving a speech to an audience filled with people like this person, what types of topics do you think they would like? What would be some things you would emphasize in a speech? What are some topics you might stay away from? Would you dress a certain way to increase your credibility for this audience?

These questions help students see how messages need to be catered to the specific audience. The instructor also asks students to give examples of other situations where audience analysis is important, helping them to come to the conclusion that in all circumstances, considering the audience is important for crafting a message. Moreover, the instructor makes the connection about how audience analysis is important for speechmaking. Specifically, just as we analyze our audience to craft a message indicating interest, we also need to analyze our audience to craft a message about an issue in which we are informing or persuading.

In addition to the above questions, this activity is also useful for talking about ethics in public speaking. Once all of the groups have shared their paragraphs and profiles, we can have a discussion about ethical application of audience analysis. For example, some questions we ask include:

- Is it right to change who you are for the sake of impressing or persuading an audience?
- Is it okay to lie in order to persuade people? Has anyone stretched the truth a little to impress people? Any examples?
- Does the size of the audience matter when considering ethical issues? For example, is it okay to stretch the truth a little with one person in the dating world, but not okay to do this with a larger audience?

Students report that they enjoy this activity because it helps them see the application of audience analysis principles to settings beyond the classroom. More specifically, students have stated that they were able to understand the importance of audience analysis when trying to persuade an audience. While the point of sending an email to a potential dating partner is often to introduce oneself, the ultimate goal in doing so is to persuade the other person to show interest. Thus students are made aware of how even small word choices can affect how a message is perceived when trying to achieve a goal.

## REFERENCES

Madden, M. & Lenhart, A. (2006). Online dating. Retrieved from http://www.pewinternet.org/2006/03/05/online-dating/

Nuwer, R. (2015). The science of online dating. Retrieved from http://www.nytimes
    .com/2015/02/17/science/the-science-of-finding-romance-online.html?_r=0
Smith, A. & Anderson, M. (2015). 5 facts about online dating. Retrieved from http://
    www.pewresearch.org/fact-tank/2015/04/20/5-facts-about-online-dating/

## APPENDIX

Getting Rich and Having Fun
Wanna join?

Name: Big Spender
Age: 24 years old
Location: Boulder, CO
Looking for: Friendship, casual dating
Interested in: Women
Education: College graduate
Occupation: Sales
Ethnicity: Caucasian
Height: 6'1"
Sign: Scorpio
Hobbies: Music, working out, making money
Dating history: No real serious relationships
Kids: *Maybe* down the road

**About me:** I recently just moved to Colorado from Jersey. I went to college at New Jersey State. (Go big blue!) I moved to Colorado with my company and am looking to meet some new people. I work in sales, so I love being around people. I'm not gonna lie ... I usually like being the center of attention and making the party happen. I love going out, making money, and having a good time. I also like working out and staying fit. My favorite type of music is hip-hop, and I love going out to clubs so I can dance.

**Ideal partner:** My ideal date would be fit and would know how to have a good time. I have dated quite a few different ladies, and I'm most impressed with women who can keep up with me on the party scene. I like a woman that can dance and looks good doing it. She would have to know how to have a good time. I want a woman that can keep up with my fast-paced lifestyle.

If you think you can be that woman, send me a message! I'd love to get together for drinks ...

Just looking for Mrs. Right ...

Name: Nice Guy 21
Age: 25 years old
Location: Kansas City, MO
Interested in: Women
Looking for: Dating, Friendship, Online Conversation, Serious Relationship
Education: Graduate Degree
Occupation: Social Worker
Ethnicity: African American
Height: 5'9"
Sign: Cancer
Hobbies: Friends, reading, volunteering, traveling
Dating history: A few girlfriends
Kids: Hopefully one day

**About me:** I guess I'm just a pretty normal guy. I'm laid back, friendly, and easy to get along with. I love spending time with my friends and family ... doing just about anything. I grew up in the KC area, so I'm able to see my family a lot and have been lucky to have the same group of best friends for many years. I went to college and graduate school in the KC area, and have only lived away when I spent a year in the Peace Corps in Swaziland, Africa. My time in the Peace Corps points to my love of traveling; I've been to seventeen different countries and four continents, mostly studying and volunteering. I work hard as a social worker and love giving back to the community. I spend a lot of time volunteering with my church, where we do a lot of work with the homeless community in downtown Kansas City.

**Ideal partner:** My ideal partner would be a woman who deeply cares for other people. She would have to be interested in meaningful relationships, and it's important to me that she has good friendships. She would also need to care about helping those who are less fortunate. I don't really care about her specific occupation or salary, but am much more interested in how she treats people. It's also a must that she has a thirst for travel and is willing to see the world with me. Ideally, I'd start talking to a woman, become friends with her, and eventually cultivate a serious relationship where we are best friends. If you're that girl, I'd love to hear more of your story. Looking forward to hearing from you.

Artistic and creative man,
looking for a best friend.

Name: OpenMindedKYMan
Age: 29 years old
Location: Lexington, KY
Interested in: Men
Looking for: Friendship, Casual Dating
Education: Some college
Occupation: Artist & barista
Ethnicity: Caucasian
Height: 5'11"
Sign: Sagittarius
Hobbies: Writing music, poetry, coffee
Dating history: Divorced
Kids: 1 daughter

**About me:** My name is Johnny, and I just moved back to Lexington. I graduated from UK a few years back, got married, and moved to Rhode Island to be closer to my ex's family. For work, I'm a freelance writer and barista. I love being around the coffee-shop scene, where ideas flow freely and people are (in general) open-minded and considerate of others. I grew up in a very religious family, and I wouldn't say that I'm religious now, but spiritual. I think spirituality is important, but I'm not a huge fan of organized religion. For fun, I enjoy writing both music and poetry, playing music, and enjoying good food and drink.

**Ideal partner:** My ideal partner would be someone who is creative, artistic, and free-spirited. I want to spend time with someone who drives me to think more deeply and will draw out my innovative side. I also want to be able to bring out his innovative side, and I want to be collaborators of ideas and beauty. I would love to be around a man who enjoys spending time with small groups of people and is okay with one-on-one time. I'm not much of a partier, so I need to be with someone who is okay with me being laid back. Last, I need to be with a partner who loves children. I have my little girl in the summers, and anyone I spend time with must be willing to accept her and put out effort to get to know her for the wonderful person she is. I'd love to hear from you if you think we might be a good fit. Cheers.

Fun, friendly, and fantastic! Looking
for romance!

Name: Funzinella21
Age: 26 years old
Location: Atlanta, GA
Interested in: Men
Looking for: Friendship, Casual Dating
Education: College degree
Occupation: Bookstore owner
Ethnicity: Caucasian
Height: 5'6"
Sign: Aries
Hobbies: reading, writing, listening to music
Dating history: No serious relationships
Kids: None

**About me:** My name is Jane, and I am a small business owner. I like to read, write, sing, and listen to music. I also like to exercise and am currently training for my first marathon in the spring! I am very involved in my church, serving in many capacities, such as Sunday school teacher and ministry coordinator. My faith is very important to me, and I am looking for someone who shares the same basic beliefs. But, most important, I love to laugh and see humor in all situations.

**Ideal partner:** I am looking for someone who is intelligent enough to carry on and enjoy good conversation, and who is laid back enough to tell a good joke. I would like someone who puts God first and seeks His will. And my ideal partner would have a flair for romance, knowing how to treat a woman and how to make her feel special. Could that be you? Let's chat!

Finding myself, finding you.

Name: yogagirl12
Age: 29 years old
Location: Philadelphia, PA
Interested in: Men
Looking for: Serious relationship
Education: Technical school
Occupation: Massage Therapist
Ethnicity: Caucasian
Height: 5'9"
Sign: Libra
Hobbies: yoga, reading, music
Dating history: Divorced
Kids: 1 son

**About me:** My name is Caitlin. Although my physical age is twenty-nine, my spiritual age is one hundred fifty. I am an old soul looking for someone who I can connect with on a physical, mental, and spiritual level. I love to practice yoga and meditate daily. I feel that a lot of the problems in the world could be solved if people would only find a way to connect with themselves. Thus yoga and meditation are very important to me. I am a vegetarian and try to eat only local, organic food. I am an activist at heart, and so I try to keep my daily practices in line with my life philosophy. I have one son, who is three, from my previous marriage, and he is the light of my world. Although my profession is a massage therapist, I know my life path has led me to this moment of raising my son.

**Ideal partner:** I am looking for an old soul like myself to spend time with and connect to. I would prefer someone who has the same beliefs as I do regarding health and sustainability practices. My ideal mate would understand the mind-body-spiritual connection and would seek to continue to develop that. If you are interested in grabbing some conflict-free coffee, shoot me an email.

Looking for Love!

Name: TXchic81
Age: 26 years old
Location: Boston, MA
Interested in: Men
Looking for: Friendship, Casual Dating, A Relationship
Education: Law Degree
Occupation: Lawyer
Ethnicity: African American
Height: 5'8"
Sign: Capricorn
Hobbies: reading, concerts, cooking, sports
Dating history: Serious relationship just ended
Kids: None

**About me:** My name is Priscilla, and I just moved from Texas to Boston, MA. I am a lawyer and practice at a local firm. I just ended a serious four-year relationship and am looking to meet new people and perhaps start something new. I like to read, go out for coffee, try new restaurants, cook, and go to concerts. I would say I am spiritual but not religious. Although I was raised Catholic, I see value in all religions. I also love sports. I am a huge Dallas Cowboys fan, and even though I now live in Boston, I am still a Texas Longhorns fan. Hook 'em horns!

**Ideal partner:** I am looking for someone who is kind, honest, intelligent, and funny. I want someone who I can be serious with and who knows how to help me have fun. As a lawyer, I can be very serious, so I need someone who knows how to help me loosen up and have fun. If you are someone who knows how to have fun, likes sports and doesn't mind me cheering for Texas teams, I might be the person for you. Feel free to contact me.

# 57

## Perspective Taking: Communicating Multiple Perspectives in Mental Health, Multiple Disciplines

*Jennifer B. Gray*
*Department of Communication*
*Appalachian State University*
*grayjb@appstate.edu*

*Neal D. Gray*
*School of Counseling and Human/Community Service*
*Lenoir-Rhyne University*
*neal.gray@lr.edu*

**History:** This activity was presented at the annual meeting of the Southern States Communication Association, April 2014, in New Orleans, Louisiana.

**Primary courses in which this activity might be used:** Interpersonal Communication, Health Communication, Counseling, Mental Health, Psychology

**Concepts illustrated:** Perspective Taking, Illness Experience, Disease versus Illness, Patient-Provider Communication, Role Playing, Social Support

### PURPOSE

Health communication, and other social science and health courses, distinguish disease, the physical manifestations of a condition, from illness, a condition as it is experienced (Gray, 2007; du Pré, 2010; Sharf & Vanderford, 2003). Perspective taking—understanding multiple points of view—is another important part of understanding the holistic portrait of illness. Both concepts are central to communication in health settings, such as mental health. This assignment addresses these ideas through applied research by having students choose a psychological condition, addiction, or mental illness and explain it from multiple points of view, including the patient, family members, providers, and friends. The research culminates in oral presentations allowing each student to (1) partially grasp an individual mental illness experience or addiction; (2) understand the impact illness has not only on patients, but also on the patient's social network and on providers; (3) understand the concept of perspective taking and multiple points of view; and (4) be exposed to information on multiple conditions.

Presentations explain the physical, psychological, emotional, communicative, and social aspects of a mental health condition from various points of view, including the patient's. (See Appendices A and B, pp. 229–232 for an assignment sheet and grading rubric, which may be customized for particular instructor discipline, interests, tastes, and needs.) Students are asked to explore not only the physical aspects of a condition, but its daily experiences and its impact on quality of life. They are also challenged to connect health communication concepts, such as illness narratives, patient-provider communication, social support, and the like, as well as concepts related to counseling and other mental health fields, such as stage of addiction or illness, bringing such concepts into clearer focus.

## EXPLANATION OF ACTIVITY

Teachers as well as your students may find that the interdisciplinary nature of the material in your course can be challenging in that there is so much to cover in so little time. When introducing the course early on in the semester, it can be helpful to mention this activity as a way to learn multiple concepts, as well as become educated about multiple conditions, in one assignment and set of course presentations. Teachers may wish to familiarize themselves with literature on multiple mental illnesses and with addiction information, as well as information on social support and patient-provider communication, prior to introducing material related to this activity. You may introduce and employ the activity as it suits your particular course through the following steps:

1) Prepare the "multiple perspectives on mental illness" presentation assignment sheet. (See Appendix A, p. 229.) Present the assignment several weeks prior to its due date. Assign groups or have students choose groups of three to four students each.
2) Have groups begin thinking about mental illnesses, conditions, or issues they may wish to research and present. Alternatively, you may offer students a group of options to choose from, such as a list of potential mental illness scenarios or individuals to studying the assignment and have them choose from that list, or have students draw from a group of conditions that you have chosen.
3) Complete lessons in class on patient-provider communication, social support, illness narratives, perspectives of patients, providers, and families, and the difference between disease and illness, the latter three being

most crucial to the assignment. du Pré's (2010) text, *Communicating About Health*, offers a comprehensive, accessible introduction to these areas for the introductory health communication course. In interpersonal communication courses, lessons on perspective taking, Watzlawick's interactional view (Griffin, 2012), denotative and connotative meaning, and other areas may be best for preparing students for the assignment. In mental health-based courses, discussions on various conditions, illness versus disease, and the role of providers versus patients may be most appropriate.

4) Introduce the idea of disease versus illness with patient illness narratives (du Pré, 2010; Sharf et al., 2011). Perhaps also offer narratives of the same illness written from different points of view. A brief lesson on Faulkner's approach to narrative from various perspectives, such as in *As I Lay Dying*, may also aid in student understanding and application.

5) Devote several class periods to the presentations. Each student group also prepares a one-page handout that includes basic information about the illness, support resources for those with the illness, and their references.

Offer students feedback through the assignment rubric/grade sheet (Appendix B, p. 231) and through a concluding discussion following all presentations. Grading is based on the balance of various components, including the evidence of understanding of the condition and population presented, the depth and breadth of the presentation of psychological, physical, and social aspects of the condition, the inclusion of course theoretical and conceptual concepts, and the professionalism of the presentation and materials.

## DEBRIEF

Following the presentations, lead students in a discussion to further enhance learning from the activity. Suggested questions include:

a. What is the difference between disease and illness?

b. What did you learn about the physical aspects of mental illness and mental health from these presentations?

c. What did you learn about the psychological, social, and communicative aspects?

d. What surprised you?

e. What are the daily experiences of some of these presented illnesses?

f. How does communication impact, help, and/or hurt the illness experience?

g. How does the illness impact the patient? The significant other? The child? The friend? The parent? The provider/physician/counselor?

h. How were the group depictions of conditions (presentations, video, readings, etc.) accurate or inaccurate? How do media portrayals of conditions affect our perceptions? Stigma? Understanding?

Students tend to enjoy this activity and are quite interested in mental health issues. Many have remarked that they "had no idea" that a condition came with so many daily struggles before being assigned to research it for this assignment. Through the perspective-taking they must employ for the assignment, they also come to realize the impact mental illness and addiction can have not only on the patient, but also on his or her social ties and network, and that the provider's perspective is also impactful. They also more easily grasp the concept of disease versus illness and greatly value the exposure to multiple mental health issues and information in a nonthreatening, enjoyable presentation format.

## REFERENCES

du Pré, A. (2010). *Communicating about health: Current issues and perspectives* (3rd ed.). New York: Oxford University Press.

Faulkner, W. (1930). *As I lay dying.* New York: Random House.

Gray, J.B. (2007). Interpersonal communication and the illness experience in the *Sex and the City* breast cancer narrative. *Communication Quarterly, 55(4),* 397–414.

Griffin, E.M. (2012). *A first look at communication theory* (8th ed.). New York: McGraw Hill.

Sharf, B.F., Harter, L.M., Yamaski, J., & Haidet, P. (2011). Narrative turns epic: Continuing developments in health narrative scholarship. In T.L. Thompson, R. Parrott, & J.F. Nussbaum (Eds.), *Handbook of health communication* (2nd ed.). Mahwah, NJ: Lawrence Erlbaum Associates (pp. 36–52).

## APPENDIX A

## ASSIGNMENT SHEET—MULTIPLE PERSPECTIVE MENTAL ILLNESS PRESENTATION

Multiple Perspective Mental Illness Presentation

To more fully understand the concept of illness experience, an important topic in health communication and a vital topic as a healthcare consumer and/or professional, you and three other students will be randomly assigned to a particular mental illness or addiction (e.g., work addiction, depression, heroin addiction, etc.), and will be asked to research its physical symptoms and its emotional, social, and psychological impact. Remember that disease is the physical manifestation of an illness, while the illness is the physical, the psychological, and the social impact of a health condition. You will also be challenged to present how this illness affects not only the individual with the condition, but also other people in his or her life. In this assignment, you must present the illness experience of your assigned illness from various points of view in a brief oral report.

These will be ten- to fifteen-minute oral reports in which you consider the daily experiences of a mental health condition or addiction, and must pick several points of view to present on the illness by portraying how the illness would affect various parties involved, such as the individual with the illness, parents, friends, spouse ... and so on?. Your group will portray the points of view you have chosen as well as the stage of the condition/illness/addiction you wish to illustrate (such as active addiction, relapse, recovery, etc.). Through your presentation of various dimensions of this illness, you will describe what the illness is in physical terms, how one would feel psychologically due to the illness, and what experiences and stressors it creates for one's daily life. You must let the audience know how the illness impacts communication with loved ones and healthcare providers; you should also note resources that may aid in coping. Your objective is to portray this same illness, this same story of mental illness or addiction, from various points of view. In brief, your oral report must address the following areas:

- The condition (could include causes, symptoms, care providers, diagnosis, treatment, medication, prognosis of recovery, obstacles to recovery, etc., depending on what you think is most interesting and/or important—remember that you should not focus entirely on the physical aspects of the condition) and its physical, mental/emotional, and social impacts
- Common experiences of those with the illness (day-to-day and overall)
- The way the condition impacts communication with care providers, family, friends ... and so on
- Support resources available to patients/clients and their family/friends

Keep in mind that this is a very brief report, and you'll likely find a lot of information on your illness. You'll have to be selective in what you include and should keep the areas above relatively balanced in terms of time spent on each, though a little more time can be spent in some areas than others, depending on how you want to structure things.

You may use visual aids and multimedia if you wish, but can also simply speak to us without any such aids. In any case, please be extemporaneous (prepared, but conversational) and keep good public speaking guidelines in mind (eye contact, vocal variety and expression, posture, volume, etc.). You may conduct your presentation in a number of ways. For instance, it may be a somewhat traditional oral report in which your group presents the elements above directly. You could have trained medical actors or standardized patients also portray parts of the illness (for instance, the physical and the emotional/social/psychological separately) and explain the condition to the class in this manner. You could have such trained folks portray a person with the illness/condition, or could portray more than one, each having a different sort of experience in dealing with the illness/condition; video clips of individuals sharing experiences of their particular conditions may also be effective, as could be fictional portrayals from film or television. You could show a video of a patient-provider interaction scene in which there is a provider and a patient, or a counseling session or intervention in which the client with the condition and several members of his or her social network are present, and in the course of the interaction, incorporate the four elements above. You could find published narratives of people telling the story of their mental illnesses or addictions, presenting each person's side/perspective of experiences with it, or you could have several other students or just your group members involved, each one reading the story one of such individual. There are of course many other ways you could do this, as long as you cover the four elements noted above. Please keep in mind that your objective is to illustrate a condition and its multiple impacts as honestly, respectfully, and sensitively as possible; refrain from portrayals that lead to caricature or stereotyping of mental illness. When in doubt about such impressions, please consult the instructor. I will also ask you to meet with me about your presentation ideas prior to the date of the class presentations. I urge you to practice your presentation and time yourselves.

The only written work required for this assignment is a one-page, double-spaced, typed handout that your group will turn in to me and that you will copy and distribute to the class following your presentation. The handout must include basic information about the mental illness or addiction (physical, social, and psychological), the manner in which the illness may affect the individual with the condition, as well as his or her social and healthcare network, support resources for those with the illness, communication issues/tips, and a reference list (using APA, 6th ed.) of the sources you looked up to explore your illness. Please look up at least five to seven sources (some may be websites, pamphlets, and interviews if you wish, but some should also be scholarly books, peer-reviewed journal articles, etc.). Another possibility as a source is to interview someone about the condition, such as a patient/client or healthcare provider, if that type of resource is available to you. Several web-based sources are listed on your syllabus that may be of help. If you have questions about where to look for this information, please ask. You will be graded based on the Multiple Perspective Mental Illness Presentation Rubric.


## APPENDIX B

### MULTIPLE PERSPECTIVE MENTAL ILLNESS PRESENTATION RUBRIC

**Names:**

**Mental Health Condition Portrayed:**

**Explained physical aspects of illness clearly**

1        2        3        4        5

**Explained psychological/social aspects of illness clearly**

1        2        3        4        5

Daily experiences/stressors/quality of life effects of illness from various points of view presented well

1        2        3        4        5        6        7        8        9        10

Social support resources presented well

1        2        3        4        5

Impact on communication addressed well

1        2        3        4        5        6        7        8        9        10

Linked illness experience well to health communication and mental illness/psychology/counseling concepts

1        2        3        4        5

Presentation Style (professionalism, volume, eye contact, expression, creativity)

1        2        3        4        5

Quality of handout (information, format), resources/references (format, quality)

1        2        3        4        5

Total:_____/50 points____

Comments:

# 58

# Going Green Dispute: A Role Play in Mediating Others' Perceptions and Potential Biases in a Conflict

*Kathleen M. Propp*

*School of Communication*

*Western Michigan University*

*kathy.propp@wmich.edu*

**History:** This activity was presented at the annual meeting of the National Communication Association, November 2015, in Las Vegas, Nevada.

**Primary courses in which this activity might be used:** Conflict, Mediation, Interpersonal Communication, Group/Team Communication, Organizational Communication

**Concepts illustrated:** Attribution Bias, Mediation, Manifest Conflict, Latent Conflict, Facilitation

## PURPOSE

When mediating conflict, strong communication skills are central to fully understanding how each person views the conflict and to facilitating a remedy for the disputants. Good facilitation includes getting participants to reveal their perceptions of the events that lead up to the conflict, what the conflict is really about, what attributions they make about themselves and the other party, and what their goals are in the conflict, which may be multiple and complicated. And all of this must occur while simultaneously managing the dialogue in a manner that shows the mediator is credible and neutral, and that also creates a safe environment for disputants to share their stories. The purpose of this role-play is to provide students an opportunity to practice all of these communication skills in a realistic context.

## EXPLANATION OF ACTIVITY

The Going Green Dispute is a three-person role-play including a student mediator, and the two disputants who are the President and Treasurer from a campus environmental group. The role-play was designed specifically to highlight the differences in perceptions and attributions that two people may bring to their understanding of an event and ensuing conflict. Both sides fully believe that they are telling the truth and being factual, but their perceptions are not equivalent. Further, the role play is designed to have a manifest (surface-level) conflict which is the issue of scheduling meetings, that is quite easy to uncover through the mediation process, but also more latent, relational issues based on the insecurities of the President, and how each of the disputants define *friendship*. The latent issues take stronger probing and insightful questions to reveal. Last, the roles have been designed to create some additional difficulties in the facilitation process with one participant wanting to dominate the conversation.

Before running this activity in the classroom, it is important to explain the concepts or theories you will be using the role-play to illustrate (e.g., how to facilitate a mediation session, attribution theory and bias, levels of conflict, and/or the role of perception in conflict). You may do this through lecture or assigned readings. For example, if you are using this role-play primarily to illustrate that conflict can occur at different levels, before having the students take part in the role-play you should lecture on manifest versus latent conflict and the cyclical nature of conflict that occurs when underlying issues are not addressed. On the other hand, if you use the role-play to build your students' skills in facilitating a mediation session, you would first need to teach appropriate interviewing techniques, mediation formats, and the importance of mediator neutrality.

After you have provided the necessary background information for your chosen focus, start the exercise by dividing students into triads for the role-play (you can use larger groups if you want more than one student to play the role of mediator). For each group formed, pass out the role of the President to one student (see Appendix A, p. 236), the role of the Treasurer to another student (see Appendix B, p. 237), and the role of the mediator (see Appendix C, p. 238). If you would like your students to take notes during the role-play, you should also give the mediators and observers, if any, the mediation note form (see Appendix D, p. 239). Explain to the students that the mediation form provides a place for them to record what they think are the most important facts that they hear, what they believe each side wants (their goals and interests), possible solutions that are offered, and a place to record the final agreement with what actions each side agrees to take. Tell all of the students they are not allowed to look at the others' roles, and give them about five minutes to read their roles and prepare themselves for the mediation session.

After they have had a chance to look over their roles, ask the students to begin the mediation and remind the disputants that they should not volunteer information unless it is asked for, and tell the mediator that his/her goal is to bring the disputants to a mutually satisfactory resolution of the dispute. Tell them that they have only fifteen to twenty minutes to come to an understanding and that they should write out their specific agreement including any actions to be taken by each side. When the mediation is done (or time is up), have the groups read through all of the roles together and have them highlight any information that the mediators were able to pull out through their interviews and then note what they did not uncover through the facilitation process.

## DEBRIEF

Typical results of the role-play are that the mediators usually uncover less than 50 percent of the stories of the disputants, focus on the surface-level conflict instead of the more latent relational issues, and struggle with how to manage the obstacle of the more dominant personality. This can lead to very insightful discussions about the difficulties of facilitating or managing the dialogue in a fair and unbiased manner, the role of perceptions and attributions in conflict, and manifest (content goals) versus latent (relational goals) conflict.

Discussion questions on mediation facilitation skills might include:

- How did you attempt to get them to tell their stories (what facilitation techniques were used)—what worked, and what didn't? Were some techniques easier to use than others? If so, why?
- What goals did you uncover for each side? What obstacles to getting the disputants' full stories did you find? What techniques did you use to overcome them? If you could do the role-play again, how might you get at some of the facts and goals that you failed to uncover?
- Were you able to maintain neutrality throughout the interview? If so, how? If not, what could you do differently?
- How difficult was it for you to remain in control as the mediator? What techniques did you use to maintain control? What other techniques might you have tried?
- Was it easier or harder than you thought to employ all of the communication skills needed to mediate a conflict? What skills were most difficult? What skills were easiest?

Discussion questions on attribution theory and bias might include:

- Having read both sides, who do you believe is telling the truth? Is it possible for two individuals to see the same event so differently and both be telling the truth?
- What attributions did you uncover that the disputants had about the other? What attributions were situational? What attributions were dispositional?

- Did you see evidence of attribution bias? How did each disputant's attributions color his/her perception of what happened?

Discussion questions on manifest versus latent conflict might include:

- Did you help the disputants uncover the solution to the scheduling problem (manifest issue)? If so, how? If not, what might have you done differently? What agreements did you achieve to address the scheduling issues?
- What were the underlying relational issues between the disputants? Did you uncover and help the disputants resolve their latent relational issues? If so, how? If not, what might have you done differently? If not, do you believe the resolution of the scheduling problem will be effective without addressing the latent issues?

It is important that through a critical and constructive discussion, you help students recognize important concepts that are demonstrated through this activity. After taking part in this role-play, students have expressed a deeper understanding of and respect for the many skills needed to mediate conflict successfully as well as the destructive impact of unrecognized latent conflict and attribution bias on conflict management.

## APPENDIX A

### GOING GREEN DISPUTE

Robin—President

You are the president of a campus environmental group (volunteer). You had been active in the group for several years before being elected president, and you felt it was a great honor. You also feel it is a great responsibility. Under the direction of the last president, the group accomplished so much that you feel that everyone will think you are a failure in comparison. You feel so much pressure to succeed, that you blame everything that goes wrong on yourself.

Recently, Chris, the treasurer of your group has not been attending meetings. You know s/he is busy, but you feel that s/he needs to establish the group as a priority. You are beginning to doubt Chris's loyalty and devotion to the group. Last week, you scheduled a meeting just for Chris's convenience and s/he didn't bother to even show up. You were furious. When you saw Chris the next day, s/he claimed that s/he had been at the meeting room and waited, but no one had shown up. You know you were five minutes late, but s/he claims to have waited fifteen minutes and didn't even text you that s/he was waiting. You think Chris is lying to you.

Now to top it all off, you rescheduled a second meeting just for Chris and s/he didn't bother to show up again. After waiting for almost a half hour, you call Chris. S/he answers the phone and tries to claim that s/he waited in the wrong room, and then went home. You know you told Chris that the room was changed, so you think s/he is lying to you again. You end up losing your temper on the phone, screaming at Chris and telling him/her that you think he/she should probably be impeached. You hang up the phone in anger.

After cooling off, you regret losing your temper. You know Chris is the best treasurer around. S/he has great ideas for fundraising and is unquestionably honest. You are not too worried about yelling at Chris because you have been friends for a long time—and friends can get away with that sort of thing. You are surprised to hear a few days later that Chris is contemplating quitting the group, and call him/her to set up a mediation session to resolve the conflict.

You are a take-charge kind of person who tends to dominate a conversation and this mediation process is no different for you. You feel it is important to speak up, and even interrupt to get your points across. You also don't pull any punches in terms of how you feel and what you say—Chris needs to understand how angry you are at his/her behavior.

Going into this mediation, your primary goals in this mediation are to get Chris to remain treasurer and to show up to meetings, but you are also looking for some validation of how hard you work as president of this group.

## APPENDIX B

## GOING GREEN DISPUTE

Chris—Treasurer

You are the treasurer for a campus environmental group (volunteer). You were active in the group for several years before being elected and feel that it was an honor. The only problem is that your primary employment has been very demanding lately and you have had to miss several meetings of your group. You feel bad about this, but feel it couldn't be helped. Part of the problem is that the group schedules everything at the last minute, and you don't have time to change your work assignments so that you can attend.

Last week, a special meeting was scheduled and you worked extremely hard to clear your schedule so that you could attend. You were furious when you sat in the meeting room for fifteen minutes past the meeting time, and no one else showed up. The battery in your phone was dead, so you couldn't even text or call the president to find out what was going on, so you left in frustration. The next day Robin, the president of the group, called and asked, "Where the hell you had been," because they had to meet without you. Robin claimed that s/he had been in the meeting room within five minutes of the allotted time, and that you hadn't been there, and that you would have texted her if you had really been waiting as you claimed. You explained that your phone was dead, so you feel that Robin called you a liar, and this hurts because you have always been close friends.

The next week, another meeting was planned to make up for the last. You cleared your schedule again, even though it was very difficult for you. You went to the meeting room and once again sat there for fifteen minutes without anyone arriving. You were so angry that you stormed out of the room and went home without even trying to contact Robin because you were afraid you wouldn't be able to control your temper. Just as you arrived at your home, you received a text. It was Robin asking where the hell you were, because they were meeting without you again. In the text, Robin claimed the meeting place had been changed, and that you knew that. S/he said that it was clear that you didn't give a damn about the group, and maybe you should quit or they might have to impeach you. You did not respond to the text because it made you so angry.

You feel extremely hurt and angry that a friend could turn on you like this. A few days later, you are pondering quitting when Robin calls and asks you to try mediation to resolve the conflict. As you are very committed to the cause of the group, you decide to give it a try, even though you feel Robin has been completely wrong and has betrayed your friendship. Given how hurt you feel, you are very reticent to speak in front of Robin and will only answer exactly what you are asked—it is much easier for you to talk about scheduling problems rather than your relational issues with Robin.

Your primary goal in this mediation is to get a formal apology from Robin, but if you don't quit, you would also like to get her to schedule meetings in a more organized fashion.

## APPENDIX C

### GOING GREEN DISPUTE

Role: Mediator

You volunteer as a mediator at a large Midwestern University. The President of a campus environmental group called Going Green has contacted you. The group consists entirely of volunteers and has no paid members. The President has asked you to mediate a dispute between him- or herself and the Treasurer of the group. You don't know any specific details about the conflict, but when requesting mediation services, the president mentioned that it had to do with the treasurer missing meetings and threatening to quit the group. You also know that the treasurer has agreed to the mediation process.

The participants in this mediation are:

- The President of Going Green, Robin Jones
- The Treasurer of Going Green, Chris Smithe
- The Mediator, a neutral third party appointed to serve in this case (You)

## APPENDIX D

## MEDIATION NOTE FORM

Party A's Name _____        Party B's Name _____

| Party A's Goals | Common Interests? | Party B's Goals |
|---|---|---|
| • | • | • |
| • | • | • |
| • | • | • |
| • | • | • |
| • | • | • |

Specific facts pertinent for resolution:

_____        _____

_____        _____

_____        _____

_____        _____

Possible solutions discussed by parties: _____

_____

_____

_____

_____

Final agreement, including actions to be taken by both disputants:

_____

_____

_____

_____

# 59

## Who Gets the Office?: Creating Conscious Approaches to Conflict

*Katherine Hampsten*
*Department of English and Communication Studies*
*St. Mary's University*
*KHampsten@stmarytx.edu*

**History:** This activity was presented at the annual meeting of the Southern States Communication Association Conference, April 2016, in Austin, Texas.

**Primary courses in which this activity might be used:** Interpersonal Communication, Small Group Communication, Organizational Communication, Conflict Management

**Concepts illustrated:** Conflict Resolution, Perspective Taking, Dialogue, Problem Solving

### PURPOSE

Conflict resolution is a difficult but rewarding process. This in-class simulation helps students explore various approaches to conflict in professional and personal settings. The objective of this activity is to compare and contrast various conflict resolution strategies within a particular context. Students will appreciate how perspective-taking and dialogue are helpful in achieving optimal conflict strategies.

This in-class simulation explores the conflict strategies of accommodation, avoidance, competition, compromise, and collaboration (Kilmann & Thomas, 1977). Integrative collaboration, in which the conflicting parties work to find outcomes that are mutually beneficial (De Dreu & Van Vianen, 2001), is often new to students. It requires conflicting parties to consider not just what their positions are, but why they hold those positions. In other words, positions are *what* we want, but interests are *why* we want it. Shifting the dialogue to one of interests, rather than positions, opens the scope of the discussion and allows those in conflict to discover optimal alternatives (Fisher, Ury, & Patton, 2011). However, as this activity demonstrates, conflict resolution is not a one-size-fits-all activity (Hocker & Wilmot, 1985).

## EXPLANATION OF ACTIVITY

This activity works best as a single-class activity. Depending on time available, the instructor may wish to conduct the activity after an in-depth introduction to conflict. Minimally, the instructor should introduce the definition of conflict before beginning the activity, as explained below.

### Preparation

To prepare students for the activity, the instructor provides students with a working knowledge of how conflict is defined and the types of typical responses. The definition of conflict as "an expressed struggle between at least two interdependent parties who perceive incompatible goals, scarce resources, and interference from others in achieving their goals" can frame the initial discussion (Wilmot & Hocker, 2007, p. 9). It is also helpful to introduce students to conflict styles. Kilmann and Thomas's (1977) framework of accommodation, avoidance, competition, compromise, and collaboration works well with this activity. Instructors may also wish to briefly review or introduce the basic concepts of active listening at this time, as this skill will be explored during the debrief portion of the activity.

### The Scenario

The instructor will break the class into five groups of about four to six students each, depending on class size. Students will read a scenario that describes a workplace dispute between coworkers, Pat and Chris, over office space. This case is provided in the Appendix (p. 243).

Students will work in groups to demonstrate what will happen if Pat and Chris use accommodation, avoidance, competition, compromise, and collaboration. To use class time most efficiently, the instructor may assign only one of the five conflict styles to each student group. For the sake of simplicity, students will assume that both Pat and Chris are using the same conflict style. After five to ten minutes of in-group discussion, students will present a brief simulation or role-play to the class in which they demonstrate what the communication process looks like if Pat and Chris use their assigned outcome. Their simulation should demonstrate how the conflict would be resolved using that outcome.

## DEBRIEF

Following the group presentations, the instructor will guide the students in a ten- to fifteen-minute discussion in which students evaluate the strengths and weaknesses of the strategies presented. The simulations will likely demonstrate the advantages and disadvantages of each of the strategies. For example, competition may seem fair and easy to implement. Using the competition outcome, students may suggest that Pat's slight seniority dictates that he/she win the office. This outcome may be effective if Chris and Pat have little time and/or interest in discussing the conflict. However, the use of competition may ignore the interests behind *why* Pat and Chris would want the office, or what may be in the ultimate best interest of the organization.

The instructor can then lead the class in a discussion about each of the simulations as examples of how these strategies work. This discussion helps students understand both the short- and long-term ramifications of using a particular conflict style. The discussion should also highlight the role of active listening during conflict. The following discussion questions may facilitate this discussion:

- In each of these role-plays, was Pat and/or Chris satisfied with the outcome? Why or why not?
- Under which circumstances would you choose to use one of these conflict styles over another?
- What, if any, are the likely benefits of using each of these conflict styles? Conversely, what are the likely costs, if any, of using each of these conflict styles?
- Which styles, if any, required Pat and Chris to listen to and consider what the other person wanted and needed? How did actively listening to the other person affect the final conflict outcome?

For simplicity, this activity assumes both Pat and Chris use the same conflict style. How would these outcomes change if each were to use a different conflict style? For example, imagine that Pat tends to use competition while Chris tends to use accommodation. Ultimately, students will recognize the way that collaboration approaches conflict differently than the other approaches. The instructor can guide them to consider the possible *interests* behind why they each want the office. In my experience, groups will suggest a collaboration that is actually a compromise. Collaboration requires discourse and creative problem solving to reach mutual advantages for both parties. For example, students in my classes have suggested that Chris has an interest in a space that is comfortable and impressive to prospective and new clients. Meanwhile, Pat has an interest in more square footage.

Astute students have suggested that removing the existing wall between Pat and Chris's current office will create more total square feet for Pat, while Chris can host clients in the corner. This solution creates optimal benefits for both parties. Certainly, other suggestions for collaborations may be equally effective.

This activity provides a hands-on opportunity for students to creatively compare and contrast conflict strategies in a simple scenario. The simulation presentations allow students to evaluate the strategies in a hands-on way. It also challenges students to think about conflict from multiple perspectives, recognizing the importance of active listening during a conflict.

At different points throughout the activity, it is important to help students recognize that no single conflict outcome will work in every situation (Roloff, 2009). Rather, effective conflict resolution requires one to think critically about the potential strengths and weaknesses of these approaches.

# REFERENCES

De Dreu, C. K. W., & Van Vianen, A. E. M. (2001). Managing relationship conflict and the effectiveness of organizational teams. *Journal of Organizational Behavior, 22*(3), 309–328. doi: 10.1002/job.71.

Fisher, R., Ury, W., & Patton, B. (2011). *Getting to yes: Negotiating agreement without giving in* (3rd ed.). New York: Penguin.

Hocker, J., & Wilmot, W. (1985). *Interpersonal conflict.* Dubuque, IA: Wm. C. Brown Publishers.

Kilmann, R. H., & and Thomas, K. W. (1977). Developing a forced-choice measure of conflict-handling behavior: The MODE Instrument. *Educational and Psychological Measurement (37)*2, 309–325. doi: 10.1177/001316447703700204

Roloff, M. E. (2009). Links between conflict management research and practice. *Journal of Applied Communication Research, (37)*4, 339–348. doi: 10.1080/00909880903233200

Wilmot, W. W., & Hocker, J. L. (2007). *Interpersonal conflict* (7th ed.). New York: McGraw-Hill.


# APPENDIX

## INSTRUCTIONS TO STUDENTS

1) Read this scenario carefully:

    **Source of conflict.** Pat and Chris have worked together for over five years. Their offices share a wall. Their supervisor calls them to her office. She says, "The big corner office has become available. I know you both have had your eye on it, and from my point of view you both deserve it—so I'm letting you two decide who gets it. Let me know by the end of the week what you decide."

    **Information about Pat.** Pat holds daily meetings with staff in his/her office. He/she often needs to access hard documents from the files stored there. Pat is generally happy with his/her job and supervisor, but often complains about needing more room for files and seating for staff. Pat has worked with the company for eight years.

    **Information about Chris.** Chris often meets with potential and new clients in his/her office. Chris thinks that these individuals would be more impressed with the company if they could meet in an aesthetically pleasing space, such as the corner office with its expansive windows. Chris wishes the company would publicly recognize his/her contributions in bringing in more clients. Chris has worked with the company for seven-and-a-half years.

2) Review the conflict strategy that your instructor assigned to your group.
3) Discuss with your small group how Pat and Chris would manage their conflict if both were using your assigned conflict strategy.
4) Create a role-play or skit that demonstrates Pat and Chris using your conflict strategy.
5) Present your role-play or skit with your class.

# Intercultural Communication

# 60

## The Sights and Sounds of Rapport-Building Across Cultures: Intercultural Interaction Analysis in *The Last King of Scotland*

*Lauren Mackenzie, Ph.D.*
Professor of Military Cross-Cultural Competence
Marine Corps University
Lauren.mackenzie@usmcu.edu

**History:** This activity was presented at the annual meeting of the Eastern Communication Association, April 2014, in Providence, Rhode Island.

**Primary courses in which this activity might be useful:** Intercultural Communication, Interpersonal Communication, Introduction to Communication, Nonverbal Communication

**Concepts illustrated:** Rapport, Intercultural Communication Competence, Paralanguage, Nonverbal Communication Categories

### PURPOSE

The value of intercultural competence for college students cannot be overstated. Preparing students for the culturally complex interactions they will face throughout their college years and beyond entails the introduction of key intercultural communication concepts and skills. The purpose of this activity is to take the educational process one step further and provide students with an opportunity to observe and discuss an intercultural interaction in context. The activity was first introduced at Maxwell Air Force Base in Montgomery, Alabama, in 2013 in an effort to connect culture, communication, and rapport building for military students with varied educational backgrounds.

One of the goals of intercultural competence is the ability to build relationships across cultures, and rapport is fundamental to this process. Defined generally as the relative harmony and smoothness of relations between people, rapport includes the following components: coordination, mutual positivity, and mutual attention (Tickle-Degnan & Rosenthal, 1990). This activity is designed to introduce a unique way in which communication skills and concepts can be applied in the classroom to better understand how rapport is developed in intercultural interactions. Students are asked to examine several communication concepts and skills: paralinguistic use and perception, the decoding of nonverbal cues, as well as the ways in which prominent symbols are used to develop rapport. As a result of participation in this activity, students are afforded the opportunity to practice and give each other feedback on a variety of communication skills in a low-threat, low-stakes environment.

The "Sights & Sounds" activity has been presented to over one thousand military students at U.S. Air Force and Marine Corps Bases and enables students to:

- Bring together the communication components associated with rapport building.
- Apply their knowledge of these components to a film-based intercultural scenario.
- Observe, listen to, and discuss the complex ways in which rapport is built and respect is communicated across cultures.

## EXPLANATION OF ACTIVITY

This activity consists of five steps and is designed for a one-hour class. The instructor begins with a review of several communication categories that impact the process of rapport building across cultures: paralinguistic use and perception (i.e., intonation, word emphasis, and volume), decoding of nonverbal cues (i.e., proxemics, haptics, and kinesics), and the different ways in which symbols can be interpreted across cultures (i.e., colors appropriate to wear at weddings and funerals, unlucky numbers, food that is good luck vs. taboo to eat, etc.).

The instructor then introduces the intercultural communication exchange between Ugandan General and Scottish Doctor from the film, *The Last King of Scotland* (MacDonald, 2006). The clip (just under three minutes) can be accessed on YouTube using the search terms "Last King of Scotland Nicholas shoots a cow." In order to provide some context for the scenario, the instructor might state: "The scenario you will see occurs as a Scottish doctor working in Uganda is called to assist General Amin—whose arm was hurt when his vehicle struck a large animal. This is the first meeting between these two men."

After the first viewing of the clip, divide students into groups of four. Distribute assigned questions (see Appendix, p. 250) for students to discuss as a group, and ask each group to designate one speaker who will present the group's responses to the class. Show the film clip again and ask each group to watch it through the lens of their assigned questions. Conclude the activity by connecting each group's responses to the nonverbal components of rapport, with an emphasis on coordination, positivity, and mutual attention. Common themes found in student responses will be discussed in the section to follow.

## DEBRIEF

Each group presents its responses based on the specific questions they were assigned. Discussion often leads to students' personal experiences with rapport building and the power that nonverbal communication has to improve or degrade the quality of a conversation. Examples of typical student responses to the questions (see Appendix, p. 250) illustrate this point and tend to revolve around three themes. First, students react to the paralanguage used by the General to convey rapport in the way he says, "Scottish!" This often leads to responses that emphasize that *how* something is said can often be more important than *what* is said. Students in the past have pointed to the *way* a supervisor or professor asks questions as an indication of respect or disrespect. Discussion typically leads to how the voice is used to sound inquisitive (sometimes rising intonation) or condescending (often falling intonation), and the cultural variation that surrounds our expectations. A second in student responses pertains to history and the *why* behind the General's reaction to learning the Doctor is Scottish. This can be an opportunity to practice the intercultural competence skill of perception checking and to ask students to think about why a Ugandan might relate better to a Scott than a Brit. The third common theme in the responses is focused on attribution. That is, the meaning of a suffering cow to a farmer who may require it for his/her livelihood versus the meaning of the suffering to a physician who may have taken an oath to alleviate suffering whenever possible. Again, the question of perspective taking may arise as a skill that could have helped the doctor anticipate the second and third order effects of his decision to shoot the cow.

The instructor can then connect the communication skills or concepts mentioned (such as managing paralinguistic use and perception, decoding nonverbal cues, etc.) to the rapport building categories of *coordination* (mimicked expressions, smooth responsiveness between conversational partners), *positivity* (smiling, touch), and *mutual attention* (direct body orientation, mutual gaze), to underscore the sights and sounds of rapport in an intercultural context. If time allows, a final question for discussion could be posed: Intercultural communication competence is defined as the "knowledge, motivation and skills to interact effectively and appropriately with members of different cultures" (Wiseman, 2003, p. 203). Was it achieved in this interaction? Responses tend to differ widely, but provide the instructor with an opportunity to remind students that the concepts *effective* and *appropriate* are largely dependent on the context of the interaction and the relationship between those within it.

Since the exercise was piloted in 2013, students have responded enthusiastically. Not only is it a memorable case study to which students can apply the communication skills and concepts they've read about and heard about in class, but it opens the door for fascinating discussions about students' own intercultural experiences. The key take away for most students is that rapport, like respect, is often communicated not just by what is said but by how it is said. They walk away from the activity with a new appreciation for the role of nonverbal communication in the rapport-building process.

## REFERENCES

Macdonald, K. (Director). (2006). *The last king of Scotland* [film]. Los Angeles, CA: Fox Searchlight Pictures.

Tickle-Degnen, L. & Rosenthal, R. (1990). The nature of rapport and its nonverbal correlates. *Psychological Inquiry*, 1 (4), 285–293.

Wiseman, R. L. (2003). Intercultural communication competence. In W. Gudykunst (Ed.), *Cross-cultural and intercultural communication* (pp. 191–208). Thousand Oaks, CA: Sage.

## APPENDIX

a) Verbal Communication: Are there any words stated during the interaction that communicated respect/disrespect? Which specific words change the course of the interaction in this scenario? (i.e., "Scottish).

b) Paralanguage: Pay close attention to the paralanguage of the doctor and the general during the initial interaction, and note how it changes as time goes on. What differences do you notice in their volume, intonation, and word emphasis as the interaction progresses?

c) Nonverbal Communication Categories: Pay close attention to other types of nonverbal communication used by the doctor and the general during the initial interaction and note how it changes as time goes on. For example, what differences do you notice in their use of space (proxemics), touch (haptics), and facial expression (kinesics) as the interaction progresses?

d) Symbols: What are the meanings of the cow, the exchanged shirts, and the pistol to the *Africans* in this scenario? What are the meanings of the cow, the exchanged shirts, and the pistol to the *Westerners* in this scenario? How might these two members of very different cultures misinterpret the symbols?

# 61

# Exploring the Relationship Between Multiple Identities and Communication Through a Classroom Art Gala

*Tara J. Schuwerk*
*Department of Communication and Media Studies*
*Stetson University*
*tschuwer@stetson.edu*

**History:** This activity was presented at the annual meeting of the Southern States Communication Association, April 2015, in Tampa, Florida.
**Primary courses in which this activity might be used:** Interpersonal Communication, Intercultural Communication
**Concepts illustrated:** Identity, Identities, Identity formation, Culture, Communication

## PURPOSE

Teaching undergraduate students about identities is worthwhile, as it can lead to more interculturally competent communicators. Furthering the understanding of the relationship between who we are and how we communicate with others is rewarding as students develop an appreciation and deeper understanding through their own engagement with the material. This activity, inspired by the "Identity Model Exercise" (Martin & Nakayama, 2014), provides a tool to help undergraduate students learn about identity and communication. This assignment encourages students to create and display a handcrafted artifact that showcases multiple dimensions of their identities. Doing so helps students explicate their own identities, illustrate their understanding of themselves, as well as explore the ways in which people communicate their identity and societal influences contribute to the formation of identity.

Understanding identities and how they are embedded in power, history, and are largely unconscious is important for understanding ourselves and the ways in which we communicate with others. Students may not understand the complexity of their own identities and often see identity as singular. They may also not fully understand how their identities influence their communication. Engaging the students in a way of knowing and expressing that deviates from the typical communication of knowledge in academia allows the students to explore other manifestations of knowledge and also value the body in its ability to create. Valuing art as the medium for the message is highly motivating for the students. This project is empowering for the students, as it increases their confidence in their own understanding of theoretical concepts and their practical skills of recognizing how their multiple identities, as well as others' identities, influence communication.

Students should be able to:

- Identify multiple dimensions of identity (race, age, physical ability, ethnicity, gender, sexual orientation, regional, religious, spiritual, national, familial, individualized, etc).
- Explain how they see their identities and how they have been constructed, including how history and power influence construction (see Martin & Nakayama, 2013; Collier, 2005; Sigelman, Tuch, & Martin, 2005; Tanno, 2012; Witteborn, 2004).
- Understand how identities impact communication.
- Demonstrate their knowledge of these concepts in relation to themselves and others.

## EXPLANATION OF ACTIVITY

Assign appropriate readings and instruct a corresponding lesson on identities. Several key topics that would be appropriate to include would be the relationship between identity formation and communication, the plurality of identity, the influence of society on our identities, the formation and ongoing development of both minority and majority identities in different cultures, as well as social, cultural, and multicultural identities. See chapter 5 in *Intercultural Communication in Contexts* as an example of content on this topic (Martin & Nakayama, 2013).

Explain to your students that the corresponding assignment for this lesson is a creative endeavor that will help them understand issues concerning identity and the part our multiple identities play in our lives and during intercultural communication. Instruct students to reflect on their multiple identities and select a minimum of four (but the number can be as many as the instructor deems appropriate). For example, students may select to highlight their sexual, racial, ethnic, gender, age, class, national, or religious identities. Students are allowed to choose which facets of their identity they wish to share, and are encouraged to consider the risks and rewards associated with the disclosure of certain identities that were previously discussed during the class unit. Students should explore and interrogate each of their selected identities and consider the following:

- Which aspects of their identities are the most important to them?
- Which identities are the most visible to others?
- Which identities are often misunderstood or misinterpreted by others?
- How these identities were constructed, including which dominant discourses have shaped these identities, and how?
- How do these identities influence communication?

Students should then create an artifact (art, craft, or other self-constructed symbol) that communicates these multiple facets of their identity, paying close attention to the points considered above. The project is a creative endeavor; thus the artifact cannot be a simple, pre-constructed slideshow or a poster board written on with a black marker, and must be more than a photo collage. Some students may resist this activity, but often accept the assignment when reassured that they will not be evaluated based on their artistic ability. It is also worthwhile to encourage students by highlighting the idea that engaging in multiple ways of demonstrating knowledge aids in a more thorough under-standing of that knowledge. Another way of inspiring students' creativity and reducing their apprehension is by bringing in past student projects as exam-ples, if available.

The constructed artifacts are then displayed during a gala-like or art exhibit event that can take place during or outside of class time. Students are invited to the art gala by formal invitation (created by the instructor), and are encouraged to interact and appreciate the "identity art" by observing and speaking with the artists.

## DEBRIEF

The artifacts are then used as a catalyst for in-depth discussion of identities, perceptions, and communication ideally as part of the closing of the gala, or as soon afterward as possible to maximize the richness of the experience. The instructor should focus on how the activity helps students analyze various aspects of a person's identity and how creating an artifact representing these identities aids in their understanding of the issues. The instructor should lead the students in a discussion of the concept of multiple identities in relationship to communication while contemplating how identities are socially constructed and related to dominant discourses (Martin & Nakayama, 2013). Additionally, instructors should review with their students the importance of identities as factors in intercultural communication to help connect this activity to the unit readings, lecture, and discussion. Suggested questions to include in this discus-sion are:

- How do you see your identities now, after creating your artifact? How do you see them in relation to your classmates' identities?
- What did you learn about yourself and your classmates from the gala?
- From your gala experience, what connections have become clearer between history, power, and your identities?
- Using an example from the gala, how do identities influence communication?

Students have had positive experiences with this activity and have recom-mended the inclusion of the assignment for future classes. In one class, a stu-dent constructed a miniature house out of cardboard, with each interior room decorated as a representation of a selected identity. Contrastingly, when con-sidering her artifact, the student also recognized that the identities shown to others must be managed and therefore decorated the exterior of the structure with representations of her own external identity as communicated to others. This distinction in her own work demonstrated that she understood the concepts of risk/reward, power, privilege, the societal pressures of identity performance, and how these factors are integral to intercultural communication. The gala discussions about her project, as well as the artifact itself, also helped other students better understand these concepts. Multiple students commented on the tension between identities we willingly share and what is more closely guarded and how that influences communication with others.

## REFERENCES

Collier, M. J. (2005). Theorizing cultural identification: Critical updates and continuing evolution. In W. B. Gudykunst (Ed.), *Theorizing about intercultural communication* (pp. 235–256). Thousand Oaks, CA: Sage.

Martin, J. N., & Nakayama, T. K. (2013). Identity and intercultural communication. In *Intercultural communication in contexts* (6th ed., pp. 169–222). NY; McGraw-Hill.

Martin, J. N., & Nakayama, T. K. (2014). *Experiencing intercultural communication: An introduction—Instructor's manual* (5th ed.). NY; McGraw-Hill.

Sigelman, L., Tuch, S. A., & Martin, J. K. (2005). What's in a name? Preference for "Black" versus "African-American" among Americans of African descent. *Public Opinion Quarterly, 69,* 429–438.

Tanno, D. (2012). Names, narratives, and the evolution of ethnic identity. In A. González, M. Houston, & V. Chen (Eds.), *Our voices: Essays in ethnicity, culture, and communication* (5th ed., pp. 35–38). New York: Oxford.

Witteborn, S. (2004). Of being an Arab woman before and after September 11: The enactment of communal identities in talk. *Howard Journal of Communications, 15,* 83–98.

# 62

## Using *The Hunger Games* to Teach Intercultural Communication

*Karen McGrath*

*Department of Communications*

*College of Saint Rose*

*mcgrathk@strose.edu*

**History:** This activity was presented at the annual meeting of the New York State Communication Association, October 2014, in Liberty, New York.

**Primary courses in which the activity might be used:** Intercultural Communication, Communication and Gender

**Concepts illustrated:** Privilege, Oppression, Race, Class, and Gender

### PURPOSE

One of the toughest challenges teachers face is how to engage students and maintain quality learning standards. One way to embrace this challenge is to ask students to actively analyze popular culture artifacts (e.g., films, TV shows, comic books, etc.), because doing so engages students and provides teachers opportunities to play to current student strengths and interests while also maintaining their own academic integrity (Boyd, 2004; Merolla, 2009; Proctor and Adler, 1991; Wilson, 2004). Simmons (2012), for example, effectively engages millennials by using *The Hunger Games* trilogy to encourage social action with her students through examination of issues of violence and domination in our world (pp. 23–28).

Since *The Hunger Games* appeals to a largely preteen-to-adult female audience, and many others who saw the film, it is a novel that invokes much student interest (young men may initially be a bit hesitant if they think it appeals to young women only, but they too ultimately enjoy the story), and has proven useful in the classroom.

While students can discuss the plot, most haven't used it to analyze intercultural concepts discussed in an assigned textbook for a formal course. Since most students indicate they rarely read books unless they are assigned for class (*Harry Potter* is an exception), I include the novel in the first few weeks of class to provide a context for intercultural concepts present in the course and to prompt students to read, apply, and analyze course content. Specifically, this activity addresses issues of privilege and oppression while also discussing other intercultural communication concepts such as identity development, values, and power, in an accessible context.

## EXPLANATION OF ACTIVITY

During the first class discussion, I introduce Linda Holtzman's (2013) "The Fabric of Oppression and Social Group Membership" model, which distinguishes people who are privileged from those who are oppressed, based on various social categories including race, class, sex, and sexual orientation (p. 27). For example, race, as a primary social category, positions whites as privileged and all others as oppressed, based on how people are positioned in the world. Peggy McIntosh's (2014) essay excerpt "White Privilege: Unpacking the Invisible Knapsack" is a terrific supplement for this activity as she acknowledges how her own whiteness has encouraged her to avoid seeing how she benefits from the system in place, including mundane events like buying "skin-colored" Band-Aids (Rothenberg, 2016). These two supplemental readings posted online focus students on issues of privilege and oppression.

To further clarify these concepts, I use the term *whammy* for those who are oppressed because it identifies social categories that don't offer as many opportunities in the social system. For example, using my own race, sex, and class as examples, I discuss how I have one *whammy* based on my sex—female. I identify myself as a white, upper-middle class female. I then give examples of sex inequity and remind them that the Equal Rights Amendment has not yet been ratified. I then ask them to think about how many *whammies* they each have, based on these three categories alone. This provides an opportunity for students to reflect on their own social positions in the world during the first week of online participation.

If you prefer full in-class meeting days, then convert the online discussions into classroom activities. If you don't wish to commit five weeks to this book, then you could assign it as an end of the semester read, and assign an analytic essay to assess student understanding, or you could even spend a week or two on the book's content and assess learning in ways you find most suitable. I prefer to slowly progress through the content to provide opportunities for repetition, which seems to aid in student learning.

Second, during weeks two through five, we discuss (via an online content management system and class discussion) Katniss and relevant others in the book. Over the course of these weeks, students are assigned key chapters in a primary intercultural textbook, such as Martin and Nakayama's (2014) *Experiencing Intercultural Communication* that focuses on nonverbal communication; identity development; the roles of different histories in our lives, especially political, national, and family histories; and also assign a collection of essays, such as Paula Rothenberg's (2016) edited book titled *Race, Class, and Gender in the US,* which offers readings focused on privilege, oppression, race, class, and gender; and, a class handout that provides more depth, definitions, and examples to further clarify key concepts (see Appendix A, p. 259). We then discuss how these concepts are present in Katniss's world and our own. (Without supplemental and primary readings and handouts that clarify these concepts, the use of *The Hunger Games* will not be as effective.) For example, we focus on how her district is positioned in terms of social class by reminding each other that "[i]n the United States, one is born into a family that can be identified as working class, middle class, or wealthy, both objectively and subjectively. These divisions denote status, expectations, location, and power as defined by access to resources" (Lott, 2012, p. 650).

For Katniss, District 12 is one where coal mining is primary for males and child-rearing and nurturing are women's roles. When a parent dies, the living parent has to adapt, as do the children, and daily survival is made almost impossible by those in charge from District One. People struggle to eat on a daily basis and hunting outside the fence is illegal, yet food sources are more readily available there; controlling resources creates power for the ruling class. We also discuss the bartering system within the districts and in the games themselves, which helps people survive their conditions, identify and use available resources (i.e., physical strength, hunting abilities, intellect, and position), and discuss how the environment (e.g., district) of which they are a part further informs class and social position.

## DEBRIEF

During each in-class discussion we clarify *privilege* as opportunities afforded to one group of people because of the social system currently in place, and note that this system is based on race, sex, class, and other social categories, such as religion; the *oppressed* are those who do not benefit from the social system in place based on those same social categories. We use current events, US and world history (e.g., Japanese internment and the treatment of Native Americans in the US, the Holocaust, refugee crises, etc.), and Peggy Macintosh's (2014) article for support of our claims. I also expand the discussion of social class by asking students to consider how President Snow is positioned and positions others via these "games," and how even the word *games* differently positions them. I then ask students to reflect on Katniss's social class, sex, and gender in discussing the hunger games so they can begin to see her *whammies* and how those might change, even temporarily, during the course of the book.

Specifically, I ask students to consider how Katniss's life differs before and after she volunteers in terms of her own privilege and oppression, assess how she feels about that, and to reflect on where she is in her identity development. Clearly, there are many intercultural concepts that can be applied to this book and prove helpful in clarifying course concepts.

In addition to class discussion, students take two short answer quizzes during weeks two and five whereby they define and analyze course concepts using examples from the novel (see Appendix B, p. 262). In week six, they are assigned an analytic essay about *The Hunger Games* that asks them to discuss how privilege and oppression are apparent in the book by focusing on either Katniss or President Snow (see Appendix B, p. 262). Specifically, they are also asked to consider how other concepts such as identity development, history, or power play out, and help contextualize privilege and oppression. What I notice is that with online discussion, class discussion, short quizzes, and exam questions, students typically demonstrate a firm understanding of the material through repetition and application. They also use course evaluations to express how helpful *The Hunger Games* was in making sense of course concepts.

## REFERENCES

Boyd, J. (2004). A different kind of [text]book: Using fiction in the classroom. *Communication Education* 53.4, pp. 340–347. Web. doi:10.10/036345203000305940. *Communication &Mass Media Complete*. 28 Jan. 2013.

Holtzman, L. (8 Feb. 2013). The fabric of oppression and social group membership. *Media Messages*. Google Books. Web.

Lott, B. (Nov. 2012). The social psychology of class and classism. *American Psychologist*, pp. 650–658. Web. doi: 10.1037/a0029369. *Academic Search Premier*. 28 Jan. 2013.

Martin, J. N., & Nakayama, T. K. (2014). *Experiencing intercultural communication— an introduction* (6th ed.) NY: McGraw-Hill.

McIntosh, P. (2014). White privilege: Unpacking the invisible knapsack. In *Race, Class, and Gender in the United States* (8th ed.). Ed. P. S. Rothenberg. NY: Worth, pp. 165–169.

Merolla, A. J. (2009). Utilizing contemporary short fiction in the interpersonal communication classroom. In *Communication Teacher*, 23(1), pp. 7–10. Web. doi: 10.1080/17404620802581869. *Communication & Mass Media Complete*, 28 Jan. 2013.

Proctor, R.F., II, & Adler, R.B. (1991). Teaching interpersonal communication with feature films. In *Communication Education* 40 (1991): 393–400. Web. *Communication & mass media complete*, 8 Feb. 2013.

Simmons, A. M. (2012). "Class on fire: Using the hunger games trilogy to encourage social action." *Journal of Adolescent & Adult Literacy* 56(1), pp. 22–34. Web. doi: 10.1002/JAAL.0099. *Communication & mass media complete*. 28 Jan. 2013.

Wilson, M. E. (2004). Teaching, learning, and millennial students. In *New Directions for Student Services*, 106, pp. 59–71. Web. *Academic Search Premier*. 28 Jan. 2013.

## APPENDIX A

### Class Handout for Gender, Race, and Fabric of Oppression

#### Sex and Gender Defined:

| Sex | Gender |
|---|---|
| Biologically determined | Culturally constructed and performed (Butler, 1990) |
| Has to do with physiology (DNA, hormones, genitalia) | Social Norms and Assumptions |
| Male/Female | Masculine/Feminine |
| Some children are born intersexed (hermaphrodites) | Performance can be androgynous |

One's sex is thought of as primary in US culture. Typically we learn to be good males and good females by performing appropriate masculinity and femininity within our specific environments. Therefore, males usually perform more masculine behaviors, and females usually perform more feminine behaviors. The cultural expectations for these gender performances differ across cultures.

### Race Defined

Biological characteristics such as the color of one's skin, one's genetic makeup, and one's hair texture are often assumed to be defining features of race. However, throughout US history, the US government engaged in racial reorganization, especially in the late 1800s and early 1900s, such that scholars tend to agree that race is not simply a biological characteristic. Instead, it is a political, social, economic, and cultural construct that can be, and has been, defined and changed over time (Hochschild, 2008). For example, Mexicans were once classified as white based on established race categories; but over time, the categories were expanded such that the cultural and economic climate changed the cultural categorization of Mexicans. Once considered white, Mexicans were then considered nonwhite, and would now have social status similar to that as blacks in the culture at that time. As we know, prior to the advent of Civil Rights, blacks were not (and still are often not) highly valued in this culture. Another example is the Chinese, whose race was declared nonwhite only after the national climate of the times changed; since so many white men were without jobs while Chinese men were working, racial categories were redefined, and by default, so were the Chinese. Therefore politics, economics, and social and cultural norms influenced, and still do, who was white and nonwhite. One final example, though not a US example, comes from the aborigines of Australia, whose children were taken from them at a young age, and should the British government declare the lighter-skinned aborigine children white, they would be educated and assimilated into white culture. However, should the children not be light enough as defined by this political, cultural, economic, and social climate, they would be trained to be house servants (women) or field workers (men) to work for the whites (see Phillip Noyce's *Rabbit Proof Fence* and Delany & Delany's *Having Our Say*).

## Types of Racism

There are two types of racism: Overt and covert, and these can happen at two different levels: individual or institutional.

The use of the following terms can be done with any *-ism* such as sexism, heterosexism (often expressed as homophobia), ageism, able-bodiedism (no physical disability), etc.

**Overt:** Blatant and obvious; not hidden, but open.

**Covert:** Subtle; often not considered an *-ism* until closer analysis is done.

**Individual:** A person commits acts against others that are prejudicial or discriminatory. These individuals may be part of a group, but are not identified as part of a formal organization or government. For example, a group of young men who all go to the same junior high school may jump a black male student because he is black, but the young men's behavior would be categorized as "overt individual racism" since it is not the school (the organization) that supports these students in these ideas and behaviors.

**Institutional:** The structure or climate of an organization, town, state, or government commits acts against others that are viewed as prejudicial or discriminatory. For example, the immigration fence to be built in Arizona or Native American children forced by the US government to attend white schools and learn white culture.

**Overt Individual Racism:** I beat you up because you are black, or I choose not to hire you because you are black (insert various race categories here).

> This can happen with heterosexism—I beat you up because you are gay.
> Or any other *-ism* (a group not in the dominant group).

**Covert Individual Racism:** I have negative thoughts about you because you are Mexican (or another race category), and therefore I don't interact with you even for casual conversation, but am not really aware that I do this.

**Overt Institutional Racism:** Jim Crow Laws, whereby the government says which fountain whites can drink from and nonwhites can drink from; "separate but equal" didn't really mean *equal*. The imprisonment of Japanese Americans immediately after the bombing of Pearl Harbor. The removal of Native Americans from their land (Trail of Tears).

**Covert Institutional Racism**: Check out who is in positions of power; check out how education funds are based on tax brackets; check out who gets hired and what policies are in place to ensure that hiring.

**Fabric of Oppression Defined**: Discussed in Linda Holtzman and Leon Sharpe's *Media Messages*, this theory suggests that in every culture there are groups that are privileged and those that are oppressed. The privileged groups have opportunities not provided to other groups because of the current social system in place and may not recognize that they benefit from the system. See Peggy McIntosh's article entitled "Unpacking the Invisible Knapsack" (as cited in Rothenberg, 2016) for further clarification. This fabric of oppression is woven throughout societies and is not easy (is often impossible given cultural mores) to reverse. In American culture, currently, the fabric of oppression looks this way where privileged groups are located on the top and oppressed groups are located on the bottom:

| White | Male | Upper | Christianity | Able-bodied |
|---|---|---|---|---|
| **Race** | **Sex** | **Class** | **Religion** | **Able-bodiedness, etc.** |
| Other(s) | Female | Middle | Other(s) | People with |
| Blacks, | | Lower | Muslims, Jews | Disabilities |
| Hispanics, etc. | | Poor | Buddhists, etc. | |

The more privilege you experience across categories, the more opportunities you will have. Those on the bottom will experience oppression (overtly or covertly), and the more categories they fill on the bottom, the fewer opportunities they will have. Who has the most privilege? White, upper class, Christian males with able bodies.

Who has the least privilege? Perhaps a Hispanic, the working poor, a Muslim female with a physical disability? The female here may experience oppression as a woman, as a person whose religion is not Christianity, and/or as working poor. Her chances to experience oppression are much greater than someone privileged in all categories.

This handout provides a context by which we can learn about other cultures and ourselves. While you may not feel privileged on multiple levels, chances are when dealing with issues of race and sex, you still reap the benefits of the system in place. One purpose for this handout is to ask you to begin to see some of this privilege and oppression in actual news accounts and through our course readings (*The Hunger Games*) and assigned videos/films.

## REFERENCES FOR CLASS HANDOUT

Butler, J. (1990). *Gender trouble*. NY: Routledge.

Delany, S. L., and Delany, A. E. (1993). *Having our say*. NY: Dell Publishing.

Hochschild J. L, and Powell, B. M. (2008). Racial reorganization and the United States census 1850-1930: Mulattoes, half-breeds, mixed parentage, hindoos, and the Mexican race. *Studies in American Political Development*, *22*(1), pp. 59–96.

Holtzman, L., and Sharpe, L. (2014). *Media messages: What film, television, and popular music teach us about race, class, gender, and sexual orientation* (2nd. Ed.). NY: Taylor & Francis.

Noyce, Phillip. Dir. (2000). *Rabbit proof fence*. Miramax. DVD.

Rothenberg, P. (2016). *Race, class, and gender in the United States* (10th ed.). NY: Worth Publishers.

West C., and Zimmerman, D. H. (1987). Doing gender. *Gender & Society, 1*, pp. 127–151.

## APPENDIX B

### Quiz 1—Short Answer Question (5 points)

Using examples from *The Hunger Games* as your guide, discuss two ways in which Katniss is considered oppressed. In your answer, be sure to define privilege and oppression.

### Quiz 2—Short Answer Question (5 points)

1. Using two examples from *The Hunger Games* as your guide, discuss how privilege and oppression are present in the structure of the actual hunger games. (2 points)
2. Using three examples from *The Hunger Games* as your guide, explain how Katniss uses her privilege or challenges her oppression regarding her gender, race, and/or class in your response. (3 points)

### Assigned Book Analysis—Take Home Essay (20 points)

In essay form, explain how *The Hunger Games*, reflects issues of privilege and oppression related to gender, race, or class, as discussed in class and in the course materials. You must cite examples from the book and also **cite at least three** distinct course materials such as videos, essays, class notes, handouts, and the textbook that help you make your case. You should choose either Katniss or President Snow as your focal point. Remember that privilege and oppression can be connected to histories, identities, power, cultural differences, etc., and may provide a strong context for your essay. This is your opportunity to demonstrate your understanding of course materials, concepts, and theories, and to write a coherent, well-supported essay. (Student samples are included in the course management system.)

# 63

## Melting Pot or Garden Salad: Draw a Metaphor

*Jacqueline Barker*
Professor of Communication
St. Louis Community College at Meramec
jbarker@stlcc.edu

**History:** This activity was presented at the annual meeting of the National Communication Association convention, in San Antonio, Texas, in November 2006. It was selected as "A Best of the Best Submission" and was designated the #1 submission that year.
**Primary courses in which this activity might be used:** Intercultural Communication, Interracial Communication, Media and Culture, Oral Communication
**Concepts illustrated:** Metaphors of the US culture such as Melting Pot, Tapestry, Tributaries, Garden Salad; Cultural Identity; Acculturation; Diversity; Global Village; Language

### PURPOSE

The purpose of this activity is to get students to learn and dissect common metaphors that describe the diversity of the United States. In the process of drawing and discussing the metaphors, students begin to see the depth of the concepts as well as related themes, issues, strengths, and weaknesses. The goals of this class activity are to:

- Learn metaphors of US American culture such as *melting pot*, *tapestry*, and *garden salad*
- Explore the functions of metaphors
- Discuss the pros and cons of existing metaphors which describe the diversity of the US American culture
- Connect the concepts of global village, identity, and culture
- Collaborate with classmates
- Present a drawing to the rest of the class to prompt discussion class-wide
- Have fun and be creative

Metaphors have long been used to describe the unique diversity of the US culture. Most students, for example, have heard of the *melting pot* concept. Although this idea is still referenced, many newer metaphors have been offered to capture the uniqueness of the US culture. Discussing the intricacies of a metaphor as well as drawing one, will allow students to grapple with deeper cultural issues such as identity, communication, separation versus integration, marginalization, power, and many other possible implications.

Additionally, simply asking students to discuss the pros and cons of abstract concepts sometimes results in a blank stare. This activity has worked well to get students to engage in a creative process, drawing. As the group formulates the physical picture of their metaphor, ideas and reflections are a natural product.

This activity engages the students in lateral thinking; rather than telling them what the final destination will look like, they discover it on their own. It also allows for an action-oriented learning through drawing, providing an opportunity for kinesthetic and visual learners.

## EXPLANATION OF ACTIVITY

For this activity, four metaphors of US culture are used. Others could be easily substituted. (This activity could easily be transformed into "Metaphors of Communication.") The four metaphors are melting pot, tapestry, tributaries, and garden salad. The four metaphors are simply mentioned but not explained in too much depth. There is material in many intercultural communication textbooks that discusses these metaphors or similar ones (e.g., Lustig & Koester, 2013). Any US cultural metaphors would be appropriate.

Give students an activity description sheet similar to the one in the Appendix, p. 265. Instruct them to form into four groups. In their group they first must *draw the metaphor* as a group. They can use whatever tools they have handy; if they have any markers, pens, or other assorted items, they can enhance their drawing in any way they choose. You can also bring paper and crayons/pencils for this activity. However, I find that having the students combine their own tools brings a cohesiveness and spontaneity to the activity.

As the group is drawing the metaphor, they also need to *brainstorm the pros and cons* of the metaphor. Students are instructed to make two lists: the advantages this metaphor offers in describing US American culture and the disadvantages it presents. After the drawings and brainstorming is complete, the groups present their artwork and pros/cons to their classmates. These presentations open the door to a larger class discussion on the various components of the metaphors, the accuracies and inaccuracies, and the important issues to consider when trying to explain the diversity of the US.

Students usually perceive this activity favorably because it is a break from routine. The drawing component allows for creativity and something out of the ordinary. Visualizing metaphors can bring additional perspectives that reading about them cannot. This activity is one of the easiest ways to bring about a discussion of the implications of all the metaphors such as growth and change, immigration issues, separatism versus blending of cultures, and many others.

## DEBRIEF

Displaying the drawings for the class and having the group explain the pros and cons opens the discussion up to the rest of the class. Usually students are quick to point out cultural problems such as the struggle for blending and maintaining one's own identity; power differences and issues, and many others. Some prompting questions can be used to bring out ideas about many related concepts. For example, I often ask the students what their favorite metaphor is and why. Also I may ask, what is the difference between the *melting pot* and the *salad bowl*? A way to carry this activity further would be to have students come up with a new metaphor to describe the United States, and produce a drawing of it along with implications, pros and cons.

Typically, students are slightly skeptical about this activity in the beginning. They sometimes need assurance that this is not an art class, and that they are not getting judged on the merits of their drawing. However, as students start pulling out pens, pencils, and markers there is a change in their approach. Often someone in the group will want to be the artist; sometimes the group will pass the paper around and each will contribute. It is exciting to watch the creative process unfold.

The brainstormed pros and cons that result from the activity are usually much more in depth than a simple class discussion tends to generate. Having to conceptualize what the metaphor looks like allows for greater connection to the abstract ideas. For example, identity is an important concept. When students compare the melting pot to the garden salad, it is very clear that the identity issue is completely different. This does allow for a more thorough examination of the identity notion.

Groups are usually impressed with their drawings and the drawings of others when this activity is over. The creative process provides a different path to understanding a concept, which allows for more learners to be affected.

## REFERENCES

Dodd, C.H. (1998). *Dynamics of intercultural communication (5th ed.)*. Boston, MA: McGraw Hill.
Lustig, M.W. & Koester, J. (2013). *Intercultural competence* (7th ed.). Boston, MA: Pearson.

## APPENDIX

## DRAW AND DISCUSS A METAPHOR

**Goals:**   Learn the four cultural metaphors
Discuss strengths and weaknesses
Report to the class
Use creativity and collaboration

Your group is assigned one of the four cultural metaphors (melting pot, tributaries, tapestry, and garden salad).

In your group, draw a picture of what this metaphor looks like. Use whatever tools you have with you, and draw one picture for the whole group. Brainstorm the strengths and weaknesses of the cultural metaphor in describing the US culture. Make two lists as a result of your brainstorming: Pros and Cons.

Report your strengths and weaknesses to the rest of the class, and be prepared to show your work of art.

# 64

## Why Are All the International Students Sitting Together in the Cafeteria?: Teaching About Cultural Adaptation Through Community Engagement

*Paula Hentz*

WORLD: *The David and Leighan Rinker Center for International Learning Stetson University*

*phentz@stetson.edu*

*Jelena Petrovic*

*Department of Communication and Media Studies*
*Stetson University*

*jpetrov1@stetson.edu*

**History:** This activity was presented at the annual meeting of the National Communication Association, November 2015, in Las Vegas, Nevada.

**Primary courses in which this activity might be used:** Intercultural Communication

**Concepts illustrated:** Cultural Adaptation, Cultural Identity, Intercultural Friendships

### PURPOSE

In 2015, the United States was a home to nearly a million international students (Open Doors, 2015). As this student population increases, universities need to ensure the successful integration of international students into American culture and classrooms. By partnering with the university's International Student Services Office (ISSO), intercultural communication students can support this growing population of international students on our campuses and apply the theory they learn in class. Semester-long engagement with international students exposes the nonlinear nature of cultural adaptation as a person experiences uprooting and a range of cultural shocks, while adapting to a new cultural context, educational system, and the need to develop new inter-personal relationships (Chen, 2003; Hwang, Bennett, & Beauchemin, 2014; Szabo, Ward, & Jose, 2015). Collaboration with the ISSO addresses this issue and enables the exchange of experiences between students in a manner that is both beneficial for all involved, but also critical of "othering" of international students who are often marked by their cultural difference (Margison, 2010). This project prioritizes the development of meaningful intercultural friend-ships to promote socially just intercultural praxis, which in turn makes it less likely that the students will treat experiences of their intercultural partners as means to an end (Ramen, 1998; Sorrells, 2010). Finally, through research and continuous interactions with their intercultural partners, students develop interpersonal skills and learn how to communicate with people of different cultural backgrounds, while paying attention to intersectionality and ways in which educational institution affects those relationships.

## EXPLANATION OF ACTIVITY

Throughout the course of a semester, students create a proposal for a proj-ect that reflects the experiences and needs of international students on cam-pus. The project could be a campus initiative, event, or media piece that the ISSO could do in the future (i.e., students are not putting this proposal into action). Examples might include a proposal for a video series on culture shock, the American Greek Life system, or challenges in US classrooms; a student-run radio show covering topics, such as international student athletes or cultural representations; a series of handouts for international students on how to move around via public transportation, get involved on campus, or use com-mon American slang terms; or a virtual peer-to-peer mentoring system.

Over the course of sixteen weeks, students work individually and in their small groups on various parts of this proposal through research, group meet-ings, attendance of events hosted by the ISSO, and interactions with interna-tional students. Of these, the most important are usually individual interviews and focus groups with international students in which participants discuss their experiences of studying and living in the US, propose the topics that should guide the group projects, and comment on them.

There are seven steps that ensure that students develop the proposal in the manner that promotes intercultural dialogue and cultural immersion.

1. The instructor builds a relationship with the ISSO prior to the start of the semester to identify goals, challenges, and the type of practical sup-port that the ISSO can offer to students involved in this process. Topics to discuss include types of projects that would be beneficial for all par-ties, time the ISSO can to commit to the project, schedule for check-in meetings throughout the semester, involvement of ISSO in the classes (e.g., attending final projects, holding a class in the ISSO building/office if possible), and organization of events, where students from the class

can meet and interact with international students in a non-classroom setting.

2. Once the semester starts, the instructor forms groups of three to four students and builds in class-time for the students to develop community among themselves (e.g., small-group class discussions, group visits to ISSO). After two weeks, groups should schedule a meeting with a designated ISSO representative to establish the scope and format of their individual and group engagement in the project.

3. By the end of the first month and in consultation with the other group members, each student crafts her or his own contract that establishes the level of individual engagement with the project. This allows students to identify the duration and format of their engagement, weekly tasks, and personal and group goals. The contract also allows students to personally invest in the project and create a list of commitments that reflect their skills, interests, and academic and personal schedules. The contract is reviewed, approved, and signed by the instructor, the ISSO, and all group members. See Appendix A, p. 271, for more details.

4. Throughout the semester, students must document their work on the project with field notes. These might include outlines of read articles, notes from group meetings, a summary of research activity, diary, interview transcripts, etc. Students can use these field notes to reflect on their interactions with international students who might be their interviewees, friends, and group members (who often also act as cultural insiders). Instructors can use the field notes to assess students' adherence to their contracts and overall engagement.

5. Students conduct research in the form of two papers. The first paper focuses on the history and the current issues affecting the international students with whom students in class are working. The second paper is an ethnographic analysis of cultural identities that are important for these international students. Through these assignments students learn about macro and micro level factors that affect cultural adaptation. See Appendix B, p. 271, for details.

6. At the midpoint students take an oral exam with their group. The exam is conducted as a semi-structured conversation in which the instructor serves as a facilitator. The purpose of the exam is for students to articulate the connections between theory and their group project. Sample questions might include "What theoretical concept helped you the most in your group project, and why?" and "Based on the theories you studied in class, what are the strengths and weaknesses of your project so far?"

7. At the end of the semester, students submit final versions of their project proposals, and orally present their project to their peers, instructor, international students, and ISSO representatives. If possible, hold the at the ISSO building or office.

## DEBRIEF

During step six, students receive immediate feedback on both their knowledge and work on the group project. For example, the instructor may ask at the end of the exam, "How will you move forward with the project using the topics discussed in class and in this exam?" and "What did you do to acknowledge the diversity of voices and experiences of your community partners?" For this occasion, students often point to the importance of examining their assumptions about the needs of populations with whom they are working, honing in on a specific topic or group of international students, getting and using the feedback on different stages of the project from international students, and expanding beyond their own friendship networks and reaching out to students of different races, nationalities, and immigration statuses. During step seven, the students and their audience are able to engage in intercultural dialogue, and cultural partners and the ISSO have an opportunity to evaluate the project, overall student's engagement, and how well each student fulfilled his or her individual contract. In the process, students receive constructive feedback and an opportunity to reflect on their own learning.

## REFERENCES

Chen, L. (2004). How we know what we know about Americans: Chinese sojourners account for their experiences. In A. Gonzales, M. Houston, & V. Chen (Eds.), *Our voices: Essays in culture, ethnicity, and communication* (pp. 266–273). New York, NY: Oxford University Press.

Hwang, B., Bennett, R., & Beauchemin, J. (2014). International students' utilization of counseling services. *College Student Journal, 48*(3), 347–354.

Margison, S. (June 27, 2010). Here's how we can end the threats to international students. *The Chronicle of Higher Education.* Retrieved February 10, 2016, from http://chronicle.com/article/International-Students-Are-at/66051/

Open Doors, Institute of International Education (2015, November 16). *IIE Releases Open Doors 2015 Data* [Press release]. Retrieved February 9, 2016 from http://www.iie.org/Who-We-Are/News-and-Events/Press-Center/Press-Releases/2015/2015-11-16-Open-Doors-Data

Remen, R. N. (1998). In the service of life. *MERIDIANS-COLUMBIA, 5,* 15–16.

Szabo, A., Ward, C., & Jose, P. E. (2015). Uprooting stress, coping, and anxiety: A longitudinal study of international students. *International Journal of Stress Management.* http://dx.doi.org/10.1037/a0039771

Sorrells, K. (2010). Re-imagining intercultural communication in the context of globalization. In T.K. Nakayama & R. T. Halualani (Eds.), *The handbook of critical intercultural communication* (pp. 171–189). United Kingdom: Blackwell Publishing.

## APPENDIX A

### INDIVIDUAL CONTRACT

**PURPOSE:** The goal of the contract is not to create more work for you, but to allow you to design very specific guidelines for yourself and your group. This will help you channel your energy and work, collaborate more successfully as a group, and minimize stress. Finally, the contract is a tool by which you will tell me how I should grade your involvement in this community engagement project, and how I should grade your group members, and how the ISSO should evaluate that engagement. This contract needs to emerge as a result of at least two group meetings, after which you can craft your individual contracts. Below you will find items you should include in your contracts:

- Name:
- Group members:
- Group goals:
- Individual goals:
- The skills and interests I can bring to this project:
- The tasks I want to complete for this group project:
- Number of hours per week I will devote solely for this project:

**Signature**

                                     **Date**

**Signatures of group members, instructor, and ISSO representative**

                                     **Date**

## APPENDIX B

### PAPER PROMPTS

**Paper #1:** Write a four-page paper in which you will **DESCRIBE** your community partner, or more precisely, a group of international students you are currently working with. The focus should be on the political, social, and cultural context, and specifically the history of this cultural group or the history of the issues this cultural group may face at our university. In other words, provide a background or a backstory you have learned from this cultural group and from your independent external research.

> TIP: Check the university library that has archives of the student newspapers and other materials that document our university's history.

**Paper #2:** Write a four-page paper in which you will **ANALYZE** cultural identities and experiences that are significant for the international students you are currently working with. The focus should be on their cultural identities (race, gender, nationality, ethnicity, sexuality, class, etc.), and the ways in which they are manifested in nonverbal and verbal communication. In other words, you should discuss the aspects of cultural identity that matter to this cultural group as its members move through the campus environment. You can present this as a story of one person, or you can advance an analysis that speaks about a particular and relevant cultural identity in general terms.

# Group and Organizational Communication

# 65

# NBC's *The Office* and Working with New Employees: A Lesson in Organizational Socialization

*Kyle B. Heuett, Ph.D.*
*Ball State University*
*Dept. of Communication Studies*
*kbheuett@bsu.edu*

**History:** This activity was presented at the annual meeting of the Southern States Communication Association, April 2016, in Austin, Texas.
**Primary courses in which this activity might be used:** Organizational Communication, Business Communication, Leadership Communication, Small Group Communication
**Concepts illustrated:** Organizational Socialization, Organizational Entry, New Comer Information Seeking Strategies, and Organizational Assimilation

## PURPOSE

Of the topics covered in organizational (or related) communication courses, socialization may be one of the most overwhelming to students due to the complexity of the socialization process. At the macro level, organizational socialization is the process of bringing new employees or members into an existing organization (Miller & Jablin, 1991; Chao, O'Leary-Kelly, Wolf, Klein, & Gardner, 1994). Breaking down the socialization process further, we find two branches of socialization. First, organizational entry is considered any attempt by the organization to help new employees learn their role and often includes such activities as new employee orientation, or pairing employees with mentors (Ashford & Black, 1996). Second, newcomer strategies constitute the attempts new employees make to learn their own role in an organization. This could include asking direct questions or merely observing others to learn more about behavioral expectations. With several strategies outlined in both organizational entry and newcomer strategies, students may find it difficult to grasp the overall socialization process and its necessity to organizational communication (Sumanth & Cable, 2011). Further, it is unlikely that students are able to draw on past experience to help make sense of the entirety of the socialization process. While students do experience some elements of socialization into student groups, community groups, sports teams, and part- or full-time jobs, the probability that students have experienced socialization in the same way or to the depth they will encounter when entering a career is low (Kramer, 2010).

This activity is designed to provide a learning activity to aid in processing the information associated with socialization using an episode of *The Office*. This documentary-style sitcom is based around a small paper company in the northeast region of the United States. Typically episodes include humorous displays of leadership, interpersonal communication, and organizational communication that serve as good examples of what should not be done in professional communication settings.

## EXPLANATION OF ACTIVITY

Prior to watching the episode, it is good to thoroughly cover organizational socialization, organizational entry, and newcomer strategies (see Miller, 2015, pp. 119–138). In the past this activity has been a success when Monday and Wednesday are used as lecture/discussion days and the episode is shown on Friday. Or to lecture Tuesday and the first half of Thursday, followed by watching the episode during the second half of Thursday's class. If class times vary, it is recommended that the first two-thirds of class time for the week be spent in discussion or lecture on socialization material, and the last one-third of the time given to completing the activity. This activity is dependent on students being able to identify organizational entry and newcomer information seeking strategies, and thus is not conducive to watching the episode first, followed by lecture and discussion. By following this schedule, information is salient to students and they do not have to refer back to notes too often as they watch the episode.

Organizational socialization is highlighted in an episode titled "The Merger." In this episode, a branch office of the company has been shut down and the remaining employees are assigned to a new branch office. The episode focuses on the first day of work for the new employees. Some of the highlights include the preparation and welcome that takes place on the part of the new office, the feelings new and existing employees have toward one another, and how the new employees react to new work situations.

Throughout the episode, several instances of socialization, organizational entry, and newcomer strategies unfold. The episode allows students the opportunity to see the socialization process and recognize strategies used by new employees and organizations. The full episode is twenty-two minutes long, and originally aired as the eighth episode of the third season. "The Merger" can be found on Netflix, purchased on iTunes for $2.99, or YouTube for $1.99, or may be available to rent as part of the season three DVDs from your university or public library.

Before starting the episode, each student should have a piece of paper and something to write with. Students are instructed to separate their paper into four equal squares by drawing one vertical and one horizontal line. The top left square is for writing down what the organization does well to help new employees socialize to the organization, and the top right square is for recording what the organization did not do well or could have done better in terms of trying to socialize new employees. The bottom left square is for recording what the new employees did well to help socialize themselves to the new organization, and the bottom right square is for recording things that the new employees did not do well or could have done better to help themselves socialize. Given the comedic nature of the show there is no lack of bad examples of what both the organization and new employees could have done better. However, there is a surprising amount of things both the organization and new employees do well.

## DEBRIEF

After the episode has completed, the remaining time is spent asking students to share examples of successful and unsuccessful socialization attempts by the organization and new employees. Initial questions to the class may be as simple as "So what did you notice?" More in-depth questions that have been successful at sustaining discussion include "What did the organization/new employees do that you would have liked if you were a new employee in this situation, and why?" or similarly, "What did the organization/new employees do that you would not have liked if you were a new employee in this situation, and why?" Instructors should make an effort to tie examples from the episode back to the previous week's lecture and connect the principles for students.

For example, the boss, Michael, plans a lunch for everyone in the office. This strategy allows new and existing employees to meet, become acquainted, and remove some of the "new person" stigma that can accompany new employees. However, Michael also reveals that only the "new people" in the office are allowed to eat the food provided. What started out as a potentially successful strategy to allow all employees to communicate quickly becomes a poor example of privileging new employees too much during the early stages of socialization.

Also, during the episode, an existing employee, Dwight, and a new employee, Andy, encounter conflict when it becomes unclear who reports to whom in the organization, resulting in competition and petty power tactics between the two for much of the episode. This example provides for some in-depth discussion of the role taking, role making, and role routinization phases, especially what can happen when the organization fails to clarify this process for employees.

I find this is a successful way to help students differentiate the material associated with socialization and both organization entry and newcomer strategies. Further questions to the class should focus in on requiring the class to critically think about what they saw in the episode and how it relates to socialization. These questions might include "So what could the organization/new employees have done differently in a given situation to help with [insert socialization element, i.e., achieving role routinization, or cohesion among new and existing employees]?" Further, instructors might ask in general what the organization, leadership, or new employees might have done differently to change a negative example to a positive one or to change a socialization tactic from a good one to a better one. These questions allow instructors to address both the consequences of successful socialization and unsuccessful socialization practices.

Using this method for engaging students in the socialization process has been quite successful in getting students to increase discussion of class principles, and is often drawn upon in subsequent discussions in class. As observed by the instructors, classes engaging in this activity tend to recall socialization strategies more easily than classes who receive the lecture only. Further, as many examples in the episode are bad examples of what should not be done during the socialization process, each of these serve as a discussion starter for students to turn these scenarios around and discuss how they might be turned into successful strategies for socialization. When writing exams, it is helpful to be able to put a short-answer question requiring students to pick an example from the episode and highlight which socialization strategy is at play, and why it was/was not successful. One final benefit of using this activity is the light-hearted nature that comes with discussing socialization via comedy. Students tend to be more open when such a major organizational communication topic is met with humor. With the array of strategies that are associated with socialization, even to cover the basics includes a lot of information and this activity seems to reinvigorate the students and allow them to see what could be labeled as serious or heavy information in a lighter way.

## REFERENCES

Ashford, S. J., & Black, J. S. (1996). Proactivity during organization entry: The role of desire for control. *Journal of Applied Psychology, 81*, 199–214.

Chao, G. T., O'Leary-Kelly, A. M., Wolf, S., Klein, H. J., & Gardner, P. D. (1994). Organizational socialization: Its content and consequences. *Journal of Applied Psychology, 79*, 730–743.

Kramer, M. W. *Organizational socialization: Joining and leaving organizations.* Cambridge, UK: Polity Press.

Miller, K. (2015). *Organizational communication: Approaches and processes.* Stamford, CT: Cengage Learning.

Miller, V. D., & Jablin, F. M. (1991). Information seeking during organization entry: Influences, tactics, and a model of the process. *Academy of Management Review, 15*, 92–120.

Sumanth, J. J., & Cable, D. M. (2011). Status and organizational entry: How organization and individual status affect justice perceptions of hiring systems. *Personnel Psychology, 64*, 963–1000.

# 66

# Convergence in the Classroom: A Speed-storming Approach to Group Formation for Projects and Presentations

*Stacy E. Hoehl*
*School of Professional Communication*
*Wisconsin Lutheran College*
*stacy.hoehl@wlc.edu*

**History:** This activity was presented at the annual Central States Communication Association conference of April 2015 in Madison, Wisconsin.
**Primary courses in which this activity might be used:** Any communication course with group projects or presentations
**Concepts illustrated:** Collaboration and Small Group Communication, Brainstorming, Public Speaking and Presentations

## PURPOSE

As the workforce becomes more collaborative in nature, many of our classrooms are becoming more collaborative, in the hope of preparing students to be maximally effective when working with others. From a teacher's perspective, students' collaborative work is at its best when they have partnered with others to work on projects involving shared passions and interests. In addition, research supports this assertion, noting that students who perceive their group as having high levels of task interdependence also have the highest levels of collective efficacy (Alavi & McCormick, 2008; Bandura, 1997, 2002). However, this ideal group is often elusive, leaving both teachers and students frustrated and even overwhelmed (Speck, 2002). Speed-storming, an idea-generation technique based on the speed-dating method of meeting potential romantic partners, offers teachers and students an efficient, effective way of identifying groups of students that will work well together (Hey, Joyce, Jennings, Kalil, & Grossman, 2009). Since speed-storming is a timed, structured, one-on-one social interaction, students can bypass the small talk, social evaluation, and lack of depth that commonly results from typical brainstorming sessions.

Instead, the conversation remains focused on the given topic, the level of conversational engagement increases, and the resulting creative collaboration is of higher quality (Hey et al., 2009).

## EXPLANATION OF ACTIVITY

This activity is best conducted the class period after the project or presentation assignment is distributed in class. Ask students to identify their own project or presentation topic ideas prior to the class period in which this activity will be used. Required resources include physical classroom space in which students can rotate through a series of face-to-face conversations, notecards or scratch paper to record ideas, a stopwatch to time interactions, and a bell or alarm to signal rotations. The whole activity takes about an hour. On activity day, begin by explaining the speed-storming procedures to the students. Divide students into two groups, one that will face the front of the room and remain stationary, and one that will face the back of the room and rotate at each sound of the bell. After dividing the students in this way, each student should have one face-to-face partner.

Explain that the purposes of each face-to-face conversation are to generate possible project or presentation ideas and to identify potential collaborators. Tell them that they will have three, four, or five minutes (depending upon the size of the class and number of rounds needed) to create a project idea and record it on teacher-provided notecards or scratch paper. Remind students that this is a timed exercise, and it is important that they rotate quickly at the sound of the bell. Announce the start of each time interaction and offer a one- or two-minute warning to help students pace the conversation. Sound the bell when time runs out, and encourage the students facing the back of the room to move quickly to the next conversational partner. Repeat this process as necessary until each rear-facing student has completed one round of conversations. Though students will not have met with every other member of the class, this procedure and the discussion to follow typically result in well-formed groups. If the results are not satisfactory, the class can proceed through another round with shuffled starting locations.

After the rotations are complete, ask students to mingle and identify the classmates with whom they found common ground or intriguing complementary perspectives. Feel free to wander among the students, and encourage those who might be hesitant or reserved to get involved; asking them a few questions about their topic interests might help them vocalize their desired partner choices. For those simply wishing to partner with friends, remind them that the goal is to form interest-based teams. Use the resulting groupings as the work groups for the assigned project or presentation.

## DEBRIEF

Close the class period by asking students to share their opinions of the speed-storming session. Typical responses reflect on the fun yet focused conversations they had that were inspired by working with a set goal and time limit. During the activity, students experience heightened levels of engagement, as they get to know their classmates better, talk about ideas that are important to them, and take part in the creative thinking process. Students also improve their ability to articulate their ideas in a short period of time, an outcome frequently mentioned during the debriefing portion of the activity. Though students sometimes find the time constraints of speed-storming stressful, they are often pleased that the resulting ideas are more specific and personalized. Finally, students form clearer opinions about potential collaborators with whom they would like to work (Joyce, 2007).

This activity offers benefits for students not only during the class period in which it is conducted but also throughout their group's completion of the assigned project or presentation. After the activity is completed and while students move forward with their newly formed groups, students find that they are more committed to their group's goals and to developing an excellent project or presentation. This outcome is a reflection of the improved task interdependence and collective efficacy cultivated by this activity. The students have the opportunity to see convergence in action!

## REFERENCES

Alavi, S. B. & McCormick, J. (2008). The roles of perceived task interdependence and group members' interdependence in the development of collective efficacy in university student group contexts. *British Journal of Educational Psychology, 78,* 375-393.

Bandura, A. (1997). *Self-efficacy: The exercise of control.* New York: W.H. Freeman.

Bandura, A. (2002). Social cognitive theory in cultural contexts. *Applied Psychology: A International Review, 51,* 269-290.

Hey, J. H. G., Joyce, C. K., Jennings, K. E., Kalil, T., & Grossman, J. C. (2009). Putting the discipline in interdisciplinary: Using speedstorming to teach and initiate creative collaboration in nanoscience. *Journal of Nano Education, 1*(1), 75-85.

Joyce, C. K. (2007). The freedom of knowing one's boundaries: How accountability, rules, limited choice, and other constraints support creativity. *Unpublished dissertation proposal,* Berkeley: University of California.

Speck, B. W. (2002). *Facilitating students' collaborative writing.* San Francisco: Jossey Bass.

# 67

## Case Study of Personal Group Work Interaction for Online Courses

*Sarah E. Wilder, Ph.D.*
*Department of Communication Studies*
*Luther College*
*wildsa02@luther.edu*

**History:** This activity was presented at the annual meeting of the Central States Communication Association April 2013, in Kansas City, Kansas.
**Primary courses in which this activity might be used:** Introduction to Communication Studies, Small Group Communication, Organizational Communication, Interpersonal Communication, Communication Theory, Online Communication Courses
**Concepts illustrated:** Group Work, Group Roles, Leadership Styles, Group Norms, Group Patterns, Group Climate

### PURPOSE

Compared to students in traditional classrooms, those taking online courses have fewer opportunities to engage in discussions that help them apply course concepts to real-world experiences (Ko & Rossen, 2004). This is unfortunate, considering that making such connections is an imperative means of enhancing content relevance (Frymier, 2002). This activity addresses such concerns by facilitating peer discussions of prior group interactions. First, by writing a case study about their own recent group experiences, online students critically reflect on communication that has *already* occurred in their lives, increasing the relevance of the content. Second, by identifying course concepts in peers' case studies and providing comments and responses to each other, students apply concepts they are currently learning. Finally, this exchange of comments with peers increases interaction to more closely resemble interactions in traditional face-to-face courses, as opposed to individually moving through online modules with no interaction with classmates.

### EXPLANATION OF ACTIVITY

Before facilitating the activity, you should have students complete any appropriate readings or coursework to prepare them to apply the group communication concepts for the unit. While the specific concepts will vary depending on your goals, course, textbook, and unit, concepts I have successfully used when facilitating this assignment include leadership styles, group roles, group norms, and group climate. Concepts can be found in a variety of communication textbooks for a wide range of courses including introductory communication courses to more advanced group communication courses (e.g., Adler & Elmhorst, 2008; Beebe & Masterson, 2012; Duck & McMahan, 2012; Seiler & Beall, 2011). When preparing the assignment explained below, use detailed prompts and keep in mind that for all prompts it is helpful to provide examples (see Appendix, p. 285). For all portions of the activity, the length of responses varies by student, but encourage students to address all elements of each prompt.

To begin, you should create small groups online of three to four students. Instruct students to write a case study detailing a recent group experience. If anonymity is a concern, allow students to use pseudonyms or apply more stringent criteria, in which group experiences must be selected from those occurring outside of the institution. To qualify, the experience must have had a specific timeframe and identifiable goals or outcomes. For example, the group project for a final grade would qualify, whereas an organizational membership with meetings but no specific tasks or projects would not.

Prompt students to first identify the timeframe and the end goal. Next, direct students to write a detailed account of the group experience, addressing as many aspects as possible including but not limited to demographic information about individuals, how many meetings or exchanges occurred, the medium of communication, and members' behaviors and communication tendencies. Last, prompt students to identify their perceptions of success. Direct students to avoid course terminology if possible, but to write with the goal of a rich enough description that group members can apply course concepts.

Once all case studies are posted, instruct students to read and write a response to each case study in their group. I recommend setting parameters online so that students are unable to see other responses until they have posted their own. Provide students with a list of questions to guide their responses and direct them to include course concepts, while being specific as to which behaviors support their analysis. Sample questions include aspects such as who emerged as a leader, what leadership style was enacted, which roles did others in the group fulfill, what norms were present, what was the group climate, how cohesive was the group, and what was their perception of success. These should be revised according to your goals and chosen course concepts.

Finally, once comments are posted, instruct students to read all comments provided to their own case studies and submit a final response. The final response should consist of three parts. First, students should react to peers' analysis and perceptions, discuss where they agree or disagree, note if they found additional or differing concepts, and provide clarification to support their reactions if more information would benefit the group in understanding that case study. Second, based on their own and their group members' analyses, they should provide advice and recommendations for improved group interaction for that group in particular and future groups in general. Third, they should provide a brief reaction to the activity, considering aspects of what they learned or surprised them about their communicative tendencies, what they learned by studying a previous interaction they had already experienced, and what they learned by reading case studies of others.

## DEBRIEF

Read the case studies, comments, and reactions, and look for emerging themes to share with the class to debrief the activity. For example, I look for things such as which concepts were most present, what types of groups did most individuals select, were students being critical and reflective in challenging themselves across the interaction, and where I can provide supplemental emphasis. The final posting from you is to debrief the activity by highlighting current themes and how that can be used to propel considerations in the future. This final posting should also include an emphasis on the importance of learning from personal experiences. Responses from students to the debrief posting are not expected. Instead, the posting is for personal reflection, and you might answer or provide some further reflection questions in addition to summarizing and highlighting various concepts. These might include thoughts such as asking how being intentionally reflective can benefit them in the future, why these groups were chosen, what leadership style may be most effective in future groups, how can one work to shift a group climate to be positive, how can students be active in considering the best role to enact in a group, and so forth. After creating the debrief summary, it should be posted for students.

Students appreciate this activity because they are better able to relate to these case studies that come from classmates who are often engaging in similar group experiences, addressing the goal of relevance. The process of working in groups with multiple prompts and expectations to respond to peers better mimics the experiences of traditional face-to-face classrooms, addressing the goal of increasing opportunity for engagement with others. Something to consider when facilitating this assignment is that it may function differently in classes with more diverse ages or backgrounds. Students may not relate as well to each other, but that may allow them to analyze group dynamics they would not have experienced otherwise. Students comment that this a favorite assignment as it enables them to critically reflect on their own experiences, visualize how the concepts may enhance productivity in future groups, and facilitates meaningful conversations in the course.

## REFERENCES

Adler, R. B. & Elmhorst, J. M. (2008). *Communicating at work: Principles and practices for business and the professions.* Boston, MA: McGraw Hill.
Beebe, S. A. & Masterson, J. T. (2012). *Communicating in small groups: Principles and practices* (10th ed.). Boston, MA: Allyn & Bacon.

Duck, S. & McMahan, D. T. (2012). *The basics of communication: A relational perspective* (2nd ed.). Los Angeles, CA: Sage.

Frymier, A. B. (2002). Making content relevant to students. In J. L. Chesebro & J. C. McCroskey (Eds.), *Communication for teachers* (pp. 83–92). Boston, MA: Allyn & Bacon.

Ko, S. & Rossen, S. (2010). *Teaching online: A practical guide* (3rd ed.). New York: Routledge.

Seiler, W. J. & Beall, M. L. (2011). *Communication: Making connections* (8th ed.). Boston, MA: Allyn & Bacon.

## APPENDIX

## CASE STUDY OF PERSONAL GROUP WORK INTERACTION FOR ONLINE COURSES

Below are the steps and prompts to facilitate this activity online.

1. **Instructor step:** After students have completed the assigned readings to have a foundation of the concepts you choose to highlight, assign students to groups of three or four. Then post the first prompt.

2. **Prompt for students:** You should write a case study detailing a recent group experience. To qualify for this activity, your group experience must have a specific timeframe (e.g., you were in the group for one semester) and identifiable goals or outcomes (e.g., you were in your group to organize and implement a fundraiser). For example, a group project with a final grade would qualify, whereas an organizational membership with meetings but no specific tasks or projects would not. First, identify the timeframe (e.g., five weeks) and the end goal (e.g., we wanted an A grade). Next, write a detailed account of the group experience addressing as many specific aspects of the group as possible including but not limited to demographic information about individuals (e.g., sex/gender, age, year in school, position in organization etc.), how many meetings or exchanges occurred, the medium of communication (e.g., email, face-to-face), and members' behaviors and communication tendencies (e.g., Sheila tended to be late; John could often be relied on to start meetings on time; we often canceled face-to-face meetings and defaulted to email communication). Last, discuss your perception of success. For instance, "The goal was an A, and the group achieved a B (somewhat successful); we completely missed the deadline (not successful); but had an excellent final product (successful)." While writing your case study, you should avoid using course terminology when possible, but write with the goal of a rich enough description that your group members can apply course concepts.

3. **Instructor step:** Once all students have posted case studies you should post the next prompt. Which concepts and questions you focus on are dependent upon the text you use and what you would like to highlight and should be revised accordingly. Examples are in the prompt below. I also recommend setting up the comments so that students can't see other responses until they have posted their own in order to reduce the temptation to mirror someone else's thoughts.

4. **Prompt for students:** Now that your group members have posted their case studies, you should read each case and write a response. In your response you should identify course concepts while answering the following questions. For each question, be sure to detail which behaviors led you to draw that conclusion. If you note any other concepts of consequence beyond the following questions, note those as well. Questions: Who emerged as a leader? What leadership style was enacted? What roles did other members fulfill? What were some norms that developed? What is the group climate like? How cohesive is the group? What is your perception of their level of success?

5. **Instructor step:** After students have posted responses to each case study, you should post the next prompt.

6. **Prompt for students:** Now that each group member has provided a response to your case study, you should read the comments and provide a final response. Your final response should consist of three parts. First, you should react to their analysis and perceptions, discuss where you agree or disagree, note if you found additional or differing concepts, and provide clarification to support your reactions if you feel more information would benefit the group in understanding your case study group experience. Second, based on your and your group members' analyses, you should provide advice and recommendations for improved group interaction for that group in particular, and future groups in general. Third, you should provide a brief reaction to the activity, considering aspects of what you learned or what surprised you about your own communicative tendencies, what you learned by studying a previous interaction you have already experienced, and what you learned by reading case studies of others.

7. **Instructor step:** Read the case studies and comments and look for emerging themes to share with the class to debrief. For example, I look for things such as which concepts were most present; what types of groups did they focus on (for instance when I've taught nontraditional students, I've seen more work experiences whereas with more traditional students I tend to see more academic experiences); were students being critical and reflective in challenging themselves (for instance, students are quick to identify leadership styles and less likely to note group climates); where I can provide supplemental emphasis. The final posting from you is to debrief the activity by highlighting themes and areas to consider in the future, and to emphasize the importance of learning from personal experiences. While responses to the debrief posting are not expected since my debrief posting is for personal reflection, you might provide some further reflection questions in addition to summarizing and highlighting various concepts. These might include thoughts such as asking why these groups were chosen,

what leadership style may be most effective in future groups, how can one work to shift a group climate to be positive, how can students be active in considering the best role to enact in a group, how does being intentionally reflective about prior experience influence future experiences etc. After creating the debrief summary, it should be posted for students.

# 68

## Teaching Small Group Decision-Making Through *The Walking Dead*

*Nathan G. Webb, Ph.D.*
*Department of Communication Studies*
*Belmont University*
*nathan.webb@belmont.edu*

**History:** This activity was presented at the annual meeting of the National Communication Association, November 2014, in Chicago, Illinois.
**Primary courses in which this activity might be used:** Small Group Communication, Introduction to Communication, Interpersonal Communication
**Concepts illustrated:** Decision making, small group communication, decision-making procedures, conflict management

### PURPOSE

Making decisions is a vital component of groups in the workplace, in family and friend groups, and any setting where problems need to be solved. Keyton (2006) points out that teams regularly make decisions about topics like group procedures, relationship management, and how to best complete tasks. When done well, group decision-making can create synergy where the final outcome is greater than simply the sum of each individual part (Galanes & Adams, 2013).

Given the importance of decision making in an array of contexts, communication instructors regularly focus on the topic with their students. For example, when teaching decision-making, I regularly cover topics ranging from *how* groups make decisions to *evaluating* the decision-making process. One way that instructors can explain various aspects of decision-making to students is utilizing hypothetical scenarios. Popular hypothetical scenarios used in the classroom regularly include survival situations, such as being stranded on a desert island or surviving a spacecraft crash. The current activity builds on past hypothetical decision-making activities by providing an updated and culturally relevant survival scenario. Specifically, students are asked to make decisions as a group about items that would help them survive a zombie apocalypse.

The idea for the activity comes, in part, from the recent popular culture fascination with surviving the zombie apocalypse. In recent years, there have been several movies, comic books, television shows, video games, and websites devoted to a zombie apocalypse. The Centers for Disease Control and Prevention (CDC) even joined in on the pop culture phenomenon by creating a "Zombie Preparedness" campaign to raise awareness about disease prevention and preparedness. Of particular interest to this activity, however, is the popular television show on the AMC network, *The Walking Dead*. According to Forbes (2015), *The Walking Dead* was the most popular show for adults on television, with approximately fifteen million viewers per episode. In addition to the show's high ratings, it is also critically acclaimed. According to the Internet Movie Database (2016), the show has received forty-two awards and one hundred thirty nominations.

## EXPLANATION OF ACTIVITY

1. Prior to starting the activity, cover content related to decision-making. Specifically, I draw from Galanes and Adams (2013) to cover topics like dealing with conflict in groups and decision-making procedures.
2. Divide students into small groups of three to five students.
3. Explain to students that they will have to make decisions as a group to survive the hypothetical situation of a zombie apocalypse.
4. Discuss the popularity of the zombie apocalypse in society and show students a trailer of the popular television show *The Walking Dead* (trailers can be found by searching for "Walking Dead trailer" on YouTube.com or amc.com.). You can also show students the CDC Zombie Preparedness website if time allows. Students can help fill in the blanks of the show's synopsis to their classmates, if needed.
5. Read and/or project the following hypothetical situation to your students:

   *You and your group have returned from a wilderness camping trip to discover that the zombie apocalypse is actually happening. You hear on the radio the virus that brings the dead back to life is spreading rapidly and will reach your area within the hour. You and your friends decide you should get away from populated areas and return to the wilderness for safety and to figure things out. All of the stores in your area have already closed, so you can only take the items left over from the camping trip and items at your apartment/dorm. Your group only has one vehicle with you, so you must fit the group and your items in the vehicle.*

6. Project the list of items, or write them on the board, so each group can see them. Explain that each group has access to fifteen items and that they can only fit seven—about half of the items—in their vehicle. Explain that their task is to decide which items they will bring with them and then to rank their order of importance. Here are the items:

   *box of canned food (six cans), twenty feet of nylon rope, family-sized tent, air mattress, hammer, two-way radio, three sleeping bags, fishing materials (rod/reel & plastic bait), magnetic compass, five-gallon jug of water, two signal flares, large knife, first aid kit, GPS receiver, camping lighter*

**7.** Give each group ten to fifteen minutes to pick their items and rank them in order of importance. Tell students to be ready to discuss and defend their decisions.

**8.** Ask each group to share the items they chose, how they ranked the items, and their rationale for doing so. You can compare and contrast how each group ranks their items on the board.

## DEBRIEF

After each group has shared their items and rationale for decisions, have groups discuss course content related to decision-making. You can discuss the questions as a whole class, within the groups, or a combination of both. Example questions include:

- What procedure(s) did your group use to decide on your items?
- How did your group finalize its decision?
- How did your group handle disagreements and conflict?
- Did you notice any behaviors that hindered the decision-making process?
- How would you rate the effectiveness of your decision-making? What might you do differently in the future?

After debriefing on specific elements of the decision-making process with the class, I finish the activity by discussing the importance of group decision-making. I always review content presented in class prior to the decision-making activity. The activity and debriefing usually takes thirty to forty minutes to complete.

While teaching small group, interpersonal, and introductory communication, I've used a variety of hypothetical decision-making survival scenarios, and none have been better received than this one. Students are able to connect the dots between course content and the activity. In addition, student participation for the activity is exceptionally high. In sum, the activity is both engaging and effective.

## REFERENCES

Centers for Disease Control and Prevention (2015, April 10). *Zombie preparedness.* Retrieved from http://www.cdc.gov/phpr/zombies.htm

Galanes, G. J. & Adams, K. (2013). *Effective group discussion: Theory and practice* (14th ed.). New York, NY: McGraw-Hill.

Internet Movie Database (2016). *The walking dead: Awards.* Retrieved from http://www.imdb.com/title/tt1520211/awards

Keyton, J. (2006). *Communicating in groups* (3rd ed.). New York, NY: Oxford.

St. John, A. (2015, March 30). *"Walking dead" episode 516 draws 15.8 viewers, posts record rating for TWD series finale.* Retrieved from http://www.forbes.com/sites/allenstjohn/2015/03/30/walking-dead-episode-516-draws-15-8-million-viewers-posts-record-ratings-for-twd-series-finale/

# 69

# Developing a Team Contract as a Means to Understand, Apply, and Reify Small Group Communication Concepts

*Nicole A. Ploeger-Lyons*
*Department of Communication Studies*
*University of Wisconsin – La Crosse*
*nploeger-lyons@uwlax.edu*

**History:** This activity was presented at the annual meeting of the Central States Communication Association, April 2015, Minneapolis, Minnesota. It was a top-ranked submission.
**Primary courses in which this activity might be used:** Introduction to Communication, Small Group Communication, Team Communication
**Concepts illustrated:** Stages of Group Development, Conflict, Communication Climate, Leadership, Assessing Group Performance

## PURPOSE

The announcement of group projects in the classroom is generally met with sighs, groans, and looks of disgust or dread. Most of the students I have taught have similar reactions because of poor past experiences working in groups. This attitude and mindset—that groups are horrible—is unfortunate, because great outcomes can come from working in teams. If students are encouraged to dig deeper into their analysis of why they hate group work, they can see that what makes or breaks a group—regardless of its task—is often the quality of their communication. Rather than assuming group members know how to communicate with each other and assuming that everyone expects the same from each other, I find that it behooves students to discuss their communication expectations (i.e., engage in metacommunication) before they focus on the group task itself.

While helpful, the idea of groups developing their own group or team contract from scratch is not groundbreaking. However, with an instructor-developed template that incorporates small group communication concepts as the *basis* of the contract, students must (a) understand the concepts; (b) think about what the concepts look like and sound like in each of the five stages of group development; and (c) speak their desired group norms and expectations into being within their actual groups. In other words, they reify these small group communication concepts; through their metacommunication, they make the seemingly abstract ideas concrete.

## EXPLANATION OF ACTIVITY

I recommend at least one full class period for this experiential learning activity. The materials are minimal. To form my contract template (see Appendix, p. 294), I used what I believe to be the most critical components of small group communication as described in the basic course textbook used at my institution (O'Hair & Wiemann, 2012). Students prepare for this class period by reading excerpts of the textbook that correspond with the concepts found on the team contract template. Also, they should download the template before the given class period and have at least one group member bring a laptop to class so that they may type their responses into the contract template and submit it at the end of the class period.

I randomize students into small groups that they will work in for a class project and presentation. This activity—the development of a team contract—is to occur in the class period *after* they get their group assignments and engage in icebreakers. The team contract template is broken into five sections, one for each stage of group development. Thus, the first set of questions in the template relates directly to the communication that ought to occur in the *forming stage* of development (e.g., come together, exchange names and contact information, get to know one another, create a team name). For the *storming stage*, the questions focus on how groups will encourage productive conflict and engage in and manage all conflicts. When discussing the *norming* set of questions, students really start to engage in metacommunication. What will they do and say to encourage positive, interdependent communication? What will shared leadership look like for them? How will they recognize, stop, and/or prevent groupthink from occurring? How will they handle social loafing? What does an ideal group member say and do? For the *performing* questions, students answer questions about how they will hold themselves accountable to their contract. They discuss what a successful performance will look like. Here, they also describe how their firing process will unfold, should they deem it necessary to fire a group member. Lastly, it is important to highlight to students that the group is not done after their presentation. They must engage in the *adjourning stage* in which they meet post-presentation to evaluate their performance and the entire group communication process.

Students use the entire class period to negotiate their contract amongst the group members. Essentially, they are foreshadowing what they want their group communication to be like throughout all stages of group development and throughout their entire project. By signing the contract at the end of the class period, they are committing to uphold the contract as created and specified by the group. During this process, the instructor ought to visit with each group frequently to encourage them to think about why they are making the decisions they are making, to elevate their understanding of the concepts in action, to promote critical thinking, and to help facilitate their process. Additionally, because of the instructors' experiences and frame of reference, they will likely find holes or weaknesses in the contract that will be helpful for students to revisit before signing.

An alternate way to do this activity is to have each group member complete the contract on his or her own. Students would come to class with a contract containing only *their* expectations, allowing them to engage in more complex group decision-making since each person has already codified his or her own beliefs. Their negotiation from individually derived contracts to an agreed-upon group contract would likely allow students to practice their conflict management and negotiation skills. Further, these conversations could be recorded, allowing students to later analyze their own group communication skills and to identify concepts in action (e.g., social loafing, groupthink).

## DEBRIEF

In addition to the instructor's small group facilitation throughout the activity, it is helpful to engage in a class-wide debrief, asking the following questions: 1) Why is it important to understand the communication that occurs in each stage of the group process? 2) Why is it important to engage in metacommunication *before* beginning work on the group task? 3) What do you think will be your biggest challenge in holding yourselves to the standards you have set forth in this contract? 4) How can you use this contract formation process and small group communication knowledge to your benefit in everyday life and in other groups to which you belong? To evaluate this activity, consider both (a) the students' process (i.e., their communication during contract development); and (b) the students' product (i.e., the contract itself) and whether it is complete and accurate.

## REFERENCES

O'Hair, D., & Wiemann, M. (2012). *Real communication: An introduction* (2nd ed.). Boston, MA: Bedford/St. Martin's.

## APPENDIX

## DEVELOPING YOUR TEAM CONTRACT

You will be immersed in group communication throughout your group project and presentation. For group success, morale, and motivation, it is helpful to plan your communication strategies, hopes, and norms. What do you expect from each other? What will you not tolerate? How will you create cohesion? How will you manage conflict? What will you do if a group member is loafing?

Through discussion, together complete the following worksheet that draws upon important concepts from your reading. You will each provide an electronic signature. Submit one copy for your group. Once approved, it will serve as your group contract.

**Forming:** In the first stage of group development, you come together, get acquainted with each other, and strive for acceptance and unity.

1) What are all team members' names, phone numbers, and emails?
2) What is your team name?
3) What are your common goals? *Specifically*, what do you hope to accomplish together (i.e., go beyond, "We want an A")?
4) How will you achieve a sense of belonging amongst yourselves? How will you convey that to the class?
5) What are five things you all have in common with each other?

**Storming:** You'll likely experience conflict in your group. How will you handle conflict?

1) What is productive conflict and how will you ensure you manage conflict productively? What conflicts will you encourage? What type of conflicts will you avoid?
2) When conflict arises, what strategies will you want to use or avoid?
   a. Escapist
   b. Challenging
   c. Cooperative
3) What is a supportive communication climate? What specific strategies will you use with each other to ensure a supportive climate during conflict situations?

**Norming:** Your group norms and patterns of behavior start to emerge and are recognized as the "group's way of doing things" in terms of your actions, roles, and leadership.

1) How will you manage the interdependent nature of your group communication? In other words, your communication, behaviors, and actions affect the other individuals and the group as a whole. What will you do to ensure the interdependent communication is positive?
2) I want you to use shared leadership in your project. What does that mean? What will shared leadership look like in your group? What roles will you each take on?

3) What is groupthink and what steps will you take to prevent it or recognize and manage it if it happens? What are specific techniques you can use?

4) How will you handle social loafing? Directly? Indirectly? As it arises? Through which channel of communication?

5) How will you establish a norm of cohesiveness? What will you do and say? What will you not do or say?

6) What does an ideal group member look like within your group? What do they do and say? What do they not do or say?

7) When and where will much of your group work occur? How will you manage the group meetings? What will you do to ensure they are productive and worthwhile? How often will you meet face-to-face? What technology will you use?

**Performing:** In this stage, you are busy accomplishing the tasks at hand.

1) How will you hold yourselves accountable to the contract as laid out above?

2) What will a successful performance look like for your group?

3) If you deem it to be necessary, you can fire group members, meaning they will meet with the instructor to determine an appropriate route moving forward. Very clearly and specifically lay out your process for firing member(s).

**Adjourning:** How will you evaluate your performance overall? As a group?

1) Schedule a post-presentation meeting. In the space below, create an agenda for that meeting. At a minimum, you'll want to address the following: strengths, weaknesses, what would be done the same way, what might you do differently? This is not just in terms of your presentation performance, but also your group communication skills throughout the process.

# 70

# Sources of Power and the Impact on a Small Group: An Activity to Help Students Experience the Impacts and Effects of Power and Power Imbalances

*John R. Katsion*
*Department of Communication and Mass Media*
*Northwest Missouri State University*
*johnkat@nwmissouri.edu*

**History:** This activity was presented at the annual meeting of the National Communication Association Conference, November 2012, in Orlando, Florida. It was a top-ranked submission.

**Primary courses in which this activity might be used:** Small Group Communication, Fundamentals of Communication (Hybrid approach), Interpersonal Communication, and Persuasion

**Concepts illustrated:** Small Group Communication (general), Power in Small Groups, Sources of Power in Small Groups, Expertise Power, Resistance to Power, Strategies of Defiance

## PURPOSE

An interesting topic in small-group communication is the way power manifests itself in the interactions within a group. Students know about this concept, but sometimes they find it hard to see how power plays itself out within group interactions. This activity gives students a short experience that helps them understand the effects of power in small group situations, specifically sources of power, ways to defy power, and the power of privilege in society. This activity can be used in any class where issues of power in communication are covered, but it works best within a small-group communication context. In teaching the section on power in small-group communication, I felt that I needed something to help students not only intellectually understand the impact of power, but to experience the various sources of power, to feel the effects of authority, and the ways people in groups tend to resist power.

Specifically, this activity helps students experience the following within a group setting: information power, expertise power, and rewards/punishment power. It also gives students a chance to look at ways people in groups resist those types of power and the impact the various forms of resistance and non-resistance can have on groups (Rothwell, 2010). Last, through this activity students experience the broader implications of the power of privilege in society, specifically issues of privilege and fairness.

## EXPLANATION OF ACTIVITY

Before class, create a slightly difficult five-question trivia quiz, with a tie-breaker in case of a tie, that you will show as a PowerPoint or as an overhead (see the Appendix, p. 299, for the one that I use). In class, place the students in groups of five to seven. Then explain that you will be playing a trivia game, where each team will compete against each other to answer the most questions out of five. Tell the winning team that they will get to decide a punishment for another group in the class. Some of the students will want to know what the exact punishment is, but do not let them know. Keeping it secret usually increases their desire to win so that they can avoid any penalty, and it can also be an interesting addition to post-activity discussion. Remember that while the winning team gets to decide who will be punished, they do not decide on the way they are punished, as that has already been determined.

Begin the quiz. Each group has one minute to decide on an answer for each question. After the minute is up, reveal the correct answer, and then find out which team(s) got the question right. Move on to the next question and follow the same procedure. After the final question is answered and the winning team is determined, ask students to discuss in their groups the concept of information and expertise power. Specifically, they might consider:

- Who held the informational/expertise power in deciding which answer the group was going to choose? Help them notice how the informational/ expertise source of power heavily impacted whom the group looked to for leadership at that moment. Some groups, for example, might have one person who is a history major, or is a fan of popular culture, who is able to answer important questions. Other groups might have two or three students who seem to share that power. A lot of groups want to say they all shared the power, but this is where you need to have them take a better look at their group interactions, and to be more specific.
- Was there a clash over whose information you were going to listen to? How did you resolve that clash? What does that say about the way this form of power works? Most groups respond that they just went with the group member who knew the answer and that there was no argument; other groups sometimes clash if they have a leader who does not want to share power.
- If you use established groups, have them discuss how informational/ expertise power may have moved leadership from the emergent leader

of the group. Did the leader mind? Did the current leader of the group end up being the informational/expertise source of power anyway? Were they the actual source of knowledge, or did the group just defer to their role as leader? If you have groups that have been together awhile, this can lead to an excellent analysis for the group to look at how power is being distributed within the group. For groups with no history, it helps them understand how expertise can lead to power and leadership.

After this discussion, explain that we now want to look at rewards and punishment as a form of power. Ask the winning group to pick another group to punish. The group they choose to punish must come to the front of the class and do the movements to the song "I'm a Little Tea Pot." Find a video on YouTube that shows the words, and how to do the actions to this song. I usually search YouTube or Google using the terms "I'm a Little Teapot," "I'm a Little Teapot Actions," or "I'm a Little Teapot with lyrics." The group that is chosen then comes forward and completes the punishment. At this point most groups come forward and willingly comply, but they may drag their feet, or one member may put up a fuss. Allow them to complain, and even refuse to comply, but make sure to make note of their acts of defiance, as this will help the discussion to follow.

## DEBRIEF

To debrief, I lead a class discussion around the issue of rewards and punishment as a form of power.

- What did it feel like to have the power to punish? How did you choose whom to punish? This is a question that can only be answered by the winning team. Usually the choice to punish another team is based upon the fact that people from the winning team know members of the team they punished, and they want to have fun with their friends. If you are dealing with groups who have been together for a semester, the choice may come down to a genuine dislike of the other group.
- What did it feel like to be punished? This is a question that only the punished team can answer, and usually elicits responses of how unfair the activity is, or how the randomness of it all seems so unfair.
- As a form of power, should punishment ever be used? Under what circumstances might it be an effective form of power? How might it be destructive? This is a good question to have the groups discuss themselves, and then share their responses with the whole class.
- Why did the punished group comply? Why did they not resist the punishment? What does this say about the power of authority held by the instructor in the classroom, or the pressure to conform within the group? I have found that this question is the one that leads to the most discussion, and is the most fruitful in terms of getting students to think about issues of rewards and punishment.

- For those who did resist the punishment, what resistance strategies did they use? It is important to keep the punishment section as lighthearted as possible, but to still maintain the sense of discipline required for the students to experience the effects of punishment. This is where you can have the class reflect back upon the strategies of resistance that were being used by the group chosen for punishment.

I have found that the student response to this activity has been positive and that it has helped students to understand the various forms of power and the effect power has on the community of a small group and broader issues of power and privilege.

## REFERENCE

Rothwell, J. D. (2010) *In mixed company* (7th ed.). Boston, MA: Wadsworth Co.

## APPENDIX

### TRIVIA QUESTIONS

Note: The asterisk marks the correct answer. Be sure to remove it before showing these to the students. I usually copy and paste these and put them into a PowerPoint presentation.

1. Who lived at 221 B Baker Street in London?
   a. The Prime Minister of England
   b. Sherlock Holmes *
   c. The Queen
   d. The Chancellor of the Exchequer

2. What do the opposite sides of a dice add up to?
   a. 7 *
   b. 8
   c. 6
   d. It's never the same

3. When did the American Civil War end?
   a. 1769
   b. 1800
   c. 1865 *
   d. 1869

4. What is the capital of Australia?
   a. Sydney
   b. Melbourne
   c. Adelaide
   d. Canberra *

5. Who was the director of the film *Psycho*?
   a. Steven Spielberg
   b. Alfred Hitchcock *
   c. Paul Newman
   d. Martin Scorcese

**Tie-Breaker**
**(If Needed)**

1. Which philosopher said, "The unexamined life is not worth living"?
   a. Aristotle
   b. Plato
   c. Socrates *
   d. Descartes

2. What is the name of the Simpsons's family dog on the show *The Simpsons*?
   a. Santa's Little Helper *
   b. Trixie VonRuffle
   c. Spotolicious
   d. Eddie

# 71

## "Is That Work Related?": The Implications of Staying Connected Through Technology at Work

*Jeremy P. Fyke*

*Department of Communication Studies*

*Belmont University*

*jeremyfyke@gmail.com*

**History:** This activity was presented at the annual meeting of the Central States Communication Association, March 2012, in Cleveland, Ohio.
**Primary courses in which this activity might be used:** Business/ Managerial Communication, Organizational Communication, New Communication Technologies in the Workplace, Small Group Communication
**Concepts illustrated:** Information and Communication Technologies (ICTs), Leadership, Employee Communication, Work-life Balance, Managerial Control

### PURPOSE

Given the ubiquity of information and communication technologies (ICTs) in today's workplace, it is important that students entering the work force be mindful of the benefits and drawbacks of technology. Demands on employees' time necessitate multitasking, despite the benefits of staying focused on one task at a time (MindTools, n.d.). Students need fresh and vivid examples of the myriad situations that could arise in which they are likely to be distracted by technology in the workplace. Furthermore, this activity highlights the ever-blurring lines of public and private life in the information and technology age (Ford, 2011). Thus this activity takes students to a familiar scene: One where tasks are to be accomplished while personal and professional communication via technology presents constant interruptions. The purpose of this exercise is to illustrate the dynamics, tensions, and complexities surrounding the integration of personal (i.e., non-work-related) and professional (i.e., work-related) ICTs in the workplace.

## EXPLANATION OF ACTIVITY

### Preparation Outside of Class

First, using the class roster, divide the class into two groups—group one: personal technology use; and group two: professional technology use. Next, you will need to construct a simple PowerPoint slide deck with a slide for several students in the groups. (To save time, rather than create a slide for each student, you can create fewer, but try to have roughly an equal number of slides per group.) Some of the slides will contain personal technology distractions, while others will contain work distractions (see Appendix, p. 304, for more examples). For instance, personal distractions could contain something like "Jenna! You got an email from Mom: '*Hey sweetie, can you email me that recipe for those cookies you baked last week?*' Please flip your paper over and write a recipe with five ingredients and steps for your perfect cookies," or "Brandon, you got a text message from your girlfriend: '*Why is there a picture of you with your ex? The pic was from last week!*' Take out your phone now and type a five-sentence response to explain yourself." It is important to tell students to play along with the examples (e.g., "If you do not have a girlfriend or mom you communicate with regularly, just pretend"). Work distractions could include "Alex: You need feedback on a final report you put together for your latest project at work ASAP. Flip over your paper and write a response to your co-worker asking for suggestions. Limit it to five sentences." Insert a sound effect for each changing slide (e.g., cell phone ring, email sound) to get the students' attention. Print out an activity for each student to work on in class (e.g., word search, Sudoku).

### Executing the Activity

In class, divide the students into the two groups and *only* tell them their group *number*. Next, assign one student to be the supervisor. (Make sure the supervisor is not one of the students for whom you made a slide.) Take the supervisor away from the class and explain his/her role: "Imagine that the students are employees and you are their supervisor. The employees will have various tasks (e.g., word search, Sudoku) they need to complete in fifteen minutes. Walk around the room and feel free to ask workers what they are working on, keeping in mind that they are at work. As you walk around, notice if they are productive at accomplishing the tasks they have been given. Keep an eye out for the technology they are using. If their technology is hindering their production, you may put them on 'probation' by taking their activity away. Please do not look at the projector screen during the fifteen minutes."

Return to the classroom and explain directions to the class: "Welcome to The Sudoku Factory. Your job is to complete Sudoku puzzles from 8 a.m. to 5 p.m. every day. ____ is your supervisor. You will be given a puzzle (your "work") to complete. Be sure to finish your work in the next fifteen minutes. Each time you hear a sound, please look up at the screen. If your name appears, be sure to follow the directions. If your supervisor addresses you, you should respond as you would in a normal work setting." (Rather than Sudoku, you can substitute in other "work" for the students, such as word search or crossword puzzles.)

Hand out the activities (i.e., Sudoku work) to the students (i.e., employees) and tell them to begin working. As the students are working change the PowerPoint slide about every minute. Have the supervisor begin monitoring employees. Keep track of time, allowing the activity to run for approximately fifteen minutes. Note: you can change the slides more often (e.g., every thirty seconds), but you will need to create more slides. It is important to emphasize that every student needs to look up at the screen each time they hear a sound, but they need to continue working unless they are prompted otherwise on the screen. You might find that changing more often is more exciting and mimics how quickly distractions really happen in the workplace.

## DEBRIEF

Debrief the exercise by connecting the activity to course concepts and research. There are several issues to be explored. First, you can discuss the ubiquity of information and communication technologies (ICTs) in the workplace and the opportunities and challenges they present (Miller, 2015). You could also connect the discussion to a recent trend in workplaces, co-working, which includes open-plan office spaces where mostly unaffiliated professionals work alongside and around each other (Spinuzzi, 2012). Questions to prompt discussion include "What was it like trying to get your work done with so much technology being used around you?" "When you were distracted, how did that impact your work?" "What are some examples where you've been distracted by co-workers?" Second, you can add an ethical layer to the discussion that spans issues of privacy and managerial control (Moussa, 2015). For instance, "How can employers monitor technology use while meeting employees' needs for autonomy?" Third, you can include the implications on work/life issues. For instance, "How has technology blurred the lines between home and work?" "How did you feel if you were using technology for professional reasons, but your usage was questioned because of those around you?" "How did you feel if you got caught using technology for personal reasons?" Finally, you can help students connect the experience in the activity to non-work situations. For instance, "How often are you able to complete school work without interruptions (e.g., Facebook, email)?" "Are you able to turn everything off in order to complete a task? Why or why not?" "What's it like when you are able to turn everything off and get things done?"

## REFERENCES

Ford, S. M. (2011). Reconceptualizing the public-private distinction in the age of information technology. *Information, Communication & Society, 14*, 550–567.

Miller, K. (2015). *Organizational communication: Approaches and processes* (7th ed.). Stamford, CT: Cengage Learning.

MindTools (n.d.). Multitasking: Can it help you get more done? Retrieved from https://www.mindtools.com/pages/article/newHTE_75.htm.

Moussa, M. (2015). Monitoring employee behavior through the use of technology and issues of employee privacy in America. *SAGE Open, 5,* 1–15.

Spinuzzi, C. (2012). Working together alone: Coworking as emergent collaborative activity. *Journal of Business and Technical Communication, 26,* 399–441.

## APPENDIX

## PERSONAL AND WORK TECHNOLOGY DISTRACTIONS

### Personal distractions

- "Jamie, your phone just buzzed and it's an alert from Instagram: 'nathansmith commented on your photo.' You'd better check it out and respond!"
- "Mary, you just got an alert on your phone from Facebook: 'Messenger: Michelle Williams. Hey, girl what are your plans....'" Grab your phone and type a quick response.
- "Brandon, you just got an alert on your phone from ESPN: 'Jimmy Walker wins ninety-eighth PGA Championship.' You'd better check out the story."
- "James, your partner just texted you: 'OMG I just saw a huge wreck right in front of me. A Porsche and an SUV. Porsche is really messed up.' Write out a response."
- "Jason, your brother just texted you: 'Dude, my car is out of gas. Help!' Type out a response telling him you're at work but can ask to leave early to help."

### Work distractions

- "Sam, your co-worker Robert just emailed his speaking outline for his sales pitch tomorrow asking for feedback. Turn over your paper and write him a few comments."
- "Jessie, you just heard a ding from your inbox. It's your boss with an important message about your presentation this afternoon. Write out a five sentence reply to her."
- "Rachel, you just got a Google News Alert about Target's data breach. You're not sure if it's relevant to another project you're working on, but you'd better check it out."
- "Mike, your next-cube-over neighbor Scott has his music on his iPod up loud enough where you can hear it. Stand up and ask him to please turn it down."
- "John, you just got an IM from a co-worker asking if you heard about the problems another co-worker was having recently. He said he's heard that HR visited him like five times. Send him a reply saying you heard but

you're not sure." (Can be debriefed as a form of workplace gossip, a common distraction.)

- "Brooke, out of the corner of your eye you can see your boss's office TV, which has last night's NBA scores on it. Write out a quick IM asking him who won the Spurs-Rockets game."

(Many of these distractions could be considered a combination of personal and work distractions. In your debrief, there is a good opportunity to discuss the blurring lines between work and home with all of the technology at hand.)

# 72

# Skunkworks!: Using Unconventional Paper Airplanes to Teach the Communication of Technical Information and Procedural Instructions

*Kurtis D. Miller*
*Brian Lamb School of Communication*
*Purdue University*
*mille518@purdue.edu*

*Marcy Lendaro*
*Brian Lamb School of Communication*
*Purdue University*
*mjlendaro@gmail.com*

**History:** This activity was presented at the annual meeting of the Central States Communication Association, March 2014, in Minneapolis, Minnesota.

**Primary courses in which this activity might be used:** Organizational Communication, Health Communication, Risk Communication, Technical Writing, Communication in the STEM Fields

**Concepts illustrated:** Audience Adaptation, Information Processing Methods, Design, Verbal and Nonverbal Print Communication, Communication Channels

## PURPOSE

Good directions mean the difference between life and death. Using a product, drug, or medical device incorrectly can result in serious injuries or complications. Despite the importance of clear instructions, we have all experienced the challenge of struggling through confusing and poorly written ones. The challenge comes, in part, from writing instructions for the widest possible variety of approaches that members of your audience will use when processing them. Some people will not look at instructions at all, some will glance over the pictures, some skim the text, and a minority will carefully read every step. Writing good instructions is a life skill that is often untaught.

Students enjoy that this activity allows them to engage in creating something during classroom time and clearly connects the class content with prescriptive readings about procedural instruction design and instruction design research (e.g., Eiriksdottir & Catrombone, 2008; Fukuoka, Kojima, & Spyridakis, 1999; Harvey, 2008; McCroskey, Valencic, & Richmond, 2004; van Hooijdonk & Krahmer, 2008). They also like that it allows them to exercise and improve specific communication-relevant skills. With appropriate discussion, students see writing clear and effective instructions as an important skill in their future careers.

## EXPLANATION OF ACTIVITY

To conduct this activity, you will need a stack of several identical, unusually shaped sheets of paper, at least two sheets for each student, and a single target for the class. Using unusually shaped paper requires students to solve the problem creatively and produces a much wider variety of designs than standard paper. We used scrap paper chopped on an oblique angle in a paper chopper. We used a hula-hoop as our target, but any similar object will work. The target needs to be fairly large.

Students take on three roles successively: designer, producer, and pilot. Students first act as the designer. In this role they are given one of the oddly shaped sheets of paper and allowed two to five minutes to prototype a paper airplane. Once they have settled on a prototype, the students use a sheet of notebook paper and write instructions for how to re-create their aircraft. Allow up to ten minutes for the creation of instructions. Encourage the students to provide as much detail (text, illustrations, etc.) as they can. You may wish to make it clear that student aircraft should not be a wadded up ball of paper.

Next take the prototype aircraft—these prototypes will not be used again. Students are now taking on the second role of the producer. Randomly select pairs of students to exchange instructions. Pass out the second identical sheet of unusually shaped paper and allow students two to five minutes to create the aircraft described by the instructions they received. Taking up the prototypes requires the students to rely on the instructions by removing the prototypes as a reference.

Finally, have the students give the aircraft they produced to the students who designed the prototype and wrote the instructions. The designer gives the aircraft its maiden voyage by trying to fly it through the hoop from a distance of approximately two meters.

## DEBRIEF

Typically, there are several examples of paper airplanes that are very different from what their designers expected and one or two that are exactly correct.

Most are similar to what was expected, but it is common for a single important step to be omitted. The simplest airplane designs are often reproduced most successfully. Engage the class in discussion, asking questions such as: What challenges did you face in following the instructions? Which parts of the directions did you pay attention to? Which parts did you ignore? What parts did you find confusing? In what ways do you think the instructions for more successful teams were different from less successful teams? How good did you think the directions you wrote were before you handed them off? Did you get the aircraft you expected?

A document reader can be used to show examples of more and less successful sets of instructions so students can identify characteristics of good instructions. Variations on this activity include returning the prototypes so students may compare them with the final product, having students discuss their experience in pairs in front of the class before flying in place of class discussion, using groups of three, and flying planes for maximum distance rather than using a target (Caldwell & Millen, 2009).

Many students are surprised to discover how the aircraft they get back is different from what they expected. It is common for students to discover the many opportunities for miscommunication in procedural instructions. A significant source of confusion they identify is a lack of images in instructions. Students are often surprised to learn that their partner did not carefully read through their directions or missed important steps because they were skimming the page. This provides an important opportunity to discuss ways to make written instructions friendly for the wide variety of reading approaches used by the end user.

## REFERENCES

Caldwell, C. A., & Millen A. E. (2009). Social learning mechanisms and cumulative cultural evolution: Is imitation necessary? *Psychological Science, 20*, 1478–1483. doi:10.1111/j.1467-9280.2009.02469.x

Eiriksdottir, E., & Catrambone, R. (2008). How do people use instructions in procedural tasks? *Proceedings of the Human Factors and Ergonomics Society Annual Meeting, 52*(8), 673–677. doi:10.1177/154193120805200814

Fukuoka, W., Kojima, Y., & Spyridakis, J. H. (1999). Illustrations in user manuals: Preference and effectiveness with Japanese and American readers. *Technical Communication, 46*(2), 167–176.

Harvey, G. (2008). Designing procedural instructions: 5 key components. *Information Design Journal, 16*(1), 19–24.

McCroskey, J. C., Valencic, K. M., & Richmond, V. P. (2004) Toward a general model of instructional communication. *Communication Quarterly, 52*(3) 197–210. http://dx.doi.org/10.1080/01463370409370192

van Hooijdonk, C., & Krahmer, E. (2008). Information modalities for procedural instructions: The influence of text, pictures and film clips on learning and executing RSI exercises. In *IEEE Transactions on Dependable and Secure Computing, 51*(1), 50–62. http://dx.doi.org/10.1109/TPC.2007.2000054

# 73

## Identifying Organizational Values for Customized Career Communication

*Rose Helens-Hart, Ph.D.*
Fort Hays State University
*rhhelenshart@fhsu.edu*

**History:** This activity was presented at the annual meeting of the Central States Communication Association, in April 2016, in Grand Rapids, Michigan.

**Primary courses in which this activity might be used:** Business Communication, Communication Skills, Organizational Communication

**Communication illustrated:** Employment/Career Communication Customization, Organizational Identity, Organizational Values

### PURPOSE

Résumés, cover letters, mock interviews, and career fairs are foundational assignments used in business, organizational, and communication skills courses. Cliché terms and phrases in career communication such as *team player, hard worker, leadership skills,* and *communication skills* litter career documents and create one-size-fits-all employment profiles, which do little to help students stand out among their peers (Bovée & Thill, 2016). In an attempt to mitigate this, students are taught that it is essential to customize their career documents and related communication for the specific job calls and organizations to which they are applying. Most students, however, will be asked only to submit a single version of their career documents or participate in one mock interview or career fair during a semester. Thus it is difficult to assess their abilities to identify the values of particular organizations that they would refer to in future career-related communication. To help them understand the process of recognizing organizational values, this activity asks students to examine organizations' websites and identify evidence that supports the use of certain key terms in their documents and orientations toward specific organizational values.

### EXPLANATION OF ACTIVITY

This activity can be assigned as an online discussion board or be completed in a fifty- or seventy-five-minute class period. Students need to have laptops

309

or other devices to access organizations' websites or the instructor can print copies of websites if needed. Instructors should be careful to include important, information-rich pages of the websites, such as those that contain mission statements, staff profiles, career opportunities, and recent organization news. These will allow students to craft a clearer picture of organizations' espoused identities.

To begin the activity more quickly, instructors can preselect a number of organizations' websites for students to analyze. Using the websites of organizations that have posted jobs on university job boards or who have confirmed they will be attending a university career fair encourages students' engagement with these resources and organizations.

Before completing this activity, students should understand and be familiar with (a) common organizational values ("Company culture," 2013; Lencioni, 2002) and (b) the importance of customizing career-related communication (Bovée & Thill, 2016). It may be helpful first to analyze a website or a mission statement together as a class or provide an example for online students. Place students into groups of three or four and assign them an organization's website to review. Depending on the time you have allotted for the activity, you may assign more than one website. For online courses, you can assign virtual groups or have students examine a website on their own. Each group (or student) should be assigned a different organization. Offer students the following questions to guide their review of the websites:

1. What is your initial impression of this organization?
2. What terms and ideas are repeated or visually emphasized through color, placement on the page, or font type?
3. What kinds of images are used on the website?
4. Using your knowledge of organizational values, what values do these terms, ideas, images, and designs represent?
5. What do you think are ideal qualities of an Organization X employee?
6. What experiences could you highlight on your résumé or cover letter to show you possess these qualities?

## DEBRIEF

After students have discussed these questions in their groups, have one or more representatives of the group share their findings with the class so that all students benefit from learning about multiple organizations. Findings can be posted to a discussion board in online courses. Guide students in the discussion and ask follow-up questions to elicit their interpretations. For example, why might the repetition of the phrase *family-owned and operated* lead you to believe the organization values *loyalty* or *family*? Table 1 shows some of the key term/value pairings that have been produced from this activity.

If students are struggling in their small groups to think of their work experiences and activities as related to the perceived organizational values, I suggest

**TABLE 1.** Sample key terms and organizational values pairings

| Key Terms | Associated Organizational Values |
|---|---|
| Family-owned | Loyalty, family, hard work |
| Fast-paced | Competition, independence |
| Putting the customer first | Personal relationships |
| Community-oriented | Sustainability, collectivism |

that they brainstorm generally the job duties and skills that could support these values, and then compare them with their past work experience. From this exercise, links tend to emerge enough for them to be able to contribute to classroom discussion. Students later refine these skills and experience descriptions in their career documents and communication after we discuss more nuanced writing techniques, such as using action verbs and focusing on highlighting successes and outcomes that demonstrate performance (Bovée & Thill, 2016; Isaacs, n.d.). Table 2 shows how some students framed their experiences and skills (after they had completed additional work to develop their career documents) to represent the organizational values and preferred language originally identified through this activity.

**TABLE 2.** Sample customization efforts

| Perceived Organization Values | Customization effort |
|---|---|
| Loyalty, family, collectivism, hard work | A student applying for a financial planning internship highlighted in his cover letter how his experience working on his family's farm taught him the value of hard work and the importance of wealth management and caring for his community. |
| Competition, independence | A student applying for a sales position included athletic awards/titles she received as a student athlete on her résumé to demonstrate her competitive drive. |
| Trust, personal relationships | A student who approached a local bank recruiter at a career fair had worked seasonally to pick fruit and sell it at roadside stands. In her conversation, she mentioned how her employer had trusted her to handle hundreds of dollars in cash sales and that she had developed customer service skills interacting with regular customers. |

Students tend to enjoy this activity for several reasons. First, it is a nice break from what might otherwise be a dry lecture or unit on career document formatting. Second, students appreciate the applied nature of this activity. They become familiar with an organization they will see at a career fair or who is currently hiring, so the work is more immediately useful to their careers. After this activity, students are required to prepare cover letters and résumés in response to real job or internship calls and must write thank-you letters to their mock interviewers. *Customization*, as an evaluation criterion, is included in my grading rubrics. I have noticed an increase in customization efforts, particularly for the cover letter and thank-you letter assignments, which are submitted after this activity.

Students mentioned that having a better idea of what specific recruiters and interviewers might be looking for made them more confident in their application materials and interactions at the University Career Fair and mock interviews. They have reported back from career fairs and mock interviews that recruiters were impressed by their familiarity with the organizations, which boosted their self-esteem.

## REFERENCES

Bovée, C. L., & Thill, J. V. (2016). *Business communication today*. Boston, MA: Pearson.
    "Company culture: An inside look at 100 core values from 15 winning companies." (2013). Retrieved from http://yfsmagazine.com/2013/02/01/
    company-culture-an-inside-look-at-100-core-values-from-15-winning-companies/
Isaacs, K. (n.d.). 9 work history resume writing tips. Retrieved from http://www
    .monster.com/career-advice/article/write-a-winning-employment-history
Lencioni, P. M. (2002). Make your values mean something. Retrieved from https://
    hbr.org/2002/07/make-your-values-mean-something

# Ethics and Citizenship

# 74

# Goal-Directed Graffiti: Using Chalk Quotes for Critical Thinking About Free Expression

*Terri Toles Patkin*

*Eastern Connecticut State University*

*Department of Communication*

*patkin@easternct.edu*

**History:** This activity was presented at the annual meeting of the National Communication Association, November 2013, in Washington, D.C.
**Primary courses:** Communication Law, Communication Theory, Political Communication, Mass Communication
**Concepts illustrated:** Freedom of Expression, Medium Theory, Information Dissemination, Censorship, Time, Place and Manner Restrictions

## PURPOSE

This project emerged as a way for students in my Communication Law & Ethics class to mark Freedom of Expression Week. The goal of the assignment was to encourage students to contemplate big-picture issues relating to the First Amendment and freedom of expression. Students were asked to write their favorite quote about free speech with chalk somewhere on campus.

While freedom of speech is the best known of the five freedoms guaranteed by the First Amendment—religion, speech, press, assembly, and petition—a startling number of Americans are unable to name even that right (Newseum, 2015). This activity facilitates greater general knowledge of issues of free speech by bringing freedom of expression to public attention, and additionally allows communication students to explore questions of when and where expression may legally be limited.

The boundaries for categories of unprotected speech and the ethical implications associated with these sociopolitical decisions frame numerous historical and contemporary controversies (Fraleigh & Tuman, 2011). Theoretical work concerning freedom of expression includes absolutism theory (positing that the government may present absolutely no barrier to speech), balancing theory (in which freedom of expression is balanced against other constitutional rights such as the right to privacy or national security), marketplace of ideas theory (an economic metaphor focused on the search for truth), and access theory (emphasizing the need for media content to represent a broad spectrum of society), among others (Pember & Calvert, 2013). Drawing connections between philosophical writings about freedom of expression and everyday life can be challenging for some students; this activity provides a hands-on opportunity to make theory more accessible.

## EXPLANATION OF ACTIVITY

I bring a box of sidewalk chalk (available at most dollar stores) to class along with this directive: "Exercise your freedom of speech and raise awareness about free speech issues! Find a great quotation about freedom of speech or censorship. Write this quote (include author attribution) in chalk somewhere on campus. Put your initials somewhere near the quote. You can add drawings or other artistic flourishes if you want. Take a picture of your final product and send it to me." Time the assignment to coincide with a period of dry weather so that the quotations remain visible for several days. Most students will use a popular search engine to seek out the quotes; encourage them to dig deeper than the first few that appear, or to vary their search terms to include specifics such as censorship, political speech, or free speech in fields such as music or publishing. The requirement for author attribution provides a convenient opportunity to reinforce professional standards for citation of sources.

Establish ground rules appropriate to campus culture: no obscenities, only use removable material such as chalk, write only on sidewalks or in public areas. If your campus has regulations regarding chalking or posting material, it is important to contact the appropriate Student Affairs office in advance of the assignment.

Having the student photograph the completed work is essential. Some students include themselves in the picture, some apply visual esthetics learned in other courses, and some simply take a snapshot of their quote. Even students who do not own phones that can transmit images are likely to know someone who can help them out or they may own a digital camera. In the event that the student cannot comply with the photo requirement, alternatives are offered, but no one has ever reported a problem. Anecdotally, I find that requiring students to email me the photos often opens the door to further email communication throughout the semester; many times, students will follow up to share current events related to class content via email. Be sure to clearly establish a convention for identifying these emails in your inbox, such as a subject line reading something to the effect of "[name] [course] [quotation photo]."

## DEBRIEF

I collect the photos and share them in a slideshow in class, which leads to lively discussion as students recognize quotes scattered around campus. After the slideshow plays once, we go through it again slowly, with each student speaking briefly about their chosen quote, and why they chose it and the location for chalking it. Typically, either the source of the quote (from Voltaire to Beyoncé) or its content strikes a chord with the student. Popular entries typically include George Washington's "If freedom of speech is taken away, then dumb and silent we may be led, like sheep to the slaughter," and Frederick Douglass's "To suppress free speech is a double wrong. It violates the rights of the hearer as well as those of the speaker." Students clearly put some thought into the placement of their quotation: Abbie Hoffman's variation of "You can't shout fire in a crowded theater" appeared near the drama department, and a quote about money was placed in front of the entrance to the financial aid office.

Since many campuses have some sort of regulation regarding placement of chalk quotes, some students may deliberately or accidentally violate those rules. This opens an avenue for discussion of censorship and appropriate time, place, or manner restrictions on expression. Students may examine the official policy and consider its underlying rationale as well as the implications of the policy. Might there be exceptions that could be granted? Does the policy present a truly content neutral regulation of campus speech?

Instructors may wish to consider contacting the campus newspaper, television station, or University Relations office to get some publicity for this activity, as it fits nicely into the creative classroom theme for a news story.

In addition to selecting the quotation and displaying it, students can be asked to complete various extension assignments demonstrating their knowledge of theories or concepts relating to the quotation. This could range from a short response paper based on their own or another student's quote to a historical précis of the original context of the quotation and its relation to the topic at hand to a detailed analysis of the ways in which the quotation fits into a larger conceptual framework, such as freedom of expression or political communication. Class members can be encouraged to note others' quotes around campus, stand near their chalk quote and discuss it with passersby for some period of time, or the entire group could even spend class time on a "field trip" visiting the quotes while holding a discussion about them. Students are asked to reflect on how this activity may have altered their understanding of free speech and the constraints within which it operates. Clearly, the activity could be adapted for a variety of classes simply by altering the topic for the quotes.

The chalk activity serves as a springboard to building a sense of community in the classroom, and students appreciate the opportunity to express their creativity in an alternate format. Many students remark on the course evaluation form that this was by far their favorite class activity; one term, we celebrated the continued presence of a single quote in the parking garage months later when we gathered for the final exam.

## REFERENCES

Fraleigh, D. and Tuman, J. S. (2011). *Freedom of expression in the marketplace of ideas.* Thousand Oaks, CA: Sage Publications.

Newseum Institute. (2015). *2015 State of the First Amendment Survey.* Retrieved from http://www.newseuminstitute.org/wp-content/uploads/2015/07/FAC_SOFA15_report.pdf

Pember, D. R. and C. Calvert. (2013) *Mass media law* (18th ed.). New York: McGraw Hill.

# 75

# Ethical Reasoning in Action: Using 8 Key Questions to Facilitate Group Decision-Making

*Timothy C. Ball*
*School of Communication Studies*
*James Madison University*
*balltc@jmu.edu*

**History:** This activity was presented at the annual meeting of the Eastern Communication Association, April 2015, in Philadelphia, Pennsylvania.

**Primary courses in which this activity might be used:** Interpersonal Communication, Organizational Communication, Health Communication, Intercultural Communication

**Concepts illustrated:** Ethical Reasoning, Critical Thinking, Active Learning, Circle Process, 8 Key Questions

## PURPOSE

College students are and will be faced with increasingly complex decisions. Often these decisions are ethically complicated with implications that require sophisticated reasoning abilities they do not yet possess. For example, decisions made by individuals in the banking and mortgage industries plunged the world into the Great Recession (Petruno, 2009). Others made by political and military leaders to continue the wars in Afghanistan and Syria (DeYoung & Ryan, 2015) resulted in a mass exodus of people from that region to safer places in Europe and the Americas. Still others made by police officers in the United States have resulted in the death of countless young people, which in turn sparked public outrage and protests (Kindy, 2015).

The goal of this activity is to provide students with a framework or reasoning process they can use when dealing with ethical situations. Specifically, this activity teaches college students how to develop their reasoning abilities through the use of 8 Key Questions (Alger, Sternberger, & Goldstein, 2013). The expectation is that when given a specific scenario to deal with, students will be able to identify appropriate considerations for each of the 8 Key

Questions. Alternatively, students should be able to provide specific considerations that are raised or a rationale that is implied when applying every key
question to an ethical situation or dilemma.

## EXPLANATION OF ACTIVITY

To begin, introduce students to the 8 Key questions (to find the questions, type
"James Madison University 8 Key Questions" in an internet browser). These
questions focus on *fairness* (How can I act equitably and balance all interests?);
*outcomes* (What are the short-term and long-term outcomes of actions?); *responsibilities* (What duties and obligations apply?); *character* (What actions will help
me become my ideal self?); *liberty* (What principles of freedom and personal
autonomy apply?); *empathy* (How would I respond if I cared deeply about those
involved?); *authority* (What do legitimate authorities—experts, law, my god[s]—
expect of me?); and *rights* (What rights—innate, legal, social—apply?).

After reading about the key questions, have students read a short case study
or scenario that provides them with an ethical dilemma. Case studies and scenarios can be found in textbooks (e.g., Christians, C. G., Fackler, M., Richardson,
K. B., Kreshel, P. J., & Woods, R. H., Jr., 2016) and on websites (e.g., the University of Southern California's Levan Institute for Humanities and Ethics or the
Markkula Center for Applied Ethics at Santa Clara University).

Then introduce them to a circle process (Pranis, 2005). Specifically, have
them break into groups of five to eight and encourage each group to sit in a
circle while expectations are established—everyone turns their cell phones off,
shares, and engages in active learning (Bonwell and Eison, 1991).

In addition, the use of talking pieces (these can be tokens of some kind) is
important to the circle process, and there are rules governing their use. First,
whoever is holding the talking piece is the only one who should be speaking.
Other members of the group should focus their attention on the speaker. Second, students should pass the talking piece around the circle and share their
thoughts about the eight questions and the scenario. Third, students always
have the right to pass the talking piece to someone else. The circle is designed
to be a safe space to openly share thoughts and experiences, question assumptions, and challenge others in a respectful way. Using the 8 Key Questions, a circle process provides students with a framework for making reasoned decisions.

To help them identify appropriate considerations, use multiple rounds so
that students can understand and apply the 8 Key Questions to the scenario.
In Round One, give students three minutes to reflect individually on the questions and apply them to the scenario. Ask students to determine which key
questions are most relevant for this scenario and explain their rationale. After
everyone has had a chance to share using the talking piece, have the group
decide what three questions most apply to this scenario. Each group should be
prepared to share their top three questions and why they chose them.

In Round Two, have the groups discuss which questions were the most
important. Each group must come up with an answer and be prepared to share
it with the larger group. Have groups report on what they would do in the

scenario and to explain why. Encourage the groups to reflect on and articulate how their decisions match up with the 8 Key Questions. In Round Three, have the groups discuss whether using the 8 questions changed their considerations and/or the discussion they had about the scenario.

## DEBRIEF

Some groups spend a great deal of time discussing which one of the questions is most relevant to the scenario and why. Oftentimes they will agree that there are three questions that are most relevant to the scenario being discussed. Other groups spend less time discussing the key questions and move more quickly to making a decision. It is difficult to determine in advance which groups will be more deliberative and which groups will be more decision-driven.

In the end it is important for the groups, after having reported what they would do, to move from asking, "What would you do?" to the more challenging "What is the right thing to do, if there is a right thing to do?" Asking "What makes it right or not?" brings the 8 Key Questions into play and demonstrates the reflective nature of the ethical reasoning process.

## REFERENCES

Alger, J. R., Sternberger, L., & Goldstein, B. (2013). *The Madison collaborative: Ethical reasoning in action.* Harrisonburg, VA: James Madison University.

Bonwell, C. C., & Eison, J. A. (1991). *Active learning: Creating excitement in the classroom.* ASHE-ERIC Higher Education Report No. 1. Washington, D.C.: The George Washington University School of Education and Human Development.

Christians, C. G., Fackler, M., Richardson, K. B., Kreshel, P. J., & Woods, R. H., Jr. (2016). *Media ethics: Cases and moral reasoning* (9th ed.). New York: Routledge.

DeYoung, K., & Ryan, M. (2015, Dec. 22). As bombing in Syria intensifies, a debate about the rules of engagement. In *Washington Post.* Retrieved from https://www.washington-post.com/world/national-security/as-bombing-in-syria-intensifies-a-debate-about-the-rules-of-engagement/2015/12/22/d9dece84-a823-11e5-bff5-905b92f5f94b_story.html

Kindy, K. (2015, May 30). Fatal police shootings in 2015 approaching 400 nationwide. *Washington Post.* Retrieved from https://www.washingtonpost.com/national/fatal-police-shootings-in-2015-approaching-400-nationwide/2015/05/30/d322256a-058e-11e5-a428-c984eb077d4e_story.html

The Madison Collaborative: Ethical Reasoning in Action (n.d.). *The eight key questions (8 KQ).* Retrieved from http://www.jmu.edu/mc/8-key-questions.shtml

Markkula Center for Applied Ethics (n.d.). *Ethics cases.* Retrieved from https://www.scu.edu/ethics/ethics-resources/ethics-cases

Petruno, T. (2009, Dec 31). Stock market closes the books on a 'lost decade.' *Los Angeles Times.* Retrieved from http://articles.latimes.com/2009/dec/31/business/la-fi-stocks31-2009dec31

Pranis, K. (2005). *The little book of circle processes: A new/old approach to peacemaking.* Intercourse, PA: Good Books.

University of Southern California Levan Institute for Humanities and Ethics (n.d.). *Ethical dilemmas, cases, and case studies.* Retrieved from http://dornsife.usc.edu/levan-institute/dilemmas-and-case-studies

# 76

## Using Jon Stewart's Appearance on *Crossfire* to Teach Students About (In)Civility and the Elaboration Likelihood Model

*Angela M. McGowan*
*State University of New York at Fredonia*
*Department of Communication*
*mcgowan@fredonia.edu*

**History:** This activity was presented at the annual meeting of the National Communication Association, November 2012, in Orlando, Florida. The G.I.F.T.S. was a top-ranked submission.
**Primary courses in which this activity might be used:** Argumentation and Debate, Communication Ethics, Communication Theory, Persuasion, Political Communication, Public Speaking, Rhetorical Criticism
**Concepts illustrated:** Civil Discourse, Elaboration Likelihood Model, Persuasion

### PURPOSE

In 2004 Jon Stewart appeared on CNN's *Crossfire* and charged that the thirty-minute debate show was "hurting America" (Feist, 2004). Stewart maintained that the show's co-hosts were hurting America by engaging in uncivil discourse. Similar to Stewart, Darr (2011) argued that discourtesy in the public sphere weakens America's policy-making process and diminishes the quality of political discourse. Incivility, such as rhetoric heard on *Crossfire,* is the antithesis of productive debate because incivility stifles dialogue (Loomis, 2000). CNN's president agreed with Stewart's assessment of the show, and attempted to move the cable news channel away from the "head-butting debate show" by cancelling *Crossfire* (Carter, 2005). This segment offers a means for exploring (in)civility and its connection to a person's motivation and ability to process a persuasive message.

As opposed to uncivil language that is associated with "unproductive personal and partisan attacks" (Evans & Oleszek, 1998, p. 27), "civil language makes compromise across partisan and ideological lines possible" (Uslaner, 2000, p. 35). Civility can be conceptualized "as a set of standards for conducting public argument" (Darr, 2011, p. 604). Scholars generally argue that civility is an important characteristic of public deliberation in our democracy (Ivie, 2008).

In addition to learning about civil discourse, Stewart's appearance on *Crossfire* teaches students about message processing. Persuasion theories, such as Petty and Cacioppo's Elaboration Likelihood Model (ELM), clarify how people's attitudes guide decisions and behaviors. The ELM is a dual-processing model of how attitudes are formed and changed (Petty & Cacioppo, 1986). When people are motivated and have the ability to think logically about the content of a message, elaboration is high, and people are more likely to take a central persuasive route. While participating in the activity, students process Carlson, Begala, and Stewart's messages through the central route, because they watch the video and read the transcript to assess the message's content.

Conversely, if a message recipient relies on cues such as the source's perceived credibility and the quality of the way in which the message was presented, he or she may not elaborate on the message through critical thinking (Petty & Cacioppo, 1986). In this activity, students explain how aspects of the segment, including source attractiveness and likeability, can influence whether the audience accepts the position advocated in the message. As a result, students learn that civility can be assessed through examining central cues, namely the actual arguments being made, and peripheral cues such as the interlocutor's nonverbal behavior.

In sum, this activity helps students see that when dialogue is squelched, central processing is more difficult, whereas peripheral cues might function to promote and/or stifle dialogue. On one hand, an interlocutor who uses incivility might repress dialogue by distracting the speaker or by diverting the audience's attention so that they cannot centrally process a message. On the other hand, an interlocutor may foster dialogue by remaining still during the opposition's speaking time, thereby promoting central processing on the part of the undistracted audience.

## EXPLANATION OF ACTIVITY

The lesson and activity use theory and practice to enhance students' abilities to engage in civil discussions and recognize how persuaders construct and process messages. The activity typically requires two fifty- to seventy-five-minute class sessions. The instructor spends one day lecturing on the psychology of persuasion, ELM, and civil discourse, and executes the activity on the second day. He or she must have access to a computer, the Internet, a projector, and audio speakers.

### Part 1: Lecturing on the psychology of persuasion, ELM, and civil discourse

1. Using the ELM, explain the dual processing approaches, why different processing modes might be used, and the results of those processing modes on attitude change (see Petty & Cacioppo, 1986).

2. Discuss civility and how polarized thinking and discourse create false dichotomies that suggest deeper divisions than might actually exist.
3. As a class, choose a definition of *civil discourse*. The instructor may want to search communication journals and books for possible definitions and/or ask students to create their own definition (see Darr, 2011; Loomis, 2000).
4. Use the definition of *civil discourse* to have students generate a list of times that they participated in uncivil discourse. Have one student write his or her list on the board and then ask students to either add to the list or place a checkmark next to situations that they too experienced.

**Part 2: *Crossfire* Activity**

1. Provide background on *Crossfire* and mention that it was cancelled because of Stewart's criticism of cable news shows ("Jon Stewart vs. *Crossfire*," 2012).
2. Distribute two handouts, including the show's transcript ("Jon Stewart's America," 2004) and a worksheet that lists discussion questions (see Appendix, p. 326).
3. Have students spend between seven and eight minutes reading the segment's transcript and reviewing the discussion questions and then provide clarification if they have questions.
4. To locate the segment, go to YouTube and search "Jon Stewart on Crossfire" and select the 14:14 second video posted by Alex Felker ten years ago.
5. Play the fourteen-minute *Crossfire* segment (Feist, 2004).
6. Ask students to form groups of four.
7. Referencing the list of uncivil discourse that is written on the board (see Part I, Step 4), ask students to connect their own experiences to situations that they observed during the show. For instance, students may notice that similar to the television commentators, they too have engaged in name-calling, marginalized other viewpoints, and refused to discuss the topic with those who opposed their perspective.
8. Students should first respond to the discussion questions on their own, then with their group, and then share their responses with the class. For example, students answering Part 1, Question 2 on their own have identified Stewart's source credibility as a reason to support his argument. However, those who had never heard of Stewart focused more on the glitzy television set and the commentators' wardrobes.
9. As a class, examine the ways in which students can enact civil discourse. When answering Part 2, Question 2 on their own, students listed compromise and cooperation but as a group they noted the importance of respecting others' viewpoints as legitimate and mutual respect as ways the co-hosts could have used civility.
10. Collect the students' written answers to assess whether or not they fully grasp the ELM, uncivil discourse, and the connection between the two concepts.

11. Conclude the activity by reminding students that understanding the principles of persuasion are vital to being an informed citizen. Moreover, students should be reminded that enacting civil discourse, such as treating others with respect both in language and in deed, relies on a person's motivation to centrally process the interlocutor's argument.

## DEBRIEF

Following each groups' shared responses, the instructor should facilitate a class discussion that examines the ELM and civil discourse. By completing the activity, students understand how attitudes affect oneself and other people, objects, and issues, and gain insight into how persuasive messages are received and the ways in which listeners hear, interpret, and respond to messages. During the class discussion, students identify specific peripheral and central processing cues that influence their abilities to process Carlson, Begala, and Stewart's messages. By answering questions such as "How did the commentators induce change without the audience scrutinizing the true merits of the information?" and "What conditions fostered the audience's motivation and ability to engage in issue-relevant thinking?," students illustrate how an audience organizes, categorizes, and understands messages as well as the basic processing underlying the effectiveness of persuasive communication. The hope is that students realize that civil discourse requires that interlocutors rely less on peripheral processing and more on giving careful and thoughtful consideration to the true merits of the information being presented.

In addition to focusing on other people's motivation and ability to carefully interpret messages, students also connect their own experiences to situations that they saw during the show. In so doing, students discover how communication behaviors that encourage peripheral processing at the expense of central processing are "hurting America," hindering productive debate, stifling dialogue. By asking students to critically assess how they respond to messages, students identify how compromise, consensus building, and verbal respect create a civil environment. It is easy to be distracted during a debate, and since distraction hinders a person's ability to scrutinize messages, students better understand what causes them to process peripherally. Therefore, the post-video conversation enhances students' awareness of their own cognitive processing and the role that central processing plays in fostering civility.

## REFERENCES

Carter, B. (2005, January 6). CNN will cancel 'Crossfire' and cut ties with commentator. *The New York Times.* Retrieved from http://www.nytimes.com/2005/01/06/business/media/cnn-will-cancel-crossfire-and-cut-ties-to-commentator.html?_r=0

Darr, C. R. (2011). Adam Ferguson's civil society and the rhetorical functions of (in) civility in United States Senate debate. *Communication Quarterly, 59,* 603–624. doi:10.1080/01463373.2011.614208

Evans, C. L., & Oleszek, W. J. (1998). If it ain't broke bad, don't fix it a lot. *PS: Political Science and Politics, 31*, 24–28. Retrieved from http://www.jstor.org/stable/420428

Feist, S. (Executive Producer). (2004, October 15). *Crossfire* [Television broadcast]. Washington, DC: CNN Broadcasting System. Retrieved from http://www.youtube.com/watch?v=aFQFB5YpDZE&feature=player_embedded

Jon Stewart's America. (2004). *CNN Crossfire*. Retrieved from http://transcripts.cnn.com/TRANSCRIPTS/0410/15/cf.01.html

Jon Stewart vs. Crossfire. (2012). *Time*. Retrieved from http://content.time.com/time/specials/packages/article/0,28804,1884499_1884515_1884462,00.html

Ivie, R. L. (2008). Toward a humanizing style of democratic dissent. *Rhetoric & Public Affairs, 11*, 454–458. doi:10.1353/rap.0.0061

Loomis, B. A. (2000). *Esteemed colleagues: Civility and deliberation in the U.S. Senate.* Washington, DC: Brookings Institution Press.

Petty, R. E., & Cacioppo, J. T. (1986). *Communication and persuasion: Central and peripheral routes to attitude change.* New York: Springer-Verlag.

Uslaner, E. M. (2000). Is the Senate more civil than the House? In B. A. Loomis (Ed.), *Esteemed colleagues: Civility and deliberation in the U.S. Senate* (pp. 32–55). Washington, DC: Brookings Institution.

## APPENDIX

### DISCUSSION QUESTIONS

### Part 1: Elaboration Likelihood Model

1. According to the ELM, how might Carlson and Begala receive Stewart's message if they were processing from the central route? Use specific examples from the transcript to support your response.
2. If processing from a peripheral route, what cues might influence the way the message is received? Use specific examples from the *Crossfire* video and its transcript to support your response.

### Part 2: (In)Civility

1. Do you agree with Stewart that these shows are hurting America?
2. Keeping in mind Stewart's plea, "See the thing is, we need your help. Right now, you're helping the politicians and the corporations ..." ("Jon Stewart's America," 2004), brainstorm between three to five ideas for how the co-hosts could have had a discussion of political topics using civility.

# 77

# Communication, Choices, and Consequences: Patrice's Problem, or a Case in Organizational Communication Ethics

## W. Thomas Duncanson
Department of Communication
Millikin University
tduncanson@mail.millikin.edu

**History:** This activity was presented at the annual meeting of the Southern States Communication Association, April 2013, in Louisville, Kentucky.

**Primary courses in which this activity might be used:** Organizational Communication, Communication Ethics, Introduction to Communication Studies

**Concepts illustrated:** Principle of Publicity, Moral Agency, Organizational Isolation, Technological Fix, Exit or Voice

## PURPOSE

Many instructors teach ethics by the discussion of cases. There is also a long tradition of teaching organizational communication by case. Cases are excellent ways to plausibly frame what might otherwise seem to students to be hopelessly abstract problems. Students tend to make quick assessments of the problems in the case, and then benefit from a class hour walking back those hasty remarks as they consider the complex features of the matter and as the instructor skillfully advances the discussion through fresh questions and the introduction of new concepts and literature. The most useful cases have enough drama to get and keep the students' interest and have enough detail to seem real and to make the characters sympathetic. The best cases have enough complexity to give students an opportunity to do some genuinely critical thinking about what is relevant to the question being asked, and enough layers to give students the experience of drawing careful distinctions.

This case (see Appendix, p. 331) is probably most suitable for a course in organizational communication where not a great number of class hours are to be dedicated to ethics, and the instructor seeks to raise a number of core issues and concepts efficiently.

In this exercise, students will learn the principle of publicity: To be ethical, a behavior or contemplated course of action must be capable of public statement and defense (Bok, 1978; Rawls, 1971).

Bok's "test of publicity" is one of those great propositions where good communication becomes good ethics and vice versa. The central idea is that unless there is some exceptional circumstance, we should only do things we can explain and justify to others. The corollary is that barring some exceptional explanation, dishonesty and secrecy are wrong. The practical take-away for students is that in organizations, workers should not become isolated from explaining their work and work decisions from other members of the organization, and form a sense of what it would mean to explain themselves to people outside the organization.

## EXPLANATION OF ACTIVITY

This case concerns an industrial engineer named Patrice who faces difficult choices around an issue of submitting a fraudulent product certification. This class activity lends itself to informal discussion, formal debate, and written response. Because this case is detailed it might best be distributed in a previous class so that students have enough time to read it. Instructors might have it read aloud and take time to explain specifics in the case, especially when students are not strong readers. The instructor would rightly select her or his own specific objectives and determine the best evidence of student learning, and articulate most clearly the rationale for why this exercise meets larger curricular goals of your institution concerning critical thinking, ethical reasoning, or democratic citizenship.

## DEBRIEF

Do details about Patrice's family matter in analyzing this problem—is there anything we can say, for instance, about the health or hopes of Patrice, her husband, and her children that are more than a nuisance or distraction from the real questions in this case? In the same way, do details about the economy or news about Patrice's industry change at all the way one should approach this situation? When Sarah approaches Patrice with an unforeseen concern about the well-being of her son and other soldiers, is this evidence that we must be open to new information in analyzing moral questions, or is this an irrelevant distraction from the central problem in this case?

Does this case represent a classical dilemma between the duty to tell the truth and the happiness of one person's community, organization, family, and self? Or does a conflict of dreary, noble, sacrificial, duty versus vital prosperity misstate the problem? In fact, is this only a choice between doing the right thing, and compromising one's self and one's community—making it harder for all the community's members to behave with integrity?

Patrice is advised to commit fraud, one form of dishonesty or deception. Every deception seems to be based on the idea that one can short circuit the other person's powers of reason—that one can make a perfectly normal, healthy, educated, other-regarding person think wrongly, by giving them misleading information to think about. In doing so, we hope to protect ourselves from some sort of negative judgment—dissent, disapproval, or blame and punishment. Do you think there is any realistic hope that Patrice's fraud will work?

This problem is set in recent times, when the nation has soldiers faraway in combat, and in a kind of organization some people would find very realistic. Patrice and her colleagues, as the story is told, would prefer to be immunized against fear of job loss, and protected from the more outrageous forms of quarterly measured profit motivation. They would prefer to be good engineers without worrying about other matters. Patrice's problem is presented as the tragic exception in a relatively morally innocent life. Today, does Patrice's sort of problem seem melodramatic (exaggeratedly dramatic), because today millions of workers are under constant, daily pressure to violate their sense of morality—assigning people unfair interest rates, denying people services for which they have contracted, selling others things they themselves know to be in some sense defective, working diligently to give the consumer less or to hook them on things that are not good for them, misleading and avoiding those who would be economic referees and public advocates? It has been said that when we face these pressures in our work, we feel as if we only have two choices, to exit or voice (Hirschman, 1970)—but Patrice does not want to quit or speak out. Does she have a third option?

In moral dilemmas such as Patrice's the wicked supervisor is presented as an unchangeable given. This supervisor seems to act freely without any fear of consequence. Although this makes for good storytelling, are there really such characters in our organizations? If Patrice can only comply or lose her job, she is not much of a moral agent, not a free person herself who has her own sanctions she can deliver. We might choose to think of this using a vocabulary of *power*. Are there things organizations can do, using ombudspersons, creating protective whistle-blower policies, or something else, that can even out the power disparity between Patrice and the supervisors?

The federal government plays an important role in this case. People in business routinely blame the Feds for seemingly illogical things they do, and hating the federal government as a total *other* has become a feature of American public life. Anything believed this widely and repeated this effortlessly deserves careful questioning, especially in a system of popular sovereignty. In Patrice's case, the government is the client, the potential prosecutor, and the potential judge, and these last things in several possible ways from administrative hearings to criminal prosecution. How can we as students studying Patrice's case recuperate the concept of the federal government as an honorable actor and partner with whom we struggle for justice?

To read Patrice's story is for some readers to hope for, to root for, a techno-logical fix. If Patrice can make a legitimate engineering solution to the prob-lem, her moral dilemma goes away. If we had enough technical fixes, we could make all of our moral problems go away, up to and including the loss of life itself. We would simply reverse death. Critique our belief in these fixes.

Patrice is anxious; ultimately she cannot sleep. Prominent thinkers such as Nietzsche in *Thus Spoke Zarathustra* (1978) and Cioran in *A Short History of Decay* (1998) use a good night's sleep and insomnia, sometimes ironically, as moral measuring devices. Patrice's moral life leaks out of her body. Her head aches. What is the significance of the emotional dimension of our moral lives?

Bok in the book *Lying* writes at length on the principle of publicity. We ordi-narily do not do what we are ashamed to tell others we are doing, unless, of course, we are secure in our secrecy or deception. Organizationally, one of the best ways out of problems such as Patrice's might be to create greater, more deliberate, even more formal collegiality among the Grinder engineers and those who supervise their work. We notice in the case, Patrice's project begins as a kind of joke with her peers, and she grows into a more and more isolated position in the company over this work. Silence becomes a morally unfortunate feature of the problem. If the project were vetted each morning at a team meet-ing, if there were dozens of eyes and ears playing a part and taking responsibil-ity for the outcome instead of just Patrice, there could almost never be a scene in which the individual is ordered to commit fraud. And if a dozen engineers can look one another in the eye and say out loud in a meeting they will commit fraud together, then we have a completely different case than the one Patrice has presented here. How can publicity and collegiality be systematically used to improve the moral climates of our organizations?

Patrice's problem takes us back to questions of communication. Agnes Heller in her book *General Ethics* (1988) argues that we need ethical *theory* and not just ethical philosophy. She meant by that, we need to mesh our best think-ing about society making with our formal ethical thought. Surely, communica-tion studies are a part of that theorizing. Patrice's communication—her sense of hierarchy, isolation, inability to disagree—must be understood and addressed in understanding the problem.

## REFERENCES

Bok, S. (1978). *Lying*. New York: Random House-Pantheon.
Cioran, E. M. (1998). *A short history of decay*. (R. Howard, TRANS.). New York: Arcade.
Heller, A. (1988). *General Ethics*. Oxford: Basil Blackwell.
Hirschman, A. O. (1970). *Exit, voice, and loyalty: Responses to decline in firms, organizations, and states*. Cambridge: Harvard University Press.
Nietzsche, F. (1978). *Thus spoke Zarathustra* (W. Kaufmann, trans.) New York: Penguin.
Rawls, J. (1971). *A theory of justice*. Cambridge: Harvard-Belknap.

## APPENDIX

## PATRICE'S PROBLEM

It is the present, and the place is the American mid-south. Patrice is a forty-four-year old engineer at Grinder Works, a company spun off from Detroit's Behemoth Motors in a deal which saw Grinder purchased by its own top managers and some private investors, and moved from Michigan to a new office and plant complex in a small city in western Tennessee. Behemoth is a comprehensive ground transportation company with several nameplates of automobiles and consumer trucks, detached over-the-road diesel trucks, industrial diesel engines, locomotives, earth moving equipment, farm tractors, military and other specialized vehicles, motorcycles, lawn care equipment, and more. Grinder Works is the industry-leading manufacturer of concrete mixing equipment; it was owned and operated by its founding family in Michigan until the founder retired in 1963 and sold out to Behemoth. Grinder Works is in the third phase of its corporate life; it has tried to keep its reputation for top-of-the-market machines and a steady cycle of lucrative defense contracts.

Behemoth is organized by the United Auto Workers, but the new Grinder Works has no bargaining unit. Patrice and the other managers and engineers who moved to the new facility from the Detroit area have good wages and benefits, but they are anxious about compensation because salaries have been stagnant in recent years and there is talk of asking the line workers to take a small pay cut in the name of global competitiveness. Non-union workers such as Patrice happily bought Behemoth stock by payroll deduction. But times have changed, and under private ownership, there is no Grinder Works stock to buy.

Patrice's title is Industrial Engineer but in fact, she only has little more than a year of college credit from a community college. She worked into her title with Grinder by being dedicated to the organization, perceptive about the needs of specific projects, and proficient in mathematics. Patrice has felt trusted and valued at Grinder, but feels much less secure in her job since the company broke off from Behemoth. She knows she could be replaced by a four-year degree-holding engineering grad, hired at the company every spring. She gets along well with these young, college-educated engineers from the University of Memphis and Mississippi State, but there is no faking that she does not have a degree.

Last year Patrice was assigned an unusual project. Grinder Works got a contract to deliver one thousand desert-camouflage, gasoline-powered, concrete mixers to the United States Army for use in combat zones. This would have been a routine matter, except that the procurement officer at the Department of Defense had asked for some design variations for durability, and had added that all heavy equipment must meet revised noise pollution requirements. If the equipment does not meet those requirements on delivery, the contract is void. Patrice was assigned to make the concrete mixers noise-level compliant.

These noise requirements and the very idea of noise pollution seems like a trivial matter in an industry that usually sells its products on horsepower and durability, and her co-workers tease Patrice about the absurdity of a quiet cement mixer. They rolled their eyes about stupid government regulations. Patrice evaluated every part in the machines, isolated every rattle and hum in the devices, and considered all the materials used in the parts. Patrice even made a study of the constituents of concrete in the vague hope for less clattery gravel. She tested jerry-rigged mufflers and baffles, held long talks with her supervisors and the cost containment people on material substitutions, scrutinized engine size, etc. Most of her efforts had negligible impact on the decibels the mixers produced; the most effective noise suppression tactics weakened the machines for heavy-duty use, putting them in clear violation of other aspects of the contract and unacceptable to carry the proud Grinder name. Some of the most obvious solutions would have been so expensive they would have pushed the unit cost of the concrete mixers far above profitability on the contract. As the project has ground on, Patrice has spoken to her co-workers about it less and less, and they cheerfully help her save face by talking about SEC football and the latest craze in reality television when she is around.

Patrice checked out everything she could on sound and sound engineering from the small Grinder Works Library, then spent a day at the University of Memphis Library, and privately came to the anxiety-laden conclusion that the solution probably lay in six years of engineering by a top team of university specialists, not six months by her and the two technicians assigned to support her on the project.

Like the rest of us, Patrice does not live in a social bubble of work. She has a forty-six-year old husband who works intermittently as a truck driver, and two teenage sons who are pointing toward college. This family's lifestyle and aspirations depend on Patrice keeping her job. There is an unpleasant change in the air. People who have always understood the necessity of the fight against terrorism are questioning the war, and the economy has flattened. In Patrice's town, people have said since Grinder arrived, they can tell how the economy is doing by the number of unsold concrete mixers in the Grinder Works parking lot. Right now, there are three long rows of mixers lined up there. Every job, every contract, is important now. Patrice unconsciously measures these troubles, and the sum is not looking very good.

One late afternoon when Patrice is going over the latest trial reports at her desk, Sarah, who is about her age and works afternoons in the Grinder reception area, stopped by and asked, "How's it going, Patrice?"

Patrice spun her predicament as best as she could saying, "It is pretty grim today, but we're trying something new tomorrow."

Sarah looked at her and said, "I hope you get this figured out. You know my son Robbie is over there, and they get sniper fire all the time. Quieter machinery that doesn't draw as much fire might save some of our soldiers' lives." Sarah turned and headed back to the reception.

Draw fire! Save lives! Patrice had never thought of it that way. She thought she was meeting a stupid government requirement, maybe saving the hearing of some old retired construction equipment operators in the far off future. Patrice's head ached.

Patrice's bosses' boss made an appointment to see her, asked her to bring the project file and all of the test reports. Patrice almost always enjoys a good night's rest, but tosses sleeplessly the night before the meeting, which goes badly. She feels like a little kid being called to the principal's office at school for a scolding and worse. There is something slightly crazy about being held personally accountable for the laws of nature, the state of noise technology, the economics of construction equipment, and the terms of a contract she herself had not made—but there was the glaring supervisor making it so. It came down to this: On the delivery date, Patrice would sign the noise-level certification, whether or not the mixers met the standards. She would prepare data that supported this certification. If she did not, she would be fired as an incompetent engineer. Or so the supervisor implied in unmistakable code and euphemism, just veiled slyly enough to protect himself in court.

Seeing no hope for a timely technological fix, what should Patrice do? Should she commit a federal contract fraud and sign the certification, or should she refuse to do so, and be fired?

# 78

## The Ethical Speaker: A Discussion of Ethical Concerns Facing the Public Speaker

*Rita Rosenthal*

*Communication Department*

*Boston College*

*rosenthr@bc.edu*

**History:** This activity was presented on a G.I.F.T.S. program at the Eastern Communication Association Convention, April 2008, in Pittsburgh, Pennsylvania.

**Primary courses in which this activity might be used:** Public Speaking, Persuasion, Rhetorical Theory

**Concepts illustrated:** Ethical Considerations, Ethical Perspectives

### PURPOSE

When asked what constitutes an ethical public speaker, students will often define it as a speaker who does not lie or cheat. This activity helps students understand that a number of ethical concerns may arise during a speaking situation, and recognize that the decisions speakers make can have important consequences. It is geared to helping students make their ethical decisions in a more robust manner.

### EXPLANATION OF ACTIVITY

During the second or third week of the course, students are asked to discuss ethical concerns facing communicators (see Appendix A, p. 335). By way of example, the first two prompts provide students with an opportunity to focus on the attribution of sources. The goal is to get students to identify why we cite sources in speeches and presentations. For example, I will ask the class if they cite sources in discussions with their friends. While they generally find this question amusing, students eventually note that they attribute certain information to television programs or Internet sites. A student may tell a friend that they "saw 'X' on ESPN." We build upon this, moving to the importance of source attribution in class and public speeches. Students are required to include specific reasons or examples for their viewpoint.

Once students are involved in the discussion, the instructor should move on to several of the other ethical concerns. For example, if the students seem reticent, I move on to the prompt concerning the use of profanity in a speech. That topic always enlivens the discussion. The amount of time spent on each topic is determined by the flow of the discussion. The entire activity can take as little as thirty minutes, but if students are engaged, it can last for a ninety-minute class period.

Playing the role of devil's advocate can enhance the discussion. If students have a strong view about one item, I try to give an example of when that view may be questioned. For example, students generally find that lying in a speech is "very unethical." As devil's advocate, the instructor might then ask, "Is it permissible for the president of the United States to lie in a speech to protect national security?" This provides students an opportunity to consider different ethical perspectives. It also helps them feel more comfortable verbally stating a difference of opinion.

## DEBRIEF

At the end of the discussion, a number of ethical perspectives are introduced to the class including the religious, human nature, political, dialogical, situational, legal, and social utility perspectives (Larson, 2009). After considering each, the instructor should go through the prompts on the handout a second time, examining which perspective is most consistent with particular responses provided by various students during the discussion. The goal of the debriefing is to show that ethics can be viewed from a variety of perspectives and different ethical constructs can result in contradictory ethical conclusions.

The final part of the debriefing is to show that while there are no ethical absolutes, there are ethical rules that pertain to the particular course, in terms of best practices for speeches and presentations. At this point, I hand out Johannesen, Kinkugel and Bryan's (2000) list of general ethical guidelines (see Appendix B, p. 336), and I present my view of ethical public speaking (e.g., students must cite sources in their speeches).

## REFERENCES

Larson, C. U. (2009). *Persuasion: Reception and responsibility* (Rev. ed.). Belmont, CA: Wadsworth.

Johannesen, R. L., Valde, K. S., Whedbee, K. E. (2008). *Ethics in human communication* (Rev. ed). Long Grove, IL: Waveland Press.

Johannesen, R. L., Allen, R. R., Linkugel, W. A., Bryan, F. J. (2000). *Contemporary American speeches: A sourcebook of speech forms and principles* (Rev. ed.). Dubuque, IA: Kendall/Hunt Pub.

## APPENDIX A

Place yourself in each of these three situations: a discussion with your peers, a speech delivered in class, and a publically delivered speech. Which of the following constitute very ethical, ethical, unethical, or very unethical behaviors in each of these situations?

1. Paraphrasing a source without giving credit to the source.
2. Using a direct quote without giving credit to the source of the quote.
3. Changing a quoted source's name to a source that would be more acceptable to the audience.
4. Using only a portion of a quote to justify a claim while disregarding the rest of the quote, which negates the claim the source is really making.
5. Using a speech totally written by a speechwriter.
6. Using a hypothetical example, but portraying it as a real example.
7. Basing an argument strictly on emotional appeals.
8. Using profanity to highlight a point.
9. Using a speech to promote conflict and tensions that may lead to public unrest.
10. Labeling a person or idea with terms having negative or evil meaning.
11. Deliberately lying about a condition in order to calm a person or an audience.
12. Failing to inform the audience that he or she represents another person or group.

## APPENDIX B

1. Do not use false, fabricated, misrepresented, distorted, or irrelevant evidence to support arguments or claims.
2. Do not intentionally use specious, unsupported, or illogical reasoning.
3. Do not represent yourself as informed or as an expert on a subject when you are not.
4. Do not use irrelevant appeals to divert attention or scrutiny from the issue at hand.
5. Do not ask your audience to link your idea or proposal to emotion-laden values, motives, or goals to which it actually is not related.
6. Do not deceive your audience by concealing your real purpose, by concealing self-interest, by concealing the group you represent, or by concealing your position as an advocate of a viewpoint.
7. Do not distort, hide, or misrepresent the number, scope, intensity, or undesirable features or consequences or effects.
8. Do not use emotional appeals that lack a supporting basis of evidence and reason, or that would not be accepted if the audience had time and opportunity to examine the subject themselves.
9. Do not oversimplify complex, gradation-laden situations into simplistic two values, either-or, or plural choices.
10. Do not pretend certainty where tentativeness and degrees of probability would be more accurate.
11. Do not advocate something in which you do not believe yourself.

# 79

## Smoke and Mirrors?: Using *Thank You for Smoking* to Teach Persuasion and Ethics

*Jennifer B. Gray*
*Department of Communication*
*Appalachian State University*
*grayjb@appstate.edu*

**History:** The activity was presented at the annual meeting of the Southern States Communication Association, April 2009, in Norfolk, Virginia. It was a top-ranked submission.
**Primary courses in which this activity might be used:** Persuasion, Rhetorical Theory, Criticism
**Concepts illustrated:** Persuasion, Persuasive Speech Tactics, Ethics

### PURPOSE

Beginning communication students sometimes confuse persuasive communication with manipulation. However, persuasion is inherently amoral; the speaker may have ethical or unethical goals and tactics (Cope & Sandys, 2010; McCroskey, 2005). This classroom activity for the public speaking classroom, using the film, *Thank You for Smoking*, allows students to discuss transparent versus manipulative approaches and the importance of persuasion with underlying ethical speechmaking goals. The goal of the activity is to have students begin to examine the objectives of persuasion within the context of ethical speechmaking by watching a scene from a film *Thank You for Smoking* and discussing the persuasiveness of the speaker, Nick Naylor, as well as his ethics.

Students are exposed to a persuasive speaker who uses unethical speaking tactics when viewing and examining the scene through class discussion. Based on this scene, portrayed with clarity and humor, students are able to see that the objective of persuasion is to convince the audience to attend to and perhaps accept one's argument, but not at any cost. Ethical and unethical persuasive approaches are demonstrated to be very different.

## EXPLANATION OF ACTIVITY

You should rent the DVD of the film *Thank You for Smoking* and show the scene "Meet Nick Naylor." Preface the scene with a brief discussion of speech ethics and some background on the character in the film. Specifically, Nick Naylor is the chief spokesperson for big tobacco. He gets paid to talk. In the scene, Nick addresses an audience (in the studio and the viewership watching at home) of a talk show. Prior to the scene, he provides a narration of what he really thinks about cigarettes and his job (he believes he has killed more people than Attila the Hun, knows how harmful cigarettes are, that he spins the truth, he is right because he shows that others are wrong, etc.). He is then shown pandering to the audience, and turning the issue of cigarettes and cancer on its head, focusing on how individuals having cancer and dying would just reduce customers for him, and how the industry is developing programs "for the children."

After viewing the scene, you should begin a discussion of Nick's job, his methods of persuasion, his ethics, what he says versus what he believes, his delivery, and how he relates to his audience. Depending on the desired focus, the scene may be used for various types of discussion regarding message and delivery, as well as speech ethics. In the ethics discussion, you should try to emphasize that "with great power comes great responsibility," and that in a persuasive speech, one should be convincing, and bring others to at least attend to, if not totally accept, one's argument, but *not* at any cost (such as lying, debunking other positions in an unfair or manipulative manner, etc.). Other, more ethical speechmaking strategies may then be discussed, such as the combination of emotional and logical appeals, based on solid factual information and ethical pathos (Dillard & Pfau, 2002; Johannesen, 2002; Lucas, 2007).

## DEBRIEF

The viewing of the scene and the discussion of ethics makes clear the distinction between persuasion through ethical and unethical means, and ways in which persuasive speech tactics may indeed be unethical if one's goals are not ethical. Nick's true feelings about his professional position are directly juxtaposed to his speechmaking tactics in the scene. One can also discuss persuasive strategies that are ethical in contrast to those employed by the film's character. Questions for discussion may include:

1) Name at least one unethical approach that Nick uses in his speech. How does this strategy align with his goals and values? Can you name another manipulative tactic Nick could have used?
2) Can Nick employ ethical persuasive strategies with his current goals behind the speech? If so, can you name one strategy he might use during the talk show?
3) What would be one possible ethical goal in a speech made by a tobacco spokesperson such as Nick? What would be a transparent persuasive strategy Nick could employ in this case?

Students normally at first describe Nick's professional position as fun, until they begin to discuss ethics and his true feelings (as revealed in the scene) versus his points made in a public forum. Students usually also come to a realization of the difference between ethical and unethical persuasive goals and strategies and discover what may happen when one is not true to one's ethics in speechmaking; they may then recognize Nick's tactics during the scene as unethical. A variation in the activity may be to place the students into groups and have them discuss ethical responses to Nick Naylor's argument.

## REFERENCES

Cope, E. M., & Sandys, J. E. (Eds.) (2010). *Aristotle: Rhetoric* (1st ed.). Cambridge, MA: Cambridge University Press. Cambridge Library Collection. Retrieved August 2, 2016 at http://ebooks.cambridge.org/ebook.jsf?bid=CBO9780511707421. http://dx.doi.org/10.1017/CBO9780511707421

Dillard, J. P., & Pfau, M. (Eds). (2002). *The persuasion handbook: Developments in theory and practice.* Thousand Oaks: Sage.

Johannesen, R. L. (2002). *Ethics in human communication* (5th ed.). Prospect Heights, IL: Waveland.

Lucas, S. E. (2007). *The art of public speaking,* (9th ed.). Boston, MA: McGraw-Hill.

McCroskey, J. C. (2005). *An introduction to rhetorical communication* (9th ed.). New York: Routledge.

# VI

# Rhetoric

# 80

## Dinner and Movie: Introducing Students to Rhetorical Criticism

*Christopher M. Duerringer*
*Department of Communication Studies*
*California State University, Long Beach*
*christopher.duerringer@csulb.edu*

**History:** An earlier draft of this activity was accepted to the 2016 meeting of the Southern States Communication Association in Austin, Texas.
**Primary courses in which this activity might be used:** Rhetorical Criticism, Critical Approaches to Popular Culture
**Concepts illustrated:** Rhetorical Criticism

### PURPOSE

Discussions among scholars in the field of rhetorical studies have yielded a number of useful criteria for evaluating good criticism. To begin, nearly all hold that good criticism should in some sense illuminate experiences and phenomena that have previously gone unnoticed or undervalued. New understandings produced by rhetorical criticism can contribute to larger scholarly conversations about human communication (Foss, 1983); to our ability to richly experience politics and culture (Brummett, 1984; Hart and Daughton, 2004); and to our appreciation of the appeal, significance, and sophistication of individual texts (Palczewski, 2003).

There also seems to be consensus about *how* criticism should be done. Although it is not scientific inquiry, good rhetorical criticism should manifest its own kind of objectivity by transparently developing and applying an appropriate theoretical perspective (Hunt, 2003). Brummett (2003) agrees, suggesting that good criticism provides a clear statement of purpose and ought to satisfy "the promises and intentions made in the statement of purpose" (p. 364). And Palczewski (2003) looks for critics who leverage a theoretical vocabulary that will "clarify more than it obscures" (p. 388).

Unfortunately, when students arrive in a course in rhetorical criticism, they often associate the word *criticism* with disparagement or disapproval. Certainly, that is the way the word is most often deployed in broader American culture. Thus it is incumbent upon instructors to help students develop a fuller appreciation of criticism, at least within the context of rhetorical studies. This activity offers students two familiar metaphors by which they may better know what criticism can mean.

Although students may be new to rhetorical criticism, they are undoubtedly consumers of other kinds of popular criticism. They frequently make expert use of their smartphones, tablets, and laptops to search out ratings of goods, services, and culture. They consume, and often produce, reviews and ratings on popular smartphone apps like Yelp, UrbanSpoon, and movie rating websites RottenTomatoes and IMDB. The goal of this activity is to prompt students to make explicit their tacit understandings about what makes a piece of criticism (even of a hotdog or the newest action movie) more useful or better than another one.

## EXPLANATION OF ACTIVITY

### Preparation

Spend some time combing through popular review websites for user reviews of local eateries and films. It is helpful to have reviews that span the gamut from the most vivid, detailed, and thoughtful to brief, spiteful, and arbitrary complaints. Wine tasting notes often make for excellent examples of vivid description. Reviews of classics and cult films make excellent choices as well. Collect enough examples to provide small groups of four to five people with a range of reviews from the most detailed and useful to the least.

### Initial Instructions

1. Divide students into small groups and distribute a set of reviews to each.
2. Instruct students to read the reviews and discuss amongst themselves which reviews are the best.
3. Ask students to rank the reviews and be prepared to explain their justifications for these rankings.

### Class Discussion

1. Ask each group to nominate one member to stand and briefly address the class. Each group should show the rest of the class the reviews they read and provide their rationale for ranking them as they have.
2. After all the groups have presented, ask the students to suggest common criteria that the groups used to rank reviews. Ask the students, "What benefits should I get out of a good review?"
3. Lead students in synthesizing group answers into a consensus about the qualities and benefits of a good review.

## DEBRIEF

In my classes, students generally arrive at specifications that sound quite similar to our expectations of good rhetorical criticism. They rank most highly reviews that have rich descriptions; arguments about the value of the wine, restaurant, or film; are well written; and are entertaining. They like reviews that give them a perspective not only on the specific food or film, but also on what makes for good food or film more generally. They like original perspectives. The lowest ranked reviews are generally those that are vague, brief, rife with grammar and spelling errors, baseless, or needlessly vicious. Sometimes students may quite like a nasty review on the basis of its humor; this is not a problem. Good criticism ought to entertain the reader with style and tone appropriate to the subject matter.

Now, I make the point of the exercise explicit: "What we call reviews are, at their best, acts of criticism. This is the kind of thinking you'll be doing in this class—studying, describing, appreciating, and making arguments based on evidence about the value of something. But instead of wine or a cheeseburger, you'll be reviewing texts that influence and persuade."

This activity is designed to deliver two benefits: First, to make explicit some qualities of good rhetorical criticism; and second, to make students more comfortable with the expectation that they will perform rhetorical criticisms of their own. I find that the criteria that students laud are quite similar to those commended by rhetoric scholars. Like the film review that helps us understand why we love a cult classic, good rhetorical criticism should produce explicit knowledge from implicit understandings about eloquence, storytelling, ideology, and the power of language via a case study. Just as we do not value baldly arbitrary and personal reviews of restaurants, scholars call for criticism that begins with a clear declaration of purpose and develops appropriately toward that end.

Burke (1984) argued that "all living things are critics" (p. 5). Every one of us continually interprets symbols, makes discriminations about the meaning, quality and value of these symbols, and forms judgments on the basis of these understandings. When rhetorical criticism is presented as an extension, a specialization, and a more reflective kind of this activity, students can recognize themselves as already-practicing critics with an intuitive sense of the qualities that make criticism useful.

## REFERENCES

Brummett, B. (2003). Double binds in publishing rhetorical studies. *Communication Studies, 54*, 364–369. doi:10.1080/10510970309363293

Brummett, B. (1984). Rhetorical theory as heuristic and moral. *Communication Education, 33*, 97–107. doi:10.1080/03634528409384726

Burke, K. (1984). *Permanence and change: An anatomy of purpose* (3rd ed.). Berkeley, CA: University of California Press.

Foss, S. K. (1983). Criteria for adequacy in rhetorical criticism. In *Southern Communication Journal, 48*, 283–295. doi:10.1080/10417948309372571

Hart, R. P. & Daughton, S. M. (2004). *Modern rhetorical criticism* (3rd ed.). London: Pearson.

Hunt, S. B. (2003). An essay on publishing standards for rhetorical criticism. *Communication Studies, 54*, 378–384. doi:10.1080/10510970309363295

Palczewski, C. H. (2003). What is 'good criticism'? A conversation in progress. *Communication Studies, 54*, 385–391. doi:10.1080/10510970309363296

# 81

## Teaching Narrative, Identification, and Criticism

*Christopher J. Oldenburg*
*Department of Communication and Rhetorical Studies*
*Illinois College*
*chris.oldenburg@mail.ic.edu*

**History:** This activity was presented at the annual meeting of the Central States Communication Association, April 2009, in St. Louis, Missouri.
**Primary courses in which this activity might be used:** Communication Theory, Political Communication, Persuasion, Argumentation and Debate, Rhetorical Criticism
**Concepts illustrated:** Narrative, Identification, Persuasion, Rhetorical Criticism

### PURPOSE

The objective of this activity aims to effectively illustrate how narrative is a central strategy available to public speakers for promoting Kenneth Burke's Identification Model of Communication. Narratives told in the specific context of American political discourse are examined. Burke's conception of identification is often either oversimplified or explained in elevated, abstract, theoretical terms. As a consequence, undergraduates in entry-level communication courses miss out on the significance the dynamic process of identification plays in public address. Since most students grasp the conventions and rhetorical impact of narratives, this exercise uses anecdotes told by political leaders (particularly presidential candidates) to explicate the Identification Model of Communication. Thus, interpretations of what is going on in the narrative (e.g., characters, word choice, appeals to values and emotions) lend themselves to robust discussions about how political rhetors foster identification.

### EXPLANATION OF ACTIVITY

Begin with a brief definition and explanation of Kenneth Burke's Identification Model of Communication. For Burke, identification is essential to human communication. He argues that our need to identify is born out of division.

347

Humans are separated from one another biologically, socially, politically, and symbolically, and consequently, desire to identify via communication in order to vanquish division. One of Burke's simplest and most pellucid examples of identification occurs when "the politician who, addressing an audience of farmers, says, 'I was a farm boy myself'" (1969, xiv).

In *Dramatism and Development*, Burke outlines more detailed strategies of identification. It is applied in at least three ways. First, he describes usages that highlight the speaker's humility. For example the rich politician "tells humble constituents of his humble origins" (p. 28). In other words, this is the *I'm really just like you* move. Contemporary examples of this include images of George W. Bush removing brush on his Crawford farm, Ron Paul driving a tractor with his grandson in his lap, Obama rolling up his sleeves, Mitt Romney donning dungarees while washing his own laundry, and Hillary Clinton doing shots of liquor in an Ohio working-class bar.

The second strategy Burke refers to as involving the workings of antithesis. This is also known as the merger/division, us/them, friends/enemies maneuver. Where allies dispute, antithesis can rally them around antipathy for a common enemy. Finally, the subtle use of the word *we* has tremendous identificatory power. Burke explains, "As when the statement 'we' are at war includes under the same head soldiers who are getting killed and speculators who hope to make a killing in war stocks" (p. 28).

After this brief orientation to the concept and some illustrative applications of identification, divide students into five groups. Provide for students a compilation of seven or eight different anecdotes (see Appendix, p. 350) used in campaign stump speeches, convention addresses, or debate responses. (This works best when you have a good mix of anecdotes told by both Republicans and Democrats.) Have them read closely and critically all anecdotes told by politicians in a variety of speech contexts. Then, after allowing adequate time (fifteen to twenty minutes) for analysis, discussion, and deliberation within their own group, have each group pick one anecdote and explain how the speaker attempts to engender common perceptions and feelings among the audience.

Prompt students to think about how the audience might share the speaker's experiences, values, fears, friends, enemies, desires, dreams, and ideologies—that they are in effect, bound together in community (Burke 1969). In other words, what identifications are produced that facilitate social cohesion or connect the speaker and audience to something larger and more comprehensive? Students may employ the three aforementioned identification strategies outlined in Burke's *Dramatism and Development*: a) Humility, b) Antithesis, c) Transcendent "We."

## DEBRIEF

After about twenty minutes, have a reporter from each group articulate those key passages in the anecdotes that make identificatory appeals. Ask the reporter to explain why they selected the parts of the narrative they did, and how identification is functioning in those sequences. Also, encourage students from other groups to weigh in on the particular anecdote being discussed. Typical questions asked during the discussion could be: Who is the target audience? How are the narrative components of characters, action, conflict, resolution, theme, etc. crafted to produce identifications? Of the speaker's appeals for unity, what corresponding divisions are evident? What familiar, cultural myths, archetypes, and commonplaces are reinforced? What larger discursive formations and ideological constructs shape the group identity the audience is invited to see themselves as part of? Pay attention to word choice and connotations. What other rhetorical figures engender identification? How are the appeals of ethos, pathos, and logos used to court the audience?

Several insights from students fork from this activity and analysis. Most students are surprised by how unnoticed identification is in political contexts and that it often dwells in the dull, daily reinforcements of life. They remark at the cyclical nature of identification's mergers and divisions and the implications that has for political discourse. Students note how effective identification is when packaged in an anecdotal form, mainly because of how familiar we all are with narrative conventions. Finally, some students contend that the major thrust of anecdotal identification's rhetorical power works to make claims about the speaker's person (credibility, likeability, electability, etc.) more so than about the veracity of political reality.

This exercise works well in accomplishing two essential goals. First, it helps students grasp the theoretical and practical applications of how narrative and identification work together. Anecdotes work well primarily because they are short in length, thus allowing students to stay focused and more critically engaged. Second, it introduces students to rhetorical criticism by asking them to evaluate closely the persuasive purpose of narratives used by political leaders. The various interpretations of each group promote a mutual respect for diverse opinions and ideas.

## REFERENCES

Bush, G. W. (2004, Sept. 30) *The first presidential debate*. Washington, DC: Commission on Presidential Debates. Retrieved from http://debates.org/index.php?page=september-30-2004-debate-transcript

Burke, K. (1969). *A rhetoric of motives* (3rd ed.). Berkeley, CA: University of California Press.

Burke, K. (1972). *Dramatism and development: The Heinz Werner lecture series*. Barre, MA: Clark University Press.

Clinton, W. J. (1992, Oct. 11). *The first presidential debate*. Washington DC: Commission on Presidential Debates. Retrieved from http://debates.org/index.php?page=october-11-1992-second-half-debate-transcript

Clinton, H. (2008, Aug. 26). *Democratic National Convention keynote address*. Retrieved from http://www.americanrhetoric.com/speeches/convention2008/hillaryclinton2008dnc.htm

Cruz, T. (2016, July 20). *Republican National Convention address*. Retrieved from http://www.huffingtonpost.com/entry/ted-cruz-speech-full-text_us_579020dfe4b0bdddc4d320b0

McCain, J. (2008, Oct. 15) *The third presidential debate*. Washington, DC:
    Commission on Presidential Debates. Retrieved from http://debates.org/index.
    php?page=october-15-2008-debate-transcript
Obama, B. (2004, July 27). *Democratic National Convention keynote address*.
    Retrieved From http://www.americanrhetoric.com/speeches/convention2004/
    barackobama2004dnc.htm
Obama, B. (2013, Feb. 12). *Fourth State of the Union address*. Retrieved from http://
    www.americanrhetoric.com/speeches/stateoftheunion2013.htm

## APPENDIX

### Bill Clinton, First Presidential Debate, 1992:

And just remember this folks. A lot of folks on Medicare are out there every day making the choice between food and medicine; not poor enough for Medicare-Medicaid, not wealthy enough to buy their medicine. I've met them, people like Mary Annie and Edward Davis in Nashua, New Hampshire. All over this country, they cannot even buy medicine. So let's be careful. When we talk about cutting health care costs, let's start with the insurance companies and the people that are making a killing instead of making our people healthy (Clinton, 1992, para. 86).

### George W. Bush, First Presidential Debate, 2004:

You know, I think about Missy Johnson. She's a fantastic lady I met in Charlotte, North Carolina. She and her son Bryan, they came to see me. Her husband PJ got killed. He'd been in Afghanistan, went to Iraq ... I told her after we prayed and teared up and laughed some that I thought her husband's sacrifice was noble and worthy. Because I understand the stakes of this war on terror. I understand that we must find Al Qaida wherever they hide. We must deal with threats before they fully materialize. And Saddam Hussein was a threat, and that we must spread liberty because in the long run, the way to defeat hatred and tyranny and oppression is to spread freedom. Missy understood that. That's what she told me her husband understood (Bush, 2004, para. 245).

### Barack Obama, Democratic National Convention, 2008:

You know, a while back—a while back I met a young man named Shamus in a V.F.W. Hall in East Moline, Illinois. He was a good-looking kid—six two, six three, clear eyed, with an easy smile. He told me he'd joined the Marines and was heading to Iraq the following week. And as I listened to him explain why he'd enlisted, the absolute faith he had in our country and its leaders, his devotion to duty and service, I thought this young man was all that any of us might ever hope for in a child. But then I asked myself, "Are we serving Shamus as well as he is serving us?" (Obama, 2008, para. 24)

## Hillary Clinton, Democratic National Convention, 2008:

You allowed me to become part of your lives, and you became part of mine. I will always remember the single mom who had adopted two kids with autism. She didn't have any health insurance; and she discovered that she had cancer. But she greeted me with her bald head, painted with my name on it, and asked me to fight for health care for her and her children. I will always remember the young man in a Marine Corps T-shirt who waited months for medical care, and he said to me, "Take care of my buddies. A lot of them are still over there." And then, "Will you please take care of me?" And I will always remember the young boy who told me his mom worked for the minimum wage that her employer had cut her hours. He said he just didn't know what his family was going to do. To my supporters, to my champions, to my "Sisterhood of the Traveling Pant Suits," from the bottom of my heart—thank you. Thank you because you never gave in and you never gave up (Clinton, 2008, para. 8).

## John McCain, Third Presidential Debate, 2008:

You know, when Senator Obama ended up his conversation with Joe the plumber—we need to spread the wealth around. In other words, we're going to take Joe's money, give it to Senator Obama, and let him spread the wealth around. I want Joe the plumber to spread that wealth around. You told him you wanted to spread the wealth around. The whole premise behind Senator Obama's plans are class warfare, let's spread the wealth around. I want small businesses—and by the way, the small businesses that we're talking about would receive an increase in their taxes right now. Who—why would you want to increase anybody's taxes right now? Why would you want to do that, anyone, anyone in America, when we have such a tough time, when these small business people, like Joe the plumber, are going to create jobs, unless you take that money from him and spread the wealth around? (McCain, 2008, para. 48)

## Barack Obama's Fourth State of the Union Address, 2013:

Each of these proposals deserves a vote in Congress. Now, if you want to vote no, that's your choice. But these proposals deserve a vote. Because in the two months since Newtown, more than a thousand birthdays, graduations, anniversaries have been stolen from our lives by a bullet from a gun—more than a thousand. One of those we lost was a young girl named Hadiya Pendleton. She was 15 years old. She loved Fig Newtons and lip gloss. She was a majorette. She was so good to her friends they all thought they were her best friend. Just three weeks ago, she was here, in Washington, with her classmates, performing for her country at my inauguration. And a week later, she was shot and killed in a Chicago park after school, just a mile away from my house. Hadiya's parents, Nate and Cleo, are in this chamber tonight, along with more than two dozen Americans whose lives have been torn apart by gun violence. They deserve a vote. They deserve a vote. Gabby Giffords deserves a vote. The families of Newtown deserve a vote. The families of Aurora deserve a vote. The families of Oak Creek and Tucson and Blacksburg, and the countless other communities ripped open by gun violence— they deserve a simple vote. They deserve a simple vote (Obama, 2013, para. 87).

## Ted Cruz, Republican National Convention, 2016:

Just two weeks ago, a nine-year-old girl named Caroline was having a carefree Texas summer—swimming in the pool, playing with friends, doing all the things a happy child might do. Like most children, she took for granted the love she received from her mom, Heidi, and her dad, a police sergeant named Michael Smith. That is, until he became one of the five police officers gunned down in Dallas.

The day her father was murdered, Caroline gave him a hug and kiss as he left for work. But as they parted, her dad asked her something he hadn't asked before: "What if this is the last time you ever kiss or hug me?" Later, as she thought of her fallen father, and that last heartbreaking hug, Caroline broke down in tears. How could anything ever be OK again?

Michael Smith was a former Army ranger who spent three decades with the Dallas Police Department. I have no idea who he voted for in the last election, or what he thought about this one. But his life was a testament to devotion. He protected the very protestors who mocked him because he loved his country and his fellow man. His work gave new meaning to that line from literature, "To die of love is to live by it."

As I thought about what I wanted to say tonight, Michael Smith's story weighed on my heart. Maybe that's because his daughter, Caroline, is about the same age as my eldest daughter and happens to share the same name. Maybe it's because I saw a video of that dear, sweet child choking back sobs as she remembered her daddy's last question to her. Maybe it's because we live in a world where so many others have had their lives destroyed by evil, in places like Orlando and Paris and Nice and Baton Rouge. Maybe it is because of the simple question itself:

What if this, right now, is our last time? Our last moment to do something for our families and our country? Did we live up to our values? Did we do all we could? That's really what elections should be about. That's why you and millions like you devoted so much time and sacrifice to this campaign.

We're fighting, not for one particular candidate or one campaign, but because each of us wants to be able to tell our kids and grandkids, our own Carolines, that we did our best for their future, and for our country (Cruz, 2016, para. 3–6).

# 82

# Teaching the Value of Narratives in Speeches Through Analysis of Presidential Campaign Discourse

*Kevin T. Jones*

*Department of Communication, Journalism, and Cinematic Arts*
*George Fox University*
*kevinj@georgefox.edu*

**History:** This activity was presented at the annual meeting of the National Communication Association, November 2015, in Las Vegas, Nevada.

**Primary courses in which this activity might be used:** Public Speaking, Oral Interpretation, Language, Persuasion, Political Communication, Rhetorical Criticism, Communication Theory

**Concepts illustrated:** Narratives, Storytelling, Public Speaking, Audience Analysis, Audience Adaptation, Emotions

## PURPOSE

Narratives play an important role in what makes us human. Fisher (1984a & 1984b) refers to human beings as *homo narrans*, or storytelling animals. Narratives allow humans to persuade, inform, and entertain. They tell us about our past, highlight human motivations, illuminate cultural ideals, and illustrate facets of a culture by identifying its themes and showing cultural differences (Jaffe, 2013).

Since narratives are such an important part of what it means to be human, it is beneficial for speechwriters to embrace the role and use of narratives when preparing a text. Stories create connection (Cassady, 1994), and therefore good speakers will work hard to make sure they connect with their audience through the use of narratives. This exercise is designed to demonstrate the effective use of narratives in a presidential campaign. Seeing the effective and ineffective use of narratives allows students to better grasp not only the value of a good narrative, but also see how a good narrative frames an entire message.

## EXPLANATION OF ACTIVITY

Before beginning this activity, it is helpful to preface the conversation with a qualifier that this activity is **not** a political critique or discussion of either candidate's policies or political careers. Some students feel compelled to argue for or against a particular *person*. Students need to be reminded that they are only evaluating and comparing two *texts* for the use of narrative. Nonpartisanship needs to remain a central focus of the discussion. Once some ground rules of this nature have been established, the instructor can proceed with the activity.

In July 2008, *Time* magazine asked presidential candidates John McCain and Barack Obama to each write a five hundred-word essay defining *patriotism*. After providing the class with foundational material on narratives (reading, lecture, etc.), the instructor can provide the two essays for the class to read. Full-text copies of each essay are available at *Time.com* using the search phrase, "McCain and Obama on Patriotism." It is helpful to begin with Obama's essay since it uses narrative the best (Obama, 2008).

Obama begins his essay with a story about his mother reading the Declaration of Independence to him as a young boy. This story portrays Obama as a person who is dedicated and devoted to the foundation of the United States. He continues with a story about the horrors of murder surrounding an election in Zimbabwe. This story illustrates the freedom of open elections that we enjoy in the United States. The story is gruesome and horrific, but graphically illustrates Obama's point via a narrative. The piece concludes with an echo back to his opening story about reading the Declaration of Independence as a child and how his life is the epitome of the "American Dream"—coming from disjunctive meager roots and rising to the presidential campaign stage.

After reading and discussing Obama's definition of patriotism, the class can read McCain's definition of patriotism (McCain, 2008). The McCain version reads more like a dictionary definition and does not reflect a strong use of narrative. McCain defines the term and then proceeds to provide examples of patriotism, but with general references and no specific narrative to engage the audience.

## DEBRIEF

Following a reading of Obama's answer to the prompt, a discussion can follow with questions about the role of narratives in the text. Since good narratives include background, characters, and a plot (beginning/middle/end), the instructor can ask the class questions such as "Can you identify a background?" (Opening paragraph); "Can you identify any characters?" (Obama's mother, Obama, the wife of the Zimbabwe Mayor); "Can you identify a plot—is there a beginning, a middle and an end?" (Yes, the opening story of the Declaration of Independence is the beginning, the Zimbabwe story and other references are the middle, and the end is Obama's echo back to his opening story).

After reading McCain's essay, the instructor can ask the students the same questions asked of Obama's piece—"Was there any background, characters, or plot?" Some students may try to connect some statements to the criteria for a narrative and a case may be made for some semblance of a narrative here or there, but any narrative identified is not as clear as Obama's. Most students see the lack of connection between the content and the criteria for a narrative.

It is helpful at this stage of the activity for the instructor to guide the discussion in a way that helps students discover how McCain missed many opportunities in which he could easily have turned several statements into a narrative. For example, when McCain referenced communities such as "the Boy Scouts, the Girl Scouts," the instructor could ask the class, "How could McCain have turned this statement into a narrative?" The goal of this line of questioning is to show the students that McCain could easily have noted an experience he had on the campaign trail with any one of the groups he referenced (i.e., "Just last week when I was in Iowa, I met with boy Scout Troop 205 and we talked about ..."). When McCain spoke of Arlington Cemetery, the instructor could ask the students, "Rather than just stating, 'One cannot go to Arlington Cemetery and see name upon name, grave upon grave ...,' how could McCain have turned the statement into a personal narrative?" Arriving at an answer, such as having McCain state, "The last time I was at Arlington, and I stood there and I saw name upon name, grave upon grave ..." could have transformed the cemetery statement into a personal narrative.

By guiding the students through the text and asking the types of questions noted in the previous paragraph, the class is able to discover how narratives can be far more captivating, entertaining, and engaging, and can allow a speaker or text writer to lead an audience in many directions. This point can open a discussion on the ethics of using narratives in a text. How and when does the use of narratives become unethical? How do we determine when a narrative is ethical or unethical? This discussion can go in many different directions based upon available time and how well the class has been prepared on ethics.

Additionally, this conversation lends itself to an excellent discussion on the role of narrative probability and fidelity. Fisher (1978) notes that as natural storytellers, humans are inherently aware of narrative probability, or what constitutes a coherent story. The Obama and McCain essays provide the opportunity to see a coherent and an incoherent story side-by-side. Fisher further notes that narrative fidelity is the ability of an audience to assess whether or not a story rings true based on the stories the audience knows to be true in their own lives. Obama's essay provides stories that the audience can evaluate and judge to be true, such as a mother reading to her child or the horrific injustices like the Zimbabwe election situation that can be seen around the world on a regular basis. McCain's essay fails to provide a similar tone of fidelity. The discussion of these two speeches may continue based upon time and how well the students are equipped with effective tools for analyzing the use and role of narratives.

There is no polling data available that this author could find connecting the role of narratives and voter turnout in the 2008 presidential campaign. However, Obama's definition of patriotism reflected the type of speeches and rhetoric he used on the campaign trail. Since human beings are *homo narrans*— storytelling animals—and the introduction to this essay identified how narratives connect a speaker to an audience in a special way, Obama's use of narratives could be argued to have played a role in his landslide victory.

Political pundits attribute part of Obama's success to his ability to attract such a large percentage of the eighteen- to twenty-nine-year-old vote. In 2008, Obama carried 66 percent of this age group, while John Kerry in 2004 only carried 54 percent of the eighteen- to twenty-nine-year-old vote (PewResearch.org). These numbers could not have been achieved without Obama creating some sort of connection with the public/audience. This connection indicates a clear transmission of ideas, images, and emotions (Cassady, 1994). While there is no way to definitively link Obama's use of narratives to any of his campaign victory numbers, the plausibility of the influence cannot be ignored.

## REFERENCES

Cassady, M. (1994). *The art of storytelling: Creative ideas for preparation and performance.* Colorado Springs, CO: Meriweather.

Fisher, W. R. (1984a). Narrative as a human communication paradigm: The case of public moral argument. *Communication Monographs, 51,* 1–22.

Fisher, W. R. (1984b). The narrative paradigm: An elaboration. *Communication Monographs, 52,* 347–367. doi: 10.1080/03637758509376117

Fisher, W. R. (1987). *Human communication as narration: Toward a philosophy of reason, value, and action.* Columbia, SC: University of South Carolina Press.

Jaffe, C. I. (2013). *Public speaking: Concepts and skills for a diverse society* (7th ed.). Boston, MA: Wadsworth.

McCain, J. (2008, July 7). A cause greater than self. *Time, 172,* 29. Retrieved from http://content.time.com/time/magazine/article/0,9171,1818217,00.html

Obama, B. (2008, July 7). A faith in simple dreams. *Time, 172,* 30. Retrieved from http://content.time.com/time/magazine/article/0,9171,1818217,00.html

PewResearch.org. (November 5, 2008). Inside Obama's sweeping victory. Retrieved from www.pewresearch.org/2008/11/05/inside-obamas-sweeping-victory/

Polkinghorne, D. E. (1988). *Narrative knowing and the human sciences.* Albany, NY: SUNY Press.

# 83

# Selling Guilt: Using Kenneth Burke to Teach Critical Readings of Advertising

*C. Wesley Buerkle*

*Department of Communication & Performance*

*East Tennessee State University*

*buerkle@etsu.edu*

**History:** This activity was presented at the annual meeting of the Southern States Communication Association, April 2012, in San Antonio, Texas.

**Primary courses in which this activity might be used:** Communication Theory, Persuasion, Popular Culture, Rhetorical Criticism, Media and Society

**Concepts illustrated:** Kenneth Burke's theories, Guilt, Advertising Strategies

## PURPOSE

Descriptions of Kenneth Burke's work appear in almost every textbook surveying communication theory, yet to many students his work seems vague at best, and esoteric at worst. Ironically, Burke's contemporaries heralded him for weaving together analysis of popular culture and classic philosophy (Nichols, 1952). Drawn from Burke's (1966) "Definition of Man" on how humans use language and his discussion of guilt (1965; 1984), the activity highlights the ways in which advertising often invokes a sense of inferiority in consumers/citizens as a means to promote purchasing behavior. For Burke (1965), guilt existed when we feel we are not living up to expectations. Feeling shameful for our failings, we are motivated to alleviate the guilt (i.e., seek redemption) through appropriate sacrifices, such as investing money and time in the purchase and use of a product.

Using Burke's theories we can help foster students' critical reception of advertising in the effort toward promoting a more informed and ethical citizenry (Brummett & Young, 2006). From the activity students will 1) grasp how our use of language shapes our understanding of ourselves and our place in society; 2) gain a critical awareness of the advertising messages that bombard them; 3) develop a vocabulary to discuss advertising; and 4) understand an important portion of Burke's theory of communication. This activity works as a scavenger hunt in which students can share their discoveries in class the same day, the next day, or even through your course's online management system in the discussion board.

## EXPLANATION OF ACTIVITY

*Man is*

    *the symbol-using (symbol-making, symbol-misusing) animal,*

    *inventor of the negative (or moralized by the negative),*

    *separated from his natural condition by instruments of his own making,*

    *goaded by the spirit of hierarchy (or moved by the sense of order), and*

    *rotten with perfection. (Burke, 1966, p. 16)*

**Man Is:**

In "Definition of Man" Burke (1966) articulates principles about how humans use language in a manner that that makes people feel inferior to each other. Each line from his definition stems from the prompt "Man is" and ties in nicely to a discussion of how advertising leads consumers to feel guilty about themselves, needing to redeem their shortcomings by purchasing the products advertised. For each of Burke's observations students should locate print ads, billboards (captured using mobile phones), or television commercials (through YouTube or corporate webpages) to share with the class to illustrate the concepts.

***The symbol-using animal (symbol-making, symbol-misusing).*** Students should locate advertisements that demonstrate the ways in which humans express feelings, history, and ideas through words and other symbols. These may be images that convey the sense of *cool*, suggest relational bliss or dissatisfaction, or what is (un)desirable without any words at all (e.g., relying on commonly understood nonverbal cues, camera angles, lighting, and color). Students might find an example like Hyundai's 2016 Super Bowl commercial "Ryanville" to discuss how the commercial communicates that Ryan Reynolds is an ideal of masculinity without ever saying so with words.

***Inventor of the negative (or moralized by the negative).*** Here, encourage students to find ads that emphasize selling us products by reminding us what we should fear becoming. Students may want to talk about the ways in which social morals are developed by demonstrating a person or state of being to avoid. They may locate commercials like DirecTV's 2015 advertisements featuring Rob Lowe saying, "Don't be like this me," referring to his alter ego's "painfully awkward Rob Lowe" or "super-creepy Rob Lowe," that paint the picture of socially undesirable personalities who use an inferior product.

**Separated from his natural condition by instruments of his own making.**   Many students will gravitate toward commercials that promote beauty and other personal-care products that guilt us for our bodies becoming undisciplined, smelly, or older. When they share what they found, push students to consider the ways in which the products make people ashamed of their nature as animals, preferring us to use products that perpetuate an image of how bodies should look and act by overcoming natural processes (e.g., skin-care products that call themselves "age defying").

**Goaded by the spirit of hierarchy (or moved by the sense of order).**   Students may want to simply find an advertisement that emphasizes its product is the best, but push them to consider the ways in which the differences among some brands' products—say luxury vehicles—split hairs over superiority, making the title *best* important for its own sake. Many students may locate advertisements that emphasize the importance of maintaining the appearance that one is as good as or better than their neighbors, encouraging purchases for the purpose of maintaining a respected social status.

**Rotten with perfection.**   The advertisements students locate here should exemplify the theme in advertising that costumers should never be content with what they have, such as the Lowe's (home improvement center) motto that demands we "Never stop improving" or commercials that admonish us to "Never settle." Here you may need to help students differentiate between observations about appeals being superior to others (hierarchy) versus the inability to ever be satisfied with one's current state (perfection).

## DEBRIEF

Ask students to think about the patterns they notice in the advertisements (e.g., Do you see certain values, attitudes, or goals expressed or notice attributions of the blame?). You may discuss Burke's (1965; 1984) belief that we absolve ourselves of guilt through mortification (making sacrifices, such as forgoing certain foods for a thinner body) or scapegoating (blaming others, like accusing temptations of sabotaging weight-loss diets, as Weight Watchers's Momentum campaign did). You might also share Condit's (1994) observation that Burke's "Definition of Man" is just that, an understanding of how men see the world, which may lead to discussing the extent to which the advertisements serve men's interests, values, and perspectives.

Engaging Burke's theories about language can help our students develop as critical thinkers and informed citizens. As the U.S. faces crises of consumer debt, depression/anxiety, and eating disorders, teaching an awareness of the potential for advertising to make us feel inferior to others because of our lifestyle or inadequate because of our bodies is as valuable as ever.

## REFERENCES

Burke, K. (1965). *Permanence and change*. Berkeley, CA: University of California Press.

Burke, K. (1966). Definition of man. In *Language as symbolic action: Essays on life, literature, and method* (pp. 3–24). Berkeley, CA: University of California Press.

Burke, K. (1984). *Attitudes toward history*. Berkeley, CA: University of California Press.

Brummett, B. & Young, A. M. (2006). Some uses of Burke in communication studies. *KB Journal, 2* (2). Retrieved from http://kbjournal.org/communication

Condit, C. M. (1994). Framing Kenneth Burke: Sad tragedy or comic dance? *Quarterly Journal of Speech, 80*, 77–82.

Nichols, M. H. (1952). Kenneth Burke and the "New Rhetoric." *Quarterly Journal of Speech, 38*, 133–144.

# 84

## Social Justice on Ice: Lessons from the *Sporting News* about the Rhetoric of Victimage

*Alena Amato Ruggerio, Ph.D.*
*Department of Communication*
*Southern Oregon University*
*Alena.Ruggerio@sou.edu*

**History:** This activity was presented at the annual meeting of the Western States Communication Association, February 2006, in Palm Springs, California.

**Primary courses in which this activity might be used:** Persuasion, Rhetorical Criticism, Communication Theory, Communication Ethics, Sports Communication

**Concepts illustrated:** Dramatism, Tragic Frame of Acceptance, Victimage, Scapegoating, Comic Frame of Acceptance

### PURPOSE

When students first learn about Kenneth Burke's theory of dramatism, they can mistakenly assume the brutalities of tragic rhetoric are limited to genocidal dictators. It is important, therefore, to stress that tragedy is sometimes a precursor to, but more often a substitute for, physical violence. Moreover, beginning students sometimes attribute tragic rhetoric to individual malice, not recognizing the systematized *Othering* unconsciously embedded in the communication of well-intentioned people—including themselves. This activity encourages self-reflexivity about the tragic frame of acceptance by working through what appears at first glance to be an innocuous print ad that eventually reveals homophobia.

### EXPLANATION OF ACTIVITY

Assign a reading that introduces Kenneth Burke's theory of dramatism, such as chapter 23 of *A First Look at Communication Theory* (Griffin, Ledbetter, & Sparks, 2014), which describes the rhetorical frames of acceptance within our existing social system that shape our own and others' perspectives, interpretations, and actions. In class, divide up the students and ask each group to summarize one of the stages of the tragic frame: Human language gives us the capacity for the negative, which leads to feelings of division from others and guilt for falling short of a hierarchical ideal, which are transferred to the scapegoated Other, who is literally or symbolically sacrificed to bring about redemption and purification (Burke, 1959). Students will recognize the communication strategies of the Third Reich in the stages of victimage. In addition to German politics and economics, rhetoric contributed to the environment in which genocide felt natural and inevitable to certain audiences. But examples of tragic rhetoric cannot stop with the Holocaust.

Hand out copies of a full-page advertisement from the *Sporting News* magazine featuring a man wearing a clown suit hooking a hoop between his hand and foot, and the words, "We're not sure what the hell is going on here, but you'll never have to read about it.... Our focus is sports. And only real sports. That's what we promise. That's what we deliver. And that's why dedicated sports fans like you turn to our magazine, SportingNews.com and Sporting News Radio." (For a copy of the ad, contact the author at Alena.Ruggerio@sou.edu)

Once everyone has examined the ad, lead a discussion on the following questions: What is the person in the photo doing? How can you tell? What is the purpose of this ad? Who is the audience? What do you know about the rhetor? In my years of teaching, nobody has recognized the man or been familiar with his story. This fits with the text of the ad, which relies on his anonymity to make its point.

Ask students to identify some of the written and visual elements of tragic rhetoric that frame the clown as an Other, including the words, "We're not sure what the hell is going on here" and "only real sports"; the photo's limited color palette that distances the viewer from the person depicted, and the cropping of the photo to focus on the costume and makeup to the exclusion of any identifying information about the man or his task. At this point, disclose that the ad is a parody of the U.S. Figure Skating Hall of Fame honoree Rudy Galindo, winner of multiple national and world championships. Search YouTube for "Rudy Galindo Send in the Clowns" to see a video of his performance. Cue the clip to the 2:41 minute mark and stop at 6:58, bypassing the narrative package and ending as Galindo strikes the pose mocked in the *Sporting News* ad.

Then reveal that in 1996, Galindo became the first out gay man to win a U.S. National Championship, despite discrimination by conservative judges who hindered his career (Braverman, 2014; Longman 1996). Galindo is also a Ryan White Award-winning activist open about being HIV-positive and losing a brother and two coaches to AIDS (Longman, 2000). Repeat the words of the ad to emphasize the bigotry expressed in what might have originally been read as humorous. Point out how the *Sporting News'* tragic-frame rhetoric negatively depicts figure skating as silly by ignoring the power and skill of the athlete and instead creating a photo that exaggerates the clown costume, and ridicules the masculinity of the skater by focusing on the absurdly painted face, tactics used to abuse gay men. By deriding what it has coded as effeminate, the magazine has—intentionally or not—hailed the latent (or active) homophobia of its audience.

The coverage of the homophobia surrounding figure skating during the 2014 Olympics proves the ad's salience today (Braverman, 2014; Jones, 2014), but it originally ran in the *Sporting News* from approximately 2001 to 2003. At that time, the *Sporting News* sought to differentiate itself from its competitor, *Sports Illustrated*. The implication that the *Sporting News* only focuses on the "real sports" of football, basketball, baseball, and hockey is a jab at *Sports Illustrated*, whose broader coverage includes "feminized" sports such as ice skating and gymnastics. Even excluding Galindo's personal sexual orientation, the Othering in this ad is grounded in cultural homophobia.

Given that we cannot control the rhetoric of the magazine, the classroom focus now shifts to how the students can themselves embrace a comic viewpoint when articulating persuasive messages on social justice issues. Offer a short description of the comic corrective, Burke's rhetorical genre of humbly seeking common humanity and admitting mistakenness as an alternative to victimage (1969). Emphasize that the process of comic rhetoric begins with introspection regarding each of us as a rhetor and extends to a systemic critique of the artifacts of communication we encounter each day.

## DEBRIEF

Ask a series of questions to add depth to the students' thinking: Is the tragic rhetoric in the ad worse when Galindo's identity and backstory are known? How could an ad for the *Sporting News* have contrasted itself against *Sports Illustrated* in a way that avoided the tragic? For instance, the message could have been explicitly stated: "We at the *Sporting News* focus on American football, baseball, basketball, and occasionally soccer and hockey, whereas our competitors at *Sports Illustrated* have a broader scope." Can the quest for consubstantiality—those points we have in common with others, even if only our fellow humanity—prevent us from becoming unwitting parties to victimage? What is the best way to remain mindful of choosing identification moment by moment? As a follow-up assignment, consider inviting students to submit contemporary examples of tragic rhetoric and the comic corrective from their own media consumption.

Student reactions to this lesson might vary according to the culture of the campus, especially for certain religious or military institutions of higher education. At my public liberal arts university in a blue state, students often cite this as their favorite day of instruction and dramatism as the most valuable concept from the course. I am proud to say a student has never denied the scapegoating in the ad, nor disparaged Rudy Galindo after our in-class analysis. Instead, their minds in recent years have turned back to warfare. The lesson has sparked class conversations on Iraq and Afghanistan, sometimes with students indignantly denying any utility in speaking of terrorists as anything but evil monsters requiring American extermination.

I step back and wait for another student to voice a comic response (most dramatically, a student from Germany once described her country's post-war introspection and cautioned that U.S. foreign policy could benefit from a similar dose of comic-frame humility). Then I briefly sketch some limitations of the comic corrective: It is never a permanent cure to human division, every time one constructs a *we*, another *us* is created, comic rhetoric functions within an established social system rather than facilitating its dismantling, and rhetoric ceases where violence begins.

This lesson emphasizes that the tragic frame of rhetoric enables not just physical slaughter as in the Holocaust, but also countless daily mini-tragedies enacted symbolically. Students will complete this lesson understanding that tragic messages do not have to be intentional to be harmful. On the part of the rhetors, it is unlikely that the creators of the *Sporting News* ad consciously intended their message to be so vicious. And on the part of the audience, without mindfully choosing the comic corrective, we are all constructed as accomplices to victimage. After being profoundly moved by this activity, my student Hamish Hinton returned to class with a new tattoo of the words "embrace the comic, reject the tragic" written in the shape of an infinity symbol to remind himself to perpetually engage in the identification that counteracts hate.

## REFERENCES

Braverman, B. (2014, Jan. 30). Why is the world's gayest sport stuck in the closet? *BuzzFeed*. Retrieved from http://www.buzzfeed.com/blairbraverman/why-is-the-worlds-gayest-sport-stuck-in-the-closet?utm_term=.rmmy3QNjj#.ic9Dk2w55

Burke, K. (1959). *Attitudes toward history* (3rd ed.). Berkeley, CA: University of California Press.

Burke, K. (1969). *A rhetoric of motives*. Berkeley, CA: University of California Press.

Griffin, E., Ledbetter, A., & Sparks, G. (2014). *A first look at communication theory* (9th ed.). Boston, MA: McGraw-Hill.

Jones, A. (2014, Jan. 31). The frozen closet. *Newsweek*. Retrieved from http://www.newsweek.com/2014/01/31/frozen-closet-245138.html

Longman, J. (1996, Jan. 22). National championships: A soap opera in sequins. *New York Times*, p. C1.

Longman, J. (2000, Apr. 10). Galindo facing H.I.V. with candor and style. *New York Times*, p. D6.

# VII

## Persuasion, Argumentation, and Advocacy

# 85

## Whatchamacallit: An Exercise for Understanding the Power of Symbols

*John S. Seiter*

*Department of Languages, Philosophy, and Communication Studies*
*Utah State University*
*john.seiter@usu.edu*

*Jennifer Peeples*

*Department of Languages, Philosophy, and Communication Studies*
*Utah State University*
*Jennifer.peeples@usu.edu*

*Matthew L. Sanders*

*Department of Languages, Philosophy, and Communication Studies*
*Utah State University*
*Matt.sanders@usu.edu*

**History:** This activity was presented at the annual meeting of the National Communication Association, November 2015, in Las Vegas, Nevada. It was a top-ranked submission.

**Primary courses in which this activity might be used:** Interpersonal Communication, Organizational Communication, Persuasion, Rhetorical Criticism

**Concepts illustrated:** Language, Labels, Symbols, Connotation, Audience Adaptation, Sapir-Whorf Hypothesis, Persuasion

### PURPOSE

When the people at "Fairtilizer," an online music company, were deciding what to name their business, they might have understood that symbols, including names, are arbitrary and, technically, cannot be wrong. One has to wonder, however, whether they anticipated the negative associations their company's name might conjure up (e.g., fertilizer; fair [as in so-so]; passing gas) (see Forrest, 2014). Considering there are roughly five hundred thousand new businesses in the United States every month (Gabler, 2015), such mishaps are not surprising. With a better understanding of the power of symbols, however, business owners might be able to avoid them. The purpose of this exercise is to help students understand the power of symbols by asking them to invent and evaluate names for their own hypothetical companies.

## EXPLANATION OF ACTIVITY

Start the exercise by creating a list of company names that students say they either like or dislike. Examples of ones we like (but they may not) include Google, Twitter, JiffyLube, Verizon, and PayPal. Besides Fairtilizer, we dislike Fashism, the name of a mobile app that allowed people to solicit fashion advice from other users (Forrest, 2014), and Walmart. Based on this discussion, ask students if they think a company's name is important. Why or why not? Possible answers include the role names play in developing first impressions, product branding, and creating positive or negative feelings. Here you might note that many companies think names are important. Indeed, companies that specialize in naming other companies are known to charge as much as $80,000 for their services. With that in mind, ask students to imagine that they are one of several applicants trying to secure a career in such a company. As part of the hiring process, they will become part of a naming team, which must prove itself by inventing and evaluating two names for a hypothetical company.

Break students into groups and ask each group to select (from a list you provide) or invent a type of company to name. Phone books can be a good source of examples. Classes we have taught include companies that feature massage therapists for pets, dating websites for the elderly, professional laughers, mobile dentists, and private detectives. Next, provide guidelines. For example, gurus in the naming industry recommend names that are short (five to ten letters), simple, and recognizable (e.g., Hasbro, Starbucks, Apple, Exxon) (see Gasca, 2014).

Moreover, rather than simply describing what a company does (e.g., International Business Machines) tell students to consider names that convey the company's unique personality or philosophy (e.g., what do the names *Puma* and *Amazon* convey?) and ones that intrigue or stir emotions (Keller, 2014). To brainstorm, students can consider using a thesaurus, finding rhymes, or searching glossaries for root words or interesting jargon (Watkins, 2014). Most important, they should consider the audience they want to appeal to and adapt accordingly.

Next, give your students fifteen to twenty minutes to invent two names for their company. Then ask each group to pitch their names to the rest of the class (about one minute per name). After both names have been pitched, class members should discuss which of the two names they prefer. What particular characteristics of names did they like? Why? As an alternative, groups can simply present their company names without a pitch, allowing the class to comment on and evaluate the name alone.

## DEBRIEF

Debrief with your students by connecting the exercise to concepts, theory, and research. You might, for example, define connotation and ask or remind students about the meanings they associated with companies. You might also talk about the Sapir-Whorf hypothesis (Sapir, 1949; Whorf, 1956), which suggests that language determines how we understand and perceive the world. Ask your students whether this exercise supports that hypothesis. Why or why not? Finally, ask students to think about other contexts in which labels might influence perceptions and behavior (e.g., when using euphemisms, when labeling people using stereotypes, and so forth). What does this tell them about the power of symbols?

## REFERENCES

Forrest, C. (2014, April, 15). The 15 worst startup names of all time. *TechRepublic.* Retrieved from http://www.techrepublic.com/article/the-15-worst-startup-names-of-all-time/

Gabler, N. (2015, Jan. 15). The weird science of naming new products. The *New York Times Magazine.* Retrieved from http://www.nytimes.com/2015/01/18/magazine/the-weird-science-of-naming-new-products.html?_r=0

Gasca, P. (2014, June 23). 3 tips for naming your business in the modern, mobile world. *Entrepreneur.* Retrieved from http://www.entrepreneur.com/article/234845

Keller, A. (2014, Nov. 26). A great name tells you more than just what the company does. *Entrepreneur.* Retrieved from http://www.entrepreneur.com/article/239076

Sapir, E. (1949). *Culture, language and personality.* Berkeley, CA: University of California Press.

Watkins, A. (2014, Oct. 17). 5 must-use tools for brainstorming company names. Retrieved from http://www.entrepreneur.com/article/238601

Whorf, B. L. (1956). *Language, thought, and reality.* New York: John Wiley & Sons.

# 86

## Not Sold in Stores!: Using Infomercials to Teach Persuasion Theory

*Brett Lunceford*
Independent Scholar
*brettlunceford@gmail.com*

**History:** This activity was presented at the annual meeting of the Southern States Communication Association, April 2013, in Louisville, Kentucky.
**Primary courses in which this activity might be used:** Advertising, Integrated Marketing Campaigns, Persuasion, Small Group Communication, Strategic Communication
**Concepts illustrated:** Language, Persuasion Theory, Presentation Skills, Research

### PURPOSE

Infomercials have permeated the media landscape for decades and when pressed, students will admit to having watched and even enjoyed certain ones. Because of their ubiquity, communication scholars have found this genre of persuasive discourse to be a useful way to teach such topics as public speaking (Lane, 2009), critical listening (Johnson-Curiskis, 2009), and logical fallacies (Marietta-Brown, 2011). Although infomercials are often the subject of derision, the reality is that they do, to some extent, fulfill their persuasive intent (Martin, Bhimy & Agee, 2002). In this activity, students create an infomercial to gain and demonstrate mastery of persuasion theory. Although this activity is geared toward persuasion, I have used a similar assignment in my small group course with a different theoretical focus. As such, this assignment lends itself to adaptation.

### ACTIVITY

This assignment can span an entire semester or as one assignment among several. In my persuasion class, we cover a broad array of persuasion theories from both the rhetorical and social science traditions. Students form groups early on and remain in the same group for the duration of the semester. The students are tasked with creating an infomercial for a product, either real or imagined. The only stipulation is that it cannot be a product that already has an infomercial. The goal is for students to create an infomercial crafted for maximum persuasive power. There are two parts of this assignment: the presentation itself and the documentation.

For the presentation, students perform the infomercial in front of the class. Each infomercial is fifteen to twenty minutes long and students can bring in props if they wish. Limit video in the presentation to no more than four minutes to avoid having the project become a video editing exercise and to highlight oral presentation skills. Explain that most infomercials seem to follow Monroe's Motivated Sequence of attention, need, satisfaction, visualization, and call to action (see O'Hair, Stewart, & Rubenstein, 2012, pp. 383–386), which provides a framework for them to follow. Record each infomercial with a digital video camera.

The second part of the assignment is the documentation. Explain that drawing on a wide variety of theories will lead to a better infomercial and thus a better grade. Within the documentation, have students describe strategies that the group employed in the presentation and how they applied theories of persuasion in their infomercial. Ask them to explain in detail why they chose those theories and how they used them. For example, students have often used the Extended Parallel Process Model when drawing on fear appeals in order to highlight audience susceptibility to the problem while explaining how their product helps the viewer effectively neutralize that threat. In order to do this, many have drawn on evolutionary models that demonstrate that social proof appeals ("the best-selling product of its kind!") work particularly well with fear appeals (see Griskevicius et al., 2009).

Caution students that the documentation should not be an afterthought, and they should be documenting their choices for the infomercial along the way. Students have taken different approaches to using theory in the documentation, with some writing the script and then determining if it is theoretically sound, and others using theory to drive the production of the script. In my class, I heavily front-load the general theory portion, so students are introduced to a wide variety of theories very early in the class. You can leave the format of the documentation up to them, but suggest the form of an annotated script. Explain that the more detail they provide, the better their grade will be, and encourage them to go beyond the readings explored in class. This encourages them to delve into the databases to find more research.

## DEBRIEF

The assessment of the presentation is similar to that of most group presentations, focusing on how polished the presentation was, how well the group members worked together, and how well they employed persuasive strategies within the infomercial itself. Once the students have completed the infomercial presentation, have them watch the video as a group and determine what they did well and what they could improve upon. Within two days, each group should meet with the instructor to discuss how they used theories of persuasion in their infomercial.

For example, if they use humor, ask them why humor would be persuasive in this particular case. If they use sex appeal, ask them why they did so. For example, students often begin with the assumption that sex sells, but the research actually demonstrates that it only works in particular ways for particular products (see Reichert, 2002). Having students back up their choices with research forces them to closely examine strategies that are often taken for granted. Every element of the infomercial should be scrutinized for its persuasive impact.

When I use this project in my persuasion course, I meet with each group and offer them the opportunity to persuade me concerning the grade that they think that they earned. However, this persuasive attempt must be backed up with research that demonstrates that they had included sufficient research and theoretical depth.

## REFERENCES

Griskevicius, V., Goldstein, N. J., Mortensen, C. R., Sundie, J. M., Cialdini, R. B., & Kenrick, D. T. (2009). Fear and loving in Las Vegas: Evolution, emotion, and persuasion. *Journal of Marketing Research 46*(3), 384–95.

Johnson-Curiskis, N. (2009). Importance of effective listening infomercial. *International Journal of Listening, 23*(2), 167–170.

Lane, S. (2009). The audience adaptation infomercial speech. *Communication Teacher, 23*(1), 37–40.

Marietta-Brown, A. (2011). As seen on TV: Teaching fallacies through infomercials. *Communication Teacher, 25*(3), 127–130.

Martin, B. A. S., Bhimy, A., & Agee, T. (2002). Infomercials and advertising effectiveness: An empirical study. *Journal of Consumer Marketing, 19*(6), 468–480.

O'Hair, D., Stewart, R. A., & Rubenstein, H. (2012). *A speaker's guidebook* (5th ed.). New York, NY: Bedford/St. Martins.

Reichert, T. (2002). Sex in advertising research: A review of content, effects, and functions of sexual information in consumer advertising. In *Annual Review of Sex Research, 13,* 241–273.

# 87

## The *Law & Order* of Using Effective Sources to Build an Argument

### Mary Beth Asbury

*Department of Communication Studies and Organizational Communication*
*Middle Tennessee State University*
*MaryBeth.Asbury@mtsu.edu*

### Virginia B. Jones

*Department of Communication and Journalism*
*Arkansas Tech University*
*vjones7@atu.edu*

**History:** This activity was presented at the annual meeting of the National Communication Association, November 2007, in Chicago, Illinois. It was a top-ranked submission.
**Primary courses in which this activity might be used:** Public Speaking, Argumentation, Advanced Public Speaking, Persuasion
**Concepts illustrated:** Research, Source Credibility, Building Arguments

### PURPOSE

One of the values of a communication class lies in helping students realize and demonstrate the importance of applying communication concepts to everyday, real-life situations. However, one concept that students have a hard time understanding and demonstrating is the use of credible sources when building an argument. Instructors are frequently bombarded with Internet and/or non-scholarly sources because students cannot draw the connection between the credibility of the source and the credibility of the information conveyed by the source (Grimes & Boening, 2001; Davis, 2003). In addition, students have difficulty understanding how to integrate their sources to make the most effective argument. If students could see how sources are used in everyday situations, they could potentially understand why they are so important and how to integrate them effectively in a persuasive argument. One way for students to understand the importance of using credible sources in building arguments is by showing them how sources are used in situations outside the classroom.

Television and movies have often been used in the classroom to effectively engage students and demonstrate concepts through examples (Clark & Salomon, 1988; Plowman, 1988). The NBC drama *Law & Order* serves as an effective tool to demonstrate how to find and use credible evidence to build and support an argument. Please note that for this assignment, the original *Law & Order* is preferred over *Law & Order: SVU* and *Law & Order: Criminal Intent*, because the original version gives equal time to the police and the district attorneys. The other versions tend to primarily highlight the police side of criminal justice.

While *Law & Order* is a fictional drama, the story lines are borrowed from news headlines across the country; however, these headlines are often exaggerated or sensationalized (Eschholz, Mallard, & Flynn, 2004). Thus, although students may not be viewing a situation as it actually happened, the purpose of the activity is to show how learning how to find *good* sources is not just a part of giving a speech or writing a paper; these skills transfer to other areas of life.

The link between the classroom expectation for presenting credible evidence and the real world situation of evaluating the evidence offered makes *Law & Order* a particularly powerful tool in teaching source credibility. By seeing how the police officers and district attorneys find and use evidence, students are able to see what types of evidence are considered credible and how the evidence is used to build an argument for the prosecution. In this way, students will understand why and how finding and using credible evidence is important beyond the scope of a classroom.

## EXPLANATION OF ACTIVITY

The NBC drama *Law and Order*, created by Dick Wolf, first aired in 1990, and is one of the longest-running series in television history (NBC.com, 2008). This series focuses on the criminal justice system from two different perspectives—the police and the district attorneys (NBC.com, 2008). The show is split into two segments. The first half hour focuses on the police side, following the police's efforts to catch a perpetrator of the crime. The second half hour focuses on the legal side, looking at how the district attorneys use the evidence presented by the police to build a case against the defendant(s). Episodes usually conclude with a jury verdict.

To demonstrate the importance of credible sources and how they support the arguments used in the judicial system, an entire episode of *Law & Order* is shown during a class period. This activity is completed after the lecture and readings regarding finding sources and source credibility and is used as a way to reinforce content that students have read and discussed in class during lecture time. The entire episode will take about forty-five to fifty minutes to view. If one is teaching a fifty-minute class, the episode will take the entire class period. The worksheet (see Appendix, p. 376) can be given as homework and discussed the next class period. Or the instructor can choose to limit the amount of the program shown in class, in which case the questions may need to be modified. Students are expected to answer questions that focus on how evidence is used.

Some episodes of *Law & Order* that are effective for this activity are as follows:

- Season 11, Episode 8: "Thin Ice"
- Season 10, Episode 2: "Killerz"
- Season 5, Episode 22: "Switch"
- Season 6, Episode 8: "Angel"
- Season 5, Episode 3: "Blue Bamboo"

## DEBRIEF

To debrief, go over each question as a class and ask students how this particular question applies to argumentation: What would they have done differently if they were the lawyers? Would they have found other types of sources? Were Internet sources used in the court case? If they were, how were they used? What types were used? Were they credible? How does this relate to your work? What are other instances outside the classroom where credible sources are important?

Students' answers to the questions tend to focus primarily on what they saw in the drama and are not connected to making an argument. Through discussion, the instructor can help students make the connection to using sources to create an argument. For example, with the first questions "What types of evidence do the detectives use to make their case to the district attorneys? Which is the strongest?," students typically list physical evidence and witnesses. Once we get a list of the types of evidence used for that case, we talk about how these types of evidences fall under different *types* of sources for their own arguments, for the more varied the types of sources the police and the district attorneys have, the stronger their case. For instance, having DNA evidence plus an eye witness account makes the case stronger as opposed to simply having one or the other. The same can be said for argument creation, in that having two different types of sources, such as statistics and expert opinion, which support an argument is better than having just one. In addition, this question leads to a discussion about witnesses and credibility.

On the show, if a witness is not credible but gives solid information, the police or district attorneys try to find another witness who can say something similar but who is credible. This concept of corroboration extends to research for speeches by students, and is especially valuable for online research. Students finding information that might be correct but lacks strong credibility can then seek out corroborating information from a credible source.

Through this activity, students are able to see that finding and using credible sources is not just an activity that is relegated to academics. These skills can be applied in other areas, including careers.

## REFERENCES

Clark, R. E., & Salomon, G. (1988). Media in teaching. In M. C. Whittock (Ed.), *Handbook of research on teaching* (3rd ed.). New York: Macmillan.

Eschholz, S., Mallard, M., & Flynn, S. (2004). Images of prime time justice: A content analysis of "NYPD Blue" and "Law & Order." *Journal of Criminal Justice and Popular Culture, 10*(3), 161–180.

Davis, P. M. (2003). Effect of the web on undergraduate citation behavior. *Portal, 3,* 41–52.

Grimes, D. J. & Boening, C. H. (2001). Worries with the web: A look at student use of *web* resources. *College & Research Libraries, 62,* 11–23.

NBC.com. (2008). *Law & Order.* Retrieved July 11, 2008, from http://www.nbc.com/Law_&_Order/index.shtml.

Plowman, L. (1988). Active learning and interactive video: A contradiction in terms? *Programmed Learning and Educational Technologies, 25,* 289–293.

## APPENDIX

1. What types of evidence do the detectives use to make their case to the district attorneys?
2. What types of evidence do the district attorneys accept from the detectives? Are there certain kinds of evidence they can legally use? Why?
3. How do the district attorneys use the police's evidence to build their case?
4. In the courtroom, what is the most persuasive piece of evidence that both the prosecutors and defense attorneys present? Why?
5. How does the defense attorney counter the evidence used by the prosecutors?
6. What witnesses are put on the stand, and why is their information considered credible?
7. What happens when two of the credible sources conflict (i.e., when one witness says one thing and one says another)? How would you resolve this conflict if you encountered the same problem while researching for your own work?

# 88

## Apples to Apples with a Twist: Practice for Constructing a More Effective Argument

### Lindsay Harroff

Department of Communication Studies
The University of Kansas
785-864-3633

### Cassandra C. Bird

Department of Communication Studies
The University of Kansas
785-864-3633

**History:** This activity was presented at the annual meeting of the National Communication Association Conference, November 2014, in Chicago, Illinois.

**Primary courses in which this activity might be used:** Introductory Public Speaking, Persuasive Speaking, Argumentation

**Concepts illustrated:** Persuasion, Toulmin Model, Modes of Proof (Ethos, Pathos, Logos), Main Parts of a Speech, Audience Analysis

### PURPOSE

In most communication courses, lessons on how to construct an argument and give an effective persuasive speech typically include a variety of models and complex concepts. While the Toulmin Model, three modes of persuasion, and logical fallacies are all necessary and useful concepts, students often struggle to understand their practical application. In creating this activity, we wanted to provide students with a fun and engaging opportunity to apply these concepts and develop their argumentation and general speaking skills. Additionally, this activity is easy for instructors to adapt and focus on specific challenges their students are having with constructing an effective argument. By engaging in this activity, students will have an opportunity to practice constructing persuasive arguments, demonstrate an understanding of what makes a complete argument, and apply the three modes of persuasion within an argument.

## EXPLANATION OF ACTIVITY

This activity is based on the popular game *Apples to Apples*, which can be purchased at most retail stores. Before completing this activity, students should understand (a) the components of a complete argument, (claim, warrant, evidence); (b) the three modes of proof (ethos, pathos, logos); and (c) basic concepts of preparing a persuasive speech (structure/organization, delivery, audience analysis, etc.). The activity can follow a brief lecture on one or more of these concepts and be completed in twenty to thirty minutes. For best results, however, devote an entire class period to the activity. Students typically become more engaged after the first couple of rounds, and performance continues to improve with each round. Therefore, the more time there is to play, the better.

At the beginning of class introduce the activity by telling students they will be playing the popular game *Apples to Apples*, but there is a twist. In the original game, the judge for the round picks a "green apple" card (which features an adjective and several synonyms) from the top of the deck, and reads the card aloud. The other players choose the "red apple" card (which features a noun) from their hand that they believe best matches that round's "green apple" card and places it face down. The judge shuffles the facedown cards so nobody knows who played each one and chooses the red apple card they think is the best match for the green apple card. Of course, the criteria for *best* depends on the judge. In this activity, instead of the cards being played anonymously and the winner chosen based on the judge's personal opinion of best, students must defend their card as the best choice using effective techniques of persuasion and argumentation.

Divide students into groups of three or four. Deal seven red apple cards to each group. Explain that you will be the judge for each round and will pick the winner based on the best argument presented, not your personal opinion of the best match. Draw a green apple card, read it aloud, and give students one minute to prepare. Specifically, each group should discuss and choose the red apple card they believe is the best match and then construct an argument to defend the match. After one minute, a spokesperson for the group presents the argument. The spokesperson should rotate each round. After considering all the arguments, you choose the winner based on which group made the best argument and explain your decision.

To get a feel for the game, play the first round with only the general parameter that the best argument will win. For subsequent rounds add more specific parameters. For example, the winner will be the group that makes the best use of *pathos*, establishes the strongest *ethos* in their argument, or uses the most descriptive language. Alternatively, you can ask students to identify all the parts of the Toulmin Model in their argument (Toulmin, 1958). As students become more comfortable with the activity, make the requirements harder. For instance, require students to develop a complete introduction or identify three main ideas they might use if constructing a full speech to defend their choice. For more involved rounds, groups may need longer than one minute to prepare.

Since this is an in-class activity, you may choose to award participation points depending on students' contributions. However, students typically do not need any additional incentive to participate. Given the highly subjective nature of the judging, which can be a useful issue to discuss when you debrief, we do not recommend awarding extra credit to the winning team.

For advanced or larger classes, rather than have the instructor determine the winning group, assign one team of students to judge each round and defend their choice using communication and argumentation concepts. The judging group can rotate with each round.

## DEBRIEF

As Hogan, Andrews, Andrews, and Williams (2014) state, "there is no simple list of rules defining a 'good' argument" (357–358), the debrief is an excellent opportunity to discuss how students and the instructor determined what counted as a good argument. Debrief your students by connecting the activity to essential concepts, theory, and application using the E.D.I.T. (Evaluate, Describe, Interpret, and Transfer) model, a method of asking questions based on Bloom's *Taxonomy* (Kolb, 2014).

### Evaluate

One benefit of this activity is it allows for debriefing throughout play. After each round, ask students to discuss the strengths and weaknesses of each group's argument. Then give your own explanation as to why you chose the winner. Especially for rounds with specific criteria, such as including all parts of the Toulmin model, it is important for the instructor to discuss why an argument may have won on these grounds, even if other arguments may have been stronger in other respects (i.e., may have had stronger pathos, used more descriptive language, or even been more accurate).

### Describe

- What was the most difficult part of engaging with this activity? Why?
- What considerations did you take into account in developing your argument? How did these considerations evolve as the game progressed?
- In what ways did your audience (both your classmates and the judge) factor into your decision-making and the arguments you constructed? Who influenced your arguments the most?

**Interpret**

- What does this activity demonstrate about the importance of the Toulmin Model (Toulmin, 1958)?
- How do modes of proof influence argumentation?
- What is most important: ethos, pathos, or logos? Defend your answer.
- How does adapting to your audience strengthen arguments? How can it weaken arguments? How do you determine the appropriate balance of adapting to your audience without pandering or grandstanding?

**Transfer**

- How will the experience of this activity influence your future presentations or papers?
- How is this experience inauthentic to the "real world," and what can you learn from your experience?
- What changes to this game would have made it easier to create a more robust argument?

Students typically enjoy this activity, are very engaged, and construct creative arguments. By asking these debriefing questions, the instructor can ensure students not only have fun but also make connections to important class concepts and consider how they can apply the skills and lessons they learned through the activity in their future public speaking situations in and out of class.

## REFERENCES

Hogan, J. M., Andrews, P. H., Andrews, J. R., & Williams, G. (2014). *Public speaking and civic engagement* (3rd ed). Upper Saddle River, NJ: Pearson Publishing.

Kolb, D. A. (2014). *Experiential learning: Experience as the source of learning and development.* New York: Pearson Education.

Toulmin, S. E. (1958). *The uses of argument.* New York: Cambridge University Press.

# VIII

## Mass Communication and Media

# 89

# Teaching Students to Become Curators of Ideas: An Exercise in Applied New Media Literacy

*Corinne Weisgerber*
*Department of Communication*
*St. Edward's University*
*corinnew@stedwards.edu*

**History:** This activity was presented at the annual meeting of the International Communication Association, June 2013, in London, UK.
**Primary courses in which this activity might be used:** Communication Technology, Social Media, Computer-mediated Communication, Internet and Communication
**Concepts illustrated:** Digital Curation, Personal Learning Networks, Digital Literacies, New Media Literacy

## PURPOSE

Although *curation* has become somewhat of a buzzword, it does provide a powerful metaphor through which to view and understand the role of the twenty-first-century educator and the way our students learn in the digital age. More than that though, it also describes a process that encompasses key new media literacies, which we should teach our students if they are to succeed in an information age (Jenkins, 2006; Rheingold, 2012). The activity described in this paper was designed to help students develop these new media literacies by teaching them new ways to discover, critically evaluate, and curate information from social media sites as well as other online sources.

Hobbs (2010) has identified five digital and media literacy competencies. These competencies include the ability to (1) access information, (2) analyze and evaluate messages, (3) create, (4) reflect, and (5) act. The semester-long activity described below was designed to address all five of these competencies by creating a learning experience that turns students into curators of ideas.

## EXPLANATION OF THE ACTIVITY

This assignment was developed for my Social Media course but it could easily be adapted for a number of communication courses. The assignment requires students to find web resources on a topic of their choice, choose the content most salient to that topic, tell a story by arranging that content in a compelling manner, and share that creation with people outside of class. The assignment comprises two steps.

### Step 1: Identifying a topic area and building a personal learning network

In the beginning of the semester, students are asked to identify an area of social media they want to learn more about. Past project topics have included areas such as personal branding, social media for nonprofits, measuring the success of digital campaigns, and developing a content strategy for small businesses. This aspect of the assignment can be easily tailored to other classes by shifting the focus of the topics to areas that are relevant to that particular field. In order to ensure that all topics are relevant to the course, I require students to submit their topics for approval. Once their topics have been approved, I ask students to identify experts in their chosen topic area who are active on social media platforms such as Twitter, blogs, and social bookmarking sites.

I usually set aside two class periods to train students in how to locate these experts and how to subscribe to their information streams. The idea of this part of the assignment is to teach students to create a personal learning network (PLN) which will support their independent learning needs (Butler & Weisgerber, 2011) and which will connect them to information and resources that have been vetted by other Internet users, not just a search algorithm. In other words, the PLN the students are tasked with developing is designed to help them discover valuable information through a social network. In the process of building this network, students learn how to make information find them instead of using traditional means such as Google searches to go out and find information.

If time allows, I suggest scheduling a brief progress report a few weeks later to gauge the students' progress in setting up a viable PLN, to provide feedback so that they can tweak their PLN if necessary, and to discourage slacking off. As part of that progress report I ask students to select five experts they have identified thus far and to provide examples of useful information they have received from each of these experts. For instance, a student who set up a PLN around the topic of Facebook for nonprofits reported that she had thus far identified 43 experts on Twitter and that her top five experts on that particular social media platform included Beth Kanter (@bethkanter), Nancy Schwartz (@nancyschwartz), Sandy Guerriere (@sandyguerriere), Tim Webster (@timwebster), and CharityHowTo.com (@charityhowto). She talked at length about how much she appreciated Beth Kanter's tweets and the resources they contained. The example she showed the class was a tweet by Kanter linking to a blog post on what the Facebook brand page redesign, which was about to roll out later that week, meant for nonprofits. Since this redesign had not even gone into effect yet, I probably would not have covered this topic in my Social Media class that semester. In this case, the student's PLN helped connect her to highly relevant information while simultaneously teaching her how to stay abreast of emerging trends and developments in social media. I also encourage students to engage the experts they have identified online by commenting on their posts, asking a question related to the post, or simply re-sharing the post. While these engagement attempts aren't always successful, often enough the experts will respond to the students' questions or comments. Students often report that these online engagements provided extra motivation to delve deeper into the topic area.

### Step 2: Curating the information received through their networks

Once students have set up their PLNs and have started a habit of checking their network for new information, I introduce the actual curation assignment. I usually set aside one class period to discuss the concept of digital content curation. For an introduction to content curation, I suggest reading Kanter's (2011) primer on the topic and Rosenbaum's (2011) *Curation Nation*. During that class period, I break down and explain in detail the eight distinct steps of the curation process: find, select, editorialize, arrange, create, share, engage, and track (Weisgerber, 2011). I based these steps on an article by Scoble (2010) on the seven needs of real-time curators. I then go over the assignment and tell students that they need to curate the information from their PLN the way a museum curator would curate an art exhibit. I instruct them to sift through the resources received through their PLN to discover the significant and relevant, to bundle those ideas together, to contextualize them for a world audience and to share and track the level of engagement through a social media platform. I explain that the point is to add value and a personal perspective to these resources, not just to re-share them as is.

The following student example nicely illustrates how this can be accomplished. In this case, the student used the curation platform Storyful to curate some of the best resources on the topic of branding she had discovered through her PLN (http://storyful.com/meredith/23768). Reflecting about the project, the student wrote:

> I'm a journalist, but over the past three months I've transformed into a Twitter branding expert. When approaching the topic of branding on Twitter, I started from square one and honestly did not even know what a brand was, much less how to develop one on Twitter. If this describes you, you're on the right website. With the help of experts in the field, I've compiled a one-stop shop for learning how to brand on Twitter.

The remainder of the page includes a write-up on branding which seamlessly weaves together two videos, five tweets, eight links, and six visuals—all of which were shared by members of the students' PLN.

I suggest that students use a free curation service such as Scoop.it, paper.li, or Storify for the creation step. I also encourage them to follow the eight steps to successful content curation we discussed in class. Students are asked to submit the following deliverables at the end of the semester:

- the URL to their curation (Scoop.it, paper.li, or Storify URL)
- a two- to three-page report explaining (a) how they tracked their curation, (b) how they tried to host a conversation around its content, and (c) how successful they were at disseminating it

In order to help students understand how I will evaluate these two deliverables, I provide them the following grading criteria:

1. Selection process: Curated resources are significant and relevant to the topic
2. Editorial process: Contextualized content, added your own perspective
3. Arrangement: Sorted/ranked content, paid attention to juxtaposition
4. Creation process: Professional looking end product that credits each source
5. Level of engagement: Attracted an audience & comments
6. Tracking: Successfully tracked your curated content
7. Quality of the report: Addressed all three questions listed above in the required two to three pages

## DEBRIEF

Knowing how to discover information, how to critically evaluate it, how to group it into meaningful units, how to add context to it, how to transform it into a new story, and how to share this new creation online, engage others in a conversation around it, and track the overall success of that endeavor are all important new media literacies this assignment tries to foster. This activity is likely to be perceived as challenging at first, but with the right amount of guidance, students quickly understand that they are indeed capable of successfully completing all eight steps of the curation process. Rather than providing a formal debriefing session at the end of the semester, I check in periodically with students and encourage them to reflect on the steps they are currently working on. I may ask them to describe how they discovered a particular resource to be included in their curation, or request that they share some strategies they have used in order to identify new experts to follow. Later on in the semester, I may ask about ways in which they have successfully engaged experts online or tracked the reach and spread of their curation.

Through this activity, students learn to locate and filter interesting, relevant content, and they also gain valuable experience in acquiring a series of other new media literacy skills necessary to succeed in this technologically mediated world (creating online resources, engaging audiences, using Internet metrics to track success). The assignment allows them to take pride in the product of their learning and to share it with a world audience. It gives them a sense of completion and provides them with a way to document their progress throughout the semester. This progress log in turn enables me to determine whether or not the assignment accomplished its learning objectives. On a more practical note, the assignment also allows students to get a feel for the technologies that are changing the way we communicate, rather than just learning about them.

## REFERENCES

Butler, S. & Weisgerber, C. (2011). Empowering 21st century learners through personal learning networks, pp. 249–268. In P. Ferris (ed.), *Teaching and learning with the net generation*, Hershey, PA: IGI Global.

Hobbs, R. (2010). *Digital and media literacy: A plan of action.* The Aspen Institute Communications and Society Program, Washington, D.C.: The Aspen Institute.

Jenkins, H. (2006). *Confronting the challenges of participatory culture: Media education for the 21st century.* Chicago, IL: MacArthur Foundation. Retrieved from http://www .newmedialiteracies.org/wp-content/uploads/pdfs/NMLWhitePaper.pdf

Kanter, B. (2011, October 4). *Content curation primer* [Web log message]. Retrieved from http://www.bethkanter.org/content-curation-101/

Rheingold, H. (2012). *Net smart, how to thrive online.* Cambridge, MA.: MIT Press.

Rosenbaum, S. (2011). *Curation nation: How to win in a world where consumers are creators.* New York: McGraw-Hill.

Scoble, R. (2010, March 7). The seven needs of real-time curators. Retrieved from http://scobleizer.com/the-seven-needs-of-real-time-curators/

Weisgerber, C. (2011). *Building thought leadership through content curation.* [PowerPoint slides]. Retrieved from http://www.slideshare.net/corinnew/ building-thought-leadership-through-content-curation.

# 90

## Learning Fundamentals of Public Relations via WordPress

*Regina Luttrell*
*Department of English Language and Literature*
*Eastern Michigan University*
*rluttrel@emich.edu*

**History:** This activity was presented at the annual conference of the Central States Communication Association, March 2012, in Cleveland, Ohio.
**Primary courses in which this activity might be used:** Intro to Public Relations, Advanced Public Relations, PR Writing, Social Media
**Concepts illustrated:** Strategic Communication, Audience Adaptation, Persuasion, Community Engagement

### PURPOSE

Blogging has earned itself a positive reputation as a pedagogical tool for educators across multiple fields of study (Kang, Bonk, & Kim, 2011). Given that the majority of today's students gravitate toward these types of technologies, professors could well benefit by incorporating social networking sites into the learning pedagogy (Dede, 2005). Generations X, Y, and Z have different expectations and learning styles than previous generations. The Internet-savvy generation values the ability to use the Internet to create a self-paced, customized, and on-demand learning path inclusive of multiple forms of interactive, social, and self-publishing media tools (Baird & Fischer, 2005; Dede, 2005; Hurlburt, 2008). This ideology is moving educators to enter a new phase in teaching. With this shift toward an increased student-centered, technologically rich, socially fertile environment that promises breakthroughs across the educational spectrum, researchers are citing changes for students and professors. Blogging combines essential aspects every public relations practitioner must master with a natural venue for learning.

A significant component of any public relations course includes essential theories of communication and examining the role of the PR practitioner as well as incorporating the principles and practice of effective media relations; media writing, understanding a news story, use of visual images, and working with press. Within the social media arena, blogs have emerged and altered the way organizations communicate and oftentimes complement traditional efforts put forth by PR practitioners (Barnes, Lescault, 2012). Blogging is a natural aspect within the communications profession, particularly for those going into the field of public relations; therefore, it is vital that students learn how to blog, blog correctly, and understand the components of blogging. The goal of this assignment is to combine course material with an activity that teaches students these necessary skills.

## EXPLANATION OF ACTIVITY

For this activity, all students are required to create and launch their own blog and to post on it throughout the semester. At the conclusion of the course, the blog helps students reflect on their progress and growth throughout the semester.

Students are divided into "blog clusters"—a group of no more than four students each. All students must blog and respond to those in their blog cluster on a weekly basis. The students are instructed to research and analyze articles based on the chosen subject matter or topic and what they have learned in the textbook and through class discussions. Students must incorporate peer-reviewed articles as well as multimedia elements such as videos and photos. The articles must pertain to the practice of public relations, social media, marketing, or communication. Students are encouraged to research the history of public relations, PR theories, or current topics trending in the PR industry. The majority of the blog entry should provide an analysis of the content, rather than simply summarizing the article's main points or ideas. For example, students can research an article about Edward Bernays and then begin the blog entry by stating whether they agree or disagree with his place in history.

Provide a list of possible topics for the students to choose from. These include the following:

> PR Pioneers: Bernays, Ivy Lee, Kendrix, Page, Berger, Barnum, Creel, Denora 'Denny' Griswold, Harlow; History/Origins of PR; Shift in PR—Social Media, Contemporary Media, IMPR; Global PR; Theories of PR, Ethics of PR; or students can choose a company who excels at PR, or one that doesn't: Starbucks, Zappos, Walmart, Southwest Airlines.

The initial post must be at least five hundred fifty words, and responses to blog cluster classmates at least two hundred fifty words. Every post must contain an attention-grabbing headline, an original image that supports the post, tags and categories that describe each post, and two sources beyond the textbook to support the points made within the blog (for grading guidelines, see the Appendix, p. 392).

## DEBRIEF

With an increase in introducing and mastering digital literacy skills both inside and outside of the college classroom, assignments such as this enhance educational experiences for students. Technology in the classroom is one way in which professors can involve students in their learning. We know that instruction is most efficient when students can actively engage in the materials (Dede, 2005). This assignment builds upon the method of inquiry-based learning that focuses on knowledge acquisition driven by student query and investigation (Semma, 2016). The benefits of inquiry-based learning include an increase in student engagement, information retention, student responsibilities, and critical thinking skills. This assignment helps students establish connections between a specific subject matter and outside course materials. To that end, when discussing the content of this assignment, I challenge my students with using the three-pronged approach of query-based learning (Nixon, 2010):

1. What did you learn?
2. What surprised you?
3. What did you want to know more about?

The three questions are open-ended so that students can share what they have learned, but also encourage class discussions. As the instructor, I am able to probe further by asking more in-depth questions based on individual topics. I try to pose questions, problems, and scenarios for students to engage with, but ultimately it is up to the student to investigate, research, and arrive at conclusions independently (Dede, 2005; Semma, 2016). For example, one student compared the Hazelwood Coal Mine fire of 2014 to Ivy Lee's handling of the coal mining rebellion of 1914 in Colorado known as the "Ludlow Massacre." I asked my students to think about what communication techniques were used in 1914 versus 2014. Then I asked them to determine whether or not the basic principles of crisis communication have changed between the one hundred years of each occurrence. In this particular discussion, one of the conclusions students came to was that the need for educating and training management in the fundamentals of crisis communication was a necessity in 1914, and is still a need one hundred years later. Discussions vary based on topics. That is why the three-pronged approach of query-based learning works so well.

Inquiry-based learning requires professors to move away from the conventional didactic practices emphasizing the acquisition of information and knowledge, rather than building knowledge. The professor's role changes from lecturer to facilitator while students become active participants in their own learning (Semma, 2016).

This activity appeals to a wide range of learners. Students are engaged in the material, are able to think creatively, critically, and analytically. Students today are fluent in multimedia and gravitate toward experiential learning, guided monitoring, collective reflection, and personalized educational experiences. This assignment is ideally suited for this audience since it challenges the students to think, allows freedom to research ideas that interest individual students, and incorporates principles of public relations.

## REFERENCES

Baird, D. E., & Fisher, M. (2005). Neomillennial user experience design strategies: Utilizing social networking media to support "always on" learning styles. *Journal of Educational Technology Systems, 34*(1), 5–32.

Barnes, N. G., & Lescault, A. M. (2012). The 2011 Inc. 500 social media update: Blogging declines as newer tools rule. Center for Marketing Research, University of Massachusetts, Dartmouth. Retrieved February, 4.

Dede, C. (2005). Planning for neomillennial learning styles. *Educause Quarterly, 28*(1), 7–12.

Dieterle, E., Dede, C., & Schrier, K. (2007). "Neomillennial" learning styles propagated by wireless handheld devices. Ubiquitous and pervasive knowledge and learning management: Semantics, social networking and new media to their full potential, 35–66.

Kang, I., Bonk, C. J., & Kim, M. C. (2011). A case study of blog-based learning in Korea: Technology becomes pedagogy. *The Internet and Higher Education, 14*(4), 227–235.

Nixon, B. (2010). T.O.W.: Topics of the Week for #PRCA2330. Retrieved from http://publicrelationsmatters.com/2010/05/11/t-o-w-topics-of-the-week-for-prca2330 /

Semma, M. (2016). Ways to Encourage Inquiry Based Learning. Retrieved from http://blog.tophat.com/inquiry-based-learning/

## APPENDIX

Once a student completes an individual blog entry, I will provide an analysis of the assignment and post it to our learning management system. Students are graded on the following:

Critical Reading/Analysis ☐          Critical Thinking ☐          Quality of Entries ☐

Community of Practice ☐          Grammar, writing ☐

The following rubric is also used in evaluating the assignment:

| Rating | Characteristics |
| --- | --- |
| 10 | *Exceptional.* The blog entry is focused and coherently integrates examples with explanations or analysis. The entry demonstrates awareness of its own limitations or implications, and it considers multiple perspectives when appropriate. The entry reflects in-depth engagement with the topic. Responses to blog cluster classmates are engaging and reflective. |
| 8 | *Satisfactory.* The blog entry is reasonably focused, and explanations or analysis are mostly based on examples or other evidence. Fewer connections are made between ideas, and though new insights are offered, they are not fully developed. The entry reflects moderate engagement with the topic. Responses to blog cluster classmates are somewhat engaging and reflective. |
| 6 | *Underdeveloped.* The blog entry is mostly description or summary, without consideration of alternative perspectives, and few connections are made between ideas. The entry reflects passing engagement with the topic. Responses to blog cluster classmates are not developed and superficial in nature. |
| 4 | *Limited.* The blog entry is unfocused, or simply rehashes previous comments, and displays no evidence of student engagement with the topic. Responses to blog cluster classmates lack focus and in-depth responses. |
| 0 | *No Credit.* The blog entry is missing or consists of one or two disconnected sentences. Responses to blog cluster classmates were not given or were superficial at best. |

# 91

# Is it Really JUST Twitter?: Agenda Setting in Social Media

## T. Kody Frey

College of Communication and Information
University of Kentucky
terrell.frey@uky.edu

## Nicholas T. Tatum

College of Communication and Information
University of Kentucky
nick.tatum@uky.edu

## Anna-Carrie Beck

College of Communication and Information
University of Kentucky
anniebeck@uky.edu

**History:** This activity was accepted for presentation at the annual meeting of the Central States Communication Association, April 2016, in Grand Rapids, Michigan.
**Primary courses in which this activity might be used:** Basic Communication Course, Introduction to Communication, Communication Theory, Media Effects
**Concepts illustrated:** Agenda Setting Theory, Perspective Taking, Known and Imagined Audiences, Media Framing, Current Events, Critical Thinking

## PURPOSE

Littlejohn and Foss (2010) explain that agenda-setting theory is concerned with the ways in which the press selectively frames the news to the general public. With limitless stories for the media to cover, the theory suggests that there has to be some criteria for selecting what receives coverage (especially when only using 140 characters; i.e., Twitter). This purposeful selection of news plays a significant role in shaping public opinion. According to Shaw and McCombs (1977), "considerable evidence has accumulated that editors and broadcasters play an important part in shaping our social reality as they go about their day-to-day task of choosing and displaying news" (p. 15). In other words, the process of agenda setting establishes the significant images and salient issues in the minds of the public. Littlejohn and Foss (2010) explain that the media has this ability because they "as gatekeepers of information, make choices about what to report and how to report it. Therefore, what the public knows about the state of affairs at any given time is largely a product of media gatekeeping" (p. 282).

Twitter offers a timely, relevant media platform to demonstrate agenda setting to social media entrenched students. Twitter has been used to increase community and interaction within the college classroom (Parcha, 2014). As Tyma (2011) notes, "with the desire for more and more campuses to develop their online or hybrid curricula, expanding our pedagogy to include real-time technology in the classroom not only makes sense but can also be done with little or no additional technological investment" (p. 1). Thus Twitter represents an ideal platform for teaching agenda setting and assessing online credibility and bias in the classroom.

Although more empirical research is needed to secure the role of Twitter as a developing data source in agenda setting (Vargo, 2011), past studies provide a glimpse into the notable role that this service may play in shaping attitudes and opinions. For example, Parmalee (2013) found that journalists and editors use tweets from politicians to shape their coverage of political events. To better understand the ability of the media to frame certain events and bring specific issues into public salience, students should experience agenda setting in social media firsthand. Therefore, the purpose of this exercise is for students to compare and evaluate the credibility of various sources representing differing perspectives on Twitter. In addition, this assignment will show students that the messages they send online often reach audiences far beyond their expectations.

## EXPLANATION OF ACTIVITY

The assignment is divided into four segments. Begin by instructing students to pick a currently relevant issue that they are passionate about or find interesting. Ideally, the topic should be related to a current event of public importance, political prominence, or international recognition. For example, students could choose to examine the way different media outlets from around the globe constructed the disappearance of Air Asia Flight QZ8501 (see Appendix, p. 396), the emergence of the Zika virus in Rio de Janeiro on the eve of the 2016 Olympic games, the controversial rhetoric surrounding the 2016 Republican and Democratic National Conventions, or the fatal shooting of police officers in Dallas, Texas, occurring concurrently with a protest by Black Lives Matter, all of which remain important both domestically and internationally.

Next, inform students that they will research their chosen topic using Twitter. Students must collect at least ten tweets from ten different sources that they feel are credible. Students will copy their selected tweets and organize them into a document, as shown in the appendix (see p. 396). During the assignment, encourage students to collect tweets that represent different information or various perspectives regarding the topic.

After collecting their tweets, student will write a two- to four-page double-spaced paper reflecting on the perspectives they encountered. Reflections should focus on answering the following questions: What different perspectives did you encounter? What characteristics of a tweet make it credible? What role does bias play, if any, in the way various sources present information? How has your opinion influenced or informed by reading other people's tweets? After the completion of the table and reflection paper, students will bring their completed assignments to class to serve as a resource for an in-class discussion.

## DEBRIEF

The final component of the activity involves a class discussion of the students' experiences. Ultimately, students should be debriefed by connecting their own examples to issues of agenda-setting theory, persuasion, and source credibility. This conversation serves as a way for students to consider, discuss, and synthesize the deeper implications and impact of social media on current issues. The class discussion should focus on dialogue considering the following questions: In a society dependent on information, how do you decide what to believe? How does this relate to your position as a citizen in a democracy? Out of all the sources, who do you think gave the most credible information? Why do you choose to believe that source?

The activity also presents instructors with an opportunity to engage students in conversations about relevant social justice issues. For example, if students choose to analyze different perspectives on the failed military coup in Turkey in 2016, the instructor may be presented with an opportunity to move beyond social media to discuss important issues like the state control of media, the role of the Turkish military, or the involvement of the U.S. in future Turkish affairs. Alternatively, instructors might ask their students what they learned from this activity that might change the way they approach social media as a source of information.

## REFERENCES

Littlejohn, S. W., & Foss, K. A. (2010). *Theories of human communication*. Long Grove, IL: Waveland Press.

Parcha, J. M. (2014). Accommodating Twitter: Communication accommodation theory and classroom interactions. *Communication Teacher, 28,* 229–235. doi: 10.1080/17404622.2014.939671

Parmelee, J. H. (2013). The agenda-building function of political tweets. *New Media & Society, 0,* 1–17. doi: 10.1177/1461444813487955

Shaw, D. L., & McCombs, M. E. (1977). *The emergence of American political issues: The agenda-setting function of the press*. St. Paul, MN: West Group.

Tyma, A. (2011). Connecting what is out there!: Using Twitter in the large lecture. *Communication Teacher, 25,* 175–181. doi: 10.1080/17404622.2011.579911

Vargo, C. (2011, August). *Twitter as public salience: An agenda-setting analysis*. Paper presented at the AEJMC annual conference, St. Louis, MO.

## APPENDIX

| EXAMPLE: AIR ASIA FLIGHT QZ8501 | |
|---|---|
| **Source** | **Tweet** |
| Aljazeera English @AJEnglish | Bad weather has forced divers trying to identify sunken wreckage from the crashed **AirAsia** jet to abort the mission http://aje.io/qmqg |
| Wall Street Journal Asia @WSJAsia | BREAKING: #**AirAsia** didn't have permission to fly route on day of crash, Indonesia says http://on.wsj.com/1EXQnJe |
| The Straight Times Online Mobile Print (STOMP) @stompsingapore | **AirAsia** flight QZ8501: Ice was a likely reason for crash http://bit.ly/1zLx8dG |
| Mashable @mashable | Thirty-four bodies recovered, bad weather blocks divers from **AirAsia** crash site. http://on.mash.to/149vPN5 |
| Astro AWANI @501Awani | Bandung-bound **AirAsia** flight stalled due to technical glitch—**AirAsia** Indonesia CEO http://ow.ly/GLkK9 #QZ7633 |
| David Koenig @airlinewriter | #**AirAsia** passengers "spooked"—sixty refuse to reboard after plane returns to gate with electrical problem. http://bit.ly/17aYeUy #QZ8501 |
| Sputnik @SputnikInt | Bad weather in #**AirAsia** #QZ8501 flight crash zone threatens rescuers' lives http://bit.ly/17aTgHD |
| CBC News @CBCNews | Families of #**AirAsia** victims pray in #Indonesia as bad weather prevents divers from reaching wreckage on ocean floor: http://www.cbc.ca/1.2889221 |
| Business Insider @businessinsider | The **AirAsia** plane crashed due to ice chunks in the engine, weather experts believe http://read.bi/14mno1B |
| The Japan Times @japantimes | **AirAsia** boss credited for deft response to tragedy http://jtim.es/GKGGo |

# 92

## The Narrative Machine: Constructing Narratives and Deconstructing Ideology

*Scott M. Walus, Ph.D.*
*Department of Communication Studies*
*Eastern Illinois University*
*smwalus@eiu.edu*

**History:** This activity was presented at the annual meeting of the Central States Communication Association, April 16, 2015, in Madison, Wisconsin. Additionally, it is currently used in a wide variety of courses at Eastern Illinois University.

**Primary courses in which this activity might be used:** Media Production, Mass Communication, Communication Theory, Public Relations (both content creation and criticism), Media Literacy, Electronic Journalism, Visual Communication, Television Criticism

**Concepts illustrated:** Narratives, Internal Coherence, Symbols, Ideology, Semiotics (Paradigms/Syntagms)

### PURPOSE

Few communication acts are as ubiquitous as constructing a narrative. As Roland Barthes (1977) suggests, narratives are "simply there like life itself" (p. 128). After any moment happens in life, only the symbolic form remains, and the narrative begins. In narrating an event, individuals include certain actions and symbols in the sequence of events and omit others. At that moment, they have constructed a narrative and this narrative logic (of cause and effect) differs greatly from the randomness of experience. With the proliferation of new and emergent media, the line between producer and user has greatly diminished. This new hybrid of producers constantly encode and decode mediated messages as part of a participatory culture (Jenkins, 2009) that prompts audience members to constantly switch between using media and producing it. In this convergent, multi-platform environment, students are constantly prompted to both create their own stories as well as contribute to existent ones in the forms of photo sets, short videos, and brief textual bursts. Given the current ecosystem of media and communication channels, students will spend their lives narrating in both professional and personal contexts. Therefore it is imperative for students to learn not only how to do so effectively, but also some of the ideological underpinnings of their symbol choices.

## EXPLANATION OF ACTIVITY

Students should come to class having read a foundational article on narratives. I use excerpts from Fiske (1987) and Barthes (1957, 1972, 1977) to provide this base. Start the class by discussing the importance of narratives, tailoring it to the subject matter of the course. For example, in my public relations new media course, I link to brand narratives and demonstrate how they promote an engagement not considered by analytics. Specifically, we compare brand narratives that provide a chronology to ones that detail a conflict that the organization must overcome. We then discuss how narratives, like the latter type, will draw more interest regardless of the medium on which they appear. In my introduction to mass communication course, I take a more general approach about narrating's selection and omission process. We begin by surveying the ubiquity of narratives, from television commercials (the protagonist has a problem [hunger, frizzy hair, stress] and is offered a solution by the product or service) to social media (digital bursts that provide the ongoing narrative of an individual or organization). Next we watch a one-minute news package and compare who and what have been included to the options from material reality. Throughout, I emphasize that narrating is a purposeful process.

After demonstrating the ubiquity and importance of the narrative, have the students take out any three objects of their choosing from their personal effects. In my classes, students typically select objects such as keys, jewelry, smart phones, books, writing utensils, snacks, and clothing accessories. With the objects in front of them, inform them that they will construct a story about the three objects and tell it to a partner of their choosing. Give them one minute to take some notes, and then deliver the story to their classmate.

After they have told their stories to each other, put the following on the board:

_____ and then _____ and then _____.

Most of their stories followed a pattern similar to this, in which the relationship between the objects is connected weakly through these conjunctions (e.g., The alarm clock on my phone went off and then I made a coffee and then grabbed my keys to go to class). Introduce them to the narrative machine, which looks like the following:

_____ but then _____ which resulted in _____.

In this structure, derived from the work of Roland Barthes, a narrative is a causal series of events consisting of an *enigma* (the status quo of the world that makes a reader want to find out what happens), the *delay* (the disruption of this order and the complications that this disruption causes), and a *climax* (a final act of resolution). Their revised story will have the following structure:

- Here is the scenario with this object. Something interesting is happening to keep us listening.
- But the second object causes a disruption.
- This disruption causes complications to this scenario (the original world and object) that results in the need to use the third object to resolve the story.

Have them revise their initial story in written form using the structure provided. Give them a few minutes to complete these revisions, and then inform them that they will be co-constructing a new narrative with a classmate.

Have students pair up and select three of their combined items in order to generate a story based on the narrative machine. Inform them that it must have both coherence and causality, meaning that each element is essential to the story, and that prior actions cause later ones. As they discuss their new narratives, circulate the room and inquire about their narratives, with an eye on the relationship between all three objects. As you circulate, make sure that the causal elements are happening and that *and then* cannot be substituted as a conjunctive.

An example of a revised story from a class went as follows: As Macho Man Randy Savage and I stood outside of the cockpit, we looked at the keys we had just found (enigma). As we tried to infer the keys' purpose, a man who recognized Savage as a villain from the wrestling ring threw hot coffee on him (disruption). This caused Savage to fall over me and to violently burst through the cockpit door. The man rushed toward us, and the plane began to shake as we all fought for the keys (complication). The plane's turbulence caused the pilot to bump her head (complication) and the plane began to dive out of control. I struggled with random controls while Savage dispatched the deranged man. Needing to get the plane out of a nose dive, I searched the model of the plane on my phone. One of the search results was a picture of one of the keys on the ring. It was the key for the autopilot function, and the page had the instructions for engaging it. Savage tossed me the key and I put the plane in autopilot mode (resolution).

Now, solicit three examples from the class. After each story, provide feedback in drafting the narrative, making sure that the second object disrupts the first, and that the third object results as a direct consequence of what happened from the first. If you have the time, have them select groups of three, and repeat the exercise where each student contributes one object. The repetition of the process helps strengthen their narrative skills.

## DEBRIEF

The discussion after the exercise should help students make connections between their producing and reading habits as well as theoretical foundations for the form and function of mediated messages. By learning the concept and then deploying it, refining it multiple times, and hearing multiple variants of it, it allows for a deeper and more diverse understanding of the concepts of narrative enigmas, narrative causality/internal coherence, and paradigms/syntagms. During this time, the class should discuss the logic of why they constructed a narrative in a particular manner through their use of a narrative enigma and narrative causality/internal coherence. How did they revise their narrative to make an audience want to hear the entire story? Students should differentiate the enigma from an attention-getter in the sense that an enigma causes an audience to ask a question (e.g., What are the keys for? What is my classmate doing on a plane with Randy Savage?). How did they make each object relate to one another through causality and coherence? Here they should focus on how the objects advanced the story (e.g., The coffee caused the protagonists to burst through the cockpit) and how the story would fall apart if a piece was removed. Next the class should discuss syntagmatic and paradigmatic choices they made to construct this narrative. Some questions to guide the conversation can include the following: Why did they select certain objects in their group and omit others? (e.g., The greater possibilities of keys and a phone as opposed to a notebook and pen). Why did they order the objects in the manner that they chose? (e.g., The mythological value of keys instead of a phone). Why did they have certain characters use objects in certain ways? (e.g., Coffee as a weapon by an antagonist demonstrates his nefarious nature and the intrigue caused by a professional wrestler being involved). Why did certain objects lead to certain actions in the story? (e.g., By selecting a phone to save the day, it demonstrates the cultural belief of connectivity and safety through technology). It is ideology that provides the unspoken logic for the aforementioned questions. As the class deconstructs narrative logic, the role of ideology in their symbolizing becomes apparent.

The link to ideology in storytelling demonstrates how narratives are shared and the important role of social construction in meaning and narratives. In asking students why they selected certain individuals' ideas and omitted others, the culturally driven co-construction process of creating and sharing meaning becomes clear. By co-constructing narratives and understanding causality, as well as the role of ideology in narrative linkage, students gain a complete understanding of this deceptively simple communication act.

## REFERENCES

Barthes, R. (1972). *Mythologies.* (A. Lavers, Trans.). New York: Hill and Wang. (Original work published 1957.)

Barthes, R. (1977). *Image-music-text.* New York: Hill and Wang.

Fiske, J. (1987). *Television culture.* London: Methuen.

Hefland, J. (2001). *Screen: Essays on graphic design, new media, and visual culture.* New York: Princeton Architectural Press.

Jenkins, H. (2009). *Confronting the challenges of participatory culture: Media education for the 21st century.* Cambridge, MA: MIT Press.

# 93

## On the Go: Reporter Updates in the Field with Videolicious

*Jennifer Ware, Ph.D.*
*Wright State University*
*jennifer.ware@wright.edu*

## Carie Cunningham

*Department of Journalism and Multimedia Arts*
*Duquesne University*
*cunninghamc1@duq.edu*

**History:** This activity was accepted at the annual meeting of the National Communication Association, November 2016, in Philadelphia, Pennsylvania.

**Primary courses in which this activity might be used:** Video Storytelling, Intro to Video, Broadcast Reporting, Online Communication

**Concepts illustrated:** Online Storytelling, Time-based Reporting, and Social Media Strategy, Objectivity, Sequences

### PURPOSE

Field reporters often engage viewers through bite-sized—short and to-the-point—news updates that are posted to social media channels throughout the day. This activity challenges media communication students to explore and create small yet informative sequences for news reporting or documentary storytelling using available smartphones and video recording apps. This video reporting time-based exercise also teaches students to engage in mobile editing and reporting. Students are taught to report updates on the go, capturing high-quality recordings with their smartphones that show and tell the story in more than just a text update on Twitter or picture on Facebook.

### EXPLANATION OF ACTIVITY

This foundational, praxis-based activity can be completed within a 120- or 150-minute class period or as an online activity with a few modifications.

It requires the use of smartphones and the Videolicious app, which is currently available for Apple devices and, according to the developer, will be available soon for Windows and Android platforms. Students should have a basic understanding of video composition terms including close-up, medium-shot, wide-shot, and reporter stand-ups from either earlier course discussions or from prior courses.

To prepare for the activity, students should come to class having read a selection from Bazin's (1974) writings on cinema realism and sequences. Also, ask students to download the Videolicious app to their smartphones before they come to class. At the beginning of the class period, have the students watch a selection of bite-sized video news updates posted by TV station reporters to social media platforms. Instructors may want to screen capture these updates from local station Facebook pages or save the videos in their Facebook feed prior to the class period.

Bite-sized video news updates are short and to the point pieces of information about an event or activity that's currently taking place. The updates often include a reporter on camera introduction where the reporter gives some information or a developing detail about the event, additional footage (B-roll) of the event over a portion of the update, and a call for the viewers to either stay tuned or to tune in to their nightly news station for the full report. The time range of the updates is generally between twenty-five and forty seconds. For the purposes of the activity, you may want to provide a general definition of the bite-sized report and then follow the next step of the activity to enable students to discover and discuss the content and qualities of a bite-sized report.

Ask students to discuss the types of shots found within the updates and examine the reporter standup framing, shot selection, sound quality, and length of the update. Encourage students to talk about the contents of the update: What information is found within the piece? How it is structured? You might find that some updates simply contain the reporter telling viewers information, while others include additional video (B-roll) from the activity or event. Ask students to talk about which updates they thought were more successful, and what it might take to produce such a video.

Then, lead them through a discussion of Bazin's (1974) concepts of sequences and objectivity but in relation to news video reports. The selected reading is used in class to discuss the possibilities of recording moments from an event and editing the shots together so as to present the totality of that event in an objective manner (p. 92). Bazin's writings on sequences are at odds with some theories of montage and cinema realism. However, his discussion of the concepts has value for communication students who will one day work in professions such as news reporting and need to understand how sequences can be used to show a news story in an objective manner. Reporters must often record items quickly, but report events accurately by gathering and editing a variety of shots from one continuous event.

Once students have an understanding of the bite-sized update, provide them with an overview of Videolicious app and editing process. For this activity, students are asked to use their smartphones, which record in high definition, and the Videolicious app, which enables instant online posting and can be reviewed by a group of peers. Videolicious allows users to record on-screen introductions and a voiceover coupled with additional video clips recorded at the scene. There are online tutorials available for how to use the free app. These tutorials can be shown to the students and/or the instructor can use the app in class to show students how to record and edit. We encourage the instructor to show the tutorials and demonstrate the app to the students as well in order to have a model of technology use practices (Calvert, 2015).

Unlike traditional editing platforms, Videolicious allows students to edit in the field in just minutes (Holstein, 2015). Even the veteran editors used to need bulky editing software and machines to cut together broadcast quality video. Now, students and professionals can use their smartphones and (if available) an external microphone to record broadcast quality materials. This type of technology is something many students will use in their professional careers as Hearst owns the app. Thus it is important for students to learn how mobile storytelling enables professional media communication.

At this point in the activity, the instructor will introduce how students will now use Videolicious in the field to create a bite-sized update of an event. Students are then sent out for an on-location update at an on-campus activity or off-campus event for the online version (a student handout can be found in the Appendix, see p. 404). They must complete their bite-sized update within a forty-five-minute to one-hour time frame. This includes videotaping B-roll, recording their reporter stand up, and editing the recorded materials into a sequence using the mobile application.

Having completed the on-location portion, students return to the classroom to debrief and examine their video bite-sized updates. The updates are not formally graded, but are discussed in class. This learning activity is used to introduce students to the concepts and technical expertise required for a future project, where an instructor can then require a bite-sized update as part of a full-package assignment.

## DEBRIEF

Students take a few minutes to write a series of reflection statements. Question prompts might include the following: "Think about the story you told about the event. How did you choose to focus on this aspect?" and "Tell us about what worked well for you when you were out in the field. Now think about what you feel didn't go so well. What might you do differently next time?" Reflection statements enable students to record how their experience went and note what additional shots they might gather for a future field update. Students are prompted to think about how bite-sized updates, even though they are short and to the point, can still be used to present a large amount of information to the public through visuals and sounds.

Finally, the class discusses their overall experiences with the field reporting activity in order to learn from the challenges and opportunities faced by mobile reporting with limited time and equipment. This can be an in person or online discussion activity. Suggested topics include equipment errors, scriptwriting challenges, reporting different angles, B-roll selection, timing, and sequencing.

We have found through this activity that students generally prefer that their standup portion be recorded either by another person or with the phone on a tripod, but they enjoy the overall experience of the time-based activity. Some students will feel rushed through this assignment, but learn that through more experience and time management, these reporter updates become easier for them to create.

Later in the semester, we ask students to create a 1:30 news package. As a component of this larger assignment, students must also create and turn in a bite-sized update that is recorded while they are gathering footage for the main story. This activity provides the foundation for them to do so with greater success. As an alternate assignment, you might consider having students record five to six bite-sized updates throughout the day of a local festival or ongoing event.

For the online version, students must choose an event or activity to cover and use a forty-five-minute to one-hour time limit during the event coverage period. Instructors should search local station Twitter and Facebook pages for video reporter updates and screen record them to show in class or post online for students.

## REFERENCES

Bazin, A. (1974). The evolution of the language of cinema. In G. Mast & M. Cohen (Eds.), *Film Theory and Criticism: Introductory Readings* (88–102). New York, NY: Oxford University Press.
Calvert, H. (2015). Letting go of stand-alone technology: How to blend technology into literacy situations. *The Reading Teacher 69*(2), 147–155. doi: 10.1002/trtr.1373
Holstein, L. (2015, Dec. 10). Created with Videolicious: Local Market adds rooftop beehives. Retrieved from https://videolicious.com/blog/2015/12/created-videolicious-local-market-adds-rooftop-beehives/

## APPENDIX

### STUDENT HANDOUT/ACTIVITY PROMPT

### On the Go: Reporter Updates in the Field with Videolicious

The 6 p.m. news producer has sent you to an event. You are now on location and it's 2:15 p.m. The news producer has asked you to create and upload a bite-sized update about the event to the station's social media page. The goal is to keep the public informed about activities at the event, but also to encourage them to watch the 6 p.m. news for the full report. You have _____ minutes to videotape several shots of B-roll at the event, record a short standup, and edit your first bite-sized update. Your producer is counting on you!

## Guidelines

Record a variety of wide-shots, medium-shots, and close-ups at the event. You'll use these in your mobile update. Record your reporter stand-up using the Videolicious app. The update should be bite-sized—only twenty-five to forty seconds—and provide some information about what's happening at that moment. You'll also want to invite viewers to tune in at 6 to hear more. Using the app, edit your B-roll over the reporter standup. Review your update, and export the standup. Then upload it to the class social media page or bring the completed update with you back to the classroom.

**Your update must be: twenty-five to forty seconds in length and include:**

- An on-screen reporter standup. Tell us some of what's happening at the event. Good storytelling is key. Remember, this is bite-sized update, so you do not need to tell the whole story.
- A variety of B-roll, show the audience what's happening. Include a variety of wide and mediums shots and close ups. Show us the activities taking place.

# Research Methods

# 94

## Five-Star Ratings: Using Funny Amazon Product Reviews to Teach Students About Validity and Reliability

*Lisa K. Hanasono, Ph.D.*
*Department of Communication*
*Bowling Green State University*
*LisaKH@bgsu.edu*

**History:** This competitively selected activity was presented at the annual meeting of the National Communication Association, November 2014, in Chicago, Illinois.
**Primary course in which this activity might be used:** Communication Research Methods
**Concepts illustrated:** Reliability, Validity, Critical Thinking

### PURPOSE

Students often struggle to understand and differentiate the concepts of validity and reliability in communication research methods classes. This fun and engaging class activity uses everyday customer reviews to teach students the importance of using valid and reliable data. It also challenges students to use their critical thinking skills while shopping on popular websites like Amazon. By completing this activity, students should be able to (a) define and differentiate the concepts of validity and reliability, (b) explain the importance of using valid and reliable data in the decision-making processes, (c) use their critical thinking skills to evaluate the validity and reliability of customer reviews.

### EXPLANATION OF ACTIVITY

#### Introduce the Activity (Five to ten minutes)

At the beginning of the class meeting, I tell my students to imagine that they plan to buy an expensive flat-screen television from Amazon today. They have a budget of $700. Given the expensive nature of this purchase, it is important to get the *best* deal possible. Working in pairs, I give students approximately five

**409**

minutes to go online and quickly research Amazon's inventory of flat-screen televisions (Amazon Electronics, 2014). Once the five minutes are done, I ask my students to indicate which product they would like to purchase. Next, I ask my students how they arrived at their purchasing decision. Inevitably, some students will admit that they looked at some of the television's online reviews on Amazon.

### Review the Concepts of Validity and Reliability (Five to ten minutes)

Drawing from the assigned reading—I use chapter 9 of Davis, Powell, and Lachlan's (2013) *Straight Talk about Communication Research Methods*—I quickly review the concepts of validity and reliability with my students. In general, *validity* refers to the accuracy of a person's observations while *reliability* refers to its degree of consistency or ability to be replicated.

### Application (Fifteen to twenty minutes)

Next, I challenge students think more critically about the validity and reliability of customer reviews on Amazon. To demonstrate the fallibility of Amazon's customer review system, I show them a collection of funny product reviews,[1] such as customers' sarcastic comments about the usefulness of a book entitled *How to Avoid Huge Ships* or people's outlandish testimonials and jokes about a product called Uranium Ore (Amazon, 2014). The website features humorous and often outlandish comments from consumers. For example, a customer wrote the following review about a gallon of Tuscan whole milk, *"Tuscan whole milk can be re-arranged to say 'I'll know mustache.'* Coincidence? I think not" (Amazon, 2008). A customer who allegedly bought a UFO detector wrote, "I don't know if this is a scam or if mine was broken, but it doesn't work and I am still getting abducted by UFO's on a regular basis" (Amazon, 2013). After my students and I read through a few of these outlandish comments, I ask my students to explain how these reviews might lack validity and how they knew which customer review was valid or not. Students usually acknowledge that the comments may not be truthful because many of the bizarre reviews are not designated as "Amazon verified purchases" on the product's website and some of the reviews are illogical, unbelievable, or appear disingenuous.

Next, we explore the concept of reliability. In addition to featuring customers' comments, Amazon reveals each product's rating on a five-star scale and indicates the number of customers who have contributed to its rating. Linking back to the opening activity, I ask my students to revisit Amazon's television department. Together, we find a product that has over fifty reviews and another television that has only one or two reviews. After my students compare the ratings of the two products, I ask my students to (a) identify which

---

[1] Instructors may locate additional examples of customers' comical comments by going online and using the search phrase, "Funny Amazon Product Reviews."

product has more reliable ratings, (b) explain how they were able to determine the reliability of each product's ratings, and (c) discuss the risks of depending on only one or two customer reviews. During this discussion session, students identify several limitations of relying on products that lack a sufficient number of reliable reviews. For example, students usually note that the product's seller or a representative from the product's company might have written one exceptionally positive review for a product.

## DEBRIEF

Subsequently, we explore how customer reviews can lack both validity *and* reliability (five minutes). Using the classroom computer, I open the webpage for Amazon's Nicodemus Coffin Bed (2014). The featured product on this webpage features a hoax-like bed in the shape of a coffin. Its amusing description states: "Sleep peacefully in this Gothic inspired Casket bed … use it as a coffin when the time arises. Constructed of solid pine with a removable lid … with a burgundy velvet interior atop a 6" thick mattress" (para. 4). I use this product for this class activity, because the casket bed isn't supposed to be taken seriously.

As the instructor, I click on the "Write Customer Review" link and show my students how easy it can be to write a false review. (It is important to note that I never actually submit a fake review with my students; I simply demonstrate how open and accessible the review process is.) Next, I ask my students to (a) discuss how customer reviews on websites like Amazon may lack validity or reliability, (b) explain how they can determine if a customer review is both reliable and valid, and (c) identify additional information they can use to research a product and make a smart purchase. With time permitting, my students and I revisit our original Amazon search for flat-screen televisions, and I invite them to find examples of real reviews that demonstrate a sufficient level of validity and reliability.

Overall, students enjoy this activity. They find the wacky and funny Amazon products and customer reviews to be very entertaining, yet relevant to their everyday lives as online shoppers. At the end of the activity, I challenge students to consider how the concepts of validity and reliability can guide their decisions on other popular review sites, such as Yelp, Rate My Professor, and Rotten Tomatoes. By completing this activity, they realize some of the dangers of relying on customer reviews when purchasing products. Moreover, they gain a more nuanced understanding of the concepts of validity and reliability.

## REFERENCES

Amazon. (2008). Tuscan dairy whole vitamin D milk, gallon, 128 oz. Retrieved from https://www.amazon.com/Tuscan-Whole-Milk-Gallon-128/dp/B00032G1S0/ref=cm_lmf_tit_2

Amazon. (2013). "'UFO detector' for sale on Amazon—and it's getting great reviews."
    Retrieved from http://io9.gizmodo.com/ufo-detector-for-sale-on-amazon-and-its-
    getting-g-1482005539
Amazon. (2014). Funniest Amazon product reviews. Retrieved from http://
    www.amazon.com/Funniest-Amazon-Product-Reviews/lm/RM0256CJKINZJ.
Amazon Electronics. (2014). Televisions and video. Retrieved from http://
    www.amazon.com
Amazon's Nicodemus Coffin Bed. (2014). Customer reviews. Retrieved from
    http://www.amazon.com/MHP-The-Nicodemus-Coffin-Bed/product-reviews/
    B001CHK3YI/ref=dp_top_cm_cr_acr_txt?showViewpoints=1
David, C. S., Powerll, H., & Lachlan, K. A. (2013). *Straight talk about communication
    research methods* (2nd ed.). Dubuque, IA: Kendall Hunt.

# 95

## Conversation Analysis Using StoryCorps Dialogue

*Lance Brendan Young*
*Department of Communication*
*Western Illinois University-Quad Cities*
*LB-Young@wiu.edu*

**History:** This activity was presented at the annual meeting of the National Communication Association, November 2014, in Chicago, Illinois.

**Primary courses in which this activity might be used:** Qualitative Research Methods in Communication, Interpersonal Communication, Nonverbal Communication, Communication Theory

**Concepts illustrated:** Conversation Analysis, Vocalics, Facework, Dialogism, Systems Theory

### PURPOSE

Conversation analysis (CA) is a specific analytical tool used in the social sciences for more than fifty years (ten Have, 1999). Insightful conversation analysis requires skill, but any student of communication can easily master the fundamentals. Indeed, few reach adulthood without engaging in daily rudimentary CA, as when we reflect on our interactions and wonder, "What went on in that conversation?"

Teaching students how to answer systematically the "What is going on here?" research question helps them not only to better appreciate the complexity of interpersonal communication, but also to better craft and respond to messages during their own conversations. For this reason, this simple conversation analysis assignment works on multiple levels and can be integrated into a variety of courses. It was designed for a course in qualitative research methods, in order to demonstrate how researchers can use even a brief exchange to reveal discourses shaped by language and nonverbal communication.

The assignment could also be adapted for use in introductory courses to demonstrate the intricacies of mundane meaning making. Teachers of communication theory and interpersonal communication could use it to demonstrate theoretical concepts, particularly those related to facework (positive and negative face), dialogism (centripetal and centrifugal discourses), and systems theory (one-up, one-down, and one-across messages). Finally, teachers of non-verbal communication could use it to demonstrate that a message without nonverbal (conversational) markers differs from one with those vocalic characteristics in place.

This assignment requires students to produce an original conversation analysis of a brief dyadic exchange between two people recorded by StoryCorps (2015). StoryCorps is an excellent source for text to analyze because the topics are simultaneously profound and relatable, the absence of distracting visual cues focuses attention on vocalics and text, and both audio and transcribed versions are freely available. On completion of this assignment, students will have gained:

1. An understanding of the goal and uses of conversation analysis;
2. Initial mastery of conversation analytic conventions, including line numbering and Jefferson Transcript Notation; and
3. An appreciation of triangulation, relying on multiple analysts examining the same or similar transcripts.

## EXPLANATION OF ACTIVITY

The instructor first should discuss an example of a simple conversation analysis, pointing out whether the conversation is more cooperative or more competitive overall, and which specific turns at talk support that characterization. Simon Moss (2008) provides one good online source. A brief article by Nevile and Rendle-Short (2009) provides a humorous analysis as an alternative. When students are prepared, the instructor should proceed.

First, the instructor assigns each student a different preselected conversation available at StoryCorps.org. Conversations available online are presorted into themes and include photos of the participants. The instructor should select dyadic conversations with at least ten turns at talk within one of the themes (e.g., friendship or identity). Selecting a single theme for the class will enhance comparisons across analyses. Alternatively, a class could analyze a single conversation.

Second, students create a Microsoft Word document, add line numbers, and copy-and-paste the transcripts, available by clicking "Read the transcript" on the conversation page. Students separate the turns of talk so that a blank line separates each turn.

Third, students listen to the recording and insert paraverbal features using the Jeffersonian Transcription System (see Psathas & Anderson, 2009). Beginning researchers should focus on pauses, emphases, overlapping talk, and vocal features like laughing, sighing, and crying. Transcription notation guides are easily found online. Christina Wasson at the University of North Texas offers guides, tips, and software links available by searching *Wasson transcription conventions.*

Next, students reread the transcript, focusing on *intuitive interpretation* of the overall conversation, asking, "What are the partners accomplishing together?" Students should use the "insert comment" feature to identify topics and themes and when they shift.

Students then read the transcript again, focusing on *individual turns*. The "insert comment" feature should be used to identify what point is being made, how it is being made, what is not being said that could have been said, and what response is expected. Students integrate comments and interpretations, determining how the individual turns at talk contribute to their intuitive interpretation. Students determine whether the partners are saying the exact same thing, or whether each one is making a different point in a bid to establish their version of events or their understanding of a concept (e.g., friendship). Do the threads ultimately come together, or do they remain distinct? Students should focus on the words and interaction without speculating excessively about motives.

Finally, students write a two- to three-page report summarizing their analysis and submit both the annotated transcript (with paraverbal features indicated) along with their written report. Guidelines for evaluation should be shared with students and should address both the formatting of the transcript and the analysis. A D-level submission would include accurate verbal transcription and a brief summary of the conversation. A C-level submission would include minimal paraverbal indicators and a summary of ideas (e.g., events, concepts, illustrations, etc.) presented by each conversational partner. A B-level submission would include adequate paraverbal indicators (e.g., averaging two per sentence) and trace how the ideas develop or change during the conversation. An A-level submission would include multiple indicators of pauses, emphases, and vocalic features, and the analysis would consider both how the ideas develop and how each partner cooperates or competes in shaping their meaning.

## DEBRIEF

When evaluating the submissions, the instructor should note similar and divergent themes and patterns across submissions and share those with the class. For instance, conversations about both friendship and romance may focus on either the individuals' *similarity* (i.e., birds of a feather) or their *differences* (i.e., opposites attract). Or the conversation may veer from one idea to the other, or each partner may voice a different understanding of the relationship. Similarly, relationships are often portrayed as either *meant to be* or *hard work*—or both.

Students typically express surprise that analyzing a simple conversation is so challenging because much more is happening than they realize upon simply listening to it once in real-time. In class, instructors can pose questions either to individual students or to small groups:

1. Were conversational partners more cooperative or competitive in their talk? Did they converge on a common understanding by the end of the conversation?

2. How do you explain unexpected word choices (like saying "my house" instead of "my home") or anything that was not said that you might expect to be said?
3. How did the partners use clichés (like the term "fairy-tale ending") and how do clichés constrain the way people understand their own experience?
4. Did the conversation sound too rehearsed? If so, why? Because it was recorded? Because StoryCorps selected the most coherent conversations? Because the participants had likely told it before? Because it was a speech genre—a common template like the how-we-met story that most people in our culture know how to perform?

## REFERENCES

Moss, S. (2016, June 16). *Conversation analysis*. Retrieved from http://www.sicotests.com/psyarticle.asp?id=214

Nevile, M., & Rendle-Short, J. (2009). A conversation analysis view of communication as jointly accomplished social interaction: An unsuccessful proposal for a social visit. *Australian Journal of Linguistics, 29*(1), 75–89. doi: 10.1080/07268600802516392

Psathas, G. & Anderson, T. (2009). The 'practices' of transcription in conversation analysis. *Semiotica, 78*(1–2), pp. 75–100. doi:10.1515/semi.1990.78.1-2.75

StoryCorps. (2015). *StoryCorps*. Retrieved from https://storycorps.org/

ten Have, P. (1999). *Doing conversation analysis: A practical guide*. Thousand Oaks, CA: Sage.

# 96

## Which Superpower Should Students Have?: Using Buzzfeed to Teach Students How to (Re)Design Surveys

*Lisa K. Hanasono, Ph.D.*
*Department of Communication*
*Bowling Green State University*
*LisaKH@bgsu.edu*

**History:** This competitively selected activity was presented at the annual meeting of the National Communication Association, November 2014, in Chicago, Illinois.

**Primary course in which this activity might be used:** Communication Research Methods, Survey Design, Critical Thinking and Communication, Media Studies

**Concepts illustrated:** Survey Design, Types of Data, Survey Validity, Critical Thinking

### PURPOSE

Many communication and media studies programs require students to learn fundamental skills and concepts related to research methods. Although communication research classes are important, helping students make connections between different methodological approaches and practical, everyday applications can be challenging. This creative and engaging class activity uses popular quizzes on entertainment websites like Buzzfeed and Zimbio to teach students how to critique and design communication research surveys.

By completing this activity, students should be able to (a) develop survey questions to gather nominal, ordinal, continuous, and ratio level data; (b) design (and redesign) communication research surveys; (c) discuss different sampling techniques, and (d) critique surveys on popular websites like Buzzfeed.

### EXPLANATION OF ACTIVITY

This activity can be completed in one class meeting (fifty to seventy-five minutes). To help my students prepare for this activity, I instruct them to take an entertaining quiz on Buzzfeed (e.g., "Which super power should you actually have?" or "Which Hogwarts house do you belong in?"), and bring their results to our class meeting.

On the day of the activity, I first ask my students to share their Buzzfeed quiz results. This usually piques my students' interest, and they are very excited to share their results with each other. Next, I ask my students, "How *valid* do you think your results are?" Whether students accept or reject the results of their Buzzfeed quizzes, I pose the same follow-up question: "What makes you believe that the results are valid or not valid?" At this point, I open the assigned Buzzfeed quiz, and I challenge my students to think critically about the survey's questions.

To stimulate discussion, I ask them to identify the strengths and weaknesses of specific questions from the online quiz. For example, a quiz that attempts to identify readers' most desired superpower asks, "Which household chore is the worst?" (Buzzfeed, 2014, para. 2). Readers are given only four choices that range from dusting and vacuuming to car washing and pet waste removal duties. Students often critique this question because on face value, it doesn't seem relevant to the topic of superpowers. Moreover, students tend to question the limited range of survey answers. Some students indicate that they dislike all of the chores equally and struggled to only select one option. I also ask them to explain how the survey designers could improve specific quiz questions. For example, the same Buzzfeed quiz asks readers, "Choose one of the five senses" (Buzzfeed, 2014, para. 6). However, instead of featuring the five basic senses, the survey includes a sixth option titled "all of them." To revise this confusing survey item, students usually recommend the survey designers remove the sixth option so that readers would actually have to pick one of the five main senses. Alternatively, students frequently suggest that the question be phrased more specifically (e.g., "Which of the five senses do you use most frequently?").

Now that students are familiar with the nature and structure of Buzzfeed quizzes, I make the following announcement:

> *Today, I want you to imagine that you are interns at Buzzfeed's Survey Design Department. Your boss earned an advanced degree in communication studies and quantitative research methods, and she/he is dissatisfied with the company's popular culture quizzes. Working in small teams of three, you are responsible for designing or redesigning a creative and engaging Buzzfeed quiz. Each quiz should contain five questions.*
>
> *Here is the catch. Your boss recognizes the importance of collecting diverse types of data. Therefore, your survey must include questions that will yield nominal, ordinal, ratio, and continuous data. You must also explain how you plan to gather data for your survey (i.e., sampling methods).*

At this point, I usually spend five to ten minutes reviewing nominal, ordinal, continuous, and ratio level data with my students. I also review different types of samples (e.g., simple random samples, stratified samples, convenience samples, volunteer samples, snowball sampling, and network sampling) with my students. For a quick reference, please see the communication research methods textbooks by Davis, Powell, and Lachlan (2013) and Frey, Boton, and Kreps (2000).

Next, I give students twenty to thirty minutes to develop their quizzes. While they are working in small teams, I walk around the classroom, answer students' questions, and provide constructive feedback. Once students are finished, I instruct each team to trade their completed survey with another team. I give students approximately five minutes to complete the survey *and* identify which questions measure nominal, ordinal, continuous, and ratio level data.

## DEBRIEF

At the end of the activity, I help my students process the activity by leading a discussion session. The following are some questions that I recommend using:

1. How did you design your survey questions to obtain nominal level data? Ordinal? Continuous? Ratio?
2. How did you ensure that your survey was valid? Clear? Effective?
3. Earlier today, we talked about different sampling methods. If you were to collect data for your Buzzfeed survey, who would be your sample? How would you access this group of people and ensure their participation?
4. Buzzfeed offers a variety of popular quizzes that are shared on social networking sites like Facebook and Twitter. Although you might be familiar with quizzes by Buzzfeed, you have probably taken a variety of surveys outside of this class. Please provide some examples of surveys that you have taken this semester (e.g., customer service surveys, lighthearted surveys in popular magazines, surveys in communication research studies).
5. This activity featured a hypothetical scenario where you were interns for Buzzfeed. Although you might not work for Buzzfeed after you graduate from this course, there is a strong likelihood that you will need to design and create survey questions in the future for an organization, company, class, or professional project. What information might you need to gather for an organization, job, or class?

Students love this activity. They enjoy taking and critiquing the Buzzfeed quizzes, and by completing this activity they realize how challenging it can be to write effective survey questions. Moreover, they gain a more nuanced understanding of different types of data in communication research and the fundamentals of survey research.

## REFERENCES

Buzzfeed. (2014). Which super power should you actually have? Retrieved from http://www.buzzfeed.com/joannaborns/super-power-quiz

David, C. S., Powerll, H., & Lachlan, K. A. (2013). *Straight talk about communication research methods* (2nd ed.). Dubuque, IA: Kendall Hunt.

Frey, L. R., Botan, C. H., & Kreps, G. L. (2000). *Investigating communication: An introduction to research methods* (2nd ed.). Boston, MA: Allyn and Bacon.

Zimbio. (2014). Which Disney princess are you? Retrieved from http://www.zimbio.com/quiz/bibMfGO8ax1/Which+Disney+Princess+Are+You

# X

## Health Communication

# 97

## Evaluating Health Campaign Websites: A Focus Group Exercise

*Patrick J. Dillon, Ph.D.*
*School of Communication Studies*
*Kent State University at Stark*
*pdillon2@kent.edu*

**History:** This activity was presented at the annual meeting of the Southern States Communication Association, April 2012, in San Antonio, Texas.

**Primary courses in which this activity might be used:** Health Communication, Health Campaigns, Health and Mass Media, Mass Media Campaigns, Social Marketing, Communication Research Methods

**Concepts illustrated:** Evaluation, Research Methods, Audience Analysis, Computer-Mediated Communication, Persuasion, Message Design

### PURPOSE

Recent estimates suggest that adults living in the United States spend approximately ten hours each day consuming media (e.g., Internet, television, radio, etc.) content; over the course of these ten hours, people are exposed to, on average, over three hundred fifty advertisements (Media Dynamics Inc., 2014). In addition to providing an outlet for marketing commercial products and services, mass media channels are also used to disseminate messages designed to inform and influence decisions that enhance health (Centers for Disease Control & Prevention [CDC], 2011). From raising awareness about HIV/AIDS and promoting cancer screenings to educating parents about sudden infant death syndrome and seeking to reduce tobacco use among teenagers—health communication campaigns address a number of important health issues and behaviors (Silk, Atkin, & Salmon, 2011).

Health communication campaigns have long used traditional media channels to disseminate campaign messages (e.g., billboards, brochures, radio spots, television commercials, etc.). In recent years, however, websites have emerged as a (if not *the*) primary distribution channel for health campaign content—a shift that has allowed campaign planners to "utilize the full capabilities of the Internet to bring awareness to their purpose, such as web-casts, chat rooms, blogs, and informational videos" (Helme, Savage, & Record, 2015, p. 401). A key predictor of a health campaign's success, regardless of its focus or distribution channels, is pretesting potential campaign elements before disseminating them to a wider audience (National Cancer Institute [NCI], 2002; Noar, 2006). Pretesting often involves campaign planners conducting focus groups that include members of the target audience (NCI, 2002; Silk et al., 2011). The purpose of this activity is for students to gain experience conducting focus groups designed to evaluate health campaign websites.

## EXPLANATION OF ACTIVITY

Begin the activity by showing students examples of health campaign websites and soliciting initial reactions to their content and design. Tell the students to imagine that the funding agency behind a national health communication campaign has decided to create a modified version of their website designed for undergraduate students on your campus. I have, for example, used the National Patient Safety Foundation's "Ask Me 3" campaign (see NPSF.org/askme3 or search "Ask Me 3") the CDC's "Act Against AIDS" campaign (see CDC.gov/actagainstaids or search "Act Against AIDS"), and the American Legacy Foundation's "truth" campaign (see truth.com or search "truth anti-tobacco campaign") for this activity. As a starting point for this new endeavor, the agency is asking students to help them evaluate the campaign's existing website and to identify ways that it could be modified in order to better serve the campus community. In order to address these goals, the students will conduct forty-five-minute focus groups with members of the target audience (i.e., other undergraduate students).

After reviewing best practices for conducting focus groups (see e.g., Krueger & Casey, 2015), divide students into an even number of teams. In the courses where I use this activity, there are usually four or six teams of approximately five students. Explain that the focus groups will take place over two class periods (this may vary based on your course's schedule). Each team will be paired with another one. On the first day, one team will conduct a focus group and the other team will serve as the participants. The teams will then switch places on the second day. Next, assign a health campaign website to each team. Because the teams are paired together, each campaign can be assigned more than once.

Tell the students that the focus groups will begin one week after you explain the activity. Explain that, in the meantime, each team is responsible for creating a focus group script; I provide Fraeyman et al.'s (2012) focus group script (which was used to evaluate a health campaign website) as an example. Next, tell them that they must also send a recruitment email to their participants. The email should explain the purpose of the focus group, share their assigned campaign's website, and provide information regarding the focus group's time and location. Finally, have the groups select two members to facilitate the focus group.

The rest of the team is responsible for monitoring time and recording participants' responses.

The focus groups should take place during scheduled class periods; if possible, however, I recommend reserving space outside of your regular classroom to hold the groups. I have, in past semesters, secured private rooms in the campus library and student center for this activity. After completing the focus groups, ask each team to create a one-page document that summarizes participants' responses and offers recommendations for the campaign planners to modify their website for your undergraduate population. The students should then present their summaries and recommendations to the rest of the class before you debrief the activity.

## DEBRIEF

Debriefing the activity generally centers on two main topics: (a) the role of focus groups in pretesting health campaign content and (b) focus groups as a general research practice. You might, for example, ask students whether conducting focus groups to pretest health campaign content seems as valuable as the research literature suggests (NCI, 2002; Silk et al., 2002). You might also evaluate the specific findings and recommendations that the teams developed based on their focus groups. Which ones seem most helpful or valuable to designing a campaign website for students on your campus?

Next, encourage the students to reflect on the experience of facilitating and participating in the focus groups. You can ask them, for instance, what they found most challenging about the activity or what they might do differently if they could do it over again. You can also ask them to think about real-world focus groups. When might focus groups be an appropriate research method beyond health campaign pretesting? How does focus group data compare to what one might learn from alternative methods (e.g., interviews, survey, etc.)?

## REFERENCES

Centers for Disease Control and Prevention. (2011, May 10). *What is health communications?* Retrieved from http://www.cdc.gov/healthcommunication/healthbasics/whatishc.html

Fraeyman, J., Van Royen, P., Vriesacker, B., De Mey, L., & Van Hal, G. (2012). How is an electronic screening and brief intervention tool on alcohol use received in a student population? A qualitative and quantitative evaluation. In *Journal of Medical Internet Research, 14*(2), e56. doi:10.2196/jmir.1869J

Helme, D. W., Savage, M. W., & Record, M. A. (2015). Campaigns and interventions. In N. G. Harrington (Ed.), *Health communication: Theory, method, and application* (pp. 397–427). New York: Routledge.

Krueger, R. A., & Casey, M. A. (2015). *Focus groups: A practical guide for applied research* (5th ed.). Thousand Oaks, CA: Sage.

Media Dynamics, Incorporated. (2014, September 22). *Adults spend almost 10 hours per day with the media, but note only 150 ads.* Retrieved from http://www.mediadynamicsinc.com/uploads/files/PR092214-Note-only-150-Ads-2mk.pdf

National Cancer Institute. (2002). *Making health communication programs work: A planner's guide*. Washington, D.C.: National Institutes of Health.

Noar, S. (2006). A 10-year retrospective of research in health mass media campaigns: Where do we go from here? *Journal of Health Communication, 11*(1), 21–42.

Silk, K. J., Atkin, C. K., & Salmon, C. T. (2011). Developing effective media campaigns for health promotion. In T. L. Thompson (Ed.), *The Routledge Handbook of Health Communication* (pp. 203–219). New York: Routledge.

# 98

# Voice in Healthcare Interactions: Burke, Agency, and Student Experiences

*Erin F. Doss, Ph.D.*

*Assistant Professor of Communication Arts,*

*Honors Program Director*

*Indiana University Kokomo*

*efdoss@iuk.edu*

**History:** This activity was presented at the annual meeting of the National Communication Association, November 2011, New Orleans, Louisiana.

**Primary courses in which this activity might be used:** Rhetorical Theory, Rhetorical Criticism, Health Communication, Persuasion, Communication Research Methods

**Concepts illustrated:** Guided Reflection, Burkean Pentadic Analysis, Patient Agency, Healthcare Communication

## PURPOSE

Agency is an important topic in health communication, especially in the context of provider-patient communication. Patients who are given a voice in treatment discussions are more likely to respond positively to the interaction and follow the treatment (Brown, Stewart, & Ryan, 2003; Young & Flower, 2001). Using Kenneth Burke's (1969) pentad as a model, this activity asks students to analyze their own healthcare interactions and gives them an opportunity to both reflect on their agency within that situation and to have a voice in the classroom discussion. The activity draws in students who might not otherwise participate because each student has his or her own personal story to share. Giving students a chance to voice their experiences and opinions provides a meaningful way for them to interact with the concept of agency. Because they are allowed to have agency in the classroom and are encouraged to explore the role of agency in medical encounters, they form a deeper understanding of the concept and are able to discuss it in thoughtful ways.

## EXPLANATION OF ACTIVITY

For this class period, assign one of the following articles (or another article dealing with agency in healthcare contexts): Stone (1997), Young & Flower (2001), Brown, Stewart, & Ryan (2003), or Gillotti (2003). Be sure students read the article and are familiar with the concept of patient agency and Burke's (1969) pentad, the system he used to analyze situational motives according to act, scene, agent, agency, and purpose. As a tool for rhetorical analysis, the pentad often draws attention to the way one or another element is emphasized as a privileged term (i.e., the patient's body as the *scene* of an illness may be emphasized over the patient as an *agent* in control of his or her healthcare). The pentad can also be used to discuss the ratios between two different terms (i.e., asking "how does the *agent* influence the *scene*?"). Using the pentad to analyze situations in this way allows students to view their healthcare interactions with a different perspective and begin to question why the situation unfolded as it did (see Blakesley, 2002).

Begin the class period by giving students five minutes to write a few sentences about a recent healthcare experience they are comfortable discussing. Remind students they will not be asked to share details about the reason for their healthcare visit, but to focus on the communication that took place during the visit. The goal is for them to think about the rhetorical aspects of the experience rather than disclosing private health-related information. Asking students to write down their experiences at the beginning of class allows them to think of the lecture in terms of their own stories. Because of this, when they are asked a question related to the lecture, their examples come straight from their own experiences and they begin to analyze those situations before they are asked to do so. Ask them to consider issues such as: (a) Were you allowed to ask questions? (b) Did you participate in decision-making? (c) Did the provider take charge? (d) Were you satisfied with the encounter? (e) Would you go to see that provider again?

Once students finish writing their stories, spend ten to fifteen minutes introducing them to the pentad or clarifying their understanding of the theory. Be sure to focus on the connections between agent, agency, scene, and act: Specifically, how patients can be framed as the scene of the illness, rather than as an agent who is ill, and the way that characterization can influence patient satisfaction and adherence to prescribed treatment (Stone, 1997).

After reviewing the pentad, share a recent medical experience of your own and demonstrate how the pentad can be used to analyze that experience. Focus on whether you were given a voice in the interaction (*agent*) or felt like the *scene* of the disease. Talk about the *actions* you were (or were not) asked to take, and whether or not those actions were characterized as a means of altering your current situation (*agency*). Discuss how these elements affected your own satisfaction with the interaction, and your likelihood to follow through with the treatment plan outlined during the encounter.

One example I have used is a visit to the doctor for back pain. I talk about how I was treated as an agent in the encounter and given instructions not just to take medicine, but also to do exercises to strengthen my core muscles. I point out the role of agency in the situation and contrast that experience with others in which my body was treated as the scene of a problem, rather than as an agent capable of changing the healthcare situation. Because I was given the opportunity to be an agent in my own healthcare I felt empowered to act on the doctor's instructions and practice the exercises.

After discussing your own experience, divide students into small groups, two to four students per group. Ask them to go back to the medical encounter they wrote about at the beginning of class and spend fifteen minutes analyzing that interaction, specifically answering the following questions: (a) How do you see your position as agent/scene? (b) How does this affect the medical interaction? (c) How would changing your role in the interaction change the entire experience? (d) What new things did you see using the pentad to analyze your situation? (e) How could you generalize this to make a larger statement about provider-patient communication? If students are comfortable talking about their experiences, ask them to share their analysis both with the members of their group and with the class as a whole.

## DEBRIEF

Wrap up the activity by drawing the class into a larger discussion of the pentad and the students' personal experiences. Ask members of each group to share their experiences and state whether or not they felt they had a voice in the decision-making process. Ask students who they felt had agency in their medical encounter stories and why they believe that was the case. Have them define the role of agency and the ways it affects outcomes for patients, as well as providers. As a group, discuss what an understanding of agency in medical encounters may contribute to a larger understanding of provider-patient communication. Finally, have students discuss the value of the pentad as a means of analyzing situations, both in the healthcare field and beyond. In my experience, students have responded well to this activity and shared experiences both where they felt they were given agency in a situation and where they felt their bodies were treated more as a scene to be dealt with by the care provider. Students often report thinking about healthcare experiences differently when using the pentad because it helps them understand why they did or did not respond well to a doctor or follow through with the prescribed treatment. Often, students who felt they had agency to change a situation said they were more likely to act on the doctor's advice, while students who felt less agency attributed it to a focus on scene in their healthcare experience and were overall less satisfied with the results of their interactions. Additionally, students have said this activity helped them understand and remember the elements of the pentad because of the focus on analyzing and understanding their personal experiences.

## REFERENCES

Blakesley, D. (2002). *The elements of dramatism*. New York: Longman.

Brown, J. B., Stewart, M., & Ryan, B. L. (2003). Outcome of patient-provider interaction. In T. L. Thompson, A. M. Dorsey, K. I. Miller, & R. Parrott (Eds.), *Handbook of health communication* (pp. 141–161). Mahwah, NJ: Lawrence Erlbaum Associates.

Burke, K. (1969). *A grammar of motives*. Berkeley, CA: University of California Press.

Gillotti, C. M. (2003). Medical disclosure and decision-making: Excavating the complexities of physician-patient information exchange. In T. L. Thompson, A. M. Dorsey, K. I. Miller, & R. Parrott (Eds.), *Handbook of health communication* (pp. 163–181). Mahwah, NJ: Lawrence Erlbaum Associates.

Stone, M. S. (1997). In search of patient agency in the rhetoric of diabetes care. In *Technical Communication Quarterly, 6*(2), 201–217.

Young, A. & Flower, L. (2001). Patients as partners, patients as problem-solvers. *Health Communication, 14*(1), 69–97.

# 99

## Using Videos *Wit* and *Ed's Story*: *The Dragon Chronicles* to Teach Health Communication Concepts

*Deleasa Randall-Griffiths, Ph.D.*
*Department of Communication Studies*
*Ashland University*
*drandall@ashland.edu*

**History:** This activity was presented at the annual meeting of the Central States Communication Association, April 2016, in Grand Rapids, Michigan.
**Primary courses in which this activity might be used:** Health Communication
**Concepts illustrated:** Bioethics, End-of-Life issues, Gender Roles in Healthcare, Conflict/Power in Healthcare, Healthcare Worker-Patient Communication

### PURPOSE

Video has the power to highlight concepts in health communication in accessible and engaging ways. The narratives of individual people, whether real-life or fictional, expose underlying assumptions about how health and health-care function in our society. Two videos: *Wit* and *Ed's Story: The Dragon Chronicles* help students understand ideas from the course in application.

These videos may be used to cover a wide range of healthcare concepts, including professionalism, bioethics, palliative care, end-of-life issues, informed consent, roles in healthcare, the history of healthcare, gender, conflict, power, cultural sensitivity, the communication process, goals of communication, perception, language, health literacy, nonverbal, listening, healthcare worker-patient communication. Students are able to analyze each video, connecting concepts from their course readings to specific examples found in the videos. Students are then able to articulate their analysis clearly in written papers.

## EXPLANATION OF ACTIVITY

This activity utilizes two unique videos, varying in length from one hour to one and a half hours, as vehicles to explore concepts in health communication. The videos can be viewed over the course of one or two class periods. Students are assigned related course readings prior to viewing the videos. Instructors may opt to hand out the analysis prompts before viewing the video, or they may allow students to first experience the narrative as a whole prior to assigning the analysis prompts. Multiple class periods any be used to apply course concepts and theories to the examples found in the videos.

*Wit,* a film by Mike Nichols based on the play written by Margaret Edson, stars Emma Thompson as the fictional English Professor Vivian Bearing. The film chronicles Bearing's journey dealing with Stage 4 ovarian cancer. It is available on DVD and the full-length movie is also on YouTube.

*Ed's Story: The Dragon Chronicles* is the recording of a play written by Mary-Colin Chisholm and produced in conjunction with the Izaak Walton Killam Health Center. It is available in three parts on YouTube. Based on a true story, the play was crafted from the pages of a teenage cancer patient's journal, along with interviews of his family, friends, and healthcare providers. The recording is now used to train doctors at Dalhousie University's Medical School in Nova Scotia. While it is not a high-quality production, the content it provides makes it a valuable teaching tool.

## DEBRIEF

The following lists many discussion prompts that work well in class discussion. Students articulate their understanding of the characters, plot conflicts, and application to communication concepts in a three- to four-page reflection paper centering on at least three of the following prompts. Throughout this paper, students connect course concepts with examples from the video and analyze the effectiveness of communication choices. These prompts are written to directly connect with the book *Medical Communication: Defining the Discipline* by Polack and Avtgis; however, they could be adapted to fit any textbook or collection of readings.

### Discussion Prompts for the Video *Wit*

***Professionalism.*** Analyze the communication between Vivian and her primary doctor. Compare that to her interactions with Jason, the medical student. How do you see elements of the Professional Ethos and the Four Principles of Bioethics demonstrated?

***Healthcare Worker-Patient Communication.*** Analyze the communication between Vivian and her primary nurse. How did that nurse and other healthcare workers relate to Vivian? How did they relate to one another? When did they work as a team, and when did that break down?

*Gender & Communication.*   What gender differences do you see demonstrated in this movie? When do characters fit stereotypical assumptions about gender, and when do they go against those social categories? Discuss the styles the book associates with gender norms by choosing two characters from the movie and analyzing their style.

*Listening.*   Analyze the communication between Vivian and her various health-care providers in terms of active listening and mindfulness. Look for specific examples that demonstrate both good and bad listening skills. Discuss the impact those moments had on Vivian and her journey.

*Informed Consent.*   Analyze the various examples of informed consent shown in the movie. How does Vivian feel about her choices? Compare and contrast the way the various healthcare providers (doctors and nurses) interact with her and assist in her choices. What ethical issues do see in the interactions?

*Conflict & Power.*   How does aggression impact Vivian's experience with cancer and her treatment? Find examples where conflict and power were demonstrated in the interactions between Vivian and her healthcare providers or among the various providers caring for her.

### Discussion Prompts for the Video *Ed's Story: The Dragon Chronicles*

*Doctor-Patient Communication.*   Analyze the communication between Ed and his doctors. How do you see elements of the Hippocratic Oath demonstrated? How would you characterize their relationship in terms of the Paternalistic versus Mutuality Models? What impact do you think this play had on the actor, who was also a second-year medical student at the time?

*Healthcare Worker-Patient Communication.*   Analyze the communication between Ed and his various healthcare providers (nurses, physical therapists/"physio," etc.). How did the healthcare workers relate to Ed? How did they relate to one another? When did they work as a team, and when did that break down?

*Goals of Communication.*   Analyze the communication in the play using the four goals of communication: building relationships, influencing others, gaining understanding, and reducing uncertainty. Give specific examples from the play of how each goal was accomplished. Are there times you think the goals were not accomplished very effectively?

*Communication Process.*   Analyze the act of journaling in terms of the communication model, and particularly as it relates to intrapersonal communication (communicating with one's self). How is the communication process affected when words written in a private journal become a public play? Why do you think Ed's family allowed the journals to become public?

*Language.*   Analyze the ways in which language is used throughout the play. How do characters play with language? How does jargon impact their interactions or your understanding of their interactions? How do pragmatic elements like magic or taboo surface in the interactions? When does language lead to misunderstandings?

*Nonverbal.*    Analyze the interaction in terms of how nonverbal communication functioned. How were characters developed or revealed through nonverbal communication? How did the nonverbal elements enhance the action/drama? What particular types of nonverbal communication stood out most?

## REFERENCES

Bosanquet, S. (Producer), & Nichols, M. (Director). (2010). *Wit.* [Motion Picture]. United States: Home Box Office Films.

Chisholm. M. C. (Writer), & Bicom, S. (Director). (2010). *Ed's Story: The Dragon Chronicles,* produced in conjunction with the Izaak Walton Killam Health Center, Nova Scotia, Canada.

Polack, E. P. & Avtgis, T. A. (2011). *Medical communication: Defining the discipline.* Dubuque, IO: Kendall Hunt.

# Appendix

Teaching Resources

# 100

## Five Minutes of Fame: Educating Others About Communication Theories Beyond the Classroom

*Lisa K. Hanasono, Ph.D.*
*Department of Communication*
*Bowling Green State University*
*LisaKH@bgsu.edu*

**History:** This activity was presented at the annual meeting of the National Communication Association, November 2015, in Las Vegas, Nevada.
**Primary courses in which this activity might be used:** Communication Theory, Interpersonal Communication, Persuasion, Media Production, Small Group Communication
**Concepts illustrated:** Communication Theories, Annotating Primary Research Articles, Media Production, Small Group Communication

### PURPOSE

While pursuing their undergraduate degrees, students cultivate a rich set of skills and knowledge. Unfortunately, students often fail to share course-related information outside of their classrooms and campuses. Instead of spreading their newfound knowledge to the public and empowering a broader audience with information, many students' skills, research findings, and projects remain quarantined within academic spaces. This activity challenges students to use their communication skills to translate course-specific knowledge to a larger and more diverse audience beyond the classroom. In doing so, students make information more accessible to those who are not pursuing their college degrees.

In addition to sharing knowledge beyond their academic halls, students often struggle to connect theories with praxis. In this semester-long assignment, students will work in teams to become experts on a particular communication theory. They will read and annotate a collection of primary-research articles on their selected theory. Next they will work together to develop a five-minute educational video that informs the public about their theory *and* shows audience members the theory is applicable in their everyday lives. At the end of the semester, students upload their videos to a course-based YouTube channel and on Facebook.[1] In doing so, students get an opportunity to showcase their communication projects beyond the classroom. Moreover, instructors from diverse universities and colleges who teach courses about communication theories can access and use the videos to enhance their students' learning. For a list of recommended due dates and rubrics, please see Appendices A and C (see pages 439 and 440).

By completing this assignment, students should be able to (1) discuss the basic goals, assumptions, and components of a communication theory; (2) explain how scholars have researched a particular communication theory; (3) work in teams to develop a five-minute educational video about a particular communication theory; and (4) share their educational video clips on YouTube and Facebook.

## EXPLANATION OF ACTIVITY

### Preparation

At the beginning of the semester, introduce the assignment by explaining that the video project will help them become experts on a specific communication theory. You should also emphasize the importance of sharing knowledge beyond the classroom to more diverse audiences, because the people who watch the videos are often individuals who do not have an extensive background in communication studies. Moreover, many students will need to know how to explain technical information to people who do not share their educational or cultural background. Whether at the workplace (e.g., presenting technical information to managers who are not familiar with the communication discipline's theories and jargon) or volunteering in one's community (e.g., translating nuanced survey results to a nonprofit organization), there are many situations where students will need to be able to adapt their messages to individuals who are not experts in communication studies. Next, allow students to form teams of four to five people and sign up for a theory, such as cognitive dissonance theory, communication privacy management theory, or the theory of weak ties.

The assignment consists of three major components. Once students have formed their teams and selected a communication theory, they first need to cultivate a broad understanding of their selected theory's goals, major components, and practical utility. Using their textbooks (e.g., Griffin, Ledbetter, & Sparks, 2015; Miller, 2005), ask students to complete the "Getting to Know Your Theory" homework assignment (see Appendix B on p. 439).

Now that students understand the fundamentals of their selected theory, each team should work together to develop an annotated bibliography. The

---

[1] Creating a YouTube channel is free for anyone who has a computer device or smartphone and online access to YouTube. If instructors want to separate their professional and personal identities in online contexts, they could create a separate YouTube channel for their class project and elect to not post any videos on Facebook.

annotated bibliography should consist of five annotations that cite, summarize, and briefly evaluate primary research articles about their theory. Instead of reviewing textbooks, dissertations, and popular press articles (e.g., magazines and newspapers), students should limit their annotations to primary research articles, meaning that the authors present the original results from their study in the published manuscript. To help students narrow their search, it can be helpful to limit their articles to a collection of appropriate communication journals (e.g., *Communication Theory, Quarterly Journal of Speech, Communication Monographs,* and the *Journal of Applied Communication*). For more information, please visit Bowling Green State University's (BGSU) COMM 2010 LibGuide (BGSU, 2015). By completing their annotated bibliography, students will become more knowledgeable about their theory and how scholars have studied it.

Once teams have completed their annotated bibliographies and cultivated an in-depth understanding of their selected theories, they should develop the script for their five-minute videos. Students should be creative and consider how they can adapt their message to an audience of Internet users who may or may not have a college education. Students should include the following elements in their five-minute clips: (1) an introductory title with catchy music; (2) an attention getter (e.g., a statistic, story, rhetorical question, skit, or image); (3) information about the theory (i.e., identify the theory, its main goals, assumptions, components, and assertions); (4) explain how other researchers have studied this theory (hint: Students can highlight studies from their annotated bibliography); (5) show how their theory works (e.g., through a skit); and (6) end credits and relevant citations.

### Creating the Video Clips

To help students with the technical side of developing videos, I have partnered with my university's tech support staff. My students use iMovie to create and edit their videos. This software is free on any standard Mac computer. We usually spend one day in a campus computer lab where a tech staff member introduces students to the nuts and bolts of iMovie. That said, students and instructors are welcome to use any video editing software program. I recommend iMovie because it is free and user-friendly. Once students create a full draft of their videos, you can encourage them to complete a preliminary screening with you (during your office hours or during class). This will allow students to receive informal feedback before finalizing their video projects.

### Showcasing the Video Clips

At the end of the semester, each team uploads their completed video to my Communication Theory YouTube Channel² (Hanasono, 2015). Also if desired,

---

² My YouTube channel can be found by going to www.youtube.com and using the search teams "Hanasono" and "COMM 2010 spotlight videos." Videos on this channel inform viewers about theories like communication privacy management theory, social information processing theory, the elaboration likelihood model, and expectancy violations theory.

you can encourage students to post their videos on Facebook and Twitter. During our last class period (seventy-five minutes; shorter classes may need two class periods), we watch each team's video. It is a great way to celebrate students' hard work and to review for their final exam.

## DEBRIEF

After screening each video, I debrief by leading a short discussion session. I ask my students to identify the featured theory's purpose, how scholars have researched the theory, and to assess the theory's strengths and limitations. At the end of the screening session, I ask students to reflect on their own video project. Then I ask several more debriefing questions:

1. How did you adapt the content of your video to a broader audience?
2. How did the annotated bibliography help you develop your video?
3. If you could have done one thing differently (regarding your video project), what would it be?
4. How can you use social media and computer-mediated communication to showcase your videos to a non-university audience?
5. What skills did you develop by completing this project? How can these skills help you in future classes or professional contexts?

Students find this assignment to be fun, creative, and valuable. Instead of writing a long term paper that is only viewed by the instructor, students take pride in developing a video that could be viewed by hundreds of people. In fact, students often shared the link to their YouTube videos on Facebook and Twitter because they wanted their friends and family to appreciate their hard work. I've also received positive feedback from colleagues, faculty at different institutions, and graduate teaching assistants who have used some of my students' videos to teach communication theories in their classes.

## REFERENCES

Bowling Green State University. (2015). COMM 2010: Communication theory LibGuide. Retrieved from http://libguides.bgsu.edu/c.php?g=227166&p=1505765

Griffin, E., Ledbetter, A., & Sparks, G. (2015). *A first look at communication theory* (9th ed.). Boston, MA: McGraw-Hill.

Hanasono, L. K. (2015). Spotlight videos from COMM 2010. Retrieved from https://www.youtube.com/watch?v=GFhaHg9aYUE&list=PL3nkxNfZVaoz4ny2bDhTZr6H4KscCP8H4

Miller, K. (2005). *Communication theories: Perspectives, processes, and contexts.* Boston, MA: McGraw-Hill.

## APPENDIX A: LIST OF KEY TASKS AND DEADLINES

The proposed schedule is based on an undergraduate course that spans sixteen weeks. In my class, students can earn up to 200 points for completing this assignment; however, please feel free to adjust the deadlines and points to fit your section's schedule and points system.

| Task | Deadline | Points |
|------|----------|--------|
| Assign the video project and develop teams | Week 1 | 0 |
| Students collaborate with their team members to complete their "Getting to Know your Theory" worksheet | Week 2 | 10 |
| Students begin to find and read primary research articles for their annotated bibliographies | Week 3 | |
| Annotated bibliographies are due | Week 8 | 50 |
| Video editing workshop | Week 9 | 10 |
| Teams should have a full draft of their video completed | Week 12 | 10 |
| Final videos are due | Week 15 | 110 |
| Screen videos in class and debrief the assignment | Week 16 | 10 |

## APPENDIX B: TEAM WORKSHEET TITLED "GETTING TO KNOW YOUR THEORY"

Instructions: Working with your team members, use your textbook to answer the following questions. This assignment is due at the beginning of our class meeting on [DATE] and is worth ten points.

**Students' Names:** _____

**Selected Theory:** _____

1. Who created this theory?
2. What does this theory aim to do? Please identify its specific goals.
3. What are the theory's main components? How do these components interrelate?
4. How could this theory help YOU communicate more effectively in your everyday lives?
5. Evaluate this theory by identifying (a) one strength and (b) one limitation.

# APPENDIX C: SAMPLE RUBRICS

## COMM 2010: Annotation Bibliography Evaluation Sheet

**Description:** In this assignment, students annotate five primary research articles. Each of the annotations is worth 10 points.

**Students' Names:** _____

**Theory:** _____

| Requirement | Article #1: Point Value | Article #2: Point Value | Article #3: Point Value | Article #4: Point Value | Article #5: Point Value |
|---|---|---|---|---|---|
| **Citation** | | | | | |
| Citation is correctly listed in APA format | 0  1  2 | 0  1  2 | 0  1  2 | 0  1  2 | 0  1  2 |
| Article is appropriate for this assignment | | | | | |
| **Summary** | | | | | |
| Clearly identified the article's purpose | 0  1 | 0  1 | 0  1 | 0  1 | 0  1 |
| Discussed article's theory/theories | 0  1  2 | 0  1  2 | 0  1  2 | 0  1  2 | 0  1  2 |
| Explained the article's method | 0  1 | 0  1 | 0  1 | 0  1 | 0  1 |
| Explained the article's results & conclusions | 0  1  2 | 0  1  2 | 0  1  2 | 0  1  2 | 0  1  2 |
| **Assessment** | | | | | |
| Evaluated the article's accuracy and quality | 0  1  2 | 0  1  2 | 0  1  2 | 0  1  2 | 0  1  2 |
| **Mechanics** | | | | | |
| The summary & assessment were well organized & clear. | | | | | |
| The writing was relatively free of grammatical, punctuation, and other writing errors. | | | | | |
| The source was an appropriate publication for this assignment. | | | | | |
| **Total Points (___/50)** | ___/10 points | ___/10 points | ___/10 points | ___/10 points | ___/10 points |

**COMM 2010: Annotation Bibliography Evaluation Sheet**

**Students' Names:** _____

**Theory:** _____

| Key Component | Point Value | | | | | |
|---|---|---|---|---|---|---|
| **Video** | | | | | | |
| Introductory title and music were appropriate and clear. | 0 | 1 | 2 | 3 | 4 | 5 |
| Attention getter was effective. | 0 | 1 | 2 | 3 | 4 | 5 |
| Theory and its purpose were correctly identified. | 0 | 1 | 2 | 3 | 4 | 5 |
| Main assumptions were discussed. | 0 | 1 | 2 | 3 | 4 | 5 |
| Major components & their connections were presented. | 0 | 4 | 8 | 12 | 16 | 20 |
| Explained how researchers have studied this theory | 0 | 4 | 8 | 12 | 16 | 20 |
| SHOWED how the theory works | 0 | 4 | 8 | 12 | 16 | 20 |
| **General Editing** | | | | | | |
| Video was educational & creative. | 0 | 2 | 4 | 6 | 8 | 10 |
| Video was clear. | 0 | 2 | 4 | 6 | 8 | 10 |
| **End Credits** | | | | | | |
| At least five peer-reviewed sources were cited in APA format at the end of the video | 0 | 1 | 2 | 3 | 4 | 5 |
| Group members' names and copyrighted materials were appropriated cited in the video | 0 | 1 | 2 | 3 | 4 | 5 |
| **Mechanics** | | | | | | |
| The video was submitted on time and could be viewed by students in the classroom. | | | | | | |
| The video was three to five minutes in length, excluding end credits. | | | | | | |
| Total Points | | | _____/110 points | | | |

# 101

## Inviting TED to Your Class: How to Use TED Talks to Teach Public Speaking Courses

*Nathan G. Webb, Ph.D.*
*Department of Communication Studies*
*Belmont University*
*nathan.webb@belmont.edu*

**History:** This activity was presented at the annual meeting of the Central States Communication Association, April 2016, in Grand Rapids, Michigan.

**Primary courses in which this activity might be used:** Public Speaking, Introduction to Communication

**Concepts illustrated:** Audience Analysis, Visual Aids, Delivery, Persuasion

### PURPOSE

Students learn new perspectives when guest speakers present information to them (Lang, 2008). In addition, students can learn how to be better communicators when they pay attention to other speakers (Hogan, Andrews, Andrews, & Williams, 2011). Students have the opportunity to observe best and worst practices for public speaking when critiquing others. TED Talks provide students with access to examples of a variety of speeches and course content delivered by experts in a number of fields.

TED Talks, which is short for Technology, Entertainment, and Design, is a popular series of presentations given at TED conferences. Ted Talks began in 1984 and were made accessible online in 2006, reaching over *one billion* video views by 2012 (ted.com/history). With their popularity and emphasis on "ideas worth spreading," public speaking instructors would be wise to consider integrating them into their classes. Romanelli, Cain, and McNamara (2014) make the case that critiquing TED Talks can be valuable for college students because "TED presenters are often selected not only for their expertise on a given topic but also for their ability to effectively and succinctly communicate information to learners" (para. 6). I provide suggestions for two related ways of using TED Talks in a public speaking or introductory communication class.

## EXPLANATION OF ACTIVITY

First, instructors can rely on TED Talks presenters as guest speakers who elaborate on course content. Specifically, many presenters have discussed concepts that relate both directly and indirectly to typical subjects covered in an introductory public speaking course. Using TED Talks in this manner provides your students with access to different expert voices on course content. One resource instructors can use to find TED Talks related to public speaking is the TED Talk Playlist titled "Before Public Speaking ..." After using TED Talks in class for several years, I also created a list of TED Talks related to many subjects covered in a speech course. This list serves to provide a couple of options for core subjects typically covered in an introductory public speaking class:

1. Delivering a Speech
   a. *How to Speak so That People Want to Listen* (9:58)—Julian Treasure
   b. *Your Body Language Shapes Who You Are* (21:02)—Amy Cuddy

2. Ethics in Communication
   a. *Beware Online "Filter Bubbles"* (10:27)—Eli Pariser
   b. *The Greatest Ted Talk Ever Sold* (19:28)—Morgan Spurlock

3. Audience-Centered Communication
   a. *Pop Culture in the Arab World* (5:05)—Shereen El Feki
   b. *Games for Girls* (13:08)—Brenda Laurel

4. Speech Apprehension
   a. *We're All Hiding Something. Let's Find the Courage to Open Up* (9:22)—Ash Beckham
   b. *How I Beat Stage Fright* (8:03)—Joe Kowan

5. Meaningful Speech Topics
   a. *How Schools Kill Creativity* (19:24)—Ken Robinson
   b. *The Power of Vulnerability* (20:19)—Brené Brown

6. Speech Innovation
   a. *How I Hacked Online Dating* (17:27)—Amy Webb
   b. *Teach Teachers How to Create Magic* (6:54)—Christopher Emdin

7. Utilizing Data as Supporting Material
   a. *The Best Stats You've Ever Seen* (19:50)—Hans Rosling
   b. *Why Smart Statistics Are the Key to Fighting Crime* (12:41)—Anne Milgram

8. Using Visual Aids to Communicate
   a. *The Beauty of Data Visualization* (17:56)—David McCandless
   b. *Stunning Data Visualization in the AlloSphere* (6:17)—Joann Kuchera-Morin

9. Making Persuasive Arguments
   a. *How Great Leaders Inspire Action* (18:01)—Simon Sinek
   b. *Averting the Climate Crisis* (16:17)—Al Gore

10. Listening Effectively
    a. *How to Truly Listen* (32:12)—Evelyn Glennie
    b. *5 Ways to Listen Better* (7:46)—Julian Treasure

11. Using Language in Meaningful Ways
    a. *Talk Nerdy to Me* (4:34)—Melissa Marshall
    b. *The Danger of Silence* (4:18)—Clint Smith

Second, instructors can use TED Talks as example speeches. Students can critique speeches to better understand concepts and skills covered in class. For example, an instructor could ask students to watch a TED Talk and pay attention to particular elements of a speech, like the way the speaker communicates nonverbally or the speaker's introductions and conclusions. Instructors can also use a more open-ended approach to watching TED Talks by asking students to watch a speech and discuss what the speaker did or did not do well.

How one implements TED Talks into a public speaking class will depend on the classroom setting. If instructors are teaching an online or blended course, they could provide directions and a link to a TED Talk online, and then ask students to discuss the speech via a discussion board or through a written assignment. If teaching public speaking in a traditional, face-to-face setting, an instructor could provide directions, play a TED Talk, and then discuss. If teaching in a traditional setting the activity typically takes between fifteen and thirty minutes, depending on the length of the TED Talk utilized.

## DEBRIEF

How I debrief after using a TED Talk in class depends on my purpose for showing the video. If I am using the video to illustrate a certain subject in the class, then I will lead a discussion on how the video related to the topic we are covering that day. For example, if showing a TED Talk on speech apprehension, I might ask students to make connections between what the video taught us about speech apprehension, and what we read and/or discussed on the subject. However, if critiquing the delivery of a TED speaker, I would ask the class to evaluate the speaker's performance. This could be an open-ended evaluation, or I might ask the class to discuss specific elements of the speech delivery like organization, introductions/conclusions, or visual aids.

In sum, students are very engaged when watching and discussing TED Talks. Students are often able to make clear connections between what they watch on the videos and course content. In addition, students gain an understanding of what to do and not to do through their critiques. Also, TED Talks hold the attention of students and break up the monotony of certain lectures by allowing additional voices in the classroom.

## REFERENCES

Hogan, J. M., Andrews, P. H., Andrews, J. R., & Williams, G. (2011). *Public speaking and civic engagement* (2nd ed.). Boston, MA: Pearson.

Lang, J. M. (2008). Guest speakers. *Chronicle Of Higher Education, 54*(31), C2–C3.

Romanelli, F., Cain, J., & McNamara, P. J. (2014). Should TED talks be teaching us something? In *American Journal of Pharmaceutical Education, 78*(6).

TED (n.d.) *Before public speaking ...* Retrieved from http://www.ted.com/playlists/226/before_public_speaking

TED (n.d.). *History of TED.* Retrieved from http://www.ted.com/about/our-organization/history-of-ted

# 102

# I Saw It in the Movies: Using AmericanRhetoric.com to Teach Core Concepts

*Trudy L. Hanson*
*Department of Communication*
*West Texas A&M University*
*thanson@wtamu.edu*

**History:** This activity was presented at the annual meeting of the National Communication Association, November 2005, in Boston, Massachusetts. This teaching idea was developed as part of a grant provided for innovation in core courses at West Texas A&M University.
**Primary Courses in which this activity might be used:** Public Speaking, Business and Professional Communication, Introduction to Communication
**Concepts illustrated:** Speaker Apprehension, Listening, Audience Adaptation, Supporting Arguments, Introductions, Persuasive Strategy

## PURPOSE

At West Texas A&M University, we have experimented with a number of methods for providing examples of effective and ineffective public speaking to students enrolled in our basic course. We have used videos to accompany textbooks. We have linked students to publisher websites with streaming video. We have asked students to purchase a DVD containing examples of public speaking. Those approaches have met with less than enthusiastic response. We decided to turn to the American Rhetoric website (http://www.americanrhetoric.com/) and link our students (both online and face to face sections) with selected clips from famous movie speeches. Students are asked to view the clip, answer a question that requires them to apply the principle/theory being taught in class for that session, and then upload their response through the course management system. Since adopting this use of popular cultural artifacts, we have seen added enthusiasm in students and better application of the principles being taught.

## EXPLANATION OF ACTIVITY

As part of our common syllabus for the basic public speaking course, we have a class meeting grid that includes the Movie Speech assignment question and link for each movie. Students view the movie clip and respond to the question that is posed. In classroom discussion, the instructor ties students' responses to the teaching session. Because AmericanRhetoric.com also provides a transcript of the movie speech, even if a student's technology access is limited, the student can still read what was said without the accompanying video clip. All of the following movie clips can be found using the American Rhetoric search feature found on the website, http://www.americanrhetoric.com/, in the lower left-hand side of the page. Movies are listed alphabetically. In some cases, students may only be able to retrieve the audio version of the clip, but in all cases, the text of what is said is provided.

| Movie and Link | Concept Addressed |
|---|---|
| Movie Clip: *Malcolm X*. Listen to Malcolm's speech. In what ways does the speaker create unity and common ground with his audience? | Audience Adaptation |
| Movie Clip: *Legally Blonde*. In Elle Wood's graduation speech, how does she gain the attention of her audience? | Introductions |
| Movie Clip: *The American President*. Listen to President Shepherd's speech. What supporting materials does he use for his arguments in this press conference? | Supporting Materials |
| Movie Clip: *Independence Day*. Listen to the president's speech. What persuasive strategies does he use to inspire the fighter pilots? | Persuasive Strategy |
| Movie Clip: *The Great Debaters*. Listen to the arguments that James Farmer and Samantha Booke make in supporting civil disobedience in Wiley College's debate with the Harvard team. What persuasive strategies do they use? How successful are they in persuading the audience? | Persuasive Strategy |

## DEBRIEF

As part of class discussion on the assigned day for each movie clip, the instructor asks students to share their responses to the prompts. Students are encouraged to use examples from the movie speech to explain the concept featured for that class session. For example, when students are discussing techniques to use in the introduction of a speech, they need to evaluate Elle Wood's attention getter and decide if that was a good choice for the audience. Here is a sample student response to this question:

She begins her speech with a "quote-hook"; a quote that hooks the audience's attention. She then adds humor by disagreeing with a famous philosopher, with whom her quote was about. She made the audience laugh by adding her own flair to her understanding and perception of Law School and what it's taught her. She then "sunk" the audience after reeling them in by adding a serious ending to her speech to give the audience a serious note on how strenuous and deserving every-one of her fellow graduates are. Short and simple, she added her own personality and flair to a simple and serious speech, and that is how she captured her audi-ence's attention.

One student responded to the question about persuasive strategies used in *The Great Debaters* as follows:

James Farmer really gets to the audience because of how he describes how he saw a black man being lynched. This really made an impact on the crowd because of how he tied his teammates into it. He states how they are even in fear and feel shame because of what is happening to this black man. This really gets the audi-ence to listen to what he has to say and even get up to clap and the end of his speech. That even the people at home watching on TV even leaned in from their seats.

Class discussion, whether in face-to-face classes or through our web-based sections of the basic public speaking course, center on students supporting their assertions with examples from the movie clip. In guiding the discussion, instructors seek to link student responses to the core principles being taught. If a student's answer is not well supported or the interpretation provided by the student lacks coherence, then the instructor uses the response as an oppor-tunity to reinforce the concept being taught. Using movie speeches also pro-vides a relevant context for public speaking whether the example used is from *the Great Debaters* or from *Independence Day*.

## REFERENCES

American Rhetoric Movie Speeches. (n.d.). http://www.americanrhetoric.com/moviespeeches.htm

# 103

## Designated Reader in Online Discussions: An Activity to Teach About Listening as a Skill and as a Concept

*Natalia Rybas*
*Department of Communication Studies*
*Indiana University East*
*natrybas@iue.edu*

**History:** This activity was presented at the annual meeting of the Central States Communication Association in April 2013, in Kansas City, Missouri.
**Primary courses in which this activity might be used:** Interpersonal Communication, Nonverbal Communication, Computer-Mediated Communication
**Concepts illustrated and skills developed:** Listening in Online Contexts

### PURPOSE

Discussions are often an essential part of online courses, whereby students supposedly engage in meaningful conversations on suggested prompts. In reality, students often end up responding to discussion prompts as if they were addressing the instructor as their intended audience. As a consequence, they may fail to complement, critique, question, add, and develop ideas in the posts made by their peers. To address this concern, assign students the role of designated readers (Dunlap, 2009). The objective of organizing discussions with a role of designated reader is to develop students' listening skills in online conversations. The labor of listening may be invisible in online discussions (Crawford, 2009), and thus overlooked in teaching students to learn this valuable skill.

### EXPLANATION OF ACTIVITY

Before assigning the activity, discuss the notion of listening and how listening occurs in online conversations. The publications by Crawford (2009), Bostrom (2011), and Couldry (2009) are useful in defining listening for online contexts. Students can brainstorm ways to demonstrate that they are listening and to identify best practices for listening in online conversations. Identify specific types of responses that are possible in discussions and how these responses are expressed in writing (see Appendix, p. 451). It is important to orient the students to the discussion as a process that is both informal, because it echoes a conversation, and formal, because it takes place in a college course and carries a grade. Model the activity early in the semester and show students how to accomplish the role.

Divide the class into small groups of four to eight students so that each student can take the role of designated reader once a semester. The size of the group reflects the number of discussions in a given semester. If there are five discussions in the semester, five students will be the optimal size for the group. Present the discussion assignment at the beginning of the semester and explain the role of the designated reader. The designated readers are expected to read all posts in the group and direct the conversation by asking clarifying questions, promoting the intended focus on the discussion issues, suggesting alternative perspectives, or confirming the ideas expressed in the group. In addition, the designated reader provides a closing to the conversation. The closing includes a summary of the discussion; highlights the most prominent discussion topics and conclusions; points to some areas that the discussions failed to touch, needed more work on, misrepresented or misunderstood; and finally, reviews the gains from the conversation for the designated reader.

This activity may be limited by its reliance on initial examples of designated readers. However, even ineffective examples serve as a baseline for other designated readers. Another limitation may be its feasibility for smaller classes (twenty-five to thirty), as it may be difficult in bigger classes to provide opportunities for every student to serve as a designated reader. Assigning more than one designated reader per group may be a way to manage this limitation.

## DEBRIEF

There can be two layers of debriefing: at the level of concept and at the level of skill. Debriefing at the level of concept focuses on explaining the nature and process of listening as it happens in online contexts. Such debriefing can be done after a series of discussions when students have had a chance to experience online conversations in a specific course. Examine as a class: How do people listen in online contexts? What specifically do people do to demonstrate that they are listening? Compare with the discussion about listening at the very beginning of the class. It is important to note that listening finds its materialization in recognizing what others have to say (Couldry, 2009). Listening also requires a reciprocal process of dialogue with exchange of comments as opposed to the broadcasting model of speaking (Crawford, 2009). The conclusions for debrief at the level of concept emphasize the selective nature of listening and the importance of nonverbal stimuli (like organization, labeling, and clarity of writing).

Debriefing at the level of skill focuses on effective listening and occurs after the week's discussions are complete. A class announcement (weekly at the beginning of the course and bi-weekly or less often later in the course) with a few bulleted points provides an opportunity for debriefing at the level of skill. Point out which aspects of the designated reader role were effective and make recommendations for future designated readers. Note that creating critical comments and asking critical questions seem the most difficult aspects of the role. Attract attention of the whole class to the effective models of designated reader. If the existing examples need improvement, rephrase them and share these examples with students. Praise students who take the role of designated reader with heightened diligence. Comment that students become productive participants of discussions and orient their comments towards their peers, thus curating discussions in their groups. Share with students the impressions that the students change their point of view in the conversations online and become more careful, attentive, and reciprocal (Crawford, 2009) listeners. Include examples of effective comments in weekly debriefs, especially in the initial instances of designated reader, and annotate the examples.

## REFERENCES

Bostrom, R. N. (2011). Rethinking conceptual approaches to the study of "listening." *The International Journal of Listening, 25*(1–2), 10–26.
Couldry, N. (2009). Rethinking the politics of voice. *Continuum, 23*(4), 579–582.
Crawford, K. (2009). Following you: Disciplines of listening in social media. *Continuum, 23*(4), 525–535.
Dunlap, J. C. (2009). Protocols for online discussion. In P. R. Lowenthal, D. Thomas, A. Thai & B. Yuhnke (Eds.), *The CU online handbook: Teach differently create and collaborate* (pp. 101–105): University of Colorado, Denver, Colorado.

## APPENDIX

To support the conversation, provide the following types of responses in any combination or order.

- Clarifying questions: Ask to clarify ideas or explain them in other ways.

    Example: *You suggest that ethnocentrism is the reason you felt uncomfortable. Can you explain what ethnocentrism stands for and how people express it?*

- Probing questions or comments: Ask for more details.

    Example: *You argue that the conversation you participated in demonstrates implicit bias. Can you add some more details to how you observed implicit biases? What did the participants say or not say? What nonverbal behaviors did they demonstrate or not demonstrate?*

- Critical questions or comments: Ask for alternative analysis, disagree, or express other concerns with the shared information.

    Example: *You discuss that gamers do not notice that they choose the most violent options for the game. How would the author of the article we read last week respond to this observation? If parents of teenagers participate in this conversation, what would they say?*

    Example: *You define anonymity as "being unknown." I think this is a somewhat brief and simple definition; we can find it in a dictionary! The author argues that in the context of online commenting, there are different degrees of anonymity. Can you expand on your definitions as they apply to the responses in online forums?*

- Supportive: Acknowledge that you have watched, viewed, listened to the posts or presentations made by your peers and point to the most important ideas.

    Example: *I have read your post and I understand your point that you prefer to put away your cell phone when you study.*

- Confirming: Expand on ideas to confirm arguments expressed by others.

    Example: *I think you effectively analyze this situation because you point out that the speaker uses local language to show her belonging to the community. Speakers who are bilingual can seamlessly navigate varieties of speaking. Such speakers rely on their knowledge to assemble social capital and possibly empower others.*

# 104

## Poem, Picture, Prop: Enhancing Student Engagement with Style

*Stacy E. Hoehl*

*School of Professional Communication*

*Wisconsin Lutheran College*

*stacy.hoehl@wlc.edu*

**History:** This activity was presented at the annual National Communication Association conference of November 2014 in Chicago, Illinois.
**Primary courses in which this activity might be used:** Any Communication Course
**Concepts illustrated:** Student Engagement, Audience Adaptation, Creative Thinking Skills

### PURPOSE

According to Zepke and Leach (2010), student engagement in higher education is at the forefront of educational research initiatives. For example, studies have shown that intrinsically invested students learn better and enjoy the process more than their non-engaged classmates (Evans, Ziaian, Sawyer, & Gillham, 2013; Trowler & Trowler, 2010). To achieve higher levels of student engagement, teachers should emphasize individualized learning that gives students the chance to take ownership of acquiring usable knowledge (Shuetz, 2008). The purpose of the "Poem, Picture, Prop" activity is to enhance student engagement in and retention of class content through an individualized, creative, and immediate application of the current class topic.

This activity embodies the best practices in student engagement as outlined by Zepke and Leach (2010). According to these authors, teachers who want to encourage student engagement should use classroom activities that develop students' self-belief, allow students to work independently, form learning relationships with others, and create active and collaborative learning opportunities. This activity involves each of these student engagement strategies. Furthermore, this exercise is incredibly versatile, in that teachers can use it as the application activity for any classroom topic. Such flexibility saves the teacher preparation time and still accomplishes the same exciting outcomes of an engaged classroom.

## EXPLANATION OF ACTIVITY

Begin with a thorough discussion of the day's lesson, lasting approximately twenty minutes. Following this discussion, write the words "Poem, Picture, Prop" on the board. Tell students that they have ten minutes to work independently to summarize the class content for the day by writing a poem, drawing a picture, or using a prop. Students should choose the method of summarizing the content that will resonate with them the most. For example, students with the gift of rhyme should put the day's topic of conversation into verse form. Students who love to draw or see concepts represented visually should choose the picture option. Finally, students who like to think metaphorically should choose a prop from their backpacks and explain how the item represents the class content.

While the students are working on their creations, wander among them and field any questions they might have about class material and give encouragement to students who may be struggling for inspiration. Keep the environment positive and affirm students' uniqueness and creativity through lighthearted, encouraging comments.

When the ten minutes are over, ask for volunteers to share their poem, picture, or prop with the rest of the class. Remind listeners to be respectful and supportive of others' ideas; they will benefit the most when they process multiple perspectives on the day's topic. Typically, it takes the first few brave souls to warm everyone else up to the idea of presenting their work. After this initial period, however, the ideas and excitement flow freely, and the inhibitions and fear of criticism decrease dramatically. Allow students to share their poems, pictures, and props as class time permits. Keep the dialogue open by asking why students chose their respective formats, how they might add onto or change another student's model, and whether they have any questions about the class material.

As an example of past activity outcomes, in my creativity course, a student summarized a theoretical model of the creative process in poetry form and then proceeded to rap his work for the class. Several students referenced his poem on subsequent exams because it was so memorable. Another example of this activity in action occurs frequently in my professional communication course. When we review the basic model of communication, students often draw a familiar scene (baseball field, ski slope, car engine, etc.) and indicate how the features of the scene represent the components of the communication process.

## DEBRIEF

Close the class period by showing appreciation for the students' ideas and interpretations of class content. Ask students if they have any new questions about the class topic as a result of this activity and clarify any misconceptions that arose during the discussion. Encourage them to hold onto their work as a means of remembering the day's lesson.

This activity benefits a wide variety of learning styles, as it contains visual, auditory, and experiential components. Most, if not all, students experience an increased sense of engagement in the class period, largely because they are given the freedom to apply class content in a way that resonates with their personal learning styles. Students often respond to this activity with great appreciation for the varied viewpoints, creative approaches, and senses of humor that are revealed in their classmates. The benefits of this activity also present themselves when it comes time for students to recall the class content, whether in subsequent classroom discussions or on exams.

Finally, the creations that result from this activity provide a great source of self-awareness from each student, as they learn to have increased responsibility for their own learning in the classroom. Additionally, the students get to know each other better, which, in turn, contributes to a heightened sense of engagement and community in the classroom.

## REFERENCES

Evans, N., Ziaian, T., Sawyer, J. & Gillham, D. (2013). Affective learning in higher education: A regional perspective. *Australian and International Journal of Rural Education, 23*(1), 23–41.

Schuetz, P. (2008). A theory-driven model of community college student engagement. *Community College Journal of Research and Practice, 32,* 305–24.

Trowler, V. & Trowler, P. (2010). Student engagement executive summary. *The Higher Education Academy Student Engagement Project,* 1–8.

Zepke, N. & Leach, L. (2010). Improving student engagement: Ten proposals for action. *Active Learning in Higher Education, 11*(3), 167–177.

# 105

# Engaging Student-Driven Metaphors to Extend Understanding of Course Concepts

*Linda D. Manning*
*Department of Communication*
*Christopher Newport University*
*lmanning@cnu.edu*

**History:** This activity was presented at the annual meeting of the Southern States Communication Association, April 2010, in Memphis, Tennessee.
**Primary courses in which this activity might be used:** Interpersonal Communication, Gender Communication, Family Communication, Organizational Communication, Communication Theory
**Concepts illustrated:** Metaphor, Perception, Perspective Taking, Group Dynamics

## PURPOSE

All the world's a stage, and all the men and women merely players.
—Shakespeare, *As You Like It, Act II, Scene VII*

My momma always said, "Life was like a box of chocolates."
—Forrest Gump, *Forrest Gump*

'Cause, baby, you're a firework.

—Katy Perry, "Firework"

The use of language techniques like metaphors and similes to explain phenomenon is a well understood concept and common practice. In fact, entire theories revolve around the group use of metaphor; for example, Bormann's symbolic convergence theory. Lakoff and Johnson (1980) note that "metaphor is pervasive in everyday life" (p. 3) and that "[o]ur ordinary conceptual system, in terms of which we both think and act, is fundamentally metaphorical in nature" (p. 3). Morgan (2006) explains "[t]he use of metaphor implies *a way of thinking* and *a way of seeing* that pervade how we understand our world generally" (p. 4).

In sum, people use metaphors to make sense of life; students can use metaphors to make sense of course concepts.

This activity can be used on a regular basis to encourage students to take ownership of their learning. If participation is a component of the course grade, then this activity could be an assessment point. Instead of the instructor providing explanation and examples, while students dutifully copy the information as presented on PowerPoint slides, students unpack the nuances of course concepts and present their findings to the class. The instructor then clarifies, elaborates and corrects student interpretations of course material. An ancillary benefit to the instructor is that the activity can highlight gaps in the textbook's presentation of course materials.

## EXPLANATION OF ACTIVITY

This activity could best be described as a variation on the *think-pair-share* active-learning strategy (see Barkley, 2010). My variation could be labeled *team-dream-scheme*. First, the instructor assigns students to teams (groups of five to seven students) rather than dyads because more voices and perspectives enhance discussion and the unpacking of ideas. Team-based learning suggests that people learn effectively and build a sense of classroom community by working consistently in stable teams. The instructor should assign students to teams in the first week of class. (See Michaelsen, Knight, & Fink, 2002 for an extensive explanation of this pedagogical strategy.) Teams remain consistent for the duration of the marking period.

Second, teams are tasked with developing a metaphor that will be shared orally and visually with the class. Teams report publically to class to assess mastery of course concepts. For example, each team writes or draws its answer on the board. Alternatively, the instructor creates a chart of team responses to compare interpretations of issues. For example, in my introductory interpersonal communication class, I ask students to create a metaphor to explain the listening process. Students should incorporate as many dimensions or aspects of the concept as possible and are encouraged to refer to assigned class reading(s). Allow teams five to seven minutes to develop their ideas. The instructor should circulate through the classroom to verify that teams are on task and to clarify the task. The instructor should not provide feedback regarding the team's interpretation of the concept at this point. Check in with the teams at the six-minute mark to see if they need more time to develop their ideas. I often give teams additional time as needed (in two-minute intervals) to wrap up their ideas.

At the end of the metaphor development time, teams create a visual representation of their metaphor by drawing and writing on the dry-erase or chalkboard. This will take two to three minutes. Some metaphors generated by teams in the introduction to interpersonal communication class were the listening process is like (a) a child's stacking toy, (b) a snowball fight, and (c) building a house of cards on a train. Depending upon the size of the class, all teams can share their metaphors (preferred), or groups can volunteer or be called upon to share the visual representation of their response. I use this activity on a weekly basis to enhance the level of student engagement with course concepts. Regular and repeated use of this activity also creates a sense of community and collaboration in the learning environment.

## DEBRIEF

Teams share their metaphors and justify how dimensions of the assigned course concept are illustrated through the metaphor. The explanation should be succinct—about one to three minutes per team. Often the explanations add humor to the understanding of course concepts, which contributes to student retention of the information. Issues of perception and perspective taking can be highlighted when teams choose different metaphors to illustrate the same concept. Issues of group dynamics are implicitly experienced through the process and can be an explicit point of discussion when a charismatic member of the team leads the team to an incorrect understanding of the course concept. Finally, metaphors can highlight gaps in understanding. Perhaps a team does not account for a significant dimension of a concept. This gap can be addressed by the instructor in the debrief period. Alternatively, metaphors can highlight gaps in the coverage of concepts.

For example, I asked students in a gender communication course to create a metaphor to illustrate men's and women's movements in the United States. One group used a tree to show the relationships between and among the different movements. As the group explained their metaphor to the class, it became evident that they were well informed on the various facets of the first, second, and third waves of feminism, as well as pro-masculinist men's groups, but were sorely lacking in information about the pro-feminist men's groups. This lead the class to revisit the chapters on women's and men's movements presented in the course text. Closer examination showed that the textbook did not address in any detail groups in the pro-feminist movements. This simple class exercise identified a gap in the textbook I had not noticed.

In sum, I emphasize three strengths of this exercise. This activity (1) encourages student ownership of ideas, (2) builds a sense of community in the class, and (3) is memorable, which may support student retention of course concepts. For example, a student in my advanced interpersonal theories class recalled this exercise from a previous semester's gender class. I was pleased that she correctly remembered the theory from this activity and was able to succinctly explain the theory to the class, which allowed class discussion to advance to a more sophisticated discussion of the theory. Finally, for instructors who are piloting a course or a textbook, this activity can highlight gaps in assigned readings.

## REFERENCES

Barkley, E. F. (2010). *Student engagement techniques: A handbook for college faculty.* San Francisco: Jossey-Bass.

Bormann, E. G. (1982). The symbolic convergence theory of communication: Applications and implications for teachers and consultants. *Journal of Applied Communication Research 10*(1), 50–61.

Lakoff, G., & Johnson, M. (1980). *Metaphors we live by.* Chicago: University of Chicago Press.

Michaelsen, L. K., Knight, A. B., & Fink, L. D. (Eds.). (2002). *Team-based learning: A transformative use of small groups.* Westport, CT: Praeger.

Morgan, G. (2006). *Images of organization.* Thousand Oaks, CA: Sage.

# Subject Index

NOTE: The numbers in this index refer to the numbering of the activities related to the terms listed, NOT page numbers.

# Course Index

NOTE: The numbers in this index refer to the numbering of the activities related to the courses listed, NOT page numbers.